Lest We Forget

Lest We Forget

World War I and New Mexico

David V. Holtby

UNIVERSITY OF OKLAHOMA PRESS : NORMAN

Library of Congress Cataloging-in-Publication Data

Names: Holtby, David V., 1948– author.
Title: Lest we forget : World War I and New Mexico, 1916–1941 / David V. Holtby.
   Description: Norman : University of Oklahoma Press, 2018. | Includes bibliographical references and index.
Identifiers: LCCN 2017045058 | ISBN 978-0-8061-6022-1 (hardcover)
ISBN 978-0-8061-9292-4 (paper) Subjects: LCSH: World War, 1914–1918—New Mexico. | World War, 1914–1918—Social
   aspects—New Mexico. | New Mexico—History, Military—20th century. | Soldiers—New Mexico—Biography. | New Mexico—Biography.
Classification: LCC D570.85.N33 H65 2018 | DDC 940.3/791—dc23
LC record available at https://lccn.loc.gov/2017045058

The paper in this book meets the guidelines for permanence and durability of the Committee on Production Guidelines for Book Longevity of the Council on Library Resources, Inc. ∞

Copyright © 2018 by David V. Holtby. Published by the University of Oklahoma Press, Norman, Publishing Division of the University. Paperback published 2023. Manufactured in the U.S.A.

All rights reserved. No part of this publication may be reproduced, stored in a retrieval system, or transmitted, in any form or by any means, electronic, mechanical, photocopying, recording, or otherwise—except as permitted under Section 107 or 108 of the United States Copyright Act—without the prior written permission of the University of Oklahoma Press. To request permission to reproduce selections from this book, write to Permissions, University of Oklahoma Press, 2800 Venture Drive, Norman OK 73069, or email rights.oupress@ou.edu.

In memory of my parents,
who were born the year America entered World War I
Bert E. Holtby (1917–1992)
and
Myrl Barnes Holtby (1917–1954)

And for my wife, Jeanne,
whom I met and married while in the U.S. Air Force (1970–1974)
and
to our daughter, Michelle,
born in a military hospital in Europe

But of this frame the bearings, and the ties,
The strong connections, nice dependencies,
Gradations just, has thy pervading soul
Looked through? Or can a part contain the all?
Alexander Pope, essayist, c. 1733

For myself, I always write about Dublin, because if I can get to the heart of Dublin I can get to the heart of all the cities of the world. In the particular is contained the universal.
James Joyce, c. 1923

The more you press towards the heart of a narrowly bounded historical problem, the more likely you are to encounter in the problem itself a pressure which drives you outward beyond those bounds.
Arthur O. Lovejoy, founder of the
field of intellectual history, 1948

Contents

List of Illustrations • xi
Preface • xiii
Appreciation • xvii

1. Sleepwalkers • 3
2. Patriotism • 23
3. Volunteers • 51
4. "To the Colors" • 81
5. "Slept in Mud, Bathed in Blood" • 126
6. "Terror by Day and by Night" • 156
7. Living and Dying • 187
8. Veterans' Quest Stories • 216
9. Double • 248

Notes • 271
Bibliography • 307
Index of 172 New Mexico Men in Uniform • 327
Subject Index • 333

Illustrations

Figures

Political cartoon depicting threat posed by Germany • 110
Wartime poster featuring President Wilson • 111
Political cartoon commenting on women's wartime roles • 112
War bond poster: "Women! Help America's Sons Win the War" • 113
Charles Springer • 114
Draftees boarding train in Aztec, New Mexico • 115
Nuevomexicano musicians • 115
Infantryman wearing gas mask • 116
155 mm Grand Puissasnce Filloux (GPF) artillery piece • 117
USS *Leviathan* • 118
Members of 28th Division head into combat at Vesle River • 119
77th Division • 119
Unknown soldier killed in action, 89th Division • 120
Crockett brothers—sailor and soldier • 121
Charles Gooch, 8th Division, in Vladivostok, Siberia • 122
Conrad Hilton's ex-servicemen's questionnaire • 123

Cartoon depicting dilemmas experienced by citizen-soldier veterans • 124
Bulletin board in general store, Chacon, Mora County, 1943 • 125

Maps

1. New Mexico's twenty-seven counties in June 1917 • 2
2. France, the western front, and AEF cemeteries • 127
3. AEF summer offensives in northeast France, June to September 1918 • 133
4. The Meuse-Argonne offensive, 26 September to 11 November 1918 • 157

Preface

A single date—28 June—encapsulates a recurring theme of this book—what is remembered and what is forgotten. The act sparking World War I occurred on 28 June 1914, when Archduke Franz Ferdinand of Austria and his wife, Sophie, were shot to death in Sarajevo by Serb nationalist Gavrilo Princip. Exactly five years later the signing of the Treaty of Versailles ended the war. The political assassination and the diplomatic accord are dramatic, singular, and well known, especially in comparison to specifics about the five years these events bracket. An understanding of the lived reality of that war eludes most people today. For that reason the book's title is both ironic and cautionary. Let me explain that statement by relating something about myself and how I became interested in World War I's impact on New Mexico.

Although I am a New Mexico veteran, I knew nothing about the contributions of the state's soldiers, sailors, and marines during World War I. But I had often wondered why I knew no stories from that war comparable to the legacy of the Rough Riders from the Spanish-American War of 1898 or that of the Bataan death march or Navajo code talkers from World War II. Upon retiring in 2006, I thought others might want to know more about New Mexico's involvement in that first world war. For too long the war's impact has been overlooked. This book brings forward what must never be forgotten—how New Mexicans and especially combat veterans lived through the war and the years between 1919 and 1941.

After completing my four-year tour in the air force, I put aside all thoughts about the intelligence work I did, returned to Albuquerque, and resumed my graduate school studies. Nearly thirty-five years later I rekindled historical research interrupted by life, raising a family, and career but shifted my emphasis from the Spanish Civil War to New Mexico history. I assumed a slim volume on World War I would be a two-year project and serve as a kind of academic spring training to get me into condition for the topic I knew would be a major commitment of time—the story of how New Mexico became a state. I spent 2007–8 researching and writing about the home front and military life. Though it was slow going, I confidently predicted that I had those two topics about 80 percent in hand and only veterans' activities awaited my attention. That was my expectation of what lay ahead when I sent my editor my manuscript on statehood in early 2011. I could not have been more wrong, which I quickly realized when I reread what I had accumulated. I had about a thimble-full for what turned out to be a topic that was a fifty-five-gallon barrel. The statehood book took just under three years to research and write. My work on World War I has now stretched to six years, nearly three times longer than the period most New Mexicans were in uniform or obeying the dictates of wartime mobilization.

World War I resonates in American life today, which means this book's readers gain historical perspective on such diverse contemporary topics as these: aftermath of war in veterans' lives; civil liberties in times of national crisis; economic, political, and technological transformations; empire, decolonization, and America's role in the world; public opinion about federal-state relations; and race, gender, and ethnicity realigned. For each of these issues New Mexico—as a place and its people—is a conduit to universal and timeless truths about America confronting adversity abroad and at home. Probed in this book are complexities within ideas, events, and lived experiences, and each of these in turn becomes visible in the departures, journeys, and arrivals New Mexicans made between 1916 and 1941.

The early destinations often involved perilous trips across oceans to fight in foreign lands. But those who remained on the home front likewise traversed new landscapes shaped by prescriptions and proscriptions. For all who came through the war, the years between 1919 and 1941 brought more literal and figurative trips as they stepped into new futures and faced good times and bad, highs and lows, and successes, reverses, and uncertainties. But what is most pronounced in New Mexicans' voices is resilience, of adapting, and coming through—even if not always reaching the place they sought. *Lest We Forget* offers up their stories. A definition of history I often invoke is that it is an intricate web of meanings and interpretations. I hope readers find that the stories and perspectives presented here will reward their attention.

No diacritics were inserted when transcribing names from original sources in which they were omitted.

Appreciation

I first encountered the use of "Appreciation" in preference to the conventional "Acknowledgments" when reading distinguished historian Ann Laura Stoler's book *Along the Archival Grain*. At the time I did not realize how important her ethnography of archives would be for my own research, but I instantly decided to adopt the heading "Appreciation" for the same reason she employed it. I wanted to convey my everlasting gratitude to individuals and institutions for assisting me in word and deed. On a personal level, kindness and encouragement, especially from several longtime friends in Washington, D.C., along with a pair of air force buddies and their wives on the East Coast, have uplifted me during six years spent researching and writing this book.

My greatest emotional debt lies with those to whom the book is dedicated—my parents and the inspiration of their lives and my wife and our daughter, who have enriched my life for the past forty-plus years. A special familial resource has been my brother, Dr. Ralph B. Holtby, who lent personal and professional perspective gained in part from his year-long tour as a combat medic in the central highlands of Vietnam in 1968–69. I could not have assembled the illustration scans without the able assistance of my son-in-law, Chris Neiber.

Fellow historians, publishing colleagues, and friends have offered encouragement, reactions, bibliographic suggestions, and ideas when I mapped out a line of research or floated an interpretation as a trial balloon. These generous people include the following and the chapter in which they left a mark. Chapter 1:

Elizabeth Hadas, Dr. Rick Hendricks, Dr. Calvin A. Roberts, Professor Emerita Sandra Schackel; Chapter 2: Professor Emily Berman, the late Ann Massmann, Professor Richard Melzer, Dr. Marc Simmons; Chapter 3: Nancy Brown-Martinez, Professor Emerita Joan Jensen, Dr. Kathleen Kelly, Kristie Miller; Chapter 4: Catherine Davis, Professor Emeritus Charles Harris, Kermit Hill, Vicky Ramakka, Professor Emeritus Ray Sadler, Professor Emeritus David Stratton; Chapters 5 and 6: Professor Durwood Ball, Henrietta Martinez Christmas, Adam Kane, Dorothy Chavez Wiskup; Chapter 7: Tom Gutierrez, Kim Martinez, the late Dr. Robert R. White; Chapter 8: Professor Jon Hunner, Michael Keleher, Kevin Powers; Chapter 9: Professor Emeritus Richard Etulain, Professor Donald Fixico, John Grassham, the late Professor Ferenc M. Szasz. The completed manuscript was read carefully by Maj. John Kelly, U.S. Army (retired), a student of the Civil War and World War I, commanding officer of a Vietnam War combat platoon, and longtime New York National Guard officer. I am indebted to him for sharing his insights and perspective, especially regarding expectations French officials pressed on General Pershing during the Meuse-Argonne offensive.

World War I and the interwar decades are a large topic even when delimited to New Mexico. Listed in the Bibliography are archives and repositories from around the state and the nation. Collectively they are the main building blocks foundational to this book. I owe a special debt of gratitude to some in-state archivists and their staffs, including Melissa Salazar of the New Mexico State Records Center and Archives, Michael Kelly of the Center for Southwest Research and Special Collections, University of New Mexico, now retired, his successor Dr. Tomas Jaehn, as well as staff at New Mexico State University's Rio Grande Historical Collections. The assistance of local librarians and access to the collections they maintain have been invaluable, and I especially benefited from access to material at the state library, UNM's Zimmerman and Parish libraries and the Interlibrary Loan Office, the Albuquerque Public Library, and Branson and Zuhl libraries at NMSU. Staff at the Main Reading Room of the Library of Congress were most accommodating.

A select group of men and women, and the organizations and foundations they head, embraced my vision when I sought funding for research and travel and requested publication subsidy. Their willingness to invest in my quest truly made this project a reality: Dr. Tobías Durán, retired as director of the UNM Center for Regional Studies, his successor Professor A. Gabriel Meléndez, and retired Center unit administrator Marina Cadena; the Guadalupe Institute; and the Minerva Foundation—each have been exceedingly generous, and I am most fortunate to benefit from their trust and support.

I am particularly pleased to have worked again with Charles E. Rankin, Steven Baker, and Sandy See at the University of Oklahoma Press. My career in scholarly publishing seeded an understanding of how conscientious publishing professionals add value to a manuscript. My contacts at the University of Oklahoma Press have been outstanding in providing tough-minded developmental editing and copyediting, ensuring high standards in design and production, and especially vigorously beating the promotion and publicity drum. The cartographer, Tom Jonas, and the copyeditor, John Thomas, tirelessly employed their talents to improve this book, and I am fortunate to have worked with them.

A final nod of appreciation is to the late Barbara Tuchman (1912–89). Twice awarded the Pulitzer Prize for history, she published eleven books, including three on the run-up to World War I (one of which received a Pulitzer Prize). But it was her counsel in an essay reprinted in *Practicing History* (1981) that spoke wisdom to me. She said: "The writer's object is—or should be—to hold the reader's attention.... This is accomplished only when the narrative moves steadily ahead, not when it comes to a weary standstill, overloaded with every item uncovered in the research" (89). Her words were echoed in advice from my editor and one of the peer reviewers, all of which prompted my samurai editing of the original text and endnotes, after which the cutting-room floor was carpeted in paper.

Lest We Forget

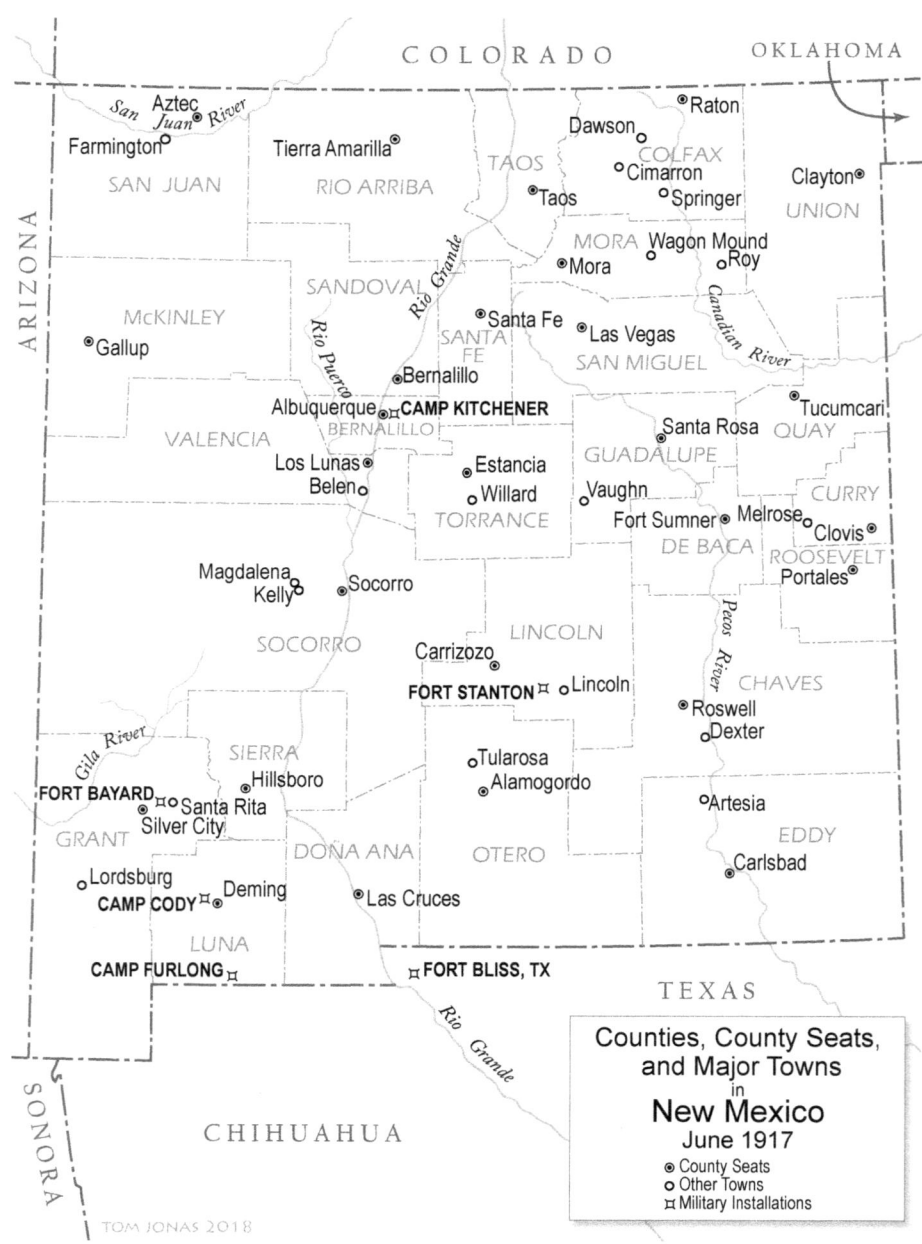

Map 1. New Mexico's twenty-seven counties in June 1917.

CHAPTER 1

Sleepwalkers

It did not happen as planned. The New Mexico legislature in early May 1917 looked ahead to the war's end and mandated publication of a *Golden Book* to "contain a detailed statement of the men who served their country and perhaps died for it" and, for civilians, an account of their "war work and other patriotic activities." Just days before fighting ceased on 11 November 1918, state officials commissioned eleven essays, nine on civilian contributions and one each on training camps and frontline duty. Three months later all but one of the essays was completed; however, "a retrenchment in state finances" canceled the book project. Five of the essays were published in the 1919 edition of *The New Mexico Blue Book,* the official register of state government. Four of the pieces discussed the home front and one described New Mexicans in the front lines.[1]

So, instead of thousands of soldiers, sailors, and marines writing about their experiences, *The New Mexico Blue Book* included just one eyewitness description of encounters with New Mexican infantrymen in the American Expeditionary Forces (AEF). Its author, Ashley Pond, founded the private Los Alamos Ranch School for boys in 1917 and was not a soldier, but rather a Red Cross volunteer in charge of a canteen just behind the trenches in the American sector of the front. His short essay, about fifteen hundred words, became the first on-the-scene battlefield narrative a civilian published about New Mexicans in World War I. It appeared two more times in 1927—as an article in the January issue of the recently launched *New Mexico Historical Review,* which in its initial issues also printed all eleven of the wartime essays, and in an edited volume titled *New Mexico in the Great War* released on the ninth anniversary of the armistice. The Historical Society of New Mexico ushered into print both the journal and the book.²

The budget cuts early in 1919 did not mortally wound the idea of gathering the military experiences of the state's men. That effort was pursued beginning in October 1919 when the state mailed a two-page questionnaire to 14,000 servicemen from New Mexico. Nearly half of the mailings went unanswered; approximately one-quarter of the letters came back stamped as undeliverable to the addressee; but about 25 percent, or 3,400 men, responded. By way of comparison, the state's rate of return as well as the number of questionnaires sent was similar to those of a pair of surveys conducted by organizations seeking to document the wartime contributions of two special populations of servicemen. About 16,000 Jewish servicemen were mailed questionnaires, and 4,719 (29 percent) were completed and returned between 1918 and 1921. Attempts to gather information on the approximately 12,000 American Indians resulted in collecting statements and receiving questionnaires from 2,846 (24 percent) between 1919 and the early 1920s.³

Expanding the Historical Record

This book returns to the original plan to have veterans and civilians from New Mexico speak about their experiences during and after World War I. To maintain the spirit of the original proposal, the current endeavor is guided by words written in February 1919 that created a compact between those who were in charge of the state's war records and future generations: "The vast depository of facts accumulated and preserved will serve the purpose of those who come after us and who will write the history of the World War [and its impact on New Mexico] in such detail as posterity will require."⁴

A "vast depository" did indeed emerge and is held today at the New Mexico State Records Center and Archives (NMSRCA) in Santa Fe. More than 110,000 pages are preserved, mostly military records. That sum more than doubles when holdings for the years 1916–41 are added from other collections, both in and out of state.

Responsibility for initially collecting wartime records fell to a tiny office known as the Board of Historical Service located in the Palace of the Governors in Santa Fe. Edgar Lee Hewett headed it, and he also served as director of the Museum of New Mexico and was a hard-charging dynamo in the capital city. Hewett's one paid assistant was Lansing B. Bloom, a Presbyterian minister. The Board had a three-person clerical staff during the war's final year and two unpaid advisors—historian and lawyer Ralph Emerson Twitchell and public intellectual and writer Benjamin M. Read. Twitchell pushed for and secured a collection of war-related clippings from newspapers statewide, and Read was the driving force behind creation of the questionnaire sent veterans. All four men were bilingual in Spanish and English, and though much of the material gathered was in English a significant quantity of correspondence and questionnaires were in Spanish.[5]

Beginning their work in October 1917, Hewett and Bloom gathered information on each soldier, sailor, and marine who, in the phrase of that era, "went to the colors." Within six months, though, a new initiative claimed an increasing amount of Bloom's attention—correspondence with families about wounded or deceased men. For the remainder of the war and nearly a year afterward, he channeled his training as a clergyman into writing empathetic letters offering heartfelt support to grieving families. He also wrote what he referred to as necrologies, or obituaries, eventually creating more than four hundred using information provided by the deceased's loved ones. His humanity revealed in these exchanges grew out of his own sorrow. His younger brother, Raymond Bloom, died of an illness just seventeen days after boarding a train bound for a Kansas training camp in March 1918.[6]

New Mexico's commitment to collecting wartime records had counterparts in twenty-five other states. But few moved on the idea as quickly as New Mexico did; it was the third state (tied with New Hampshire) to initiate collection efforts. The prime mover in urging the states to gather and preserve wartime records was the American Historical Association (AHA), an organization chartered by the U.S. Congress in 1889. The AHA worked with the federal government to form the National Board of Historical Service beginning in August 1917. Key members of the National Board were acquaintances of Twitchell and Hewett, and the latter accepted an invitation to attended the thirty-third annual meeting of the AHA to participate in an "archives conference, which will deal entirely with war records," held in Philadelphia at the end of December 1917. At that session each state was implored to collect and preserve the records of its State Council of Defense, the lead organization locally for civilian and military mobilization, with the latter activity limited to drafting men into the army. The AHA's intent had been anticipated by the New Mexico legislature's proposal in May 1917: "Make available for public use a record of the sentiments and activities of organizations and individuals . . . in the present war."[7]

In New Mexico, though, officials interpreted the phrase "public use" in a very specific way. They linked it to deep-seated resentment created during the sixty-four-year struggle for statehood. Numerous accusations that New Mexicans were unfit to join the Republic, and specifically that Nuevomexicanos—individuals born in New Mexico of Hispanic ancestry—would not be loyal to the American flag in times of crisis, continued to clutter the American public's mind. The legislature wanted evidence to be able to confront any new questions about New Mexico's contributions during the war. No such accusations arose after the armistice, and when occasional disquieting charges surfaced during the war they met immediate and forceful rebuttal. But a need to expunge all remaining doubts about New Mexicans' loyalty persisted and became the well that yielded *New Mexico in the Great War* when finally published in 1927. That book allowed New Mexico to chronicle its fealty, and for nearly two decades it stood alone as the only state-level account of civilian and military war activity. It resolutely stated its case: "Measured by the standards of wealth, population and responsiveness, its record equaled that of any state in the union and in instances its contributions to the cause exceeded that of many of the other states. In the matter of voluntary enlistments in the army and navy, New Mexico stood fifth among the states."[8]

Hewett and Bloom reported off and on to the New Mexico State Council of Defense, but relations between the two men and the head of the Council, Charles Springer, were often strained. Disagreements existed over priorities, but also personalities clashed. Springer, long a powerful figure in the state's Republican Party, was a successful businessman and used to prevailing in negotiations. Hewett likewise had an iron will and expected deference. Tensions increased significantly in the fall of 1918. Governor Washington E. Lindsey's two-year term expired at year's ended, and both Lindsey and Springer pressed hard for a publication extolling how the "War Governor" guided the state's war effort in 1917–18, especially with bond sales, food conservation, and unwavering patriotism. A compromise hammered out in the final week of the war called for including celebratory essays in the forthcoming *New Mexico Blue Book*. But by then Springer had grown weary of the Board of Historical Service, withdrew his support, and agreed with the incoming Republican governor, Octaviano A. Larrazolo, to cut the Board's funding. Springer also balked at transferring State Council of Defense records, such as they existed, to the Museum of New Mexico. Many of the Council's documents ended up in the papers of Governor Lindsey, his longtime Republican ally and fellow resident of the state's east side.[9]

Immediately after the war ended, Springer shifted his attention to a long-held desire to promote highways in New Mexico, and he presided as chair of the state's highway commission until his death in 1932. But so deep was the rift between

Springer and the Hewett-Bloom team that upon his death no obituary appeared in the *New Mexico Historical Review,* an omission permitted by its editor, Lansing B. Bloom. Just as Springer had quickly moved on in 1919, so too did Hewett. He channeled his energies into his directorship duties at the Museum of New Mexico as well as his archaeological interests. Bloom, though, continued to allot time to the war archive for seven more years while expanding his research sponsored by the museum on Spain's presence in colonial New Mexico. Publication of *New Mexico in the Great War* on 11 November 1927 marked the newly created holiday, Armistice Day, which became a national holiday in 1938 and was renamed Veterans' Day in 1954.

What Is Remembered?

Both Hewett and Bloom remained professionally active until each died in 1946. Public notices reporting their deaths omitted mention of their notable work to create and preserve the state's archive for World War I and again for World War II. Their wartime work had already been forgotten, which points us toward an important lesson. What had briefly loomed large in peoples' lives eventually faded and then lapsed from memory. The process was—and is—relentless: mortality and the steady addition of new events inexorably make transitory much of life's occurrences. Memories are a selective record of the past and are continuously edited—and even deleted. So it was that within five decades new wars eclipsed attention to World War I, and the quagmire that was the Vietnam War eroded interest in modern military history for many in the generation that came of age during the 1960s and 1970s.

Clovis combat infantryman Joe G. Wilson's urged erasing the war's memory when he completed his service questionnaire: "I was over, and am glad to get back—all [is] over now just forget it." His admonition has largely come to pass today for most Americans. World War I has been largely forgotten. The subtitle of a recent book, "The Forgotten Generation and Their Forgotten War," conveys the prevailing unawareness. Very few New Mexicans today—or any state's citizens—recall much about World War I in their community. That war has been consigned to a far corner in the attic of our national memory. But history offers a way to become reacquainted, an opportunity to reclaim from obscurity, and—most important of all—a means to understand more about ourselves by truly coming to know our past. At its most interesting history opens up stories of how the past influences and helps shape our present and future. This sense of history as a narrative linking past to present guided the research and writing of this book.

A starting point to reconnect is at the state level. Given World War I's massive scale and the demands it placed on everyone in the United States, it is fair to ask, Why study New Mexico? The short answer is that the particular reveals the universal; that is, New Mexico offers a state-level perspective on three braided processes fundamental to assessing the effects of World War I: mobilizing the home front; providing men to become soldiers, sailors, and marines and following them in their military service; and reintegrating returning veterans into the society, economy, and political life during the interwar decades. As important as those topics are, scant attention has been given to the war's effect at the state level. As a consequence, little is known about how states fulfilled the mandates the federal government thrust upon them between 1916 and 1919, and even less is understood about how a state dealt with veterans and their needs between 1919 and 1941. Thus, a study of one state has much to teach us about change in the lives of people who came to maturity during the war. The obvious focus for New Mexico is how men and women in a racially and ethnically diverse state experienced events during the war and after the armistice, especially returning veterans. But more broadly New Mexico offers a case study of economic disparity, political factionalism, urban versus rural lifeways, and gender and ethnic divisions. Although these conditions were not unique to New Mexico, they were more embedded in the war and its aftermath than has usually been recognized. Focusing on how the state responded to these challenges while coping with Washington's action or inaction sharpens our appreciation of the reciprocal influences shaping federal-state relations during three key events between 1917 and 1941: war, economic depression, and transformative public policies.[10]

One advantage of a state-level perspective is the closer look into the change wrought in the relationship between the federal government and citizens. Through a series of executive and legislative actions the federal government put in place wartime collectivism, or socialism, between 1917 and 1919. Three economic tenets central to socialism dictated relations between the federal government and its citizens: imposing national planning directed by Washington through the War Industries Board, headed by financier Bernard Baruch; substituting a command economy for free market activity, including nationalizing railroads, telegraphs, and telephones, with the greatest impact in New Mexico occurring after consolidation of railroad companies; and setting widespread wage and price controls, which dictated what farmers and ranchers earned when selling their bounty and the wages paid miners and railroad workers.[11]

A basic definition of history is the study of change over time, and New Mexico offers important evidence to situate World War I and its aftermath into two of the major trends in the twentieth century: the increased presence of the federal government in people's lives and the rise of welfare programs at the federal and state level. These two trends became permanently intertwined because of the manner in which the federal and state governments responded to veterans, especially in the 1930s. No previous study has explicitly traced the numerous ways in which veterans' demands propelled the growth of the welfare state and the expanded presence of the federal government in the 1920s and 1930s, developments that forever changed public policy in America. New Mexico had an outsized role in this transformative convergence because of two U.S. senators—old guard Republican Holm O. Bursum (1921–25) and progressive Republican Bronson M. Cutting (1927–35).

The national crisis and attendant mobilization of manpower exposed problems that could not be ignored after the armistice. One of these issues was people's poor health or, as it was often defined in that era, "the question of human improvement." Interest in bettering people's health had been on the rise under progressivism, a major political movement in the first quarter of the twentieth century. When Theodore Roosevelt campaigned as a progressive for president in 1912, he made history both for leading the Bull Moose Party and for being the first presidential candidate to pledge to enact health care for all Americans. Five years later, as Edgar Lee Hewett wrote in *New Mexico in the Great War,* "the war brought these questions [of the condition of Americans' health] to the front and in such an imperative way that they at once ceased to be debated and commanded instant attention." It became apparent by the fall of 1917 that among "men in the prime of their life, scarcely half were fit for [military] duty." During the war all military personnel were examined to detect tuberculosis, but New Mexicans received particular attention in such screenings because of the high number of the state's men infected. The manpower needs of the military and particularly, as Hewett noted, "the prospect of huge loses of the male population turned attention to the saving of infant life." New Mexico recognized its backwardness as compared to every other state in 1917–18 and focused on "the condition of children [and] their prospect for reaching useful maturity" beginning in 1919.[12]

Euro-American women reformers in New Mexico were part of a nationwide child health movement that resulted in the state's legislature creating an agency on child welfare immediately after the war. The state's American Legion posts joined forces with the women reformers beginning in the 1920s, and for twenty years thereafter child welfare remained a much larger public issue than is remembered. For example, New Mexico Legionnaires and members of its women's auxiliary had prominent roles as speakers at the American Legion's fourth annual child welfare conference attended by delegates from twelve western states in Portland, Oregon, 17–18 April 1931. The efforts of these reformers seeking to improve child well-being as the Great Depression settled over the state ought to prick our consciences. The same hurdles children faced between 1917 and 1941 persist today, as the state's senior U.S. senator Tom Udall noted in 2016: "New Mexico tragically lags behind the rest of the nation in access to healthcare, [reducing] infant mortality, school readiness, and household income, all key measures of how children and families are faring."[13]

When remembrance is understood as recalling someone or something to bring it present among us, then this book is a recovery project—uncovering long-silenced voices offering stories of sacrifice and heroism, loss and triumph, and trauma and resilience. This book makes no argument for New Mexico's uniqueness or singularity—except for the political relationship Senator Cutting had with the state's Nuevomexicano veterans. The war impacted lives in so many ways that, on one level, every American experienced it differently; however, when considered more broadly, shared experiences emerge. Three of these were situational—the home front, military service, and veterans' activities—and each of these provide a major organizational division in this study.[14]

Degrees of Change

Several events fundamentally altered New Mexico place in the world's consciousness beginning just four years after statehood. The first of these began when gunfire lashed the predawn quiet at Columbus, New Mexico, on Thursday, 9 March 1916. Nearly five hundred Mexicans loyal to insurgent leader Francisco "Pancho" Villa swarmed across the border to attack the army's Camp Furlong south of Columbus and then looted and burned the nearby town. Killed were eighteen Americans, women as well as men, including ten soldiers. The subsequent ten-month U.S. retaliation had two aspects. About ten thousand Regular Army troops undertook the "Punitive Expedition, U.S. Army," commanded by General John J. Pershing, which was resupplied from a large encampment at Columbus to which numerous New Mexico national guardsmen were posted, especially as military police. A separate military action began with a nationwide call-up of national guardsmen in June 1916. Eventually about 125,000 citizen-soldiers of the nation's reserve force assembled along the border, with Deming the site of one of the largest encampments. Both military responses were closely watched by key German military officials, who concluded that it showed that the American people and their military were wholly unprepared for full-scale war. Among the New Mexico National Guard infantrymen, 75 percent of the 750 troops were untrained, raw recruits, and Pershing's low opinion of the unit hampered their contributions in the AEF well into 1918. A notable exception was the outstanding reputation gained by the 1st New Mexico artillery battery from Roswell commanded by Capt. Charles M. de Bremond. His unit emerged from border duty with many accolades, and Pershing selected it to be among the first American artillery units to reach France late in 1917.[15]

The second event of lasting consequence occurred on Thursday, 1 March 1917. The *New York Times*—with government approval—published the threatening revelations contained in the infamous "Zimmermann telegram" intercepted between embassies in Germany and Mexico. In addition to planning to violate freedom of the seas with submarine attacks on the vessels of neutral nations, Germany sought to pit Mexico against the United States with a promise that a large swath of land in the Southwest—including New Mexico—would again fly the Mexican flag after Germany's victory. These threats to America's national sovereignty and international rights played directly into President Woodrow Wilson's evolving calculations to jettison his pledge of neutrality, which had been a key part of his reelection campaign just six months earlier. He began to angle for a new role on the world's stage, and he took America to war in the expectation of imposing his will on foreign nations through the terms of a treaty ending the conflict.[16]

In ways great and small the war also challenged—but did not fundamentally alter—existing relationships set by gender, race, and ethnicity. New Mexico's racial minorities—Native Americans, African Americans, and Asian Americans—had vastly different experiences from Euro-Americans and Nuevomexicanos in how they were permitted to support the war, particularly in whether they would be allowed to put on a military uniform. Though more than 12,000 Native Americans nationwide served in the army, only seventy were from New Mexico. Their exclusion, as explained in *New Mexico in the Great War,* came because officials "scoffed in 1917 when it was suggested to raise troops" from the state's American Indian communities. The full story of their exclusion is a complex tale of men in positions of authority fearing Native Americans would return from military service emboldened in their demand to be given the vote. About 200,000 African Americans served in the AEF, but fewer than 20 percent saw combat. The overwhelming majority were laborers, including almost all of the fifty or so African American draftees from New Mexico. Although segregation in both the army and society at large marginalized African Americans, such discrimination did not diminish the pride black communities had for their men who served. Upon returning home after having seen alternatives to their prewar circumstances, some African American men, particularly from Albuquerque, reinvented themselves with new jobs out of state. The Asian American communities in New Mexico were concentrated along the border with Mexico and in mining camps. Fewer than ten Asian Americans living in New Mexico, almost all having arrived between 1890 and 1905, were drafted. In addition, the army imported—and registered for the draft in June 1917 but never called to training camp—nearly two hundred Chinese Americans as contract laborers. They were placed at Camp Furlong in Columbus, where they resided and worked in isolation and seclusion until released to return home in 1919.[17]

How New Mexicans participated in the war and reacted to its consequences was influenced by gender and geography. Two separate, parallel statewide organizations emerged: the State Council of Defense and the Women's Auxiliary of the State Council of Defense. Each reported to national leadership in Washington, D.C., as well as assisting local representatives of two federal agencies—the Bureau of Investigation and the United States Food Administration. Euro-Americans and Nuevomexicanos were active in each organization, but Euro-American men and women—each drawn from upper middle-class backgrounds—were the prime movers in their respective defense councils.

In a predominantly rural state such as New Mexico, each organization had to overcome obstacles to enlisting help from Nuevomexicanos and Nuevomexicanas, ranging from barely passable roads to barriers of language and culture. But interethnic collaboration did occur, because every community had seen its own young men go into the military. The most successful appeals were ones where sacrifice was easily grasped as directly helping men serving their country, with Liberty Bond sales and food conservation broadly embraced. After the war the gender-based, two-tier model of participation persisted and was replicated for women in veterans' organizations and political party recruitment. But whether during wartime mobilization or during the interwar years, a small number of women, predominantly upper middle-class Euro-Americans, created within their own space opportunities to lead and advance their social and political priorities.

New Mexico's experiences during and after World War I merit attention at another level of remembrance. During the centennial of the Great War the universal appeal of stories heightens a desire to uncover the lived experiences of a century ago. When we do so we are brought face to face with two incongruous realities then and now: how war and its aftermath can unhinge society in ways that threaten the exercise of basic civil liberties, and simultaneously how people rally to defend their beliefs, their country, and the Constitution. Encountered in New Mexicans' experiences are compressed, localized versions of what the nation underwent. New Mexico offers quintessential examples of World War I's impact on civilians, servicemen, and veterans—on America—between 1916 and 1941.

The Face of War

Designation as the "Great War" stemmed from the British use of "great" to mean large or huge. That phrase echoed the French phrase *La grande guerre* (the big war), and in Germany it was identified for what it was—*Weltkrieg*, or world war. In the United States people initially called it the "Great War," but after it ended, a shift occurred and use of "World War" became increasingly common after 1930. The war pitted the Central Powers Germany, Austria-Hungary, and the Ottoman Empire (Turkey and much of the present-day Middle East) against the Allies, a worldwide collection of nations drawn into the war at varying times—and sometimes for parochial interests—during the course of its four years. The European nations France, Belgium, Great Britain, and Italy, together with Russia, were the core of the Allies, with substantial support from the United States beginning in 1917. Significant contributors to the war's global scale were the far-flung colonies of five major empires—British, French, German, Austro-Hungarian, and Ottoman—and lesser ones of Belgium and Portugal. Allied combatants (and some battlefields) spanned many continents: Asia (Japan, China, and Siam); Canada; Australia and New Zealand; the Indian subcontinent; and countries in west central, southwest, and eastern Africa. Also among Allied nations in central and southern Europe were Serbia, Bulgaria, Romania, and Greece. Nineteen Latin American and Caribbean countries joined the Allies in 1917 and 1918. In all, thirty-eight nations declared war on Germany, and eighteen of these sent troops into combat. Not until December 1917 did the U.S. Congress authorize war against Austria, and it never declared war on the Ottoman Empire.

Moreover, although the western front was the focus of much fighting, it was only one of several Euro-Asian theaters of combat. On the south side of the Alps, the Italians faced off against Austria-Hungary in northern Italy, especially in 1917–18. The eastern front pitted Russia against Germany from the opening of hostilities until, in the wake of the Russian Revolution in November 1917, the new regime signed a separate peace with Germany in February 1918. But later that year the United States and Great Britain, in a coalition with ten other countries, joined Russians loyal to the old order and fought against the new Bolshevik government in far east and northwest Russia between 1918 and 1920. New Mexicans participated in both the Russian and Italian campaigns.

"Carnage unspeakable has held humanity appalled," Edgar Lee Hewett wrote to describe battlefield deaths. The total casualties befitted the British sense of a Great War: at least eleven million military personnel and seven million civilians died as a result of hostilities. But the most haunting statistic was the worldwide death toll from the influenza pandemic of 1918–19: between fifty and one hundred million. The pandemic killed at least 650,000 in the United States, which was more than five times the 117,000 Americans who died in uniform. About three thousand New Mexico civilians died in the influenza pandemic.[18]

Of New Mexicans in uniform, 502 lost their lives in World War I: 26 percent were killed in action; disease claimed 54 percent; wounds were responsible for 13 percent of the deaths; accidents accounted for 5 percent; and 2 percent were listed as "unknown" or "suicide." These casualties became granular history. Analogous to sand churned in waves at an ocean's shoreline, the data are gritty, insistent, and cannot be ignored. So, too, do the voluminous casualty records—in compelling narratives—separate themselves from most of the 3,400 extant service questionnaires. The battlefield's casualties reveal ordinary New Mexicans doing extraordinary things. They deserve to be heard—and remembered. If this book does nothing else, I hope it allows all sacrifices from a century ago to be known and present among us always.[19]

The Granular Approach

New Mexico in the Great War embraced as a goal the "imperative that impressions of actions and conditions be put down by those who can speak as eye witnesses." Priority was given two emotionally laden scenes: "the heart-throbs of the people as they answered the summons to war" and "the feelings of brave sons as . . . can be known only to those who looked into their eyes as they marched away." Though deeply felt, the raw, human drama of such moments are almost entirely absent in first-person accounts collected by the Board of Historical Service. Frequently rote responses from servicemen on their questionnaires reduced their year or two in the military to a recitation of facts: units assigned; dates departed from training camp and arrived in France; a cramped ride in a train car that could hold either forty men or eight horses; a list of battles or duties behind the line; and discharge information.[20]

Similarly, their letters sent while in the AEF are almost eerily devoid of emotion. Strict censorship meant men almost never said anything about the war itself. Instead, four stock topics dominated the small talk in their letters: how is everyone; how goes it with the crops or herd or business; how is the weather there—here it is miserable, rains all the time, and mud is everywhere; and say hello to everyone and please, please write soon.

All of these stock topics were present in a letter Pvt. Harry M. Day sent his younger brother in mid-June, but censorship had been slightly relaxed. Thirty-year-old Day of Curry County, of medium height and build with blue eyes and dark hair, had found employment as a farm laborer in Canada and South Dakota and was in Montana when war was declared, where he registered for the draft on 5 June 1917. In July he enlisted in a Montana-based National Guard unit. In late October this unit and others were ordered to Camp MacArthur in Waco, Texas, to fill out the 32nd Division. His letter, written on YMCA letterhead, began with the ubiquitous phrase "Somewhere in France" and was dated "June 14, 1918." He immediately explained the nature of the letter: "For just this letter only they will let us tell a little. I have been in the trenches and over no man's-land more than once. Would like to tell you some experiences but I can't." The only detail of his army life he offered was this cryptic account: "Can't tell you what kind of gun I have but I haven't got the regular Army rifle [Springfield 30.06]. Have a good record shooting [the French automatic rifle, Chauchat]. Well guess I have said about all that is allowed under the circumstances." He asked his brother to "tell Mother not to worry about me. I came over here to fight and no s.o.b. Boche [German] will keep me from getting back [home] again." Day was killed firing his Chauchat while charging entrenched Germans on 1 September.[21]

The power of some personal stories lost to later generations is tantalizingly hinted at in a *Roswell Daily Record* account from mid-January 1919. When the commander of the state's National Guard artillery, Lt. Col. Charles M. de Bremond, spoke about his troops' experiences in France, he filled "every seat in the big court room" in the Chaves County courthouse. De Bremond was the first combat officer from New Mexico to return home when evacuated for medical treatment of the cumulative effects of poison gas attacks. For three hours his audience listened so intently that "a pin drop could have been heard at any time," but all that remains of his words is the reporter's description: "His talk was an intimate heart-to-heart talk, telling the little personal, everyday happenings, as well as the great big history-making events." Upon returning to Roswell, de Bremond perhaps sensed that recovery was unlikely, because he seemed driven to tell as many people as he could about his troops' military life, speaking to at least five local audiences in his first month home. But he had compartmentalized himself, revealing to civilians only common incidents of daily life and generalized accounts of strategy and tactics. On the other hand, to cadets at Roswell's New Mexico Military Institute during two hours he described "war as it was." Eleven months later he died, leaving neither a service questionnaire nor any written account.[22]

This separation of what civilians and soldiers would know about the war remained a divide rarely bridged, with one notable exception. Veterans—and the American public in general—enthusiastically embraced Metro-Goldwyn-Mayer's 1925 silent film *The Big Parade,* directed by King Vidor. He incorporated some actual wartime footage, and his scenes of the AEF before, during, and after combat are regarded as mostly unembellished depictions. In an era when films were screened for one week and then replaced, *The Big Parade* was routinely shown for many months and in some large cities for more than a year—domestically grossing more than $4.99 million (the equivalent of $69.5 million in 2017) in its initial release and becoming the highest-earning film of the 1920s. New Mexico American Legion lodges were part of a nationwide effort to have members and their families see the movie in 1925–26.[23]

Perhaps part of the reason so many ex-servicemen never broke open their experiences or shared them freely was an insight available since 1895 when Stephen Crane published *The Red Badge of Courage.* During and after the Civil War, civilians believed their loved ones marched off to battlefields ever guided by nobly chivalrous notions of valor, bravery, and equanimity. The returning veterans never disabused them of their naiveté, but Crane's quintessential novel of that war—as one scholar has argued—bridged the gap between "intellectual statement or verbal abstraction, and earned—because felt and experienced—understanding." In doing so Crane's novel "renounced the gloriousness of war" and instead presented battlefields "as violence that swirls with confusion, psychological as well as physical." Censorship aside, perhaps the most basic reason that World War I was never fully revealed to civilians was, as Crane realized, that no clear pattern, no meaningful narrative thread emerged, only unrelenting chaos.[24]

But rare flashes revealing "the heart-throbs of the people" are found—always from civilians and particularly in letters from grieving parents. One of these made its way into *New Mexico in the Great War.* The sorrow expressed dissolves all the usual buffers separating past from present. Rio Arriba County draftees assembled to depart from the railroad platform in Española in late spring 1918. Among those "who went with our young men to say our final good-byes" was the stepfather of twenty-three-year-old Silas Tafoya, an unmarried schoolteacher who had ended the term just two days earlier. With the time to board the train approaching, the two men, "each six feet tall, hugged one another as they said good-bye forever, but neither was able to hold back their tears but let them cascade freely leaving tracks on their cheeks." Private Tafoya's family remembered him as a brave, patriotic soldier whose life "was offered on the altar of Liberty and Independence" during the St. Mihiel offensive in mid-September 1918. Bloom included excerpts of the letter in his essay but provided no personal information and even left it in the original Spanish.[25]

Bloom's editorial choices were significant. Excerpting the letter and omitting biographical or other identifying information allowed him to generalize a singularly poignant, or granular, account. The particular became universal. Bloom thus elevated Private Tafoya's death to a level of meaning beyond the family's religious and patriot-tinged explanation. Remembrance became a memorial, allowing Tafoya and all deceased from the war to be present eternally. In memorializing one death, Bloom asserted a humanistic perspective to challenge the dehumanization inherent in the world's first mechanized war and its unrestrained capacity to bring death on a hitherto unimaginable scale. President Woodrow Wilson likewise had grappled with the reality of the maw of war after delivering his address to Congress on 2 April 1917. Later that evening he remarked, "My message today was a message of death for our young men." As he reflected on all that had happened on battlefields since August 1914 and what surely lay ahead, Wilson grew despondent and "laid his head on the Cabinet table and sobbed, 'as if he had been a child.'"[26]

My approach in granular history is best understood as a means to look to the past to teach us; the instructors are the very people studied and their lessons are experiences shared in their own voices. A distinguished scholar of Asian American history has catalogued where voices can be found, and my sources duplicated his: "By *voices* we mean their own words and stories as told in their oral histories, conversations, speeches, soliloquies, and songs, as well as in their own writings—diaries, letters, newspapers, magazines, pamphlets, placards, posters, flyers, court petitions, autobiographies, short stories, novels, and poems. Their voices contain particular expressions and phrases with their own meanings and nuances, the cuttings from the cloth of languages."[27]

Adopting this attention to voices continues a re-visioning of the history of World War I, but it has limits. I could not draw back the curtain on what is euphemistically known as "leisure time." The best my sources allowed was lifting one corner an inch or so to take a fleeting peak. A reference to "wine and women" in a post-armistice letter an Estancia soldier wrote a cousin implied much but confessed nothing: "I can get a pass to go to town might near anytime I want to go and sure have a time when I go for there are lots of girls and plenty to drink most anywhere you go."[28]

The collection of service questionnaires together with other documents add significantly to a general understanding of a generation of New Mexican men and women. When read closely these eyewitnesses describe a socioeconomic reality that changed little between 1900 and 1940. The state remained overwhelmingly rural, large swaths were a subsistence economy, poverty and rudimentary levels of education were all too commonplace, and for too many the meager cash economy of a farm or ranch led to little if any capital accumulation.

Lest We Forget

The phrase "lest we forget" is often used as a cautionary warning that if lessons once known are lost we are in peril of bumbling into avoidable pitfalls. The phrase is a concise but oblique version of Spanish-born poet and philosopher Jorge (George) Santayana's famous dictum in 1906: "Those who cannot remember the past are condemned to repeat it." Of the many shrouded avenues of human experience that might be illuminated by the guiding light of the past, the one that has been most discussed in recent years in terms of the lessons of World War I is what has come to be called "sleepwalkers." It refers to being unprepared and underestimating a coming crisis and singles out leaders incapable of decisive and proactive problem solving, officials who were "watchful but unseeing . . . blind to the reality of the horror they were about to bring into the world." A noted British officer and combat veteran, Robert Graves, described meeting David Lloyd George in the spring of 1916, seven months before the latter became prime minister. Graves took Lloyd George's measure, "looked closely at his eyes," and found "that they seemed like those of a sleep-walker." European rulers allowed events to pull them along toward disaster in 1914 while a distracted and powerless public watched military commanders cling to outmoded tactics that consigned millions of soldiers to death in trench warfare. The United States' year-long struggle to train, equip, and transport the troops of the AEF to France did not kindle a postwar consensus to fund the military to ensure preparedness. Instead isolationism prevailed during the interwar decades as Congress and presidents greatly reduced the military's capabilities so tortuously attained in 1917–18. Only in 1940 did scales begin to fall from leaders' eyes and a sense of urgency propel action on military preparedness after two decades of neglect. World War I as a cautionary tale of the consequences of leaders wearing blinders in treacherous times is a central lesson Afghanistan veteran and decorated U.S. Army captain (and former Rhodes scholar and West Point graduate) Craig M. Mullaney taught as a service academy instructor in 2005-8. "We studied World War I in depth," he wrote, "not because I wanted to shock them with the horrors of the trenches, but because I wanted them to see how rational statesmen had blundered into a war no one wanted."[29]

The notion of sleepwalkers is also important because it highlights five points that need to be understood about World War I. First, one hundred years later and that war is not a settled conflict. As any number of commentators have noted, there is a tragic irony that the centennial of that conflagration brings daily reminders of one of the haunting failures of the peace accord—leaving festering conflicts unresolved in the Middle East. A distinguished scholar of World War I's detritus has written, "It was in the Middle East that the most significant imperial legacies of the war are to be found." The conflicts there today are residue of misguided colonialism, which in turn unleashed local attempts at decolonization that have degenerated into religious and even tribal bloodletting. For those looking on from outside the region, as Captain Mullaney reminds us, too often we uncritically accept and act on assumptions that ought to be vigorously challenged before allowing troops to be put in harm's way. That is a timeless lesson.[30]

Second, World War I bequeathed domestic issues contested to the present. Some of these unresolved matters are recurring themes in my account; others are specific topics. Foremost among the former is the reciprocal relationship between citizens and the federal government. The war years witnessed an unprecedented expansion of federal authority that saddled everyday life with a never before imagined degree of government regulation. Take the simple act of eating a candy bar, which during the war brought two federal agencies into the picture: the Revenue Service collected a wartime tax on the sales of candy bars, and the Food Administration required candy makers to reduce the amount of sugar and use substitute sweeteners. How did New Mexicans react to the federal government's new, unparalleled empowerment? They willingly accepted these changes, as did most Americans during the war, a topic addressed at length in chapters 2-4. Why did an activist, interventionist role of government gain the people's support? One key reason was that it required widespread personal commitment and shared sacrifice. Wartime mobilization concentrated more power in the government's hands, but it also promoted personal responsibility and self-reliance. If there was genius in President Wilson's wartime socialism, it lay in the way he skillfully drew upon the main currents of civic and political discourse in early twentieth-century America. He tempered government control with individual responsibility. Wilson took the Progressive Era's penchant for federal intervention and infused it with self-reliance, a belief deeply ingrained in America's psyche—and a cornerstone of Republican principles since Lincoln's time. This formula broke down quickly after the armistice, leaving veterans to confront and navigate an American political order divided over how much responsibility the government would assume in caring for them.

War weariness and disillusionment are a third way in which soldiers' and civilians' reactions bring to mind current events. This theme became a drum beaten loudly by a number of the most prominent authors in the interwar decades, the so-called Lost Generation including John Dos Passos, e. e. cummings, F. Scott Fitzgerald, William Faulkner, and Ernest Hemingway. But lesser known writers, including some military men with extensive combat experience, likewise published novels and memoirs echoing the disillusionment trope. There exists parallel to these works, though, a body of literature that thrusts up complexity to confront anyone making broad generalizations about the nature of World War I and its impact on men in uniform. To illustrate this complexity, I briefly discuss two topics often slighted: matters of faith and the psychological (or mental health) consequences of World War I, considered in chapters 7 and 9, respectively. Trauma, of course, underlies each because mind and soul confronted violence, depravity, and death—all encountered with unimaginable frequency. Combat makes men killers, and dealing with that reality became a central psychological tension for veterans from the front.[31]

A fourth point that needs to be remembered when considering World War I is perspective. Too much attention to leaders-cum-sleepwalkers will overshadow the results yielded when we narrow our focus, which brings us back to New Mexico's part in the war. Throughout the writing of this book the admonition many writers have heard—"show, don't tell"—was in my mind's playlist; that is, I let people's accounts reveal the speakers—civilian men (chapters 2, 8, and 9), women (chapters 3, 8, and 9), and men in uniform and as veterans (chapters 4–9).

Chapter 9 is organized around this insight from a scholar of the American Civil War: "Every war begins as one war and becomes two, that watched by the civilians and that fought by soldiers. . . . In the postwar period . . . as soldiers return and the military and civilian spheres recombine, two wars must again become one in the public's understanding. At stake are the social integration or isolation of the veteran and the society's receptivity or resistance to new wars." I examine in particular "the social integration or isolation of the veteran" and argue that the "two wars" remained distinct, separate, and opposing memories for combat veterans and among their loved ones. The two "understandings" of World War I did not recombine. Instead, they were simultaneously present, or double, with implications rippling through people's lives and across the public sphere in the interwar decades. Another way to understand double is found in Colonel de Bremond's talks, which compartmentalized his experiences into separate spheres—one for civilians and another for young men in training for military service. When talking at the courthouse de Bremond spoke in generalities, but when addressing young cadets at Roswell's military institute he unmasked war as only a combat veteran could. His talks were emblematic of the simultaneous but separate realities combat soldiers carried into their civilian lives.[32]

The fifth and final issue to be addressed in considering the title phrase "lest we forget" is this: What led to the interwar generation's obscurity in New Mexico and throughout the nation after 1941? In part it was numbers: sixteen million soldiers served in World War II, four times more than in World War I. Moreover, by the 1930s the voice of World War I ex-servicemen was diffuse. The collective actions that produced legislative victories in the areas of health care and compensation benefits during the 1920s quickly shifted to individual encounters between ex-servicemen and bureaucrats over proving their eligibility in the 1930s, struggles almost always unknown to the general public. The vicissitudes of the Great Depression, especially unemployment, and the inexorable toll from mortality played their parts, too, in muting veterans' voices. The brutal suppression of the Bonus Army March in July 1932 pricked the conscience of many, but it took a new president and several more years to begin to address the demand for jobs, and not until the late 1930s did federal dollars for defense spending spur long-term employment, which in many instances required moving away from New Mexico. But there were also fewer World War I veterans, and inevitably the old order does pass. For example, at least 346 New Mexico servicemen were interred in Bernalillo County cemeteries by 1939. But perhaps it was the difference between the two wars' outcomes that pushed the World War I generation farthest into the shadows. Unconditional surrender after World War II contrasted starkly with the arc of events etched by a generation who in 1918 confidently believed that their victory would end all wars. Such was not to happen, of course, and instead the punitive terms of the Treaty of Versailles aroused resentment in most Germans, which led to the rise of Adolph Hitler, who consolidated his power as chancellor beginning in 1933 and militarized the Rhineland in 1936. A long fuse had been lit at the end of World War I, one that finally detonated in Europe in September 1939 and at Pearl Harbor on 7 December 1941.[33]

CHAPTER 2

Patriotism

Sunday, 28 April 1918, was a sunny, warm spring day across New Mexico. The favorable weather brought out large crowds at rallies in Albuquerque and Carlsbad promoting the sale of Liberty Bonds to help finance the war. But in Albuquerque a German American, W. E. Faust, employed in the local maintenance shop of the Atchison, Topeka and Santa Fe Railway, reportedly "spoke ill of our American government and refused to buy [Liberty] bonds." His coworkers considered his words and actions "traitorous" and an affront to the more than one hundred local railroad workers in the army. His coworkers seized him, abused him verbally and physically, paraded him through the streets, and "made [him] kiss the glorious stars of our flag" wrapped around him. Upon arriving at the edge of town, Faust was tarred, feathered, and kicked out of Albuquerque. The previous evening in Carlsbad a local resident, Henry J. Lang, was "given a coat of tar and feathers" after leaving a bond rally where "he cursed the members of the [sales] committee and refused to buy a bond."[1]

The two incidents frustrated Charles Springer. The consummate political insider and master of backroom deals, whom many believed to be "New Mexico's real boss," found himself in an unfamiliar position in the spring of 1918—being ignored. He shared a dilemma with defense council administrators in other states. In an atmosphere of hyperpatriotism, devotion to country and loyalty to its values were being perverted by a virulent strain of patriotism—vigilantism. In

April 1918 war fever intensified in the wake of major enemy advances in France, spawning lawlessness and mob violence against German Americans.[2]

The Atchison, Topeka and Santa Fe Railway's maintenance shop was near Las Barelas in Albuquerque, where it employed hundreds of workers drawn from the town's two largest ethnic groups—Nuevomexicanos and Euro-Americans. Collectively Albuquerque's railroad workers had demonstrated their loyalty by pledging $75,000 ($1.4 million in 2017) in the third Liberty Bond drive. But when Faust flaunted his disloyalty, his coworkers reacted in the same manner that some residents of Carlsbad had when Lang refused to buy bonds. They meted out punishment "that he will not forget as long as he lives, even if that is 100 years." *La Bandera Americana* described the perpetrators in Albuquerque as "100 percent Americans and patriots" and further claimed that the "railroad workers, one and all, make up our best citizens."[3]

Charles Springer and other public officials had a different opinion. On the Friday preceding the attacks, Springer alerted county sheriffs to be on their guard to prevent any outbreak of mob rule. The next day he, together with U.S. attorney Summers Burkhart and Governor Washington E. Lindsey, appealed to the public on behalf of the State Council of Defense to be "cool-headed, patriotic citizens" and avoid "the mob spirit and acts of lawlessness." Some in Carlsbad and Albuquerque ignored these pleas.[4]

Vigilantism

The two attacks in New Mexico on the weekend of 27–28 April 1918 illustrated recurring patriotic violence during World War I. Understanding these incidents turns on events throughout April, beginning with the approach of the first-year anniversary of the declaration of war. A lynching early in the morning on 5 April 1918 ignited a month-long spasm of vengeance-fueled attacks. The victim was Robert P. Prager, a German American baker and miner, who died in southwest Illinois very near St. Louis. Barely eighteen hours later, President Wilson was briefed on the attack by his attorney general at the cabinet's weekly meeting, and "the hope [was expressed] that there will be no repetition elsewhere."[5]

President Wilson and other officials in Washington, D.C., pressed state councils of defense into service to urge calm. Wilson's appeal also galvanized newspapers to condemn the lynching. Typical of newspaper responses were editorials in the *New York Times* and *Chicago Daily Tribune* denouncing mobs using "lynching as a demonstration of patriotism." The *Times* claimed "a fouler wrong could hardly be done America," and the Chicago paper noted that the hanging had "played out under the guise of patriotism" but was in fact "an example of the dark forces of ignorance." Many people wondered if "dark forces" had not prevailed again when, in late May, a jury returned a verdict of "patriotic murder" in acquitting the eleven defendants accused in Prager's hanging.[6]

Calls for calm and restraint did not douse the fires blazing in many people's hearts and minds. Fear and hatred were fanned beginning in late March 1918 when Germany launched a massive spring offensive that had three goals: drive the British into the English Channel; capture Paris; and end the war before the AEF could become a formidable military presence. In the offensive's opening ten weeks the Germans forced the British to retreat to the coast and pushed the front to within sixty miles of Paris, which they began regularly shelling. U.S. newspapers carried daily reports of these setbacks for the Allies, and amid the heightened anxieties, as a contemporary observed, "the lynching of Prager is regarded here [Washington, D.C.] as an instance of an aroused feeling among the American people since the beginning of the German offensive. This feeling is observed in occurrences all over the country." April 1918 also marked the beginning of the third national campaign to sell Liberty Bonds. Sales pitches ramped up patriotic rhetoric and emotions, and in Albuquerque and Carlsbad zeal quickly turned to vigilantism.[7]

New Mexicans vacillated between denunciation and approval in their opinions of mob violence. Several nights after Prager's lynching, four thousand Albuquerque residents jammed into the local armory to mark the one-year anniversary of America's entry into the war. The main speaker offered a contradictory message on violence. He told the boisterous audience that "the time has come to stop shooting men because they bear German names," but then he went on to say it was OK "to commence shooting I.W.W's.," members of the anarchist-leaning Industrial Workers of the World union. A similar mixed message appeared in the *Santa Fe New Mexican* on 18 April 1918, when it editorialized that wartime America would shun "hysterical mob violence" but then undercut itself by stating, "To be brutally frank, what America most needs at home right now is a considerable number of Hun [German] tombstones." The state's capital city newspaper condemned the lynching in Illinois but also "found it a healthy and wholesome awakening in the interior of the country" and favored having suspected German spies shot without trial. Additional vigilante actions across the state ranging from assault to tar-and-feathering occurred in Santa Fe, Deming, Gallup, and Sugarite (Colfax County) in the spring of 1918.[8]

La Bandera Americana, the state's most widely distributed Spanish-language newspaper, published in Albuquerque, carried the only press account of the attack on Faust. Monday's *Albuquerque Morning Journal* made no mention of the Sunday assault, but it did carry a brief story on Lang's tar-and-feathering. In the days immediately preceding these attacks, however, the *Journal* contributed significantly to the visceral hatred of Germans by publishing on its front page five photographic reproductions of paintings under the heading "The Huns Did This." Each inflammatory picture depicted purported incidents of German soldiers torturing, murdering, and mutilating French men, women, and children. Two of the scenes showed young French women stripped naked and impaled on bayonets in barns. These lurid images were part of systematic and widespread wartime anti-German propaganda based on reported incidents in Belgium and France in 1914 and 1915, and they tapped into primordial fears of barbarians rampaging among vulnerable civilians. The atrocities depicted in the five illustrations were distillations of stories "authenticated" by British and French officials, but within a decade of the war's end almost all these reports were shown to be unsubstantiated.[9]

New Mexicans who took matters into their own hands were both vigilantes and patriots. The very acts Springer, Burkhart, and the governor decried as lawlessness were intended to demonstrate abiding commitment to the body politic. Patriotism-cum-vigilantism was deemed inevitable by the *Albuquerque Morning Journal* in early April 1918. An editorial posited an ends-justify-the-means rationalization to explain citizens taking justice into their own hands: "Congress is now squabbling over a sedition bill which would bring within the power of the courts many offenses against the government in time of war for which there is now no punishment. Where there is no civil or military law for the punishment of spies and obstructionists, the only remedy is in mob law." Four days earlier Burkhart acknowledged his lack of authority in "many offenses against the government." He informed the assistant district attorney of Socorro County that a man arrested in the western part of that county for "pro-German utterances or disloyal remarks in a saloon" had to be turned loose because there was "no federal law under which to handle him." The assistant district attorney matter-of-factly reported to Springer on 11 April 1918 that, after the prisoner's release, "he was found hanging from a pinon tree with a barbed wire around his neck." Several days later another mob intent on hanging a vocal pro-German hotel proprietor, also in Socorro County, was foiled when the town's sheriff put the man in protective custody.[10]

Congress passed two bills during the war to protect the home front from those seeking, in President Wilson's words, to "pour the poison of disloyalty into the very arteries of our national life." The Espionage Act (15 June 1917) outlawed any interference with military preparedness, including recruitment, and the Sedition Act (16 May 1918), which actually amended the Espionage Act, prohibited expressing opinions offensive to the nation or seeking to corrupt its loyal citizens. The Sedition Act was repealed on 3 March 1921, President Wilson's last day in office, but the Espionage Act, as modified by later revisions, remains in effect today. Federal agents immediately began enforcing the Espionage Act in New Mexico, directing much effort toward so-called slackers who either evaded registering for the draft or failed to report when called, but the federal Bureau of Investigation investigated at least one desertion in which a German American convinced an African American Regular Army soldier stationed at Columbus, New Mexico, to abandon his post.[11]

Surveillance

Going to war seemed to unhinge many Americans. It was not simply that usual routines were altered everywhere on the home front. Wartime mobilization stoked anxieties unleashed by the handmaidens of troubled times—fear and suspicion. Distrust enveloped German-born residents and their descendants, but a watchful eye also fell on one's friends and neighbors. Various popular, mass-circulating magazines such as the *Saturday Evening Post* accepted illustrated advertisements from the government's official publicity and propaganda organization, the Committee on Public Information, which urged readers to inform the Department of Justice about "the man who spreads pessimistic stories . . . cries for peace, or belittles our efforts to win the war." The prevailing sense of community suddenly mutated into what has been described as "the paranoid style in American politics." In a now classic essay, the late historian Richard J. Hofstadter defined "the paranoid style" as a social pathology characterized by "angry minds" disposed toward "seeing the world and expressing oneself" in ways that were a product of "heated exaggeration, suspiciousness, and conspiratorial fantasy." Atrocity stories and rabid anti-German attacks that occurred in New Mexico and across the United States stemmed from people's conviction that the nation was "in a conflict between absolute good and absolute evil." In this struggle, according to Hofstadter, "the enemy is clearly delineated: he is a perfect model of malice, a kind of amoral superman—sinister, ubiquitous, powerful, cruel."[12]

Patriotic fervor unleashed by war gave free rein to innumerable "angry minds" and reached its most fevered pitch in episodes of vigilantism during the early spring of 1918. But the climate of suspicion had been evident earlier, and the

U.S. attorney general reported receiving daily "as many as one thousand letters" lodging allegations of disloyalty and enemy activities in mid-November 1917. To address the public's growing alarm over the parlous situation of the United States beset by domestic foes, state and federal officials enlisted the public as surveillance agents. Doing so became at times a volatile experiment in empowerment. Contributing to the difficulties of channeling the public's suspicions was an inevitable clumsiness associated with inventing ways to funnel allegations upward from citizens to various organizations conducting investigations. The proto-surveillance state—whether at the local or federal level—struggled to put in place bureaucratic structures to conduct its activities. The experiences of New Mexico's officials are illustrative of attempts to balance enlisting the public as their eyes and ears with maintaining their reins of authority.[13]

The largest nationally coordinated citizen-surveillance web, the American Protective League (APL), operated within the Department of Justice's Bureau of Investigation (BI), and it had a reported quarter-million unpaid civilian volunteers nationwide. By the time Governor Lindsey received U.S. attorney general T. W. Gregory's letter endorsing the APL's patriotic service in mid-November 1917, the group had been active in New Mexico for at least four months. The founder and head of the organization, Chicago advertising executive A. M. Briggs, sent a four-page letter to recruit a prominent Euro-American resident of Rio Arriba County on 23 August 1917. Briggs invited the individual to become chief of the local division of the APL, tasked with "assisting the Department [of Justice] in securing information of the activities of Agents of foreign governments, or persons unfriendly to this government for the protection of public property." That awkwardly worded invitation would have been understood as having various targets of surveillance. Germans in America were feared as potential "agents of foreign governments." Even though they constituted less than 2 percent of New Mexico's population, Germans "still comprised the largest single nationality among the foreign-born" nationwide. As a consequence, after 1917 "the Germans fell subject . . . to the plain and simple accusation in which every type of xenophobia culminated: the charge of disloyalty."[14]

The reference to "persons unfriendly to this government for the protection of public property" was aimed at two perceived threats: labor unions, especially the IWW, and certain Mexicans, Mexican Americans, and some African Americans believed to be loyal to a faction in the Mexican Revolution. Both groups had sparked alarm in recent years, and the specter of their disrupting the established order became the engine driving surveillance in New Mexico during the war's first few months. In the summer of 1917 the prospect loomed large in the minds of many that IWW agitators would sweep across New Mexico, shut down mines through strikes, and interrupt the wartime flow of coal. To thwart the IWW, preemptive attacks on miners occurred, first in Bisbee, Arizona, in mid-July and then in Gallup at the end of July 1917. In both towns, anti-union vigilantes rounded up miners, locked them in railroad cars, and had them hauled away. The nearly 1,300 miners deported from Bisbee in twenty-seven railway cars were deposited 200 miles to the east in the desert near Columbus, New Mexico, and thirty-four miners from Gallup were transported about 150 miles and left in Belen.[15]

The Bisbee Deportation, as it became known, was an illegal action that set in motion a series of impromptu responses. The federal government directed the army commander at Camp Furlong in Columbus to feed and shelter the deportees and keep them from disrupting local life. Over the next two months a wary Governor Lindsey received updates from a hand-picked agent who closely monitored both Columbus and nearby Deming. While calm prevailed in Columbus, Deming's local council of defense became community watchmen, a role that vastly exceeded the Council of National Defense's plans for local councils, which were expected solely to provide grassroots leadership in fund-raising, recruiting soldiers, and conserving food. But proximity to the encampment of IWW deportees prompted Deming's local council to write President Wilson at the end of July, "calling his attention to the seriousness of this matter" and demanding the miners' removal. By late September only a handful of Bisbee miners remained in Columbus. In similar fashion the Gallup miners deposited south of Albuquerque also quietly faded away.[16]

More ominous than labor unrest in the minds of many were threats from a plot to overthrow the U.S. government in the Southwest and set up a Hispanic republic loyal to the then ruling faction in the Mexican Revolution, a scheme uncovered in 1915 and pursued by the BI in New Mexico well into 1917. The length of the Bureau's inquiry is evidence that it overestimated the threat even though BI agents had abundant proof that the plot had unraveled and collapsed in the summer of 1916.[17]

The APL sought to be a line of defense against national and regional threats by creating a nationwide surveillance network. The prospective division chief in Rio Arriba County was encouraged to cooperate with the local chief of police, recruit "the big successful business and professional men in your town," and enroll sufficient numbers of volunteers "so that you will be immediately informed of any activity that may prove directly or indirectly unfriendly or not to the best interests of the Government." But the APL in New Mexico left only a scant paper trail, perhaps because it followed restraint seen in Las Vegas. There the APL leadership—the sheriff, a leading merchant, the postmaster, and a federal employee—exercised caution because their community had a history of constructive engagement with German-born residents, many of whom had been successful merchants in the area since the 1850s. Also likely is that the state's network of county councils of defense, coupled with federal investigators, provided citizens sufficient access to authorities to whom to report their suspicions.[18]

Federal Authorities

The State Council of Defense and its county councils were particularly active in the early months of the war, but they were quickly eclipsed in number and scope by the federal government's investigations. Overseeing the government's enlarged surveillance role was the U.S. attorney for New Mexico, Summers Burkhart. When war was declared, he had been a U.S. attorney for four years and was fifty-seven years old. He had broad familiarity with New Mexico based on twenty-five-plus years of legal practice in the state. His duties grew considerably during the war when post offices and the U.S. marshal's office were enlisted to assist the Department of Justice in monitoring civilians. Suddenly Burkhart had a greatly expanded purview, but what he lacked was an administrative apparatus to conduct investigations. El Paso was the nearest field office of the BI, and it handled most of New Mexico's cases prior to the war. In late spring Burkhart set about securing BI offices within his jurisdiction. Within twelve months seven BI agents, all lawyers and several of draft age, were working out of Albuquerque (three), Deming (two), Roswell (one), and Tucumcari (one). Assisting these agents were paid informants recruited among Spanish speakers in various communities.[19]

For the first year of the war, the BI agents investigated alleged violations of three federal acts: the draft (interfering with registration, failing to register, or evading induction); alien enemy registration (failing to register and violating restrictions on movement); and espionage (hindering military preparations or taking action, including mailing printed materials, that aided or supported U.S. enemies). After enactment of the Sedition Act in mid-May 1918, the BI agents in New Mexico were busy checking out reports of scurrilous utterances or other verbal attacks on the government and President Wilson. The BI also was involved in investigating crimes specific to the army training camp at Deming, including liquor sales to soldiers, trafficking in drugs, and prostitution. On a few occasions

BI agents received information from other federal employees, including forest rangers, who reported suspected draft dodgers and on one occasion arrested an alleged saboteur in Taos County in September 1918.[20]

Given that New Mexico's land mass was the fourth largest among the forty-eight states, BI agents spent much of their time on trains, in hired automobiles, and even with horse-and-buggy when that was all that was available. As a result they worked long days in the field followed by hours spent completing paperwork. Official procedures in place throughout the war required that field reports be forwarded daily to Washington, D.C., but few agents anywhere could comply once war was declared. Moreover, in New Mexico only two of the agents were fluent in Spanish, so paid informants often did follow-up with Nuevomexicanos. When investigations involved allegations of failure to register for the draft, it was necessary to verify birth dates to determine if a violation of the draft law had occurred. Because birth certificates were not issued in New Mexico in that era, and indeed hospital births were infrequent, the BI employed paid informants to track down parish baptismal records or inspect family bibles, which Protestants used to record births. Upon completing an inquiry, the informant often telephoned an agent to relay the findings, but on occasion the informant filed a report. Draft and induction cases overwhelmed BI agents; in appealing for more investigators one BI agent told his division superintendent in mid-March 1918 that "in McKinley County alone there are upwards of one hundred and fifty [draft and induction] delinquents." Socorro and Valencia Counties were also singled out as having high numbers of such cases. But the request for additional staff went unheeded.[21]

In early spring 1918, Burkhart publically acknowledged that he and his Department of Justice investigators had received "a large number of complaints about alleged disloyalty," but he also noted that "when investigated [they] proved to be without foundation." Burkhart publically urged calm to tamp down fear, but privately he vented frustration and disgust over spurious allegations. In a bitter private exchange addressed to A. Bruce Bielaski, the head of the BI in Washington, D.C., he refuted accusations made by a citizen-informant organization, the American Defense Society, at the end of January 1918. This group, with headquarters in New York City, denounced a German-born resident of Valencia County, citing information provided by an informant in Curry County. The American Defense Society then made a sweeping claim "that a small clique of wealthy men, several of whom are pro-German, in New Mexico have such overwhelming influence . . . that it is very difficult to do anything through the State officials."

When Burkhart received a copy of the American Defense Society's charges in mid-January, the individual named had already come to the attention of the BI's Albuquerque office three months earlier and been investigated. Burkhart, long a proponent of statehood, took great exception to the claim that the state was failing to fulfill its wartime duties. Calling the group's informants "unmitigated liars," he bluntly refuted aspersions cast on the new state and requested that Bielaski forward his reply to the American Defense Society.[22]

Burkhart's testiness was uncharacteristic, but his wariness over exaggerated and outright false claims was shared by BI agents under him, who frequently encountered baseless accusations of disloyalty. One of his agents investigated an alleged pro-German "plot to haul poison out through the cattle country [near Magdalena in Socorro County] to put in the feed and salt" in April 1918. The agent's field report observed wryly that there were "absolutely no facts at all on which to base the suspicions." Moreover, after interviewing the complainant, a "Baptist preacher," the agent concluded, "I found him to be a very great 'Visionary' whose imagination had been running riot."[23]

Citizens wanted to do their part to report disloyalty in all its forms: draft dodgers, or slackers; pro-German supporters; and pacifists or socialists opposed to war. Moreover, a vigilant public expected that their concerns would trigger action. It was at the intersection of public pressure and BI follow-up that Burkhart and his agents often made their hardest choices. They well understood that to the public all perceived incidents of disloyalty struck at the very heart of patriotism by rejecting sacrifice. Any word or deed that undermined sacrifice debased devotion to America by denying its highest expression—the precious, sacred gift of life willingly offered up in defense of kin and country, freedom and liberty. At that visceral level, patriotic fervor was potent and volatile, and keeping it harnessed so that it aligned with respect for and confidence in the government was a constant challenge.[24]

All the tensions inherent in this delicate balance were evident when Burkhart sent agent Joe Solanas to a hamlet in western Quay County in early September 1917. He was instructed to defuse growing hostility toward a local rancher who had repeatedly voiced pro-German sentiments and for reasons unknown escalated his inflammatory comments to include attacks on draftees just as the first men were called to training camps. He reportedly said he "hoped that every soldier that went to France would never return and that the flag was nothing but a dam old rag." Burkhart ordered the rancher arrested, but he also admitted, "[I] do not think that we can make it stick but think [it] will have good effect." Nearly a year later, Burkhart remained sensitive to perceptions that the government was not taking seriously threats posed when German sympathizers uttered antiwar sentiments. In ordering an agent to a small Nuevomexicano community in Sandoval County, he wrote, "I consider an investigation important in order to convince the native people that we are looking after disloyalty." In both these cases, Burkhart bent before the winds of public opinion and ordered an investigation, which was a show of his authority and meant to maintain order in a community. To do anything less would erode people's respect and confidence in his office and undermine their faith in the government.[25]

Always well aware of public opinion, Burkhart and his agents followed accepted investigative practices and, as much as possible, tried to be judicious. They sought to determine motive—whether an action was willful, or the result of not knowing what was expected, or stemming from other causes such as mistakes by an employer or draft board. A number of the cases Pearce Rodey investigated revealed mitigating lapses. For example, four sheepherders in Guadalupe County failed to register for the draft on 5 June 1917, but Rodey found that they were told by their employer that draft registration forms would be provided them to complete so that they did not need to leave the bands of sheep to go register. But the local draft board refused to do absentee registration and pronounced the four delinquent. Rodey noted, "As in other instances reported to me, this violation of the law was evidently based solely on ignorance, and it is evident that there will be a great many of such cases brought to light throughout the state." Burkhart advised an agent investigating six Greeks and some Austrians who had not registered for the draft in Mora County to allow "aliens who failed to register for the selective draft" to do so retroactively if their failure "was occasioned by their ignorance, but if the failure was occasioned by an intention to violate the law they should be prosecuted."[26]

But Burkhart's fairness displeased some officials. The sheriff of Chaves County, who was also chair of the county's draft board, complained bitterly to the BI division superintendent about what he saw as lax enforcement of the draft law in early November 1917: "I have not had the least encouragement from the representative of the Government [Burkhart] to prosecute a slacker after I find him and turn him over to them. . . . You say that it is the desire of the Government to rigidly enforce the selective draft act . . . but they are not practicing what they preach." The sheriff ended by saying that he "would love to rigidly prosecute each and every [slacker] case."[27]

The sheriff's disappointment was an understandable emotion, but it was wholly impractical "to rigidly prosecute each and every" draft law violation. Extremist tendencies had to be tempered—whether voiced by a sheriff or by outraged citizens. A careful investigation was preferable to rushing headlong into legal action. But when legal action was called for, the process was deliberate and thorough. Cases had to be presented to a grand jury, a true bill (indictment) returned, formal charges filed, a jury trial held, and a verdict decided. Burkhart was always wary of what might go wrong when bringing charges against a draft dodger. The perils of a trial were very much on Burkhart's mind in late June 1918 when he requested a BI agent to investigate a suspected case of perjury from Quay County. Eight witnesses had corroborated a defendant's alibi that he was elsewhere on 20 October 1917 when he allegedly "interfered with the enlistment of men of draft age in the United States army." Burkhart suspected the eight were "Socialists, as [the defendant] is, and opposed to the war." If perjury could be shown, a second trail would ensue, which is what happened on 17 January 1919 in U.S. district court in Albuquerque. Fifteen months after the offense occurred, the defendant was convicted and sentenced to two years in the federal penitentiary at Leavenworth, Kansas.[28]

Pressure for the BI to initiate more prosecutions mounted nationwide late in 1918 and into 1919. For the first time, monthly reports were required to summarize completed court cases. Five wartime-related offenses were prosecuted in New Mexico in January 1919, all involving military service. Two defendants were found guilty, with one sentenced to a year in the "Federal jail in Santa Fe" and the other sent to Leavenworth Penitentiary for two years. Two were pronounced not guilty, and the judge issued a directed verdict of not guilty in one case because "the prosecution failed to introduce sufficient evidence." In December 1918 the same court heard six wartime-related offenses, with two involving violations of the draft law. One defendant was pronounced guilty and sentenced to two years at Leavenworth; the other case was dismissed for lack of evidence. In all of these cases the defendants were Euro-Americans. Burkhart could be relentless in prosecuting draft and induction evasions, as evidenced in pursuit of such cases after the war ended and the draft was canceled. In December 1918 he authorized prosecution of a Union County Euro-American who for over a year had evaded reporting for induction and emerged only after the armistice. But the accused immediately disappeared again in December, and not until mid-September 1919 was he apprehended by a U.S. marshal in Mora and jailed to await trial.[29]

One of the first BI investigations Burkhart pursued after war was declared began in May 1917 when a U.S. Post Office inspector in Las Vegas reported on the contents of a copy of a letter he described as "very vitriolic." It had been sent by the secretary of the Socialist Party of New Mexico, Walter B. Dillon, to a number of individuals in New Mexico and urged resistance to the draft. Thus began Burkhart's longest active case, which continued until he left office in March 1921. Interest in Dillon's activities arose because of literature he sent and received through the U.S. mail. One of the provisions of wartime mobilization granted the post office three key roles in protecting the home front during World War I: censoring the mail; helping with military recruitment; and monitoring movements of enemy aliens (all Germans and Austrians who were not yet U.S. citizens or not seeking citizenship).[30]

In these surveillance activities the local post offices reported suspicious behavior to Burkhart. This provided the Department of Justice with an unequaled network of local observers, and the postmaster general, Albert S. Burleson of Texas, intended to enlist this cadre which, as a postal official noted in 1919, meant "the Government has a personal representative in every single town, village, or crossroads in the United States." On 16 June 1917, one day after passage of the Espionage Act, Burleson issued a secret, sweeping directive to all local postmasters empowering them to keep a "close watch on unsealed matter, newspapers, etc., containing matter which is calculated to interfere with the success of any Federal [Liberty] Loan [fund-raising campaign] . . . or to cause insubordination, disloyalty, mutiny or refusal of duty in the military or naval services, or to obstruct the recruiting, draft, or enlistment services . . . or otherwise to embarrass or hamper the Government in conducting the war."[31]

New Mexico had about 890 post offices in 1917, many of which were in stores, which meant official eyes and ears were attuned to comings and goings as well as conversations in communities statewide. In the heightened vigilance during the early months of the war, some postmasters in New Mexico abused the surveillance duties given them by Postmaster General Burleson. Their reports on local Germans prompted inquiries in various parts of the state, but as is inevitable in a climate of suspicious distrust most proved to be without merit. In a few instances, as one BI investigator wrote, "the whole matter is personal animosity" between a postmaster and a local resident.[32]

The most numerous reports postmasters filed involved draft-related issues. In an era when almost everyone had to go to their local post office to pick up their mail, postmasters knew who was subject to the draft, whether induction notices had been sent, and who should be away in the service but was still around or had gone missing. Postmasters throughout the state, together with local sheriffs, worked closely with BI agents by sending in tips about draft evaders or replying to BI requests for information about individuals under investigation.

This cooperation began immediately after Congress passed the Selective Service Act on 18 May 1917 and continued throughout the war.[33]

The text of the letter that triggered a BI inquiry into Dillon's activities read, in part, "I, for one, positively refuse to serve in any capacity in this war of, by, and for Wall Street and I call on you as loyal citizens . . . to also refuse to serve a government prostrated to the Money Barons of Wall Street." Thus began the first page in the file that eventually involved five different New Mexico BI agents as well as others in Arizona, Colorado, and Texas. The secretary of the Socialist Party in New Mexico continued to draw scrutiny into the 1920s after he affiliated with the Communist Party. In the two and a half weeks preceding 5 June 1917, the day set for draft registration nationwide, the BI and the Department of Justice were gripped by fears that opponents of the war would significantly disrupt this vital first step of mobilization. Any call to refuse to register threatened to disrupt a main thrust of patriotism—bringing men to the nation's defense. In this tense atmosphere, an agent was dispatched by train to Las Vegas in San Miguel County on 2 June to arrest Dillon and calm the town.[34]

After Dillon was arrested in early June 1917, he raised bail from among socialist supporters, and upon release he resumed speaking against the war. His case was presented to a federal grand jury in Santa Fe on 12 October 1917. A true bill was returned on six charges, five of which were violations of the Espionage Act for aiding in evading registration for the draft and illegal use of the U.S. mail. The sixth charge alleged he "sent obscene and filthy matter through the mails." But a few days later Attorney Burkhart informed the local BI agent that "the evidence was insufficient to properly draw up indictments in any of the charges," and on 18 October Burkhart expanded on his conclusion in a two-page letter to the BI division superintendent in San Antonio, Texas. He explained that the BI agent "through a search warrant obtained a lot of correspondence from this man Dillon which, although it showed great disloyalty on the part of Dillon, contained nothing upon which I could base an indictment. Dillon is a dangerous man and I want evidence against him sufficient to sustain a conviction." To his credit, Burkhart gave primacy to the First Amendment even in wartime, and he insisted there had to be a genuine threat that was provable to a jury before he would prosecute. In taking this position he showed greater respect for freedom of speech and civil liberties than would be exhibited by the U.S. Supreme Court in *Schenck v. United States,* a pivotal case that upheld the Espionage Act in 1919.[35]

The Dillon case showed Burkhart at his best in his legal choices, and it also revealed him to be a tenacious administrator. Between June and November 1917 three search warrants were issued for printed matter Dillon transported in trunks from town to town, and this surveillance may have had a "chilling effect," for on 9 December 1917 BI agent Rodey reported that Dillon "appears to have had a change of heart, and says that . . . he has decided not to oppose the war any longer." Dillon did nothing to attract further attention from federal agents in New Mexico in 1918, but in July 1919 he surfaced in El Paso and was linked to Russian propaganda that fueled speculation he was a communist. The accusation is not surprising given that the country was then in the grips of the Red Scare, a belief that Bolsheviks were exporting their recent revolution to America. Unlike the BI under Burkhart in New Mexico, the Texas agents used whatever means seemed necessary to track Dillon in the early 1920s, including surreptitiously intercepting and opening his mail.[36]

The Red Scare was most intense in major cities in the East, but it had a brief foray into New Mexico in May 1921, about a year after this fear had subsided elsewhere. Labor organizers identifying themselves as members of the United Communist Party circulated flyers in Clovis that called upon railroad workers to heed what "the Russian workers showed us. . . . They overthrew their Bosses' government and set up a Workers' Government." The rhetoric was inflammatory, but the United Communist Party in New Mexico had no followers. It never came to the attention of BI agents in either Texas or New Mexico, although a Bureau-wide request seeking reports on their activities sent on 14 May 1921 brought in more than two thousand pages from offices nationwide.[37]

As pivotal as were post offices in the surveillance of Dillon in 1917, most of their wartime activities in New Mexico fulfilled two other rather routine functions in support of other federal agencies. Postmasters were the initial contact for men seeking to enlist in the army and navy, after which they were sent with appropriate papers to the nearest recruitment center, either in El Paso, Albuquerque, or Denver. At least one postmaster in Roosevelt County balked at aiding military recruitment, which brought immediate protest to the BI from a local National Guard commander and a demand that he be removed, which happened.[38]

Post offices in New Mexico were indispensable to the U.S. Marshal's Office beginning in 1918. They were responsible for registering and monitoring enemy aliens. The formal nationwide cataloguing of these individuals occurred between November 1917 and April 1918, with the registration period in New Mexico falling between 4 and 9 February 1918. All noncitizen German males ages fourteen and older were ordered to report to the nearest post office, except in the cities of Albuquerque, Santa Fe, and Roswell, where the local police handled their registration.

The men had to complete a multipage questionnaire, file affidavits from U.S. citizens verifying the information provided, submit four photographs, and be fingerprinted. The penalty for failure to register was arrest and imprisonment at a camp in Utah. No cases of evasion were found in records for New Mexico, but by early October an additional ten men had come forward and registered. They were added to the list of 232 male enemy aliens the U.S. marshal compiled statewide and forwarded to Burkhart in early May. One-fifth of the enemy alien men resided in the state's three largest towns: Albuquerque (twenty-seven), Roswell (eleven), and Santa Fe (five); 189 lived in what were labeled "non-urban" areas. During early July female enemy aliens, as well as U.S. citizens married to enemy alien men, were required to register, which resulted in 135 doing so. Of the fifty-two enemy alien women living in the towns of Albuquerque (twenty-six), Roswell (twenty-three), and Santa Fe (three), thirty-five were Catholic nuns from Germany serving in hospitals or orphanages in various New Mexico towns. The remaining eighty-three women resided in "non-urban" areas. Once registered, in order to travel outside their immediate community, enemy aliens had to provide their local postmaster a written statement stating their reason for leaving, receive a permit to do so, and report themselves to the postmaster at their destination. Postmasters routinely granted alien men permits if they were traveling sales representatives or relocating to find new employment, but in the war's final months failing to register or traveling without a permit began to come to the attention of post offices and BI agents.[39]

It was but a short step from wartime fear of enemy aliens to postwar hysteria over Bolsheviks. Once passions were inflamed, it proved both easy and expedient for politicians to fan them further. An article in the *Santa Fe New Mexican* describing debate in Congress over a bill to restrict immigration highlighted how quickly New Mexico had again become a convenient prop to stir up fear of foreigners in the fall of 1919. A House congressional committee examining "immigration methods" alleged in hearings that "the Bolshevist snake lurks beyond the Mexican border, a menacing threat to the United States and a comfort to the ultra-radical disciples of sabotage and terrorism who are being smuggled into this country at the rate of one hundred a day." No such influx of "disciples of sabotage and terrorism" swept across the border and through New Mexico, but in the nation's mind such an image was easily planted during the Red Scare. Within some parts of the government, a specific fear emerged that disaffected ex-servicemen constituted a Bolshevist phalanx. The War Department maintained this position in weekly reports to the BI in 1920. Early in 1921 the national commander of the American Legion wrote to BI agent J. Edgar Hoover and urged the Bureau to continue to monitor political activity of "irresponsible" veterans' organizations. The national commander's request was consistent with the Legion's vigorous anticommunist stance, one it maintained until the end of the cold war.[40]

In assessments of America's Red Scare in 1919–20 it is worthwhile to situate New Mexico to understand the origins and evolution of this episode in the politics of fear. Numerous studies exist on the Red Scare, and two positions are clearly delineated in the literature. One is identified with Robert K. Murray, who in 1955 argued that national hysteria drove the Red Scare and that the government was forced into its actions by the public's irrational fear. A systematic challenge to that view was advanced by Danish scholar Regin Schmidt in 2000. He inverted the actors and maintained that the government, and particularly the BI, orchestrated and served as the guiding force in pursuing radicals. New Mexico's experience is a braiding of these two interpretations. Much evidence existed during the war to support Murray's view, but Schmidt's interpretation best accounts for the BI's immediate postwar activities.[41]

Council of National Defense and State Council of Defense

The State Council of Defense (SCD) emerged during a special eight-day session of the New Mexico legislature convened on Tuesday, 1 May 1917, to enact bills on four substantive issues: state and federal defense; agricultural productivity; "the expenses arising out of the emergencies of the war"; and agricultural education. So sweeping was the SCD's enabling bill that upon its passage on 8 May the legislature adjourned for the duration of the war, not meeting again until January 1919, which left Governor Washington E. Lindsey and the SCD, under Charles Springer, in charge during the war. The two men had first worked together while Republican delegates to the Constitutional Convention of 1910. Both were from the state's east side, but Springer was a stalwart among old guard Republicans and Lindsey a rising star among progressive Republicans. Springer had long been a prominent rancher in Colfax County, and Lindsey had a law practice, was active in real estate development, and served as the mayor of Portales in Roosevelt County from 1910 to 1916. Their birthdays were one day apart in December; Springer at age fifty-nine in 1917 was the older by four years. Lindsey won election as lieutenant governor in November 1916 but stepped into the governorship when Democrat Ezequiel Cabeza de Baca died in office on 18 February. Forty-seven days later Lindsey became the state's war governor. The two men worked well together on wartime issues, but their fundamental differences resurfaced as the 1918 elections neared. Springer aided other Republicans in denying Lindsey renomination.[42]

The federal government sought a nationwide network of state councils to act as local extensions of the Council of National Defense, which had been created in legislation passed by Congress on 29 August 1916 but was not organized administratively until early March 1917. Made up of six department secretaries, with secretary of war Newton D. Baker as the chair, the Council had broad authority to mobilize the nation's citizens, industry, and agricultural and natural resources in case of war. Within a week of Congress declaring war, the Council's chief administrator, Grosvenor B. Clarkson, called upon all states to form their own councils, a request that met with unanimous approval. Governor Lindsey appointed ten members on 10 May, but two quickly resigned due to other obligations. Of the remaining eight, four were Nuevomexicanos. The full membership convened only once; instead, a three-member executive committee, headed by Charles Springer and located in Santa Fe, handled its administration and programs. But rather quickly Springer, aided by general secretary Walter M. Danburg, took control of day-to-day operations. The legislature's initial wartime appropriation of three-quarters of a million dollars—a substantial amount for that era ($14.3 million in 2017)—proved more than adequate to fund the SCD during its existence.[43]

Springer and the SCD's most pressing responsibilities were to carry out national defense mandates. The National Defense Act of 3 June 1916 made civilian-soldiers in each state's National Guard the primary reserve force of the U.S. military and gave the president authority to mobilize them in time of war or during a national emergency, such as guarding the Mexican border in 1916–17. A few weeks before the New Mexico legislature created the state's council, military mobilization occurred on 21 April 1917. The New Mexico National Guard temporarily trained in Albuquerque throughout the summer until entrained to the U.S. Army's Camp Kearny near San Diego, California, in October 1917. During these months the National Guard was under the control of the SCD, and Springer and others conducted a vigorous recruitment effort.

The state's National Guard had been mustered out of service along the Mexican border just one day before Congress declared war on Germany, and when it was federalized several weeks later only forty-nine officers and thirty-nine enlisted men remained on the roster, with the latter group dramatically reduced from mid-December 1916 when there were 688 enlistees (and forty-seven officers). Concurrent with bringing over 1,200 New Mexico men into the guard, the SCD conducted draft registration on 5 June for all men born between 6 June 1886 and 5 June 1896 (ages twenty-one through thirty). Executive committee member Benigno C. Hernández, a livestock raiser from Rio Arriba County, took charge of the registration conducted by local draft boards in the state's then twenty-seven counties.[44]

He also actively participated in processing thousands of exemption requests. In early September, New Mexico began meeting the U.S. Army's quotas for delivering hundreds of drafted men to training camps. During the war, a total of 81,019 New Mexican men registered, but of these only 9,050 were inducted. In the general election held 5 November 1918, the state's voters rewarded Hernández, a Republican, by electing him to a second, nonconsecutive term as their lone member of the U.S. House of Representatives.[45]

Whereas federal officials had only a few laws to enforce and were limited to investigating violations related to these, the SCD and its local councils had a freer hand. This absence of boundaries set by legislation allowed both Springer and Lindsey to wield their authority unfettered by oversight. As a result each understood that their leadership involved applying a firm hand to steer a course through turbulence when such situations came to their attention, especially when in their respective opinions public order seemed threatened. Several local councils of defense, especially in the first nine months of the war, prompted such exercise of leadership, and in the summer of 1917 Governor Lindsey had to a rein in several county councils to defuse potential violence.

The presence of hundreds of deported IWW members in Columbus and the alarm their presence caused among members of the Luna County council of defense prompted Governor Lindsey to dispatch a special agent to Columbus and Deming to talk to all parties and tamp down rumors. He also appointed the sheriff of Columbus as the town's representative to the county's council to provide a calming voice. In doing so, the governor corralled patriotic fervor that had the potential to stampede. The governor's direct involvement likewise figured prominently in curbing labor-management conflict in Gallup. Again he used a special agent, this time the state's mine inspector, W. W. Risdon, to provide on-the-scene updates.[46]

In Gallup, as in Deming, the local council of defense had become a disruptive force with the specific aim of union busting. The state's mine inspector reported to Governor Lindsey that a local mine operator "had the [McKinley County] Council of Defense appointed and so arranged the selection that the men appointed could be dominated by him" as a step toward breaking the union in Gallup. Soon the "importation of gun men and the appointment of a lot of irresponsible men of McKinley County as deputy sheriffs" had the town on edge. It was against this backdrop that the forced removal of alleged IWW members occurred. But underlying problems persisted, and so in early September Governor Lindsey cabled the White House seeking assistance to resolve a continuing standoff between miners and mine operators. But no help was forthcoming beyond an offer to assist with mediation. Gradually, though, work resumed, and the mine inspector ended his last report to Lindsey sarcastically: the miners were left to "prate about their patriotism but patriotism to them means ... [every] man joins the union."[47]

Patriotism as righteousness framed how both union and management saw themselves in Gallup, and this self-confident certitude became woven into the fabric of citizenship during World War I. In addressing people possessed of this attitude, Springer treaded lightly to respect the sincere, though often misguided, complaints lodged by individuals and county council of defense representatives. For example, he parried the accusation made by a self-described "old-time cowboy" that a forest ranger's office in Socorro County was "run in the interest of Germany" simply because the ranger was of German descent. Springer replied diplomatically that the matter would be referred for investigation to ensure that "justice [is] done for all of the people who have ranches or cattle within the National Forest." Occasionally Springer let silence be his reply when patriotic righteousness was clearly a moral choice and not an issue of loyalty. Such was how he handled a report from Union County, which reported through its council of defense that a local "lady who is preaching in this county" was, upon their questioning, "not pro-German ... [and] says that she would like to see the United States win this war." Nevertheless they reported her for investigation because she "was not preaching for the war but that she was preaching peace." They also objected to her invoking the Sixth Commandment: "She cannot advise any to whom she preaches and speaks to take up a gun and go and shoot somebody. She considers that murder."[48]

During the first three months of its existence, the SCD moved to ensure broad engagement with New Mexicans by keeping messages in support of wartime mobilization before the public. One key organ of public outreach the SCD organized was the New Mexico Four Minute Men. It was formed on 16 August 1917, a state counterpart to the national organization founded on 16 June. A well-prepared cadre of 254 locally prominent New Mexico men delivered more than 4,500 addresses in numerous settings that drew an average audience of 167 for each speaker. Named for the four-minute interval needed to change a film reel in movie houses, this cadre of speakers delivered concise, well-prepared addresses of 400–450 words. Over the course of some thirty speaking campaigns, the New Mexico Four Minute Men urged support for all wartime mobilization measures. Though pro-German sentiment and disloyal actions were routinely condemned, the major thrust was promotion of patriotic duty through such efforts as conscription, war bond sales, food conservation, war gardens, the Red Cross, and respect for democracy and liberty.[49]

More Money: Expectations and Reality

The importance of increased crop production was mentioned in almost every Four Minute Men address in New Mexico. Likewise, it was a prominent part of President Wilson's "Appeal to the American Public" in mid-April 1917, in which he called all citizens to wartime duty and sacrifice. About one-quarter of his remarks were addressed to "the farmers of the country and all who work on the farms." A singular responsibility fell to them: "It is of the most imperative importance that everything possible be done, and done immediately, to make sure of large harvests." Such a request challenged rural New Mexicans. The legislature reported that the state produced "less than fifty per centum of the food product [excluding meat] consumed by her people" in May 1917.[50]

The state's farmers pledged to do their part, but they also requested help. Most of them had suffered through a drought in 1916 that had cut crop yield and reduced their income. Farmers in Union County were especially vocal about their needs. After a meeting in Clayton in late May 1917, they roundly criticized state officials for asking "farmers as a patriotic duty to plant unusually large crops and, at the same time, take all the risk. We believe a farmer's note, secured by mortgage on crop, should be canceled and refunded to the marker in event of crop failure not due to the fault of the farmer himself." Under the guise of wartime patriotism these farmers pressed for what amounted to premium-free crop failure insurance. Thus did the federal and state government's goal to aid farmers to increase food crops quickly became a contest of wills in which farmers thought government entities ought to "sell seed or advance money for any undertaking where re-payment was solely contingent upon success." Persistent wrangling over the terms of the loans ensued. Whereas the SCD intended to redress constricted access to capital and credit, farmers all too often simply wanted to get their hands on money that carried little or no risk to them.[51]

As soon as news of the availability of state money appeared in newspapers, letters began arriving in Santa Fe pleading for assistance outside the program's scope. On 12 May, two days after the legislature passed the $750,000 wartime appropriation. Governor Lindsey received the first of numerous inquiries from residents eager to be considered for "money to assist farmers in New Mexico." This letter and similar ones were routed to the SCD for reply, and all supplicants were told the state would not "lend cash to any person. We are, however, through our Financial Agents in the different Counties supplying seed to working farmers, taking their notes for the same." By mid-June the governor's office and the SCD had received "so many demands for money" that Springer told correspondents only $75,000 ($1.4 million in 2017) was available to help farmers secure seed. The fiscal agent in each county was responsible for ensuring that loans went "for aiding those reliable farmers who were unable to otherwise secure seed at planting time"; however, eleven months into the program the SCD realized that abuses were rampant: "farmers who had the money or could have obtained credit to finance seed requirements [instead used state money,] and such action materially depleted the funds." The anniversary of the loan program brought a sternly worded reminder from the SCD to fiscal agents that the state's loan money was "a revolving trust fund" and that the money "for use in the agricultural programme is not so much to aid the farmer, but primarily to increase production of food crops." Still, pressure for financial aid grew, especially among ranchers, and the SCD in early February 1919 announced a plan to loan them money at 6 percent interest per annum to buy feed for their livestock. But before any money could be released the legislature shut down the loan program. An SCD official explained that the legislature's action resulted from a realization that "the matter of extending aid to farmers on the credit plan was not very satisfactory."[52]

The disappointing results of the state serving as a source of credit must be understood as an early experiment with instruments of economic stimulus—but hastily conceived, underfunded, and poorly administered. These failings were recognized early on by the Taos County council of defense, which submitted a blistering critique of the state's credit initiative in early December 1917. The council's twelve members—equally divided between Nuevomexicanos and Euro-Americans—unanimously adopted a resolution to reject any "continuance of state aid to farmers," pointing out that "any man in this county who has land to farm, and will work, can get all the accommodation he may need from the local merchants or banks." Moreover, they believed that in their county the state's money would be sought by "that other class, having neither lands nor inclination to work. . . . to aid these [people] is too great a risk for the State to assume."[53]

That prediction proved accurate. A total credit of $89,938 of state money ($1.7 million in 2017) went to farmers to purchase seed, but only $38,203, or 43 percent, was repaid by the fall of 1920. Farmers in twenty-four of the state's twenty-nine counties took seed on credit, with two east side counties—Eddy and Quay—having the highest rate of default, at over 80 percent. Crop failure accounted for many defaults, and although the SCD and its agents pressed farmers for repayment, eventually the SCD absorbed all the losses in 1920. The state's credit program is an object lesson for what happens when patriotic gestures collide with human nature. The legislature and the SCD naively assumed they could boost crop productivity by waving money over the land, but in fact the yield was a bumper crop of tempted people—those who had no wherewithal along with those who had no need for credit. Each group found easy money irresistible.[54]

Whereas leaders in New Mexico stumbled in their attempts to stimulate greater agricultural productivity by providing credit for seed, the U.S. Department of Agriculture—the principal federal agency responsible for crop-related policy—had more mixed results. There was a wartime increase in productivity, but it often saddled farmers and ranchers with debt they were unable to repay. The Department of Agriculture's loan programs were authorized in 1916 in two key bills—the Federal Farm Loan Act (enacted 17 July 1916) and the Stock-Raising Homestead Act (29 December 1916). The former law enabled farmers to increase their productivity through a federal loan program to finance the acquisition of acreage and machinery; the latter bill met a long-sought request by ranchers to borrow money from the government to finance purchases of land, implements, and livestock.

A brief review of the Stock-Raising Homestead Act is a cautionary tale of unintended consequences. That federal legislation enabled stockmen to expand their ranches to 640 acres. Under this law in New Mexico, the federal government designated 950,000 acres of public domain as available, almost all "being the tier of counties on the Eastern border," and 600,000 acres were filed on in New Mexico. The federal government's generosity with land and credit enabled stockmen both to expand their holdings and to acquire cattle and calves as well as sheep, but when the war ended these loans soon became onerous in various parts of the state. For example, in northeast New Mexico, which had seen many filings under the Stock-Raising Homestead Act, an official with the area's judicial district reported to the governor in 1924 that the exodus of one-third of the residents was a consequence of debt.[55]

Perhaps the most beneficial aid provided farmers and ranchers originated in the Smith-Lever Bill signed by President Wilson on 8 May 1914. That legislation launched an educational arm of the Department of Agriculture. Created was the

Agricultural Extension Service, which provided information and consultation to rural residents through land grant colleges, including the state college in Las Cruces. Outreach was gender based: male agricultural agents aided farmers and ranchers to modernize their practices; women serving as home demonstration agents promoted the latest practices in child rearing and cooking to rural housewives. The federal government required that the state and each county contribute money to supplement the federal subvention for the Extension Service, but New Mexico had not appropriated much money for extension agents before April 1917. As a result agricultural agents worked in only ten counties, and only one home demonstration agent served the entire state. Staffing improved soon after the state legislature's special wartime appropriation in early May. Agricultural agents served in twenty-one counties by early October, and in December 1917 another county had been added to the list. Four Nuevomexicano agricultural agents served the counties of Mora, San Miguel, Santa Fe, and Taos.[56]

Efforts that linked patriotism to providing more food in New Mexico—especially wheat, corn, and pinto beans—led to dramatically improved crop yields. Between 1916 and 1919, for example, wheat production nearly tripled, from 2.1 million bushels to 6.1 million bushels, and similar increases were recorded for corn and pinto beans. Overall, the total crop value rose 65 percent, from $37.6 million in 1918 to $58.4 million in 1919. The state's farmers responded to President Wilson's challenge to grow more, but a significant incentive, too, came in the form of several new federal actions that established commodity prices above prewar levels and guaranteed purchase of all wheat that was harvested. The response in New Mexico was immediate and significant: dry land wheat farming on the state's east side, for example, grew from 113,000 acres in 1916 to 283,000 acres in 1919, putting into cultivation two and a half times as much acreage. The government's market incentives proved the best short-term stimulus among the various inducements offered, but once the war ended, it was quickly evident that expanded production benefited only farmers who did not need to carry debt or could repay loans on schedule.[57]

The national mood immediately turned against government intervention in the economy at war's end. Both President Wilson and Congress began to shut down sections of the Council of National Defense within weeks of the armistice and continued to fold it up gradually until it fully disappeared in June 1921. New Mexico's legislature balked at requests for new appropriations for the SCD in March 1919, shuttering its operations at the end of the year and closing all its accounts in the summer of 1920. The SCD, once so central to total mobilization of the home front, did see a few of its activities survive. The New Mexico legislature appropriated funds to continue county extension agents, and a cooperative agreement with the U.S. Department of Agriculture for "exterminating predatory wild animals and rodent pests" was extended. This project, in the prevailing mindset of the era, funded the systematic killing of mammals ranging from mountain lions to prairie dogs—all deemed a threat to livestock or crops.[58]

Channeling Patriotic Fervor

The subject headings written on Walter Dillon's BI files were "Disloyal" and "Socialist Agitator." These emotionally charged, pejorative labels were commonplace in the climate of suspicious distrust prevalent at both the local and national levels during and immediately after World War I. "Disloyal" had a special place in the wartime lexicon. Its use amounted to verbal vigilantism, capable of casting out someone and branding them traitors. How Americans expressed patriotism changed dramatically during and immediately after the war. Flag-waving exuberance in 1917 quickly yielded to knotty questions of how best to honor the nation and its values, issues that were imperfectly answered then and in every war thereafter. Nowhere were matters more a tangled skein than with issues of civil liberties between 1917 and 1920. Attorney Burkhart succeeded in stemming any broad-based trampling of civil liberties, but in other ways New Mexico occasionally stumbled in respecting First Amendment rights. When it faltered, politics had usually intruded. At the national level, three separate incidents in which disloyalty was invoked involved New Mexicans—two as an accuser in 1917 and 1918 and one as the accused in 1918.

On Saturday, 6 October 1917, just one hour remained in the Sixty-Fifth Congress's extra session, convened on 2 April, to deliberate wartime measures. New Mexico senator Albert B. Fall held the floor and refused to yield it to his Republican colleague from Wisconsin, Senator Robert M. La Follette Sr. Their standoff had been brewing for some time and was part of a chasm separating La Follette, a vocal opponent of the war, from almost all of his colleagues. But an unbridgeable gulf opened after an extemporaneous speech La Follette made to 15,000 mostly supportive attendees at a rally in St. Paul, Minnesota, on Thursday, 20 September 1917. In reply to one heckler, he outlined the origins of the war and affirmed that the United States "had cause for complaint" against Germany. The next day an Associated Press account of his speech appeared in over a thousand newspapers and ignited a firestorm of protest. The AP erroneously reported La Follette saying, "We had *no* grievance against Germany." Outrage swept the nation, and AP's mistake became accepted as fact by all those predisposed to see La Follette's opposition to the war as the statement of an unpatriotic traitor. A week later the Senate received a petition seeking Senator La Follette's expulsion. The following week the Senate's Committee on Privileges and Elections approved a four-member subcommittee to investigate, with New Mexico's Senator Fall as a participant. Late in the morning of 6 October, La Follette rose to speak to his colleagues. Rather than address the issue of expulsion, he spent nearly three hours denouncing the war and defending freedom of speech. Three of the four senators on the investigative subcommittee offered rebuttals, with Senator Fall being the last to speak, with only one hour remaining in the session. The front page of the Sunday *Albuquerque Morning Journal* offered readers this account of how "Senator Fall . . . sharply denounced [La Follette]" for his St. Paul address, including saying, "No more dangerous doctrine could have been preached and no more insidious utterances could have been heard from any source than those of the senator from Wisconsin." As the clock moved toward 3:00 P.M. and adjournment, Fall did allow La Follette a three-sentence comment. In it La Follette announced his intention to answer charges against him in a public forum. Ten days later he turned over a full response to Senator Fall and the investigating subcommittee and within weeks he filed lawsuits alleging libel against several newspapers.[59]

The Senate committee's deliberations on expulsion encountered delay after delay, but finally they convened on 21–22 May 1918. Eight hours of excruciatingly detailed point-and-counterpoint arguments yielded hundreds of pages of official testimony. The legalistic tone could not mask the outright hostility many senators held toward their colleague. But Senator Fall's interest in hounding La Follette had waned. And then the case evaporated two days later when on 24 May the AP admitted the error in their original story and apologized. Later La Follette won his libel suits, on 2 December 1918 the committee dropped the inquiry, and on 16 January 1919 the full Senate concurred. The recent deaths of two of Senator Fall's adult children in the influenza pandemic kept him from taking part in either action.[60]

Senator Fall likewise played a large role in a second imbroglio arising from an accusation of disloyalty. The charge was leveled in the influential *North American Review* in its issue of August 1918. In a three-page letter titled "America's Unguarded Gateway," H. R. Walmsley of Kansas City, writing under the pseudonym of Henry Wray, contended that a foreign army sweeping out of Mexico and crossing the border anywhere between Columbus and El Paso would move unimpeded up the Rio Grande Valley all the way to Colorado. "Over nearly the entire route, the enemy would be acclaimed, fed, quartered, equipped and recruited." The letter's author propounded a theory of an irredentist conspiracy funded by Germany and launched from Mexico: "A state of treason exists in this part of our country. New Mexico confidently expects to arise and join again the mother country. . . . The native population awaits the hour to strike. When some German emissary furnishes the money to some pirate in Mexico, that hour will be at hand."[61]

Wray recycled canards last used by opponents of statehood to malign Nuevomexicanos and did so maliciously to impugn their loyalty during the war. Outraged New Mexicans reacted immediately to the accusation that the state, and especially its Nuevomexicano citizens, were "essentially disloyal in sympathy." The *Albuquerque Morning Journal* and *La Bandera Americana* insisted the comments were libelous and called for legal action. The state's entire congressional delegation as well as prominent citizens such as Summers Burkhart and Charles Springer joined more than forty public officials, civic and business leaders, professional groups, and private citizens in writing to castigate the magazine. Senator Fall, a longtime subscriber, dispatched a blistering telegram on 7 August, which brought an immediate apology, and in its October issue the journal reproduced that exchange as part of a seven-page retraction and mea culpa. The vigorous rejection of Wray's article, and especially that voiced by *La Bandera Americana* on behalf of Nuevomexicanos, signaled solidarity in identity that had lay dormant since the final decade of the fight for statehood.[62]

The third incident that attracted national attention involved accusations of disloyalty lodged against publications controlled by William Randolph Hearst. As one contemporary writer noted, the SCD claimed in the pages of its *New Mexico War News* that Hearst publications in Los Angeles, New York City, San Francisco, and elsewhere exerted an influence that was "disloyal, dangerous to the morale of the people, and tends to help the enemies of the nation to succeed." No similar accusations were lodged in any other state, so why in New Mexico? A possible answer lies in partisan politics. The state's leading wartime officials were Republicans, but Democrats in the state had been beholden to Hearst since his 1903 tour during an unsuccessful bid for his party's nod as its presidential candidate. Indeed, one scholar has suggested that Democrats continued to reap dividends from Hearst's western trip when Woodrow Wilson carried the Southwest and Rocky Mountain region in the elections of 1912 and 1916. Hearst's publications became a proxy for the SCD's real target—the residual influence Hearst exercised among Democratic voters in the state in the run-up to the 1918 elections. To combat what was deemed a pernicious presence, the SCD coordinated a boycott of Hearst publications in the state. But in August 1918 a federal court in Santa Fe enjoined Governor Lindsey, the SCD, the state's attorney general, and the *New Mexico War News* from further attacks on Hearst's publications. The legal decision against the *War News* was followed quickly by "its press corps [being] crippled by the 'flu,' and [with] the end of the war in sight" the paper ceased publication. It had been published weekly since 10 July 1917, and "to emphasize its patriotism the *War News* was printed in blue ink on white paper." Its "patriotism" was for the most part public relations service on behalf of the federal government's campaigns to support war efforts, but it veered into malevolent patriotism as well as continuing a long tradition of chaotic factionalism fueling partisan attacks in going after Hearst publications.[63]

The varieties of patriotism in wartime New Mexico were on a continuum ranging from vigilantism to obedient volunteerism, from out of control to tractable. In this arc, the draft became a quintessential test of loyalty, in essence a fracture line separating those, on one side, giving patriotic obedience to the nation from those across a divide who were voicing opposition to the call to arms. Patrolling that boundary between the two sides was a heterogeneous mix of citizens along with state and federal officials, all of whom exercised their power in ways consistent with their understanding of what it meant to do one's patriotic duty. An unintended consequence of state and federal governments delegating their police powers was the unpredictability of aroused citizens, who could be vindictive as well as occasionally violent. Greater equanimity characterized the U.S. attorney for New Mexico and some in the BI, who tended to ration the use of coercion according to their understanding of laws passed in 1917 and 1918. State and federal agents could be heavy-handed, but usually theirs was a more restrained use of power than occurred elsewhere in America where hysteria often clouded judgment.

CHAPTER 3

Volunteers

President Woodrow Wilson assembled two armies simultaneously to wage war. Young men became soldiers, and the remaining men and women were to be the nation's "great service army." The president first used that phrase in his "Appeal to the American People," a letter that the *Santa Fe New Mexican*, *Albuquerque Morning Journal*, and other major newspapers statewide and across the country printed or summarized on Monday, 16 April 1917. President Wilson asked all Americans, but especially women, to embrace a great national voluntary effort that "will be serving the country and conducting the fight for peace and freedom just as truly and just as effectively as the men on the battlefield or in the trenches." Wilson's priority for the home front was to ensure an adequate food supply: "Without abundant food, alike for the armies and the peoples now at war, the whole great enterprise upon which we have embarked will break down and fail." Near the end of his open letter the president spoke directly to American women: "Everyone who creates or cultivates a garden helps, and helps greatly, to solve the problem of the feeding of the nations, and . . . every housewife who practices strict economy puts herself in the ranks of those who serve the nation. It is the time for America to correct her unpardonable fault of wastefulness [of food]." These small garden plots soon became known as Victory Gardens (as they were also called when revived during World War II). Wilson not only implored women to plant gardens to increase the quantity of food but also called upon them to be sentinels in their kitchens and reduce use and waste. These first instructions to women were reinforced when Secretary of Agriculture David F. Houston issued "a statement as to the service women can render to the nation in conserving agricultural products" on 5 May 1917.[1]

Reconstituting Patriotism

In urging Americans to lend a helping hand, "to do this great thing worthily and successfully" and to understand it "as a public duty, as a dictate of patriotism," President Wilson framed joining the new service army as a patriotic obligation. His words harkened to the way two predecessors had exercised presidential power to rally the body politic. From Abraham Lincoln's bedrock belief in preserving the Union, Wilson appropriated a call for national cohesion, and in Theodore Roosevelt's resolute moralism evident in the "bully pulpit" Wilson found an urgency and tone convergent with his own worldview as the son of a Presbyterian minister. The president's call to action resonated in New Mexico and spurred immediate grassroots organizing. A Patriotic Production League of citizens in Torrance County pledged to "increase the crop production of the county," and ranchers in Roswell began planning to increase beef sales outside the state. Likewise did the president's appeal to plant wartime gardens find a ready reception among some New Mexico women, and none more so than Isabella Ferguson of Tyrone in Grant County.[2]

Ferguson began working in early May to convert 140 acres of unused land owned by the copper mining company Phelps Dodge into a large community garden. The company even loaned her $700 to match money for seed and implements, and the county sheriff conscripted "forty or more prisoners" to supplement the voluntary labor force. At the end of May she also formed committees among English-speaking and Spanish-speaking residents to locate vacant areas with "really good land not being cultivated," which were soon planted in Grant and Luna Counties. She also wrote women in Santa Fe, Albuquerque, and Roswell to urge them to start gardens in vacant lots, which soon happened. Throughout the summer more communities joined in creating wartime gardens across the state.[3]

Ferguson's efforts intersected with those directed through a national garden movement, and though it is not clear if she was a part of that project the two thrusts were complementary. A civic group in St. Louis initiated planting public gardens in 1912, and within four years the idea had spread to a reported seven thousand cities, towns, farms, and ranches. But the garden campaign for 1917 took on new urgency when it became the first voluntary project placed under the federal government's all-encompassing umbrella of wartime mobilization.

On Sunday, 15 April, the same day Wilson released his service army letter to newspapers, the assistant secretary of agriculture, Carl Vrooman, sent a telegram to Albuquerque and other communities that had previously participated in the garden movement. He urged their continued support to help the war effort: "A million gardens planted in the cities, suburbs, and country would mean the release of millions of pounds of foods to our allies." In her garden campaign Ferguson labeled this process of freeing up food to be sent to troops and Allies "potato patriotism." Her efforts were embraced statewide, and a San Juan County home extension worker in mid-July reported that women in the Aztec area "will dry fruits and vegetables to donate to the government. They have chosen this in place of the Red Cross sewing, feeling that adding to the food supply is more in their line." In this choice, women in New Mexico repeated the experience of British women who, beginning in 1915, had made food their first priority despite their government having other goals for their service.[4]

Isabella Ferguson had unusual energy and commitment, but in other ways she was both typical and atypical of Euro-American women from the middle and upper-middle classes in New Mexico who answered the president's call to make sacrifices for their country. But service on the home front meant more than giving up something. Its larger significance lay in what it enabled Ferguson and other women to do—extend the influence women reformers had slowly accrued over five decades. They saw in Wilson's service army an opportunity to direct their energy toward achieving long-sought goals by shaping public policy to their expectations. The result, as one set of scholars has observed, was "the symbiotic partnership between the federal government and large voluntary federations [of women] that helped the nation mobilize for World War I."[5]

Drawn together in Ferguson's background, accomplishments, and wartime community voluntarism were many of the strengths and limitations of women whose patriotism was grounded in their commitment to improve society. Isabella was born in Kentucky in 1886, but after the death of her father in 1895 she spent formative years in New York City. There she became a lifelong friend and confident of Eleanor Roosevelt, serving as one of her six bridesmaids when she married her distant cousin, Franklin D. Roosevelt, in March 1905. Four months later Isabella married Robert Ferguson, who had served as an officer in Theodore Roosevelt's Rough Riders in Cuba. Seeking relief for his tuberculosis, Robert moved his family to New Mexico in November 1910. They homesteaded near Tyrone and raised their two children, whom Isabella homeschooled. She resumed volunteer charity work in 1915 at "the Club in Tyrone to which I belong called 'The Helping

Hand.'" This organization was her first women's club activity since coming to New Mexico, though she was a member of several in New York City for nearly seven years beginning in 1903, including the Junior League for the Promotion of Settlement Movements, to which Eleanor Roosevelt also belonged and was active as a participant and settlement house resident and community organizer until her marriage. Ferguson and Roosevelt had come of age in the era of New Women after 1890, an empowerment directed toward social and political change through three A's: active in public life, assertive about reform, and able to organize and lead.[6]

Beginning in the 1890s one thrust of activism among New Women was what has been called maternalist politics—infant and child health, especially reducing mortality, and more broadly child and family welfare as well as public health and safety. These were goals and programs familiar to Eleanor Roosevelt and Isabella Ferguson in their club work. But during World War I President Wilson's call for a service army pulled and pushed Ferguson, Roosevelt, Amanda Lindsey, the governor's wife, and millions of American women in a new direction—what can best be understood as mobilization politics. President Wilson's single-minded pursuit of enlisting the home front into campaigns to win the war harnessed energy already exerted toward two causes—suffrage and prohibition—club work familiar to Amanda Lindsey. President Wilson had a limited purpose in wartime mobilization politics—aligning the nation's economy and society behind programs necessary to ensure victory. This was mobilization for survival. Marshaling the home front for war became a cocreation: women accepted the president's invitation to come to the aid of their country, but they also recast mobilization to meet the goals and expectations of maternalist politics.[7]

The head of the government's program to mobilize women noted shortly after the war ended that "in war time it was found that what had been called 'women's interests,' namely food, thrift, health, morals, were the interests of a whole people and an integral part in the organization for victory." This reciprocal relationship between maternalist and mobilization politics became visible in President Wilson's actions within five weeks of America's entry into the war. Early in May 1917 the executive committee of the largest federation of women's clubs—the General Federation of Women's Clubs, which had several hundred thousand members nationwide—adopted a demand long made by temperance advocates: "The enormous amount of grain used in the manufacturing of liquors must now be utilized for bread for men and food for animals." They deemed doing so "as the fundamental step in the conservation of the physical strength and moral force of our nation." President Wilson was sympathetic to temperance arguments, and in mid-May he announced that a redrafted food bill contained a clause granting the government "power to regulate the use of grain in the manufacture of alcoholics." Thus did war abet Prohibition.[8]

New Mexico Women

New Women were key organizers in New Mexico; they were also distinctly separate from most of the women they sought to lead. In a letter Ferguson wrote to Roosevelt 22 January 1916, she presciently broached a prospect that would begin to emerge fifteen months later: "Will you be taking any part as an organizer in our women's defense project—I suppose in time, if well handled, it should get down to local organizations under larger ones & amount to a great deal—?" The Roosevelts lived in Washington, D.C., where Eleanor's husband, Franklin, was an assistant secretary of the navy. Implicit in Ferguson's question was the assumption that Washington, D.C.—and influential women there—would be at the top of a pyramid, with Ferguson and countless other women at its base. Ferguson's prediction of the creation of a vast, hierarchical network of women proved accurate. Several months before the war ended, the Women's Committee of the Council of National Defense (WCCND) reported that eleven million women were participating in 15,732 Women's Committee units throughout the country. Nearly one in five American women was mobilized in some manner within the state affiliates of the WCCND in 1917 and 1918. Two weeks after Congress declared war against Germany on Good Friday, 6 April 1917, the Council of National Defense formed the WCCND. Ferguson soon took charge of organizing Luna and Grant Counties and at the state level served as the women auxiliary's first treasurer.[9]

One of the most prominent of the New Women was Anna Howard Shaw, who was named director of the WCCND on 21 April 191. She was one of the first women ordained a minister and led a congregation in Massachusetts for a few years. She was also a physician and public intellectual, and for more than fifteen years Shaw and one of her assistants, Carrie Chapman Catt, had been principal leaders of the National American Woman Suffrage Association, which had been founded in 1890. Immediately the WCCND became an energetic and resourceful agent supporting the president's plan to mobilize America's women by "supply[ing] a new and direct channel of communication and cooperation between women and governmental departments."[10]

The women leaders of the WCCND became the commanders of the president's service army. This upper tier of leadership had extensive experience in advocacy as well as organizational and programmatic talents essential to advancing reform projects. This shared commitment to social justice and activism allowed a cadre of women to come together within weeks of the WCCND's creation. Shaw quickly had the WCCND hard at work organizing state affiliates, efforts that drew upon the decades of collaboration among women reformers under the auspices of the General Federation of Women's Clubs (GFWC). This umbrella organization had emerged in 1890 when leaders from sixty-three national and large regional women's clubs agreed to have a united presence to amplify their voice. The number of affiliated clubs increased to more than one hundred by 1917. But political infighting—bitter opposition from southern states' members to enfranchising black women and more selectively a fear of the economic consequences of shuttering distilleries and disrupting retail alcohol sales—excluded from the GFWC two key sources of talented women—activists for suffrage and for prohibition. It mattered not in 1917: Shaw, Catt, and other women drawn from those two movements were prominent in the WCCND.[11]

Amanda Lindsey, the governor's wife, received a telegram the WCCND sent on 1 May 1917 inviting her to chair her state's women's council. She was one of forty-eight wives of governors or other prominent women receiving such an invitation. Initially two vice-chairs were named in New Mexico, but when these two women realized that Lindsey delegated most daily operations to them they quickly sought a replacement and tapped Maude Prichard, wife of well-known attorney George W. Prichard and an ally of Governor Lindsey from when they served in the Constitutional Convention of 1910. A select group of Euro-American women assembled in the capital city to create the Women's Auxiliary of the State Council of Defense (WASCD) on 5 May 1917. The WCCND's telegram arrived on the opening day of the legislature's special eight-day session, which allowed Amanda Lindsey to promptly gather one Euro-American delegate from each of the state's twenty-seven counties. Most of the assembled were wives of legislators or lobbyists in town. Collectively the women who convened on 5 May were an elite counterpart to the men deliberating in the legislature. Thus it was that, two months after Congress declared war, New Mexico became "one of the first—if not the first—to mobilize its women for war service."[12]

Amanda Lindsey turned fifty-one in 1917, had been married to Washington E. Lindsey for twenty-six years, and they had three adult children. After statehood in 1912 she had become an advocate for the two issues that most roiled politics—suffrage and prohibition. She also participated in the local women's club in Portales, an affiliate of the GFWC. The governor's wife was in lockstep with her husband as a progressive Republican. In coping with her declining health—perhaps related to an unspecified cancer that took her life in 1923—she rationed her commitments, putting her energy into pushing for the state to ratify prohibition in 1918, which passed. As a result, though, she was mostly a titular figure in the WASCD throughout that year. Maude Prichard acted as de facto chair. She was ten years younger than Lindsey and proved adept at getting work done through the efforts of others. Prichard, too, was a longtime progressive Republican activist.[13]

Assembling a service army occasioned a major reorientation of voluntarism among New Mexican Euro-American women of leisure and means. The women's auxiliary was an adjunct of the SCD, which meant that Charles Springer maintained control of the budget and prescribed its organizational structure. His exercise of what many women saw as capricious paternalism resulted in friction, but Springer's fiscal control over the women's auxilliary was the norm in every state. The official history of the WCCND employed an extended metaphor of "a high wall" to describe how men's interests—"war, finance and state"—were separated from and given primacy over women's interests: "And on the side where dwelt men's interests was placed all power and dominion." The exercise of this "power and dominion" in money matters became increasingly visible beginning in the spring and summer of 1918 and continued to the end of the war in the decisions of Charles Springer. Among his actions were rejecting requests to pay for WASCD programs delegated them by the WCCND, including printing Spanish translations of food conservation literature, producing literature for initiatives pushed by the child welfare committee, and recruiting young women to become reserve nurses to be trained by the army. These WASCD requests fell into the same category as his refusal to pay for stamps and stationery—all were deemed nonessential to the war effort even though he had ample money to pay for them.[14]

A second consequential choice Springer made was imposing the SCD model of county-based councils. This arrangement departed from the community- and town-based model prescribed by the WCCND, which in May 1917 instructed chairwomen "that after your state organization is underway the organization of cities and towns throughout the state be next undertaken." The WCCND also suggested that county councils be the lowest priority, and two months before the war ended the Council of National Defense ordered that all county organizations—men's and women's—be consolidated with community-based units, a process never carried out in New Mexico. Likewise ignored in New Mexico was a WCCND mandate that women make up half of the membership of the SCD.[15]

The WASCD did, though, adhere to WCCND's instruction that each chairwoman form between thirteen and sixteen subcommittees. During the next eighteen months these subcommittees had varying degrees of activity, in large part reflecting the shallow pool from which Euro-American leaders could be recruited in various counties and an inability to build up new talent among Nuevomexicanas. The maximum number of women eligible for WASCD leadership—at the state and county level and among all the subcommittees—was slightly fewer than five hundred, a figure never attained. Quite predictably these women were drawn from a tiny pool—wives of the politically prominent as well as women active in the state's GFWC. The very real constraints county women faced were summarized by the chair of a subcommittee in Española in Santa Fe County in November 1918: "We have not been able to interest the native women [Nuevomexicanas] in the least in the work, and have had but little better success with the Americans." The writer listed several specific barriers impeding homefront work. The first hurdle cited was finances: "The lack of funds has been our greatest hindrance. . . . We have never received a penny, not even for stamps and stationery." The Española woman also mentioned the formidable language challenge: "I do not speak Spanish nor have I any way to get over the country to give the matter my personal attention."[16]

Gender division had four further gradations, and these proved key obstacles to mobilizing women in New Mexico: class, race, ethnicity, and geography. Bringing the state's female population of 169,894 (1920 census) into the nation's service army required the WASCD to engage women who had hitherto been separated—but not totally isolated—by socioeconomic, racial, cultural, and residency patterns etched onto the state long before the war. The WASCD neither confronted nor engaged the full diversity of New Mexico's population; instead, it parsed it further. Nuevomexicanas dominated the female population at approximately 95,000 (56 percent), and Euro-American women totaled about 63,000 (37 percent). These two groups, but principally the latter among its middle- and upper-middle-class members, were the women WASCD leaders sought to attract as their grassroots supporters. Neither American Indian women nor African American women were the focus of any outreach from the WASCD.[17]

American Indian women numbered about 9,300 (6 percent), and African American females numbered about 1,100 (1 percent) in 1920. When their actions were noted it was typically for accomplishments the WCSCD lauded but took no credit for guiding. American Indian women's traditional practices of drying fruits and vegetables were considered so impressive that, early in the war, Amanda Lindsey sent a series of photographs documenting their methods to Washington, D.C., in the hope that they would be reproduced and distributed nationwide, a step never taken. But perhaps their most noteworthy contribution came in buying Liberty Bonds. In the spring 1918 drive, the men and women of the Pueblo of Laguna purchased bonds totaling $23,000 ($371,353 in 2017), a level of support that elicited loud, sustained applause when announced to a Euro-American audience at a bond rally in Albuquerque. What was not widely known was the aggressive campaign the Bureau of Indian Affairs supervisor waged at the pueblo to ensure this significant financial commitment. The commissioner of Indian affairs, Cato Sells, told all agency supervisors that he expected to see "a Liberty Bond . . . in the home of every Indian and every employee of our service." The value of bonds purchased by Pueblos, Apaches, and Navajos in New Mexico is not known, but nationwide American Indians invested in excess of $25 million ($404 million in 2017). Their contribution did not result in any further contact with the WASCD.[18]

The state's African American women were found principally in urban areas but segregated from Euro-Americans. Their community was sensitive to how the white majority viewed them. When at the outbreak of war a rally attended by over four thousand Albuquerque residents lasted for more than three hours, among the speeches was one by African American minister Theodore Brinson titled "The Loyalty of the Negro." His affirmation of fealty suggests that African Americans believed they needed to refute whatever suspicions swirled around them regarding support for the war. At the level of day-to-day encounters, many African American women worked as domestics for well-to-do Euro-American families, who surely expected compliance with regulations prescribing shopping and preparing meals. The practices imposed also served as a starting point for how these regulations might be adapted in the home kitchens of domestics. The elite among African American women in New Mexico were members in Albuquerque of the National Association of Colored Women's Clubs, an organization founded in 1896 as a counterpart to the segregated Euro-American GFWC. Whatever their contributions to the service army may have been, no correspondence exists between their club and the WASCD.[19]

In New Mexico especially, geography conspired against outreach. Nationwide 51 percent (54.3 million) of the population of nearly 106 million lived in urban areas and 49 percent (51.4 million) in the countryside in 1920. But in New Mexico 83 percent (299,091) of New Mexico's 360,350 residents lived in rural areas where "distances between houses"—as one WASCD leader wrote—"are measured not by blocks but by arroyos, mountains, or mesas." The WCCND gave priority to recruiting in population centers, but Charles Springer insisted that predominantly rural New Mexico would not follow that model. Instead, WASCD's efforts were dispersed throughout all twenty-nine counties (two new counties had been organized in late June 1917).[20]

Leaders of local county WASCD activities were mostly women affiliated with the GFWC, which reflected the urban bias in these efforts. The federation in New Mexico had only three clubs in 1902—in Santa Fe, Las Cruces, and Roswell—and each gave special emphasis to establishing public libraries. When statehood arrived the GFWC had eleven affiliates, but soon the women's club movement grew dramatically, to fifty-two clubs in towns statewide by 1917. Priorities continued to include forming public libraries, and an Albuquerque women's club sponsored traveling book-lending programs in Gallup, Springer, and Hayden (Union County). Also active within the GFWC were proponents of maternalist politics—advocates of an array of reform initiatives undertaken since the 1890s to create clean, safe homes and neighborhoods for children and families and to improve health conditions for infants. In early May 1917 a national "Baby Week" promoted by the GFWC resulted in programs on their care, feeding, and well-being at clubs in Clovis, Las Vegas, Roswell, Silver City, and several in Albuquerque, and the Mountainair club discussed improving sanitation by eliminating household pests. In New Mexico only about 20 percent of the women's clubs provided volunteers to the WASCD, but these women were supplemented by volunteers from hospitals, churches, girls' and boys' clubs organized in schools, and Camp Fire Girls and Boy Scouts. Nationwide over ninety women's organizations actively participated, including civic, religious, temperance, suffrage, and educational groups. It is not possible to calculate the number of New Mexicans who participated in the WASCD, but it clearly was at least equal to the reported national average of about 20 percent, which would have meant about 34,000 New Mexican women and youngsters. The majority were Euro-American women, with Nuevomexicanas likely close to 5 percent (8,500), which is in its own way a testament to the challenges faced in drawing in the largest segment of women—rural Nuevomexicanas.[21]

Nuevomexicana ethnicity expressed in language, customs, and social views reinforced divisions of class and residence patterns. Of these variables, language was the most obvious barrier to outreach. In New Mexico the non-English-speaking population was 48.5 percent of the total, whereas nationwide that figure was about 15 percent according to the 1920 census. In rural areas, non-English-speaking women were the majority. The Nuevomexicano community of El Cerrito in San Miguel County has been extensively studied, and it was representative of such communities of the wartime era. Of its women, only 22 percent spoke English, which was a significant improvement from 1900, when no men or women in the village spoke English. Spanish literacy was 64 percent among Nuevomexicanas in El Cerrito in 1920.[22]

In predominantly Spanish-speaking San Miguel County the WASCD coordinator, a monolingual Euro-American women from Las Vegas—twenty miles north of El Cerrito—reported in August 1918 that she delegated outreach to the Spanish-speaking county agricultural agent, who "is working for me as he goes among the people." Vaulting the language barrier was a major challenge statewide, and Otero County attempted to do it with the help of a prominent bilingual Euro-American. That county's WASCD chair did not speak Spanish, "nor do I know them as a people," but she turned to "Mrs. [Albert B.] Fall, of Three Rivers, [the] state worker among the Spanish women [who] will work this county." Emma Morgan Fall, wife of the state's U.S. senator and like her husband fluent in Spanish, was well regarded among the county's Nuevomexicanas. Otero County had more than 3,800 women, almost half of whom spoke only Spanish, and reaching out to the Spanish-speaking Nuevomexicanas in the county was well beyond the capability of one bilingual woman; at least fifty such women would have been required.[23]

Gender roles were a strong determinant of social views in Nuevomexicano villages, and during the war years a Euro-American women would have encountered resistance from village leaders if she was seen as introducing change that might alter the prevailing place of Nuevomexicanas in the community. A foretaste of such conflict had flared in the Constitutional Convention of 1910 when Nuevomexicano delegates of both parties united to block efforts to empower women, particularly in opposing suffrage in political elections (but allowing it when choosing school boards). These efforts to preserve traditional power relations and hold the line against imposed social change were a product of what has been described as tradition-bound "paternalistic attitudes of the Hispanic [male] majority" prevalent in that period.[24]

Various institutions—some old and some new—were perhaps the most effective means of drawing Nuevomexicanas into the "great service army": elementary schools and their teachers, Catholic and Protestant churches, merchants setting up demonstration kitchens in their stores, and Spanish-language newspapers. Broad contact was initiated through these agents, but guesstimating actual participation is problematic. Nationwide, by early 1918 schools became the preferred site for organizing the home front on the local level. The virtues inherent in using a local school as an anchor for community outreach were described by the Council of National Defense to all state councils in early February 1918. The Council noted that schools had rooms for meetings, often were "already a social community," and were "non-political governmental units." This latter did not always obtain in New Mexico, and in general anchoring community mobilization to schools had mixed results. To prepare teachers for their role in mobilizing the home front, summer institutes of two to four weeks were held throughout the state. One of the first was in Santa Fe in early June 1917, conducted by country superintendent (and WASCD activist) Nina Otero-Warren and attended by more than one hundred schoolteachers, mostly women. By mid-July the seventeenth summer institute took place in Las Cruces. That institute's organizer, a Euro-American woman doing "food conservation [instruction] for the state," provided a Spanish interpreter "so that both Spanish- and English-speaking people might fully understand the demonstration." The focus of instruction was food conservation through canning, which tied into the garden movement. Once the school year resumed, the U.S. Food Administration presented "spirited address[es] on food conservation" to county-based teachers' association members.[25]

But the key to entrusting local outreach to teachers was the match between a community's ethnicity and that of the grammar school's teacher. Within the 1,260 grammar (or elementary) schools in the state, and an overwhelmingly female teacher corps, rapport and harmony were constantly being negotiated. For example, a Nuevomexicana in predominantly Nuevomexicano Rio Arriba County reporting on local contributions to the government's spring 1918 fund-raising drive noted that "in three school districts they have pledged three thousand dollars [$48,437 in 2017]." But the war occasioned turnover among teachers and schools underwent staff changes. Socorro County, with a predominantly Nuevomexicano population served by Spanish-speaking teachers, witnessed male teachers called to the military and "a number of competent and experienced women who have been the foundation of the educational affairs here for a number of years have found in government positions and elsewhere more congenial employment." In hiring replacements the county frequently had to settle for teachers who at best had "some knowledge of the Spanish language" and often were unfamiliar with the local community. The war afforded some Nuevomexicanas upward mobility but thereby ended their role as local cultural brokers.[26]

The head of New Mexico's newly formed Office of Cooperative Organizations, a unit of the U.S. Food Administration, wrote to "the pastors of Catholic and non-Catholic churches" in early August 1918 to request their assistance.

Admitting that "we lack literature in Spanish," he sought to enlist their help as intermediaries: "We believe that the best way to [reach Nuevomexicanas] will be to send notices, informational letters, and bulletins in Spanish to the priests and ministers" to be read during their worship services. This approach began very late in war mobilization. Also late starting—appearing only in the final six months of the war—were *cocinas de Hoover,* or demonstration kitchens. In communities large and small, grocery store owners set up a stove where local women could "teach how to cook using substitutes."[27]

Throughout the war Spanish-language newspapers provided extensive and consistently supportive aid to the federal and state governments to align Spanish speakers with mobilization efforts. Eight Spanish-language newspapers appeared at least weekly during the war, with these five the major ones: *La Revista de Taos, La Voz del Pueblo* (Las Vegas), *La Bandera Americana* (Albuquerque); *El Defensor del Pueblo* (Socorro), and *La Estrella* (Las Cruces). East side communities Mountainair (Torrance County), Wagon Mound (Mora County), and Roy (then in Mora County) likewise had local papers, albeit in a smaller format and with fewer pages. These papers had extensive, continuous news equal to the English-language press about mobilization and the war beginning in the summer of 1917.

Albuquerque's *La Bandera Americana* ("The American Flag"), the state's largest-circulating Spanish-language newspaper, endorsed wheatless baking in strident terms: "The selling of wheat is not patriotic and aids the enemy. There will not be a lack of food, but wheat has to go to the soldiers." The newspaper's readers quickly learned that the kitchen became a new front in the war. "Three times a day women have an opportunity to serve their country: by using half the sugar regularly consumed; cooking and consuming less meat than is usual; and using other substitutes in place of wheat flour." The newspaper also reminded Nuevomexicanas in a headline that "Each Bushel of Wheat Is Equivalent to a Soldier," and the accompanying article stated, "The number of men we can send into battle depends on the number of men we can feed at the front." Comparable comments appeared in Wagon Mounds' *El Centinela* ("The Sentinel"): "Our sons and brothers have joined the army to fight, to protect their country and their state. The least you can do to help is give them food—they are the ones who need to eat bread made from wheat. Do not allow anyone to say the people of New Mexico are less patriotic than those of other states." *Frijoles* (pinto beans) were the one significant cultural difference between the diets of Nuevomexicanos and Euro-Americans, and *La Bandera Americana* applauded the government's action urging substituting beans for beef.[28]

Organizing the "Great Service Army"

La Estrella (The Star), a weekly newspaper serving the Nuevomexicano community in Las Cruces, exhorted readers to "Support New Mexico's Boys" in May 1918. It pointed out that "1,485 New Mexico boys leave the state this month for military camps"—the majority headed to Camp Cody in Deming. The column pointed out that the military call-ups to date, "some 10,000 of our boys into the Army," created responsibilities on the home front, especially among mothers:

> The mothers in almost all the towns and villages will have to make more sacrifices. . . . grow more crops, help the Red Cross so they can aid the wounded boys, loan your money to the government by buying Liberty Bonds and War Savings Stamps, and save more food so it can be sent to the combatants. A soldier with an empty stomach would be better off at home than at the front. There are only certain things that can be shipped to France to feed the fighters. Wheat is the most important of these.

In the nearly fourteen months that had elapsed since the United States entered the war and the appearance of this article in *La Estrella,* the president's service army had taken shape and imposed its will on the nation. Some of the efforts were voluntary, such as making bandages or knitting "to help the Red Cross so they can aid the wounded boys."[29]

Isabella Ferguson helped found the Red Cross chapter in Tyrone. Together with her ten-year-old daughter, Martha, they were among the thousands of New Mexicans who volunteered their time and talents to the Red Cross. The state director was Albuquerque-based journalist and writer Erna Fergusson. By Christmas season 1917, the Red Cross had completed two nationwide recruitment drives that enrolled twenty-two million members, mostly women, which meant that about 40 percent of the female population had joined its ranks. It had the largest participation by women among all wartime organizations. Also enrolled during the war were eleven million Junior Red Cross members, including Martha Ferguson, many of whom took first-aid classes. The women's principal projects at the outset were sewing bandages and knitting caps, sweaters, scarves, and socks and soliciting donations to Red Cross relief fund-raisers aiding families in allied countries. A report on the accomplishments of eighty-four women in Tucumcari in mid-January 1918 is representative of Red Cross volunteers' wintertime commitment expressed in the motto "Knit Your Bit." Gathering twice a week they produced 1,440 bandages, fifty sweaters, seventy-four pairs of socks, and seven other knitted items in three and a half months. During Christmas 1918 a nationwide effort included New Mexico Red Cross volunteers who boxed and sent packages of treats to the state's AEF soldiers in occupied Germany. A delighted Nuevomexicano soldier in the army of occupation sent a thank-you letter to a Spanish-language Santa Fe newspaper and described how alone he felt "far from our country, far from our parents, relatives, and friends." But he knew he was remembered when he read the card enclosed in his parcel: "Christmas from the folks at home through the Red Cross."[30]

The American Red Cross, founded by Clara Barton in 1881, received a congressional charter in 1900, several years before Barton stepped down as its national director. When the United States entered the war, the Red Cross was able to expand rapidly because it had organizational infrastructure in leaders and local affiliates. It also had important intangibles through public presence and credibility. The government's civilian wartime mobilization initiatives had none of the qualities that the Red Cross had built up over nearly four decades. Instead, the federal government had to create new organizations to conduct its two signature programs of the service army—food conservation and fund-raising.

The Council of National Defense proposed the United States Food Administration (USFA) one day after Congress declared war and nominated Herbert Hoover as its head. He had gained international distinction for organizing food relief to Belgian refugees, and his career as a mining engineer had made him independently wealthy. On Easter Sunday, 8 April 1917, New Mexicans read that Hoover had "the important task of conserving [the] food supply." The Council and President Wilson expected the USFA to fulfill a key role in mobilizing the home front to reduce consumption of meat, wheat, and sugar. But the executive branch could only propose. Congress had to approve the Lever Act, the legislation creating the USFA and putting in place policies for the conservation of food and fuel.[31]

The Wilson administration sent its food bill to Capitol Hill in early May, where it was routed to the agricultural committees of the House and Senate and became known as the Lever bill. Immediately an impasse occurred between the executive and legislative branches of government. Foes of the legislation, mostly from Wilson's own Democratic Party, charged that the bill granted Wilson "dictatorial power." To counter this fear, Wilson invited some members of both parties to the White House in mid-May 1917 to explain his priorities. He invoked the word "control" several times in explaining "the three factors that will control the war situation." These were, in order of importance, "the actual fighting forces, control of the food situation, and control of the transportation facilities of the country." Congressional opposition centered on the Lever bill as an extension of executive power, but other of Wilson's proposed actions caused alarm, too. Yet no one foresaw that in eight months he would nationalize the nation's railroads when they did not align with the government's priorities in transporting goods and manpower. Wilson maintained that his broad uses of executive power were temporary measures needed during an "emergency crisis." But in framing solutions to current exigencies in terms of what would "control the war situation," he revealed a willingness to use executive power in ways never previously pursued. "Control" became the operative term in understanding Wilson's wartime legislation and its implementation at the state level.[32]

The president's repeated use of the word "control" when describing to congressional leaders his priorities in mobilizing the nation is best understood when contrasted with his use of "service" and "serve," which he invoked sixteen times in his "Appeal to the American People." Each was a key word in how he hoped to forge the "great service army," and each term must be approached with the realization that President Wilson "knew the power of language and obviously believed he could shape the national consciousness through his rhetoric, helping to determine the way Americans understood themselves." The "national consciousness" he sought to mold has been identified by scholars as "the ideology of voluntarism," and it was pursued relentlessly by both Wilson and Hoover. Combined in voluntarism were both control and service, and the blending of these two was fundamental to "determin[ing] the way Americans understood themselves." The righteousness of the cause, as Wilson explained in mid-April, was paramount and transcendent: "fighting for what we believe and wish to be the rights of mankind and for the future peace and security of the world." This was the banner used to rally the nation to enlist in the service army. But it was only a first step. The larger task was holding them in place once mobilized, and that necessitated control. In his address to the nation on 16 April, Wilson hinted at one change in national behavior that he would insist upon: "It is the time for America to correct her unpardonable fault of wastefulness [of food]." It fell to Herbert Hoover and the USFA to be the instruments of control over Americans' use of food. In broadest terms what occurred in voluntarism was that responding to the call to serve seemed to be a choice, thus preserving freedom of action, but in fact it was an imposed decision, and hence coercion. To enlist in the service army in matters of food was not an urgent suggestion; it was a mandate—initially veiled but fully revealed by January 1918.[33]

Food Campaigns

Three months of "hurry up and wait" followed the mid-May discussion between the president and congressional leaders. A contest of wills dominated Washington. For his part, Wilson was determined not to let congressional inaction derail moving food conservation from idea to practice. On 19 May, Wilson formally appointed Hoover as food administrator, a position he accepted on condition that he—along with national administrators and state directors—would receive no salary. The example of selfless service did not budge Congress, so Wilson wrote to Hoover on 12 June and gave him "'full authority to take any steps necessary' for the organization of the women of the country." Four days later neither chamber of Congress had reported the bill out of committee, and Wilson went public with his frustration by announcing that he would tolerate "no further delay" in initiating voluntary efforts aimed at "saving food and eliminating waste."[34]

Hoover began the next day to implement Wilson's plan, using the occasion of an address to a conference of the GFWC in Washington, D.C., to set forth his ideas. There he called upon all "housewives of America urging them to cooperate with the government." Their first act of support was to sign a Hoover Pledge card. Beginning 1 July women were asked to accept a short statement "pledging myself to carry out the directions and advice of the food administrator in the conduct of my household, insofar as my circumstances permit." A day after Hoover's speech, Congress began debate on the Lever Act, which it passed eight weeks later on 10 August—Hoover's forty-third birthday. During the seven weeks between his address to the GFWC and approval of the Lever Act, Hoover began "the organization of the women of the country" with the goal, as reported in the *New York Times,* of "enlisting every housewife in the country as a volunteer member of the food administration."[35]

Mobilizing for war meant that much happened at a fast pace, and the guiding principle became "Washington initiates and states implement." Such was especially true in the urgent need to marshal the support of women to ensure that food conservation began immediately and continued for the duration of the war. A fifteen-day Hoover Pledge drive, the first of many such campaigns during the next eighteen months, began nationwide on 1 July. The Council of National Defense printed pledge cards in English and several other languages, including Spanish. These cards reached New Mexico with only four days remaining to secure signatures and send them to Santa Fe. Distribution had been hastily arranged through the state's newly formed WASCD as well as women's clubs and church groups. The late start restricted the response to the principal cities and minimized the number of completed cards.[36]

New Mexico's experience with the Hoover Pledge cards was not unique; nationwide, less than 4 percent of all women participated in the initial pledge drive. But the WASCD persisted in its efforts, and two months later the Hoover cards were being signed throughout the state with varying degrees of success. Grant County had the highest number (1,575), with Ferguson personally recruiting 250 pledge signers, and Sandoval County was credited with a strong response, "sending in more Hoover Pledge cards than many other counties of the state." Illustrative of the varying responses are four counties—from the west (McKinley), two from the east (Quay and Curry), and in the south (Doña Ana). Quay and Doña Ana counties were active in gaining signatures, but inactivity in Curry County prompted Lindsey to seek a new WASCD chairwoman because, as she wrote, "not a single Hoover Pledge Card was sent in from Curry County." McKinley County likewise had problems that minimized signings. Its drive was "greatly hampered by labor troubles [in Gallup and nearby coal mines], thereby causing non-response by the women." The problem of rural poverty was more common in New Mexico than elsewhere but went unreported to USFA officials. Its consequence among subsistence farmers, particularly in the counties of Rio Arriba, Luna, and Grant, meant that "most of them were already eating less than the Hoover pledge required." One month into his tenure the USFA state director, Ralph C. Ely, began informing Hoover of successes but also sought help to solve local problems in food administration. Hoover was unable to aid him.[37]

In spite of this slow start, the Hoover Pledge drives became a mainstay of the government's mobilization of women. Outreach initiated by the state's superintendent of public instruction in mid-October 1917 illustrates the persistence with which this campaign was waged. He mandated that all students be given lessons on patriotism that included information about how important it was for mothers to sign the Hoover Pledge. Cards were to be sent home, and the prospect of being able to hang a Hoover Pledge sign in a home's window—a red, white, and blue card featuring spears of wheat—meant that children were expected to exert pressure on parents to secure their signatures and exhibit the family's patriotism. This school drive resulted in registering 9,863 women in October, and cards continued to be turned in during early November. A guesstimate would be that 10–15 percent of New Mexico women had signed the Hoover Pledge by the end of November 1917. Over the next eleven months, though, efforts brought the final tally to 34 percent of the state's women, about 57,000. This figure considerably exceeded the

WCCND's expectation for New Mexico, projections that placed it in the lowest of three categories based on its calculation of "percentage for Americanism and literacy." In fact New Mexico came in well ahead of states in the top tier such as New York and Massachusetts (27 percent each) and Ohio (24 percent).[38]

The Hoover Pledge cards were never an end in themselves, although this point was often lost in the initial push to secure signatures. After passage of the Lever Act authorizing the USFA on 10 August 1917, that agency took over the pledge drives. New Mexico director Ely, a lawyer from Luna County and a former chair of the state's Republican Party, was a political rival of Charles Springer. Thirteen months after Ely's appointment, Springer lodged a vituperative charge claiming Ely was a party to "violations of the Espionage Act" for encouraging criticism of the SCD as a "political tool." Shortly after this accusation, Ely resigned and left the state.[39]

Establishing the USFA's independence had been a priority from the beginning of Ely's tenure, and he quickly separated it from activities under Springer's purview. Within three months Ely recruited about 1,400 volunteers. Some volunteers served in the corps of Hoover women, whose "uniform of blue gingham with white cuffs and collars and white caps" had the effect in New Mexico of setting apart his agency from ones under Springer's control. But hostility between Springer and Ely did not preclude joint work among women volunteers from each agency. The first of several such large-scale cooperative efforts occurred at the prompting of Governor Lindsey during a "Patriotic Week" between 10 and 14 October 1917 in Albuquerque, an event that replaced the canceled state fair (which would not resume for twenty-one years) and coincided with the departure for Camp Kearny of the state's National Guard. In the exhibit hall, the Hoover women were prominent in a large booth promoting pledge signups as well as food conservation. Also present were WASCD leaders and home demonstration agents.[40]

A War Service card was presented to women age sixteen and older at the same time as the Hoover Pledge card. But unlike the short statement on the Hoover card, the service card was a half-sheet of paper with sixteen personal questions followed by 165 "Training and Experience" questions. The form originated earlier in the war when Great Britain, France, and Canada used it to recruit women into the labor force. But that was not the intent in the United States, where it was solely to provide local officials a pool of volunteers. Nationwide, it was seen quite differently and aroused great fear that, in concert with the Hoover Pledge card, it portended coercion on the part of the government. Fears of ulterior motives behind the two cards surfaced in New Mexico as well. A USFA field agent reported after touring "fifteen or more counties in the interests of the [Hoover Pledge] campaign" in early November 1917 that "he found great fear that the pledge cards would lead to the seizure for government use of the citizens' food supplies." In such conditions, widespread suspicion was inevitable. The War Service card, though, met with overwhelming rejection. The baseless assumption was that the government would force work upon women, especially to go into factories, a fear that the nation's secretary of labor, William B. Wilson, called "more or less hysteria" in May 1918.[41]

By December 1917 the emphasis of the USFA began shifting from voluntary compliance to setting restrictions on food purchases and consumption. The USFA imposed its first regulations on the kitchens and lives of American women beginning in late January 1918 when it instituted wheatless Mondays, meatless Tuesdays, and combinations of these restrictions for individual meals on Wednesday through Saturday. This schedule underwent several changes before eventually settling into wheatless Mondays and meatless Wednesdays, with some restrictions for individual meals on four other days. These limitations were accompanied by a campaign to show women how to reduce use of wheat flour and eat more chicken in place of beef. To cut in half use of wheat flour, new recipes were widely distributed that called for adding 50 percent of another flour derived from substitutes such as hominy, barley, oatmeal, rice, buckwheat, potato, and many others. By August 1918 the proportion had been altered to 80 percent wheat flour and 20 percent substitute flour. Raising and eating more poultry received special emphasis in 1918, and clubs for boys and girls taught them how to earn money by selling eggs.[42]

Merchants shouldered most of the responsibility for enforcing restrictions on consumption. They did so by imposing USFA mandates on how much they were allowed to sell to individuals or a household each week and what maximum price they could charge. Most of what they were to enforce did not require filling out forms or keeping written records, except for sugar, which was the only item that required that a "certificate" be signed by the buyer "with each purchase [affirming] that they were within the monthly allotment." The government's wartime food allocation program lasted for only one year—1918—and was implemented on a dual track. First, the USFA monitored grocery stores throughout the state using a small staff of paid employees who were supplemented by a cadre of volunteers including traveling salesmen and housewives. Second, adult education provided instruction on new practices in home cooking at sessions the USFA often sponsored jointly with home demonstration agents, volunteers from the WASCD's conservation subcommittees, or outreach through the state's newspapers and speakers' bureaus.[43]

Wartime food conservation programs, especially in 1918, became the primary emphasis of two government agencies—the U.S. Department of Agriculture Extension Service's home demonstration agents and the USFA field staff. Whereas most counties had multiple agricultural agents by the end of the war, the number of home demonstration agents lagged. As an example, Bernalillo County secured an agricultural agent in the summer of 1917, but not until April 1918 did the county appropriate funds for a home demonstration agent to begin work on 1 May. Moreover, women Extension agents were always paid less than males, and it was common for one home demonstration agent to serve multiple counties. To compensate for limited staff, the home demonstration agents eagerly cooperated with volunteers from the WASCD, and together between July and December 1917 they held no less than 685 meetings attended by 17,056 women.[44]

In a move likely linked to programmatic changes made by the WASCD, specifically a shift in priority toward fund-raising, the Extension Service altered the administration of its home demonstration program in December 1917. The close cooperation with the WASCD had enabled home demonstration agents to attract an average of twenty-five women to their numerous meetings in 1917, and the two Spanish-speaking home demonstration agents—Gertrude Espinosa and Sarah Van Vleek—made 162 presentations in Spanish in seven counties and visited more than three hundred homes of Hispanic women during 1918. But expanding outreach became a priority, which necessitated a new state coordinator of home demonstration agents. Brought in was Tura A. Hawk, who assumed her duties in December 1917.[45]

Hawk had been a home economics teacher and principal in public schools in Iowa and South Dakota for ten years before coming to New Mexico in 1916 to work as a suffrage advocate. Upon joining the Extension Service she immediately made her presence felt statewide. She convened two successful large-scale conferences in January, one in Las Cruces, where she delivered the welcoming address to hundreds of attendees, and one in Albuquerque to a similarly large audience. At the state college in 14–19 January and in downtown Albuquerque for the final three days of the month, Hawk and home demonstration agents from various counties delivered lectures and conducted hands-on cooking sessions in support of the food conservation campaign. At the Albuquerque event, organized in cooperation with the city's WASCD affiliate, Hawk's focus was on how housewives could aid the USFA, especially in its meatless campaign. After these conferences Hawk threw herself into traveling the state to convince counties to fund and hire home demonstration agents, until her next initiative—the Mother-Daughter Congress held in Albuquerque 24–29 June.[46]

The Mother-Daughter Congress enabled Hawk to share with about eight hundred New Mexico women concrete ways to fulfill an oft-repeated mantra of Herbert Hoover—"Winning the War in the Kitchen." Hawk presided over the Extension Service kitchen, which for four days offered "practical demonstrations of kitchen food conservation, the prevention of waste, [and] the using of substitutes." The USFA and the WASCD also had their own kitchen demonstrations, with the latter active again because the next Liberty Bond drive was four months away. They gave special attention to "cooking using substitutes," and members statewide were urged "to send all good tested recipes you can collect." Despite the gathering's name, the attendees were not required to have a family connection. The goal was to send pairs: "The girl must be at least 16 years old and the woman not necessarily a mother." The Extension Service planned to send one hundred pairs, the WASCD two hundred pairs, and the USFA was represented by 228 pairs. Special recruitment resulted in a large presence of "women from the remote, inaccessible regions" of many counties. All twenty-nine counties were represented at the convention, with the largest contingent (excluding Bernalillo County) coming from nearby Sandoval County, which organized car caravans for women living northwest of Albuquerque to as far away as the area around Cuba, a nearly four-hour drive northwest of Albuquerque in that era. All attendees were urged to teach others when they returned home, and at least several pairs from each county pledged to offer cooking demonstrations. Among the attendees were some fifty Spanish-speaking women, and "a large number of Hispanic-American women were busy helping out at the meeting."[47]

With four-fifths of the population rural and many living in isolated settings, home demonstration agents—even those with automobiles—needed a unique set of skills to do their jobs. The experience of one young woman is illustrative of everyday challenges. Bertha Becker, an intrepid home demonstration agent for Sandoval and Torrance Counties, was lauded in January 1918 for traveling "alone on her trips and does not depend on garages if her car breaks down forty miles from the next town, being an expert in automobile repairing." But the pace of Becker's outreach, as she noted in her report on activities in Torrance County between 30 July and 4 August 1917, was largely determined by the terrain: "The places I had to visit this week were so far apart and the roads in such a bad condition that it was impossible to hold more than one meeting in a day." Few agents were able to duplicate Becker's efforts, and typically rural outreach involved securing a driver. But the scarcity of vehicles meant that such arrangements were difficult to make in many parts of the state. For example, in Luna County one car served all WASCD volunteers, and the local chair sought in vain to "hire motors [so] they could so much more easily do the work."[48]

In the quest to bring information about wartime needs to rural women, newspaper coverage of home-front activities was of special importance. Mass communication in the era before radio (pre-1920) occurred through reading and oral transmission, and these mediums were well used in New Mexico. Out of Washington flowed English-language news for women issued from the Division of Women's War Work, a branch of the Committee on Public Information, the agency charged with creating and spreading wartime propaganda. These writers sent out between twelve and twenty stories daily to 2,861 newspapers to show "what women were doing to win the war."[49]

The Foreign Languages Press branch of the Committee on Public Information provided stories to some 745 newspapers published in fourteen languages in the United States. Although the official history of the branch reported that "96 percent of the papers availed themselves extensively of the material," the Council of National Defense urged all states to undertake their own translations of local war news and place them with foreign-language papers in their state beginning in early June 1918. In response to this request, New Mexico's SCD reported in mid-June that steps were being taken "to assist the Spanish press in New Mexico in printing more of the official war news and propaganda," but it also wondered how much might be accomplished since "practically all of the foreign language newspapers in the state already give considerable space to it." USFA administrator Ely sponsored a three-day conference of journalists that ran concurrently with the Mother-Daughter Congress in late June 1918 at which he discussed ways the state's journalists could "disseminate constantly rules and regulations from the government in regards to the production, conservation, distribution, and consumption of foods." One new avenue for such items was the Spanish-language edition of the SCD's *War News*.[50]

The power of the printed word to achieve the USFA's food conservation goals was dramatically seen in Mountainair's contributions to ensuring that wheat went to soldiers in France. An account first reported in the community's newspaper, *El Independiente,* was reproduced in Spanish-language papers statewide:

> In Mountainair a man bought a fifty pound sack of flour and a newspaper. While returning to his ranch he read in the newspaper that wheat was

needed more than ever at the [western] front. Instead of continuing on his way he went back to the store and turned over the flour declaring that he would not eat any more wheat flour until after the next harvest. The following day another man brought back ten sacks of flour. In all some 2,000 pounds were returned to the store from homes and ranches. The same thing has happened in other parts of the state.

Rather quickly "the entire town of Mountainair [vowed it] will not eat wheat until the Huns are defeated." Mountainair's citizens did not act spontaneously but rather responded to a government campaign urging wheat flour be returned to stores.[51]

WASCD: Financing the War and the Women's Land Army

The WASCD recruited its leaders from the state's GFWC-affiliated clubs but then immediately began pushing them to reinvent themselves. No longer were they limited to small, homogeneous gatherings such as their afternoon tea receptions. The WASCD required activism to accomplish its mission. Its women volunteers were expected to be agents of outreach to all New Mexicans, and no effort more exemplified this expanded purpose than Liberty Bond sales. The WASCD's participation grew steadily during the four wartime bond campaigns, and it had a prominent place in New Mexico's fund-raising during the two drives in 1918.

The U.S. Treasury Department initiated all bond drives, and regional federal reserve banks supervised and administered them. The Dallas Federal Reserve Bank supplied sales materials for contiguous states, furnished in English and Spanish. In a few instances during the first bond drive (spring 1917), Spanish-speaking women were addressed at public meetings. In Albuquerque an unidentified Euro-American professor of Spanish spoke to a "large audience in the beautiful language of Castile" and appealed to their patriotism and loyalty. The professor's address was consistent with instructions provided by the WCCND for its "Fourteen Minute Women's Speaker's Bureau," a counterpart to Council for National Defense's "Four Minute Men," and called for "arousing them in no small way to a sense of the enormity of the work to be done and instructing them as to the best methods of procedure."[52]

The WASCD began taking an active role in bond sales beginning with the second national drive (October 1917), but its involvement greatly accelerated in the lead-up to the third Liberty Bond drive in April 1918. Two trends converged to account for this expanded participation beginning late in 1917. The WASCD pivoted away from food conservation, a traditional hands-on and solitary action, and concentrated on two new missions—recruitment and fund-raising. The organization began a major push to attract new volunteers to fill all thirteen subcommittees in each county. The results can be seen by comparing leadership in the late summer of 1917 and eight months later: seventeen counties listing county-level leaders in September, of whom 199 were Euro-American women and just thirteen (6.1 percent) Nuevomexicanas. Only in Taos County were the two top leaders Nuevomexicanas. Eight months later, though, after Lindsey and Prichard had begun insisting that the WASCD do much more to recruit Nuevomexicanas, eight counties reported that twenty-six Nuevomexicanas were serving as subcommittee chairwomen.[53]

Why the sudden interest to reach out to Nuevomexicanas? It was hoped that having more of them as volunteers would increase their purchase of Liberty Bonds. The plan to sell bonds to Nuevomexicanas was explained by the chairwoman of the Women's Liberty Loan Committee on 6 April 1918: "I am today mailing to all county chairmen [chairwomen] a number of Spanish dodgers [flyers] addressed particularly to Spanish-American women. Where I was able to gauge the Spanish-speaking population, I forwarded the literature directly to the township chairman. . . . Women are to sell [Liberty Bonds] to anybody they can—men, women, corporation, societies of all kinds, but with particular emphasis laid on sales to other women."[54]

Their plan worked. New Mexico saw a steady increase in the amount it had to raise to fulfill each bond drive's quota, and they consistently exceeded their goal: May 1917, quota of $1,375,400 with subscriptions of $1,834,600, 33.5 percent greater than the goal; October, quota of $3,095,700 with subscriptions of $3,945,750, 27.5 percent greater than the quota; April 1918, $3,658,500 as the goal with subscriptions of $6,001,760, 64 percent greater than the goal; September, $3,234,300 with subscriptions of $6,170,300, 90.7 percent more than the quota. Overall, the federal government asked the state to raise $11,363,900 ($184,220,108 in 2017). New Mexicans met and exceed that amount with subscriptions totaling $17,952,410 ($291,026,400 in 2017), surpassing the total quota by 57.9 percent.[55]

Although the total sales were impressive, the results among women were skewed by ethnicity and class, as revealed in a tabulation of 613 individuals in Doña Ana County who purchased Liberty Bonds during April 1918. Of these buyers, 25 percent (156) were readily identifiable as women, and 96 percent of these were Euro-American women. Females in the county purchased $26,400 ($426,248 in 2017) in bonds, or 25 percent of the $105,850 ($1.7 million in 2017).

But just eight well-to-do Euro-American women in Doña Ana County bought $15,500 ($250,259 in 2017) in bonds, which means that they accounted for 57 percent of the total of $26,400 purchased by women. The single largest amount paid by any one woman, a Euro-American, was $10,000 ($161,458 in 2017), and half the women (78)—including almost all the Nuevomexicanas—purchased $50 bonds, for which they paid $41 ($662 in 2017) and could redeem them in five years for the full face value. A clear socioeconomic divide existed among the purchasers. The limited means of many Nuevomexicanas stemmed in large part from the adverse impact coverture had on them after 1846, when this American law denied them separate ownership of any asset upon marrying—cash, personal property, or land.[56]

Perhaps no effort undertaken by the WASCD demanded more of its women volunteers than becoming farm laborers—but on their own terms and through the Women's Land Army. This movement was based on experiences in Great Britain and Canada, and in all locales its purpose was straightforward: "to supply women [to be] farm laborers wherever they are needed." By early spring 1918, plans began to take shape to use women to replace male farm workers called into the military. During April 1918, state chairs received information about how to organize, and later that month a second letter from President Wilson and the WCCND endorsed the movement. New Mexico was one of the few states to pursue the initiative. By early June, Isabella Ferguson had been appointed to head the state's Land Army, and she promptly contacted all the county agricultural agents to help identify where women would be needed. This program coincided with Charles Springer's interest in supporting agriculture in wartime New Mexico, and he gave his blessing to her plans in mid-July and offered "assurances of my willingness to cooperate with you."[57]

It is possible that some of the more than five hundred New Mexico women who joined harvest crews in the summer and fall of 1918 were recruited from War Service cards, but more likely they were recruited through the WASCD's Land Army subcommittees, which had been initiated in early spring 1918. The largest turnout was one of the last: 250 women, working under a contract Ferguson negotiated with an El Paso grower, picked crops in October 1918. Each woman earned two dollars a day plus board and room. Other women, such as from Deming (Luna County), picked tomatoes locally and then moved into the Mesilla Valley in Doña Ana County and joined other crews in picking pears. Near Cloudcroft in Otero County a crew of fifty women, representing ten counties and laboring ten hours a day, picked, graded, and packed about 8,600 boxes of apples. The

Land Army mobilized young and middle-age women into a proto-sisterhood of laborers, where the work was seen as meaningful and necessary and controlled by women. It also set a precedent tapped again during World War II.[58]

Voluntarism and Demobilization

And then it was all over "over there." News of the 11:00 A.M. armistice reached New Mexico well before first light on 11 November. All food restrictions were rescinded within six weeks, the USFA closed its offices in the state in February 1919, and the next month the legislature refused to appropriate money for the SCD and its women's auxiliary. The collective impact of these actions meant that the "great service army" was dismantled. Women's voluntarism in the immediate postwar years rolled forward, but this time women asserted their independence in dealing with the government, especially the BI's High Cost of Living Division (HCLD), initiated a year after the armistice, and the state legislature and Congress over suffrage, ratified as the Nineteenth Amendment of the Constitution in August 1920.

USFA dictates regarding food consumption and conservation lapsed after the war's end, but the price monitoring portions of the Lever Act were actually enhanced in late October 1919. Congress passed an amendment to the act providing for fines and imprisonment for violations, and immediately the BI initiated enforcement through a "Cost of Living Campaign." This initiative continued the spirit of wartime mobilization. It enforced price regulations on numerous items deemed, in the language of the amendment, to be "food and clothing necessaries." To organize its effort, the BI adopted the bureaucratic structure used during the war, particularly separate outreach to men and women. In New Mexico the GFWC and Woman's Christian Temperance Union as well as individual women were soon invited by U.S. attorney Summers Burkhart to cooperate with BI agents and submit complaints against stores engaging in price gouging. Such reports would be turned over to the U.S. attorney or to their county's fair price commissioner, men appointed by Governor O. A. Larrazolo (1919–21), who in turn served as the statewide fair price commissioner.[59]

Participation in the men's and women's sections of the HCLD fell far below wartime levels of volunteering. New Mexico was among thirty-one states that never had a state-level head for women's activities, a post filled in only three states in the Southwest and West—Texas, Utah, and Washington. No doubt one reason for the lack of women's support was the underlying philosophy. Price monitoring became a means by which the government imposed its vision for women—a wholesale continuation of wartime privations accompanied by an antimodernist stance. Women's clubs were instructed to organize such events as "Economy Week," during which each woman was "to see how much she could go without," and two key wartime campaigns—gardens and canning—were revived. The HCLD created a pledge card containing eleven statements that bound women "by precept and example [to] emphasize the doctrine of simple living." The third statement in their pledge was "Many are feeling keenly the pressure from high prices. Wives are being forced into industry to eke out [supplement] the husband's income in order properly to clothe and feed the children. There is a grave danger that the standard of the American home will be lowered. No more important subject faces the woman of today."[60]

The specter of threats to family structure was a theme the HCLD invoked to rally support for the traditional family. Mothers were urged to bring back "simple living and high thinking" and to "use [their] influence to overcome the effect of Jazz and Joy-Riding." The HCLD's tone had been anticipated by war critic Randolph Bourne, who before he died in December 1918 predicted a moral backlash after the war against the loosening of social control. The war years had interrupted the modernist movement in America, and the postwar period resumed a general liberation of people from "old standard" values and practices. Consumerism was the new order, a time when "attention to material gain" was the ascendant "emphasis of the age." America was changing after 1919, and its signs were everywhere—from syncopated music to greater mobility via automobiles. An invigorated New Women movement was poised to seize political and economic opportunities. Abetting them in rejecting the HCLD appeals were the Supreme Court, which declared the Lever Act's amendments unconstitutional in February 1920, and the Sixty-Sixth Congress, which rescinded the Lever Act and all emergency decrees at its close in March 1921.[61]

The former leaders of New Mexico's WASCD, New Women all, turned away from the HCLD's reactionary views and instead sought a new order consistent with their priorities. For example, their reform agenda made child welfare and public health key causes, and several former WASCD leaders secured footholds for these movements in state government immediately after the war. But perhaps no legislation more epitomized clashes between the old and new orders than did women's suffrage, which had been the subject of hearings in every Congress from the Fifty-Fourth to the Sixty-Sixth (1895–1921). For New Mexico, the defeat of obstructionist senator Thomas B. Catron in 1916 provided New Mexico's proponents of suffrage an ally in Democratic senator Andrieus A. Jones (1917–27). Upon entering Congress, Jones became chair of the newly created Senate Committee on Woman Suffrage. He held the committee's first hearings between 20 April and 15 May 1917, and his committee brought to the floor a total of five suffrage bills in the next two years. The last bill, Joint Resolution 1, Sixty-Sixth Congress, passed in Congress in July 1919 and became the Nineteenth Amendment to the Constitution in August 1920.[62]

The wartime service of women had much to do with the congressional action on suffrage. In mid-February 1918, on the cusp of the third Liberty Bond drive, each party's national committee endorsed suffrage. Influencing the decision was an argument as old as the Republic itself—taxation without representation. Just over half a million women were subject to the federal income tax in 1917, and even women not paying taxes contributed to the nation through their purchase of Liberty Bonds. Leaders of the WCCND and the New Mexico WASCD were firm supporters of suffrage, and their cause had been gaining momentum since 1914. Yet the state stood alone among all the western states in not extending the vote to women. A bitter political tug-of-war ensued over the state's ratification of the Nineteenth Amendment. Nina Otero-Warren, a former leader in the WASCD, was pivotal in arm-twisting New Mexico Republicans to approve the amendment as the thirty-second of the thirty-six states required for enactment into law in February 1920. She became the Republican candidate for the state's sole seat in the U.S. House of Representatives in the November 1922 election but lost to a Euro-American male. Otero-Warren continued to hold state elected and appointed positions throughout the interwar decades. Isabella Ferguson's husband died in 1922 and she moved to Arizona, remarried, and became Isabella Greenway. She was the first woman from Arizona elected to Congress and served two terms (1933–37) in the U.S. House of Representatives as a Democrat. Maude Prichard remained active as a progressive Republican in New Mexico for a dozen years after the war, particularly as the president of the Santa Fe County board of education, until ill health, financial reversals, and her husband's death in 1935 curbed her political activism.[63]

A woman surveying contributions to the war noted approvingly in 1918 that "every woman had been drafted into the ranks of the Army of American Housewives." That a woman's word choice would be militarized during 1917 and 1918 was an understandable consequence of wartime mobilization on the home front. The seemingly benign notion of an "Army of American Housewives" in fact perfectly encapsulated the power and control the government exercised through its "ideology of voluntarism." But being mobilized did not mean women ceded fealty to causes long advocated. In fact their wartime work allowed them to attach to the president's call to enlist in the "great service army" their own long-fought campaigns involving temperance, suffrage, and a host of both municipal and maternalist projects, including child welfare and public health. Thus did women's organizations during and immediately after the war extend their strategy of acting as special interest groups seeking to shape public policy.[64]

CHAPTER 4

"To the Colors"

Proximity to Texas made it possible for five Nuevomexicanos from Tucumcari to join the Regular Army within a week of America's entry into the war. Delfino Gonzales and his cousins Jose F. and Casiano Trujillo, along with two unidentified friends, traveled to Albuquerque, enlisted, took a train to El Paso, and reported to Fort Bliss on Wednesday, 11 April 1917. Gonzales, raised by his grandfather and barely sixteen years old when he volunteered, arrived in France at the end of June 1917, served as a private in Company G, 16th Infantry Regiment, 1st Infantry Brigade of the 1st Division. Jose F. Trujillo and his younger brother Casiano lived with their parents and had worked for a year as cooks. The Trujillo brothers volunteered for the army when Jose was eighteen years old and Casiano was two months shy of his seventeenth birthday. The younger Trujillo served as a private with Gonzales, and his brother was a corporal in Company F of the 16th Infantry. These three young men were among the first New Mexicans to volunteer. Both Delfino Gonzales and Casiano Trujillo truthfully stated they were sixteen years old upon enlistment. Only later in the war did the army begin requiring parental permission for anyone under eighteen to enlist.[1]

Routes to France

Delfino Gonzales and his two cousins were part of a trickle of men who signed up with the Regular Army at recruiting offices nationwide in the war's opening weeks. The first ten days after 6 April brought in just 4,355 volunteers, yet by mid-May a total of 71,670 had enlisted. Pennsylvania led all states with 7,659 volunteers, followed by Illinois (7,327); New Mexico came in next to last with 108 volunteers, with only Vermont having fewer (42). But over the final six months of the year enlistments increased statewide, with a total of 1,594 New Mexicans joining the Regular Army in 1917. Volunteers entering the military wanted to take up arms and fight for a variety of reasons: "honor, manhood, comrades, and adventure, but especially for duty." The army signed up the majority of these early volunteers. Fort Bliss continued to receive volunteers throughout the war, but New Mexicans volunteering in 1918 went to one of two other Regular Army training sites in Texas—Camp Logan in Houston and Camp MacArthur at Waco.[2]

The navy attracted fewer volunteers, about 1,250 New Mexicans during the nineteen months of the war. Secretary of state Antonio Lucero addressed an appeal to "young men of Spanish ancestry . . . to volunteer at once in the army and navy" in May 1917. A month before this appeal, just one Nuevomexicano was among twenty-one who volunteered for the navy at a newly opened enlistment depot in Santa Fe, which reported to a recruiting office in Denver. A total of thirty-seven signed up in Santa Fe during the final week of April, with another thirteen—mostly Nuevomexicanos—expected to join in May. For all of 1917, a total of 459 New Mexicans joined the navy, with most traveling by rail to San Francisco for training, although some were sent to San Diego. The marines were the choice of a tiny fraction of New Mexicans—just seventeen during the entire war. The first from the state to become a marine in 1917 was twenty-four-year-old Palmer Ketner of Gallup, who signed up within weeks of war being declared and trained at Parris Island, South Carolina.[3]

Late in May 1917 the untrained volunteers assembled at Fort Bliss joined a core of Regular Army soldiers who had been patrolling from Brownsville to El Paso and west into Arizona in the spring of 1917. These Regular Army troops had recently completed duty with the Mexican Punitive Expedition, and they became the nucleus of the initial division of the AEF. Their commander, newly promoted Maj. Gen. John J. Pershing, sought an unprecedented division strength—28,000 soldiers and officers, twice the number in its British counterpart and four times the strength of a German division. Pershing set a high number because he expected casualties of 50 percent in each American division. Thus it was that raw recruits barely able to salute or march boarded trains heading east and arrived at New York City and Hoboken, New Jersey, in mid-June. No dockside fanfare sent them on their way; instead, great secrecy prevailed to prevent enemy agents from passing information to German submarines seeking to torpedo transport ships.[4]

There were, of course, already a small number of New Mexicans in the Regular Army, mostly in the enlisted ranks. But one officer had entered from New Mexico in November 1916—Joseph Quesenberry, twenty-two years old and from Las Cruces. After completing two years at the State College of Agriculture and Mechanical Arts in Las Cruces, he entered a Regular Army officer training school in Fort Leavenworth, Kansas. Upon completion he reported to the 37th Infantry at Laredo, Texas, arriving on the very day the United States declared war. Thereafter Quesenberry seemed destined to be one of the first New Mexicans to set foot in France. At the end of May he was assigned to the 18th Infantry at Douglas, Arizona. One day after reporting he left Douglas "on the fifth section of the six section train for Hoboken," where newly minted Lt. Joseph Quesenberry become part of General Pershing's AEF. Quesenberry boarded one of the first ships of the fourteen-vessel convoy, which brought 14,000 troops plus officers to St. Nazaire, France, arriving the afternoon of 28 June 1917.[5]

The largest number of New Mexico volunteers to make it to France in 1917, totaling at least 377, were laborers and some managers skilled in work on railroads and in forests. At least 226 railroad workers were sent to Camp Perry on Lake Erie near Toledo, Ohio, for four to six weeks, and 151 New Mexican woodsmen went briefly to American University in Washington, D.C., before being shipped overseas. Pershing realized that before he could forge combat-ready divisions he had to create an infrastructure to facilitate the steady buildup of the AEF to several million men. Atlantic ports needed to be expanded at Bordeaux, St. Nazaire, La Rochelle, and Brest to provide sufficient piers and docks to unload troop and supply transports, and the English Channel harbors at Cherbourg and Le Havre, which received a lesser number of Americans but the majority of the British troops, needed upgrading. Moreover, to move people and freight to the American sector required building or repairing more than 1,500 miles of rail lines on routes connecting the Atlantic ports to places as much as 400 miles inland from Bordeaux.[6]

New Mexico railroaders were released by their employers after Pershing's appeal to the presidents of the nation's railroads in late spring 1917. These men were permitted to leave their civilian work to enter the army as members of military-run railroad units. The first small contingent of New Mexican railroad workers were aboard the ships of the 1st Division's second convoy, which sailed at the end of July. Some among them reportedly marched in London in a parade for King George V in mid-August. When they arrived in France, they received hurried military training before resuming work they had done as civilians. Also transported to France with the crews were trains and the equipment needed for maintaining them and repairing salvageable French track.[7]

Representative of the work of these men was that of a twenty-five-year-old heavy equipment operator, Adolph Abeyta, residing in the northern New Mexico railroad town of Las Vegas. He volunteered for the army's railroad service on 23 September 1917. After some hurried training he departed for Brest on 26 December, arrived in mid-January, and was assigned to the 21st Engineers, specialists in light railway work. "The day following our arrival in France in 1918 we started construction of a standard gauge railroad . . . through a thick forest in the direction of a proposed aviation field." A month later the 21st Engineers were transferred to the American sector and assigned to light railway extension and train maintenance "on the yard at Leonval [Headquarters, Supply and Shop in their sector]. Our camp was six miles from the latter point and we walked to work there every day through heavy mud."[8]

The American, or Lorraine, sector's proximity to the Vosges and Jura forests resulted in recruiting U.S. Forest Service personnel working in New Mexico. These employees responded to an appeal Pershing made as soon as he arrived in France seeking a military-controlled forestry service of at least eight thousand men that included experienced woodsmen and unskilled laborers. The U.S. Forest Service chief, Henry S. Graves, was commissioned a major and organized two forestry regiments—the 10th and 20th Engineers. In New Mexico the goal was to find "fifty men in two weeks" during July 1917. The timetable and number sought proved ambitious, although by early September twenty-five volunteers from national forests from southern to northern New Mexico were on their way to France as members of the 10th Engineers. Three more New Mexico foresters went over with the 20th Engineers in November. Between 1 December 1917 and 20 August 1918 another twenty-two Forest Service employees from New Mexico volunteered. It took fourteen months, but New Mexico finally reached its quota of fifty foresters in the army. Almost all who entered the army's forestry unit were sent to France, but not all arrived. Charles E. Simpson from Taos, assigned to the 10th Engineers, "died of meningitis in route to France," the first of more than a dozen New Mexicans to die at sea.[9]

The 10th Engineers merged with the much larger 20th Engineers in 1918 to form the largest regiment in the AEF—360 officers and 18,183 enlisted men, more than five times larger than a standard regiment. The regiment's size was in proportion to its mission. American woodsmen were urgently needed to log and operate sawmills in forested areas from the Pyrenees, the Loire Valley, and east to the Argonne Forest and to its southeast in the Vosges and Jura Mountains. By the war's end eighty-one sawmills had turned out hundreds of millions of board feet of lumber used in 39,000 pilings for new wharves, countless railroad ties, and innumerable telephone and telegraph poles, along with lumber to erect barracks, hospitals, and warehouses.[10]

National guardsmen from New Mexico were the third contingent from the state to arrive in France, beginning in early January 1918. They had completed demobilization from their border call-up a day before the United States declared war on 6 April. Almost immediately a new recruiting campaign began, and eventually about 1,400 guardsmen reported for summer training in Albuquerque, although fewer than half that number reported in early June. The state's legislature, during its special session in May, authorized Governor Lindsey to mobilize the militia. He soon did so, and the guardsmen began reporting to a temporary summer camp on the east edge of the University of New Mexico campus on 11 June. The U.S. Army designated the training site Camp Kitchener, to honor well-known British officer and secretary of state for war Horatio Herbert Kitchener, who had died in the line of duty the previous June. That name did not sit well with the Albuquerque community, and within weeks the camp became known locally as Camp Funston, to honor recently deceased Maj. Gen. Frederick Funston, commander of the army's Southern Department. In August the army named the training camp in his home state of Kansas in his honor, and most New Mexico draftees were sent here.

The guardsmen were the first large contingent of New Mexicans to enter training in World War I. A month after the camp's opening, four counties—Eddy, Chaves, Santa Fe, and Bernalillo—had each sent more than a hundred guardsmen, and collectively they were 43 percent of all 1,149 guardsmen serving from New Mexico. Reportedly Spanish-speaking Nuevomexicanos filled four companies. Additionally, at least 250 guardsmen came from out of state, particularly from West Texas. At the Albuquerque camp officers were assigned quarters in a dormitory and worked out of offices in the administration building. The enlisted men had been expected to occupy tents, but when these could not be secured from the government Governor Lindsey authorized purchasing lumber to build barracks. Within ten days of reporting to camp, each company identified and equipped a hundred men to be construction workers, and before the end of June the enlisted men had built their quarters. Adjacent open spaces were soon trampled by men marching, with the school's athletic field used as a formal parade ground. In July digging began to create trenches to simulate the front lines and allow tactical training in trench warfare. Dummy grenade throwing was particularly emphasized. The war changed everything about University of New Mexico campus life. Seventy percent of the male students served in the military, and a total of 395 current and former students and faculty members were in uniform during the war.[11]

The first deaths of New Mexico servicemen also occurred at the National Guard summer camp when illness claimed Pvt. Wilfred Waddell on 4 July and Pvt. Faris Heath on 30 August. Waddell joined the guard in Deming in early June and succumbed at St. Joseph's Hospital to "meningitis and complications." Private Heath of Artesia likewise joined the guard in early June and died of appendicitis just before midnight on 30 August. The men's deaths are a reminder of a key statistic of the war—illnesses killed many more troops than did combat. For example, among the nearly four hundred soldiers with ties to the University of New Mexico, three died from pneumonia and only one fell in battle—machine gunner Howard E. Morrow, serving with the Canadian Expeditionary Forces.[12]

The army detached Capt. Charles M. de Bremond's Battery A of the 1st New Mexico Field Artillery, with its approximately 130 men, from the state's National Guard infantry companies shortly after it arrived in Albuquerque. This highly rated artillery unit, together with seven other artillery units from western states and one from Washington, D.C., were placed in the 41st Division, a National Guard force drawn principally from the Pacific Northwest. De Bremond's battery had its training camp destination changed three times before departing from California to Camp Greene, in Charlotte, North Carolina, on 24 September. After a brief training period, New Mexico's Battery A was designated part of the 66th Field Artillery Brigade and sent to Camp Mills, Long Island. There the combat infantrymen of the 41st Division were supplemented by eight thousand draftees transferred from the 91st Division (Camp Lewis, Washington) during November. As the infantrymen prepared to embark, the 66th Field Artillery was assigned to a different convoy. A small contingent was sent to Camp Hill in Newport News, Virginia, the embarkation port for animals. These men were to assist in transport of the horses and equipment for their 75 mm guns. Among these men was Pfc. Carl Fantacci of Roswell. The 66th Field Artillery finally left New York on 24 December, but the detachment—and horses—did not depart Newport News until mid-April.[13]

Albuquerque bid farewell to its east mesa training camp in mid-October when the officers and soldiers transferred to Camp Kearny near San Diego. Forty-eight railroad cars conveyed New Mexico's National Guard infantrymen, their equipment, supplies, and kitchens to Linda Vista, eleven miles north of San Diego, and arrived on Thursday, 19 October 1917. The New Mexicans joined guardsmen from California, Arizona, Nevada, Utah, and Colorado to form the 40th Division at 12,700-acre Camp Kearny. When the New Mexico guardsmen arrived, the *San Diego Union* devoted considerable attention to the presence of "four companies of Mexicans" among these soldiers, which prompted unidentified officers "who have been training the men" to offer reassurances that the Nuevomexicanos "form a strong part of the regiment and make exceptionally good soldiers." Even though the camp's namesake, Stephen Watt Kearny, had brought New Mexico under the control of the United States in 1846, and its Nuevomexicano residents had been citizens of the United States since 1912, they were still disparaged as "Mexicans" by San Diego's Euro-American civic and business elites, who had a love-hate relationship with the city's Spanish past and Hispanic present.[14]

Once the guardsmen arrived at Camp Kearny—or Camp Sunshine, as its commander, Maj. Gen. Frederick S. Strong, preferred to call it—they were placed into various units. Most New Mexico guardsmen were assigned to the 157th and 158th Infantry Regiments of the 79th Infantry Brigade. Other New Mexicans were assigned to these units: The 143rd Machine Gun Battalion received at least two hundred New Mexicans, and the 144th Machine Gun Battalion took in just over two hundred New Mexicans and was commanded by Maj. Etienne de P. Bujac of Carlsbad. The 115th Trench Mortar Battery had a small, unspecified number of New Mexicans. The commander of the 115th Train Headquarters and Military Police, Col. Edmund C. Abbott, was from Santa Fe; under him were New Mexican soldiers and two captains assigned to A and B Companies of the military police. A fifty-member band detachment included thirteen New Mexicans, but they were transferred from Camp Kearny to a Regular Army installation in Louisville, Kentucky, in March 1918.[15]

Occasionally an individual New Mexican impatient with endless drill convinced his superiors that he was ready for combat and should be sent overseas. One such guardsman at Camp Kearny was twenty-year-old Pvt. Eliseo Griego of Albuquerque. "Realizing that the regiment in which he had been placed would not be ready for service in France for some time, [he] applied [early in 1918] to be attached to a unit that was soon to go overseas. His request was granted and not long thereafter he was at the front fulfilling his desire to be a soldier." Private Griego was placed with the 58th Infantry, 4th Division, and "died on the battlefield" early in the war's final battle—the Meuse-Argonne offensive.[16]

At the same time New Mexico guardsmen were preparing to go to San Diego, guardsmen from North and South Dakota, Minnesota, Iowa, and Nebraska were sent to Deming in Luna County. That community had hosted a large military presence during the Mexican Punitive Expedition at a facility known as Camp Brooks, and within a week of America's declaration of war the community's business leaders began an intensive campaign to convince the army to designate Deming one of sixteen training camps for National Guard troops. The town's aggressive lobbying—including a pledge to the army's chief of staff, Gen. Hugh Scott, to provide "a free site" of 10,000 acres—combined with New Mexico's congressional delegation buttonholing War Department officials paid off in early June. Deming secured the 34th Division. Briefly known as Camp Deming, it was renamed Camp Cody to honor army scout and famous showman William F. "Buffalo Bill" Cody, who had died in January 1917. No sooner had Camp Cody welcomed the midwesterners than its new residents began writing home and complaining about "Camp Sandstorm," a moniker that stuck as the camp and division's unofficial name throughout the war. At the end of October about two thousand draftees from Nebraska and South Dakota were sent from Camp Funston to Camp Cody as part of the army's transfer of soldiers to bring National Guard camps to full force. The camp's population was augmented again in the spring of 1918 when it received several thousand New Mexican draftees, sent as part of a reshuffling of priorities in the wake of railroads coming under federal control in January 1918. The government deemed it inefficient to transport inductees far distances, and the camp began receiving men from New Mexico and nearby states.[17]

The steady addition of men to Camp Cody had a downside for the community, one addressed candidly by Amanda Lindsey in a letter to the WCCND in September 1917: "I speak very freely of the saloon and prostitution because it is a very hard and difficult problem to solve in all the army camps." Attempts to keep alcohol from passing soldiers' lips and to eliminate illicit sex were pursued but without controlling either activity. The U.S. marshal reported in late September 1917 that "the sale of liquor to soldiers in uniform . . . is considerably on the increase," and he expected matters to get worse because "there is drifting into Deming professional bootleggers." A military inquiry on "prostitution and the sale of liquor to soldiers" began after newspaper reports at the end of January 1918 claimed that "the mayor [of Deming] intended to ask the secretary of war to put the town under martial law" because he and other local officials were "unable to keep the town clean." The army, barred by the Posse Comitatus Act of 1878, could not impose martial law in the United States, so a low-grade conflict persisted between thousands of men seeking women and alcohol and fewer than ten local and federal officials determined to deny them such access.[18]

In efforts to divert men to army-sanctioned leisure activities, Camp Cody had team sports, libraries, movies, religious services, educational programs, and recreation huts staffed by the YMCA and YWCA, Red Cross, the local Masonic Lodge, and Knights of Columbus. Each of these organizations fully funded their hut, some relying on a national headquarters but others, such as the Knights of Columbus, receiving money from both national and local Catholic sources. A priest in Lordsburg, a German national, touted as evidence of his loyalty to the United States that "only one week ago . . . I went around personally to collect for the Knights of Columbus War Fund." Unfortunately his charity work did not erase evidence of pro-German statements, and he was arrested by BI agent A. R. Gere and turned over to the U.S. marshal. A memorable respite for the men at the camp were three exhibition games the Chicago Cubs played against a Santa Rita mine team on 5, 6, and 7 April 1918 in southwest New Mexico, with the final game at Camp Deming. The Cubs were on their trip home at the end of spring training in Pasadena, California. Their season ended with the Cubs being accused of "throwing" the World Series to the Boston Red Sox.[19]

Building the National Army in New Mexico

More than nine thousand of the fourteen thousand New Mexicans in uniform served with the National Army, which was newly created for draftees. The first men inducted from New Mexico began training at Camp Funston, one of sixteen National Army camps, in September 1917. New Mexican draftees in the AEF were a tiny speck among the nearly three million soldiers of the National Army, who in turn made up more than 75 percent of all U.S. soldiers by war's end.[20]

Beginning in late May, newspapers such as the *Farmington Times-Hustler* ran advertisements announcing draft registration sites based on voting precincts as well as explaining such matters as exemptions and soldiers' pay. These announcements culminated in a day-long draft registration campaign on Tuesday, 5 June 1917, from 7:00 A.M. until 9:00 P.M. All men between ages twenty-one and thirty were required to complete a draft registration card. Following this first sign-up three additional ones were held nationwide in 1918, with the final one registering men ages eighteen to forty-five in September 1918. An estimated ten million men completed forms in the first draft, and about 30,000 New Mexicans signed up in June 1917. A total of 24 million men filled out draft forms during the four registrations, including 81,013 New Mexicans.[21]

Across New Mexico Tuesday, 5 June, dawned clear and cool with slight breezes and a daytime high temperature in the upper eighties. The sun shone bright for a day of patriotic duty. Towns throughout the state took on the festive spirit usually reserved for 4th of July celebrations. Santa Fe's parade was estimated to have exceeded three thousand onlookers. In Roswell and Albuquerque at 7:00 A.M. sirens announced the opening of draft offices. Roswell's mayor, like mayors statewide, proclaimed the day a holiday and invited "all the organizations and Citizens of this City to encourage and assist in every way possible." Men in Albuquerque registered either at city hall, for those living north of Central Avenue, or at the Commercial Club if residing south of Central, but in fact registration continued for several days. A special appeal to young women in both Roswell and Albuquerque invited them to urge men to register.[22]

The mechanics of draft registration are revealed by looking at the process in Tucumcari, a town of about three thousand, a railroad maintenance center, and Quay County seat. The town fêted its 333 young men registering at the courthouse on the morning of 5 June. By early afternoon all draft forms were completed—either signed or, if an illiterate registrant, their mark of X made, and "each young man was decorated with a khaki band and red, white, and blue ribbon together with a small cardboard emblem bearing the U.S. flag in colors, and the wording, 'I have registered to serve my country.'" Beginning at 10:00 A.M. "a patriotic parade with Boy Scouts, decorated autos and many civilians was participated in." The limelight soon faded, of course, followed by a seven-week wait for the government to conduct a lottery that would determine the order in which men would be summoned "to the colors."[23]

Back in Washington, secretary of war Newton D. Baker, eyes blindfolded, drew number 258 from a large bowl holding all draft lottery numbers at about 10:00 A.M. on Friday, 20 July 1917, in the U.S. Senate Office Building. Over the next seventeen hours a cadre of officials picked one by one a total of 10,500 numbers. Registrants at each draft board had been assigned a number, beginning at one and going as high as needed to include all eligible men in the precinct. In New Mexico, out of a total population of 354,000, 23 percent completed draft forms in the four registrations. But only 9,050 (11 percent) were inducted, a number reportedly reduced by at least 550, although a figure as high as 750 is more likely because men were "subsequently discharged for various reasons" at training camps.[24]

In only two instances did voluntary enlistments in New Mexico exceed the initial draft quota—Luna and Eddy Counties—and neither had to call up draftees in the fall of 1917. Luna County volunteers exceeded the draft quota by two men;

Eddy County's volunteers were 188 greater than their quota. Not until the spring of 1918 did either county conduct a draft. But nineteen counties fell short of their 1917 quotas and had to send a total of 283 additional men in February 1918. The five counties with the highest initial quotas were Grant (218), San Miguel (213), Colfax (190), Rio Arriba (179), and Socorro (164); Grant and Colfax had majority Euro-American populations and the other three were predominantly Nuevomexicano.[25]

Almost daily for a year—and often several times each day—the U.S. provost marshal general sent officials in New Mexico telegrams, memoranda, or letters instituting or modifying selective service practices. The administrative apparatus as well as all policies and procedures to carry out the draft were being created and implemented simultaneously while also undergoing revisions and amplification. This steady stream of regulations and their changes exceeded what draft board volunteers could handle, and to deal with it each local draft board in the state soon hired one or more clerical personnel and paid them from funds approved in the May 1917 legislative appropriation. Appointed board members had initially served voluntarily, but President Wilson set a per-registrant fee of thirty cents, paid by the government and divided equally among the board members, in January 1918. In the final three months of the war, as funding for clerical staff became problematic, some draft boards throughout the state designated one or more draftees to assume clerical duties.[26]

The government used the 1910 federal census to determine potential registrants, and as the quotas filtered throughout the country New Mexico learned that it needed to induct 2,292 men to be divided into three installments sent to Camp Funston during September and October 1917. Quay County's 1910 population was 14,912 and its quota of inductees was eighty-nine. The local draft boards combed the lengthy list of lottery numbers to identify a sufficient number of men to meet their quota and called them in for preinduction screening. In Tucumcari the sheriff, country clerk, and two private citizens interviewed 201 men on Wednesday, 1 August.

The screening of Caspar Allen, the local man holding the first lottery number drawn, illustrates the winnowing process. Allen was twenty-nine years old, a railroad conductor, born in Illinois but a resident of Tucumcari, and was married with two children. By the end of the day the officials had selected eighty-nine men, but Allen was not among them. The army had assumed that half of all registrants would be passed over because of an exemption—either because their work in agriculture or industry was vital to the war effort or because a man was sole support of a wife and young children. Allen claimed the latter, and he received an exemption.[27]

Pedro Pablo Borquez held the second number drawn in the national lottery (458). He was a twenty-one-year-old farm and ranch hand hired locally, was single, and listed "stomach trouble" in seeking an exemption. The draft board denied the exemption request and sent him to Camp Funston on 12 September 1917. All men reporting for military duty underwent further medical examinations at their training camp, and Borquez was deemed physically unfit and discharged. He became one of the state's first men "who were inducted by their local boards but who by reason of physical defects were not accepted when they reached the camps."[28]

The local board's medical screening did turn away forty-five Quay County men in their first screening, which necessitated bringing in another one hundred registrants, from which only forty passed the physical examination. Overall among all draftees from New Mexico, the rejection rate was below the national average of over 50 percent. Only 20–30 percent of New Mexico draftees were rejected by draft board physicians whereas, by comparison, Arizona, Colorado, and California had 50–59 percent of draftees turned away. Among Quay County's eighty-four inductees, seventy-four were Euro-American (88 percent) and ten Nuevomexicano (12 percent). Quay County fell five short of its quota in this first call, and two other men were eliminated at camp, but fifty-seven from the county had already enlisted and were in uniform. None of these volunteers were credited toward the county's quota.[29]

Did the outpouring of support for the draft mean that Americans were eager for war? Patriotism washed across the country, but enthusiasm for the draft was not spontaneous. Elected and appointed officials at all levels of government, and especially members of each state's council of defense, cultivated public support to preempt any attempt to disrupt the process. To further minimize antigovernment hostility, the army put in place new administrative agencies to separate itself from direct control of the draft, although in fact all civilians administering the draft process were intent on meeting the army's expectations.

The first institution created to buffer the army was the national Selective Service Administration under the Office of the Provost Marshal General in Washington, D.C. It carried out the law through the second level of civilian oversight—central draft boards in states drawn to correspond to federal judicial districts. New Mexico had but one central draft board, which was headed by Benigno C. Hernández, a Republican between terms in the U.S. House of Representatives (1915–17 and 1919–21), a prominent Nuevomexicano from Rio Arriba County, and a key member of the SCD. The state draft board's executive assistant was army captain R. C. Reid, who together with Hernández divided the state into northern and southern districts. Within these districts civilian officials in towns and counties conducted the actual selection of draftees. These local boards were the third and most thoroughly civilian layer in the implementation of the draft. Of the 4,557 local boards nationwide, fewer than two hundred were in New Mexico. In addition to the four or five members of the local board, two professional bodies in each community were enlisted as adjuncts: doctors and dentists for physical evaluations and lawyers for legal representation in exemption petitions and appeals.[30]

The possibility that Hispanic Americans were overrepresented among the first draftees attracted some national attention in July 1917 when in El Paso, as sensationally stated in a headline in the *Washington Post*, "71 Per Cent Drawn from Sons of Mexico." The article noted that El Paso's population was divided about equally between "Mexican-American citizens of the U.S. and other citizens." German agents in Juárez cited this imbalance to "incite [Mexican American] citizens of El Paso against the draft," but without success. Whatever the accuracy of the data reported for El Paso, in the context of Texas's population of almost one million men of draft-eligible age, reportedly "30,000 Spanish-surnamed natives registered for the draft." Of these about five thousand Tejanos eventually were in uniform out of a population of 197,000 Texans in the military; in other words, 2.5 percent of all Texas soldiers were Spanish-surnamed.[31]

Comparable data regarding either the number or percentage of Nuevomexicanos in uniform have not surfaced; however, based on two samples—totaling 554 soldiers—more Euro-Americans served than Nuevomexicanos, at an approximate ratio of three Euro-Americans for every two Nuevomexicanos. Based on a sample of 364 New Mexican soldiers used to identify those who served in the AEF, 36 percent were Euro-Americans and 28 percent were Nuevomexicanos. A second sample of 190 men (ninety-five from each ethnic group) tallied whether they went into the army in 1917 or 1918, whether they served in the AEF, and how many were wounded in France. For the Euro-American soldiers, fifty-six of ninety-five served in the AEF (59 percent), plus one other was shipped to Russia, and thirty-six of these men entered the army in 1917 (38 percent). Thirteen of these Euro-Americans were wounded in combat (14 percent). Among the Nuevomexicanos, forty-seven of the ninety-five served in the AEF (49 percent), plus three others were sent to Russia, thirty entered the army in 1917 (32 percent), and five were wounded in combat (5 percent).[32]

No ethnic imbalance between Euro-American and Nuevomexicano inductees emerged in a survey of ten counties' draft board records from 1917–18. The ethnic distribution of inductees from seven counties throughout the state where Euro-Americans were the majority was as follows: Bernalillo, 53 percent Euro-American/47 percent Nuevomexicano; Chaves, 81/19 percent; Curry, 100/0 percent; Grant, 90/10 percent; Lincoln, 70/30 percent; San Juan, 80/20 percent; and Sierra, 55/45 percent. Three counties in which Nuevomexicanos were inducted in numbers greater than Euro-Americans were Doña Ana, Euro-Americans 33 percent/ Nuevomexicanos 67 percent; Rio Arriba, 12/88 percent; and Santa Fe, 44/56 percent. Corroborating the nearly equal ethnic distribution in Santa Fe was this statement in Oliver La Farge's history of the city: "Some 461 men from the city alone participated in all branches of military service. . . . Hispano and Anglo surnames split fairly evenly." With the exception of Curry County, no egregious pattern of either over- or underrepresentation by ethnicity emerges from these data, nor do allegations of ethnic bias on the part of draft boards appear in newspapers of the period.[33]

If no systematic pattern of ethnic imbalance existed among those who were inducted, perhaps it existed in whom among the draftees were granted an exemption? Some historians have documented, as one wrote, that "the distribution of draft exemptions in World War I tended to parallel the distribution of civilian privilege and the obligation of service fell disproportionately on the powerless and poor." In New Mexico, of course, most residents regardless of ethnicity would be considered "powerless and poor." Did they serve while the well-to-do did not? To answer that question, a 3 percent sample statewide—270 exemption forms—was examined. These records contain information on annual income and occupation that yield data to test whether the privileged manipulated the system.[34]

Great variation existed across the counties in the number of exemptions sought and granted. A draft board member from Eddy County claimed that men from his area "didn't ask for exemptions." Although that may not have been literally true, Eddy County was one end of a continuum for exemption requests. At the opposite, high, end were Socorro and Bernalillo Counties in August 1917. Because exemptions potentially were life-and-death decisions for the draftee, and a family's fate might hang in the balance, transparency and nipping rumors and innuendo became a priority for the Selective Service. All governors received a telegram from the U.S. provost marshal general on 6 August 1917 instructing them to inform all local draft boards that "the public is entitled to know the grounds upon which claims for exemption of discharge are being asked by registered men. Local boards should therefore be instructed immediately to make available to the press from day-to-day the name of persons claiming exemption or discharge, the grounds on which such claims are based and in general the number of cases that are being disposed of by the boards from day-to-day."³⁵

About a month after receipt of this message, the *Albuquerque Morning Journal* reported cryptically and caustically that "various pretexts" were offered to justify exemptions totaling 75 percent of men called in Socorro County, but no specifics were offered. The only enumeration in Bernalillo County that complied with the provost marshal's instructions came for eighty-one men granted an exemption out of 101 petitioning prior to the second induction in September 1917. The 80 percent rate of approval, when broken down, likely raised few eyebrows. The majority of instances, 69 percent, involved support for a wife and children, the latter numbering from one to five. These exemptions went to twenty-six Euro-Americans and thirty-one Nuevomexicanos. In addition, fifteen men were foreign citizens, ten from Mexico, and all were exempt. Eight cases involved special circumstances within a family, and one exemption went to an army officer already in the service. At about this same time an Albuquerque draft board granted an exemption request citing dependents—a wife, four-year-old son, and three-year-old daughter—to twenty-nine-year-old Dionisio "Dennis" Chavez, who avoided the army but fourteen years later would be thrust into the role of veterans' advocate for the state in the U.S. House of Representatives.³⁶

The number of exemptions arising from a need to support a wife and family so reduced the eligible pool of draftees that Congress soon passed legislation setting up a compulsory allotment for dependents on 6 October 1917. In this manner the government sought to provide an incentive for married men of limited means to enter the army. Each married enlisted man was to provide an allotment of at least half his pay, or no less than fifteen dollars a month, to his wife, a sum the Treasury Department matched, and the government also provided an additional five dollars for each child per month, the full allotment total not to exceed $50. (In 2017 dollars, the government's monthly contributions would be $286 and $95, respectively.)³⁷

If income is taken as a measure of status and class, then the number of exemptions granted men with annual incomes ranging from $200 to $600 ($3,800 to $11,400 in 2017) suggests no inherent bias for or against such individuals of minimal means. But also noteworthy is that no special consideration was given to men earning more than $2,000 a year ($38,000 in 2017). In fact, these individuals were usually given 1-A status, making them first in line for induction. New Mexicans earning less than $360 annually faced questions about whether they might do better for themselves as a private paid $30 a month ("a dollar a day").

If such men filed for an exemption based on their agricultural work, they most often were granted it; however, low-paid men who filed a dependent exemption form typically were inducted. New Mexico's draft boards clearly followed the Selective Service Act's intention to aid farmers and ranchers obtain laborers through agricultural deferments. But putting a man in uniform because he could earn more money in the army was consistent with the Progressive Era's spirit of assisting the less fortunate in society.[38]

Military service fell disproportionately on only one group—unmarried men regardless of income or occupation. For example, the superintendent of schools in a town in Union County, an unmarried Euro-American, had his exemption request denied, as did the single younger brother of a locally influential Nuevomexicano politician in Sierra County. These cases and others are evidence of eschewing favoritism. The board that rebuffed the locally prominent Nuevomexicano politician stated their ethical principle: "To exempt him would place the Local Board in bad light before the public and would cause severe criticism by other young men loyal and true." Exemption requests were least likely to be approved from unmarried men claiming siblings as dependents and single men approaching thirty who still lived at home. The latter group's exemption requests usually elicited annotations such as "Military service will do him good." The least frequently received request for deferment nationwide, and also in New Mexico, arose from religious conviction. During the war "64,693 drafted men filed claims for exemption on grounds of conscience. Local boards accepted the claims of 56,830." In the New Mexico sample, just one religious exemption claim surfaced, but it had no notation of disposition.[39]

At Camp Funston, Kansas

The long journey that took draftees to the western front began on a hometown railroad platform. During the first week of September 1917, the state's first draftees boarded trains in New Mexico and headed about 690 miles east. Their destination was the newly created National Army training base at Camp Funston, three miles east of Fort Riley, Kansas. Although a third of the full quota of 2,292 draftees were to be sent in early September, in fact the number leaving was a mere fraction of the 764 soldiers projected for each installment. A trickle of men from about a third of the state's counties left at the beginning of September, including Bernalillo County (six draftees), Rio Arriba County (five), Guadalupe County (four), San Juan County (three, all from Aztec), and Santa Fe County (two). Of these twenty men, fourteen were Euro-American and six were Nuevomexicano.

The state's second contingent of draftees left two weeks later, and the final, and largest, group departed in early October. Delays in building Camp Funston along with similar problems at the other fifteen National Army camps slowed the arrival of the 30,000–40,000 draftees each camp received.[40]

But for each group of draftees leaving for Camp Funston, whether few or great in number, the send-off was similar to the events reported at Silver City in Grant County: "There was a concert in the afternoon . . . speechmaking . . . and a big automobile parade to the Santa Fe [AT&SF] depot. Business was suspended during the ceremonies." The departures occasioned displays of community pride akin to ones on draft registration day in early June. But this time the flag waving gave way to heartfelt good-byes.[41]

Camp Funston was a thirty-hour train ride from central New Mexico. Men stepping off the train in Kansas were introduced to an unfamiliar world. Upon arrival the draftees were stripped and searched for contraband (typically alcohol), examined anew by doctors, issued bib overalls as a "uniform" because nothing else in the way of clothing was available in quantity, given the first of several courses of inoculations for smallpox and typhoid, and also received an anti-tuberculosis serum. New Mexicans were assigned to each of the 89th Division's four infantry regiments—353rd, 354th, 355th, or 356th—with the largest number placed in the 356th Infantry Regiment among its thirteen companies (A–M). Nearly a third of the New Mexicans had barely settled in at Camp Funston when they were put on trains and sent west to Camp Kearny. These men were part of a contingent of six thousand sent from Camp Funston, with an additional three thousand transferred from Camp Lewis, to fill massive shortages at Camp Kearny arising when physical evaluations and subsequent rejections reducing troop strength to 16,000 at the National Guard camp. Elsewhere similarly large numbers of rejected troops prompted the War Department in mid-October to order the reassignment of "78,400 men from National Army cantonments to the various National Guard divisions to fill them to war strength." Trains carrying five hundred draftees each began leaving Camp Funston for California on 25 October and continued daily for a week. The *San Diego Union* reported that "most of this first train load [of five hundred men] are Mexicans" from New Mexico and Arizona.[42]

Camp Funston had been a vast wheat field until early summer 1917, but the change made to this windswept corner of northeast Kansas paralleled the complete transformation of the men sent there. The training day began with reveille at 5:30 A.M. and ended at 9:30 P.M. Every hour of the day fulfilled some part of the army's intent to impose its own standardized habits. Nothing was overlooked. In matters of personal hygiene, the army required that all soldiers bathe at least twice a week, change all clothing afterward, and shave daily using the newly available safety razor made by Gillette. After a breakfast eaten standing up, most of the balance of the morning for many months was devoted to exercise or marching and executing drill commands on the parade field. The afternoon included more work on the parade field as well as lectures on military discipline, courtesy, and protocols. The soldiers' only scheduled time off came on Wednesday afternoon and from mid-afternoon Saturday through Sunday evening. The two-story wooden barracks to be occupied by each company of about 250 men were still being built at Camp Funston, so tents were used for two months. When finally available, the barrack's top floor was an open bay of iron cots with latrine and showers at the far end. The first floor housed the company's kitchen, mess hall, storeroom, and captain's office. Housekeeping in the barracks was ruled by "the Army way": each man quickly mastered how to make his bed and fold clothes in his foot locker. Also acquired was a coarsening of speech, what a contemporary scholar called the prevalence of "lewd language." One scholar recently claimed that the F-word gained widespread currency during World War I.[43]

The draftees at Camp Funston had much reason to swear. They were victims of the nation's unpreparedness for war. Not until Thanksgiving did heat and hot water reach Camp Funston's barracks. Pieces of the uniform continued to be distributed whenever a manufacturers' shipment arrived. But in late October as the weather began turning cold the camp commander, Maj. Gen. Leonard Wood, sent an urgent telegram to the adjutant general in New Mexico telling him, "It is imperative each drafted man coming to Camp Funston bring two suits winter underwear and advisable two changes all clothing." Just a few weeks earlier state officials were informed that incoming soldiers needed to bring two blankets to camp.[44]

The army's predicament at all its training camps was summarized by an artillery officer in September 1917: "With a million men to train at once and little or no equipment with which to make a suitable beginning, the United States [Army] will for months to come be taxed to its utmost to find suitable extemporized schemes which will permit the most to be made of these early months of preparation." Thus it was that "extemporized schemes," or improvisation, became the army's mantra. Outsourcing to soldiers the responsibility to provide their own winter clothing barely scratched the surface of training-camp problems. All other issues, though, paled before the challenge of meeting General Pershing's expectation for combat training at camp. Just six days before General Wood's appeal about winter underwear, General Pershing sent a cable to the War Department stating his priority for training the troops, one he would reaffirm repeatedly during and after the war: "The essential principles of war have not changed, that the rifle and the bayonet remain the supreme weapons of the infantry soldier and that the ultimate success of the army depends upon their proper use." But these weapons were not available in 1917, so the army made do with what was at hand. Wood was cut in the shape of a rifle, and larger planks and barrels became a common substitute for field artillery. Still, Camp Funston's men, to some extent, were luckier than soldiers at other camps that fall, including two in Georgia: at Camp Gordon the 82nd Division trainees "were given 4-inch [thick] boards and told to cut out a rifle"; for the 28th Division, at Camp Hancock, there was "only one bayonet for every third man."[45]

For men who had attended college and sought to become officers in the new National Army, a first class of candidates entered training in mid-May 1917, with twenty-eight New Mexicans commissioned after completing three months' training at the Presidio of Monterey, California, in mid-August. As their training came to a close, San Francisco's famous Fairmont Hotel fêted the candidates with a gala dance, "enlisting the prettiest girls of the community to see that every young man was given a personal welcome." Five New Mexicans were reported as among the dancers: Conrad Hilton of San Antonio; John McFie Jr. of Gallup; and from Albuquerque Charles H. Lembke, J. Wickliffe Miller, and Charles Frederick Luthy. All but Luthy served in the AEF, and he was awaiting transport to France when the war ended. All five had characteristics common among candidates in the first several classes of officer training: they had graduated from college, were experienced in leading others, and were between their mid-twenties to mid-thirties, with Hilton the oldest in his group of five at age twenty-nine and three others twenty-seven. A few Nuevomexicanos entered later officer candidate classes. The newest specialty in the army—the Aero service—accepted Miguel A. Otero Jr. and Julius Sanchez, both college graduates. When accepted, Otero was twenty-five and Sanchez twenty-three, and each served in France but flew no combat missions.[46]

Luthy and Sanchez were plucked from the enlisted ranks and sent to officer training camp, as was another man who would become the state's most distinguished combat hero of the war—Harry Rogers. Born 4 March 1891, Rogers was orphaned at an early age and raised by his grandparents on a farm near Lakewood, ten miles south of Artesia. He left school after the eighth grade to help on the farm, but he continued to read and study on his own. Finally in early 1913, at age twenty-two, he began high school, finished in six months, and that fall entered William Jewell College, at the time a Baptist-affiliated institution in Liberty, Missouri, fifteen miles north of Kansas City. Rogers graduated with honors in 1917, took a job in Nebraska, and enlisted in the Regular Army in mid-August 1917. He was five feet, eleven inches tall, weighed 185 pounds, and quickly gained acceptance among his cohorts by playing right guard on the company's football team. But he never fit into barracks life and particularly disliked profanity and gambling.[47]

Three weeks into his training he wrote his aunt in Lakewood: "We don't have any too many good influences [at camp], and I'm going to try to use all we have and shut out the bad." By early November his football team had won most of its games, and Rogers decided to get away from enlisted life and applied for officers' training. Once accepted Rogers was sent to a Regular Army officers' training camp at Oglethorpe, Georgia. There life was much more to his liking, and he told his aunt that the other candidates were "a fine bunch of men—morally as well as physically. Vulgarity and profanity are avoided and interesting conversation in moments of leisure is the rule." Soon, though, Rogers was quarantined for two weeks during a measles outbreak. Afterward he went to a training camp in Chattanooga, Tennessee, which he completed in late April. He immediately took a train to an embarkation camp near New York City, boarded a transport ship on 30 April, and arrived in France on 14 May 1918. On the eve of sailing he wondered if he was "fated to find a grave in the sacred soil of France." He was.[48]

By late summer 1918, Camp Funston and Camp Cody were receiving a new wave of draftees to replace soldiers shipped overseas in the previous six months. The new arrivals had much better living and training conditions than the camps provided in their first four months. Among the improvements were new visual aids for rifle and artillery training. Beginning in the spring of 1918, members of the Taos Society of Artists and other interested Taos-area artists volunteered "to help the soldier boys [of New Mexico] by producing range finders for Camp Funston and Camp Cody." The artists produced twenty painted canvasses measuring fifty inches by seventy inches that depicted countryside and villages in northern France and Belgium. These scenes became props used in training riflemen and machine gunners "to find the range, how to estimate distances, how to detect 'cover,' how to designate strategical points, and how to make maps." They were also used in instructing officer candidates about local topography and landscape on and near battlefields. Although each painting served utilitarian ends, they had considerable artistic merit and were exhibited briefly at the Museum of New

Mexico before being sent to training camps. These twenty "Range Finders," as the show was named, formed the second major art exhibition in the new museum, which had opened in late November 1917.⁴⁹

Medical Problems in Forging an Army

During the fall and early winter of 1917, as the men from New Mexico marched mile upon mile with replicas of rifles, the winds drove rain and then snow across the thousands of acres of Camp Funston. By January the temperature had dropped to minus thirty degrees, and all outdoor training was suspended, replaced with drills and lectures held indoors. Few new draftees arrived that winter, but diseases came in force. Dysentery had made brief forays in early fall, but as winter settled in the dreaded three M's laid siege to Camp Funston: mumps, measles, and meningitis—all highly communicable and the more so for many New Mexicans from rural areas who lacked immunity. Mumps was the most prevalent: 1,402 cases in January 1918 and 1,992 stricken in February. The camp infirmaries were overwhelmed, and even the large hospital at nearby Fort Riley filled all of its beds. As miserable as were conditions at Camp Funston, it is surprising that not a murmur of protest was heard from New Mexicans reporting on their military experiences; however, state officials more than filled the soldiers' silence with complaints about medical issues, specifically diagnoses of tuberculosis among New Mexico soldiers.⁵⁰

This winter of sickness had been preceded by a period of attrition tied to medical examinations at Camp Funston. Three counties with predominantly Nuevomexicano populations—Rio Arriba, San Miguel, and Socorro—had, respectively, draftee rejection rates at Camp Funston of 34 percent, 20 percent, and 21 percent in October–November 1917, for a total of eighty-nine soldiers out of the 382 drafted from these three counties—all due to tuberculosis. Some counties with Euro-American majorities had no draftees rejected because of TB. When local physicians volunteered to give draftees preinduction physicals, they had no familiarity with the standards set by the army. As a consequence, Regular Army physicians at training camps routinely turned aside men who had passed their draft board's physical examinations. Army doctors were better diagnosticians than local physicians, especially in identifying what was called "incipient tuberculosis." In fact, the lack of diagnostic competency among draft board physicians was a general problem, although officials in New Mexico seemed unaware that local-board physicians everywhere were inept at identifying major diseases. As a consequence, there were high rates of medically related rejections at all camps. Venereal diseases accounted for the rejection of 196,000 soldiers in the first year, and 24,000 draftees and national guardsmen were sent home diagnosed with TB.[51]

The army was determined to identify and discharge "those men who show the least tendency toward the disease [TB]." The phrase "least tendency" meant that respiratory illnesses such as bronchitis and pneumonia were seen as precursors to "incipient tuberculosis." Removing men deemed susceptible to TB, especially before they entered the AEF, became a matter of great urgency. Charged with handling the disease in the camps was Col. George E. Bushnell, a Regular Army career officer who, beginning in June 1917, headed the Division of Internal Medicine of the Office of the Army's Surgeon General. An 1880 graduate of Yale's medical school, Bushnell contracted tuberculosis while training to be a physician, and when he commanded Fort Bayard hospital near Silver City from early 1904 to June 1917 he became the army's leading authority on its diagnosis and treatment. Once in Washington, D.C., Bushnell lost no time "fine-combing" draftees and national guardsmen by unleashing "hundreds of specialists in the care of tuberculosis ... [to conduct] rigorous examinations in all of the military camps."[52]

Given the frequency with which Nuevomexicanos failed their training camp physicals, it did not take long for medical discharges to become politicized. Governor Lindsey and others in the state began to view the rejections as evidence of prejudice against Nuevomexicanos. Lindsey did not level that charge publicly but instead began with oblique criticism in mid-December after an inspection of Camp Kearny. He criticized camp officials for putting men in jeopardy because of a "destitution of Army supplies" and in particular "clothing and bedding." Four months after the war ended, when Lindsey was no longer governor, he was named to a national committee to investigate conditions that gave rise to high rates of TB, with New Mexico the first site the committee visited. But during the war the governor saw the army's handling of the disease through the narrow lens of bias.[53]

For about five months civil-military relations over conditions in training camps remained a simmering dispute in New Mexico, but they heated up nationally in this period. Between 12 December 1917 and 29 March 1918, the U.S. Senate's Military Affairs Committee held hearings to investigate the War Department's progress made in equipping and training soldiers and tending to their well-being. A week into the hearings the army's surgeon general, William C. Gorgas, released a report on disease epidemics at four training camps, including Camp Funston. He reported that in these four camps "insufficient clothing, overcrowding and bad sanitary conditions" were largely responsible for "disease epidemics." At Camp Funston lack of warm garments was cited as "hav[ing] contributed largely to the spread of pneumonia," which in two months had stricken 189 soldiers and killed forty-three—the highest such figures in all the camps. Because the army regarded respiratory ailments, including pneumonia, as a predictor of susceptibility to TB, Camp Funston was an incubator for medical conditions that resulted in dismissing men. For New Mexico, tensions over dismissals from training camp boiled over in the spring when a second wave of draftees had high rates of rejection at Camp Cody and Camp Kearny. By mid-March at Camp Cody the army was publicly calling for improved sanitary conditions, including garbage collection and disposal, better storm drainage, and removal of trash on vacant lots.[54]

What pushed state officials to react bitterly to tuberculosis-related dismissals at the training camps was a letter Lindsey received from Bushnell, dated 23 May 1918, that claimed the state's Nuevomexicano soldiers posed two serious problems undermining their usefulness in France:

> Experience with a number of races has shown that semi-civilized individuals remote from cities, if subjected to the unhygienic conditions of large cities of aggregations of men, may develop an acute and often rapidly fatal form of tuberculosis. It would, therefore, seem probable that the experience of the Mexicans [i.e., Nuevomexicanos] is an illustration of this general law. If this is true, it would not appear wise that such men should be sent to Europe where they could certainly be exposed to tuberculosis infection and where their presence would therefore be a burden rather than a benefit.

Elsewhere in the letter Bushnell employed the same conjectural argument—built on racist assumptions expressed in the conditional tense—to question Nuevomexicano loyalty and patriotism:

> There is another condition in which the cities of New Mexico and Arizona differ from the other portions of the United States, that is, the presence of a very considerable percentage of Mexicans among the [draft] registrants.... [They] constitute a body of men in which German sympathizers could readily be incorporated with difficulty of detection. For these reasons they would not appear to be well suited for duty overseas.[55]

Bushnell's explanation conformed to epidemiology for tuberculosis as it was understood in that era, but his assessment amounted to an affront to the state. His letter arrived amid heightened sensitivity over the possibility that Nuevomexicanos would not be allowed to serve as combat troops. That prospect brought to the fore two deep-seated resentments: negative stereotypes employed against Nuevomexicanos in statehood debates, and opposition to sending more than a token number of Nuevomexicanos to Cuba in the Spanish-American War of 1898. Many Nuevomexicanos looked on military service as a duty that statehood conferred and that had been too long denied. But their rate of rejection raised questions about whether once again Nuevomexicanos might be thwarted in their desire to fight for their country and to prove both their loyalty and manhood.[56]

Bushnell's letter arrived shortly before Camp Kearny rejected two hundred New Mexicans, the majority of them Nuevomexicanos, because of tuberculosis. Governor Lindsey could do nothing to challenge the decision, but he did initiate an effort through his medical aide to convince "the Government that the care of these men is incumbent upon the Government." A month later the army's surgeon general announced that New Mexico soldiers who had contracted TB in camps would be sent to sanatoriums for three months at the government's expense. They could extend their stay if further treatment was prescribed. A perceived need to respond to public opinion also likely prompted General Strong, commander of Camp Kearny, to make a goodwill gesture on the 4th of July. He reassured New Mexicans that the state's troops were well regarded and told the state's adjutant general, James Baca, that "the New Mexico troops in the [40th] division continue to do excellent work." He also said that "the Spanish-Americans are learning to speak English . . . [and] are well spoken of by all their commanding officers."[57]

At the end of July the War Department received a report after an inspection of Camp Cody in Deming by a state official. During May and June more than 1,500 New Mexicans had been sent there, but "a large percentage [were] rejected from this camp [on] account of physical disability." The inspector, Captain Reid, was cohead of the state's selective service, and he candidly admitted that "as nearly as I can ascertain, our Spanish-Americans were not highly desirable in that camp." He then offered this recommendation:

> I think that better results would be obtained, that is from our viewpoint, were you to assign the New Mexico Troops to some mobilization camp other than Camp Cody, preferably Camp Funston or Camp Travis [San Antonio, Texas, both National Army camps]. We in New Mexico are of the opinion that it would be no more than fair to our native boys to be assigned to a Company Commander who could speak their language

and who would be familiar with their racial characteristics. The War Department, however, seems to have different views.

Among the "different views" in Washington was that soldiers were desperately needed in France to blunt the recently launched German offensive. The army rendered moot Bushnell's views on Nuevomexicanos when it sent the 89th, 40th, and 34th Divisions to France between May and September 1918.[58]

Development Battalions

English was the language of the army, but its soldiers included nearly 500,000 immigrant draftees from forty-six nations, and many of them had little or no command of English. In addition there were twenty-five languages spoken by American Indian soldiers and nine among Hawaiian soldiers. Spanish, though, was the most common of all non-English languages spoken by native-born Americans. In the confusion of tongues that was the military in 1917–18, how were commands and instructions to be followed? Camp Funston became a leader in creatively dealing with this polyglot population. Almost as soon as the camp opened, linguistic disarray yielded to military order. Two New Mexicans became formative figures in Camp Funston's training of Spanish-speaking draftees: Francis G. Townsend of Aztec, San Juan County, and Dario Lucero of Cerrillos in Santa Fe County.[59]

Townsend celebrated his twenty-third birthday at Camp Funston on 12 November 1917, and occurring at about the same time was his assignment as a trainer-translator. A stock raiser and butcher, Townsend had spent one year as a cadet at Roswell's New Mexico Military Institute, which likely was why he was chosen as one of the three initial draftees from Aztec sent to Camp Funston on 4 September 1917. These first men arriving at camp were trained with an eye toward identifying those most likely to succeed as instructors. Townsend was selected after about nine weeks of intensive training and, when the transfer of soldiers to Camp Kearny was completed, he was made drill sergeant. "I was drilling whites and also Mexicans [Nuevomexicanos] as I could speak Mexican [Spanish] good." Townsend drilled a platoon of fifty mixed recruits, which meant he provided instruction and commands in both languages before signaly for their execution. This form of instruction sufficed for a few months until the formation of new companies exceeded both the supply of bilingual men and the time to prepare them to be trainer-translators. By December it was evident that a new, systematic approach was needed, and this brought two changes. For Townsend it meant a new set of assignments as a roving translator: "I was sent to the receiving station as interpreter for Mexicans. I also interpreted at the Infirmary and other places throughout the camp."[60]

The second change involved bringing in draftees to serve in a new training unit, one created specifically for non-English speakers. In launching this initiative Camp Funston officials sought the assistance of draft boards in New Mexico to help with the manpower requirements of what became known initially as a "development company" but was soon referred to as a "development battalion." Likely the first Nuevomexicano to be recruited was Dario Lucero, who grew up near Cerrillos and worked in nearby Madrid at a coal mine prior to the war. He was married and his daughter was born while he was in the army. Upon reporting to Camp Funston in early January 1918, at age twenty-five, Lucero immediately separated himself from his fellow draftees. Part of what set him apart may have been his natural bearing, which the army saw as indicative of leadership potential. Physically Lucero was rather average—about five feet, six inches tall, of medium build, with brown eyes and black hair—but he applied himself to mastering what he called "the military life." His diligence, military bearing, and bilingualism impressed his superiors, who quickly assigned him as an instructor in the newly formed development battalion. He performed well, received three quick promotions, and by early fall was a sergeant.[61]

Creation of the development battalion grew out of a need, as the army's surgeon general stated, "to deal with those [men] who were unfit for full duty from either physical, mental, or educational defects." As training camps filled with draftees, the army's attention was drawn first to special training needs for "the reclamation of incipient physical defects in the large mobilization camps." Such calls came initially from "orthopedic surgeons" at Camp Kearny and Camp Cody, respectively, on 23 November and 15 December 1917, each of whom noted that "foot conditions present an enormous problem at the training camp." What started with attention to the feet soon spread upward to "defects" elsewhere in the body as well as to educational deficiencies, especially lack of English skills. Rather quickly the development battalion became a burgeoning entity that divided its training into medical and nonmedical interventions. By early summer 1918, seven separate categories of medical cases were placed into discrete sections of the development battalion. Nonmedical issues referred to a development battalion fell into four categories "with the following priority: 1) enemy aliens; 2) allied aliens; 3) mental[ly] deficient; 4) non-English speaking."[62]

Lucero reported to Camp Funston seemingly at an inauspicious time—as a winter of sickness descended in early January 1918. But in fact timing was in his favor. Lucero's army service encapsulates how Camp Funston addressed its linguistic polyglot. Bilingual soldiers provided instruction three hours a day in the morning for native-born speakers of Spanish to prepare them to follow instruction in drill and military commands. They marched and did other military drills in the afternoon. Several months after Camp Funston began its development battalion, the army instituted a pilot program in Georgia for training foreign-born soldiers "who are unable to speak the English language and are out of touch with American institutions and ideals." The approach and results of this program were indistinguishable from Camp Funston's project aimed at native non-speakers of English.⁶³

Also in January 1918 another language issue emerged—training Spanish-speaking draftees from Puerto Rico. In this instance, rather than take an assimilationist approach the army opted for isolation, largely because of the number of troops involved—17,000 in what became the 94th Division. When the Puerto Ricans balked at being transported for training to South Carolina and placed under officers and instructors who spoke only English, the army decided to train them on their island home. But the army never resolved how they might be deployed in the AEF, so they spent the war apart and in training.⁶⁴

A massive German offensive launched on 21 March 1918 prompted calls for more American troops to be sent to France, with Camp Funston ordered to begin sending its draftees to embarkation camps within forty-five days. The first large contingent of Nuevomexicano soldiers from Camp Funston left on 21 April and landed at Brest on 24 May. For about a month these new troops received cursory combat training, and during that period another improvised arrangement enabled Spanish-speaking infantrymen to be included in the instruction. Twenty-eight-year-old Pfc. Luther P. Garcia of Greenville, Union County, who had been a cook on the troop transport, was called upon to become a temporary trainer-translator. He had been a shipping clerk prior to the war, and he enlisted in the hope of becoming an officer in the Medical Corps. He reached the medical training section at Fort Riley on 20 March 1918 and soon began his training, but on 21 April he was among several thousand men identified as ready for overseas duty. Once his troop transport arrived in France,

> after two day's rest at Brest we entrained for Blois, France [seventy-five miles southeast of Paris and a city of 24,000 during the war] where I performed some of my most important duties in the Army. Being possessed of the Spanish and English languages I served as instructor for the Spanish-American soldiers of the southern counties of the state of New Mexico,

telling them and instructing them how to work in the battlefields and to prevent the effects of the enemy's weapons, and instructing them in the use of the different kinds of gases and the effects of it. Later we were sent all over France. I and eighteen more were sent to the northern Western Front.

Once disbursed to combat units, Nuevomexicanos with limited or no ability to understand English relied on comrades, or "buddies," to explain commands.[65]

Throughout the war some New Mexicans, including Captain Reid, had called for training Nuevomexicanos in units solely for Spanish speakers. By late summer 1918 this approach was tried. Fifty men from Bernalillo County, forty-four Nuevomexicanos and six Euro-Americans, gathered in Albuquerque's Robinson Park late in the afternoon on Tuesday, 27 August 1918. There city and county dignitaries praised them as patriots and, according to *La Bandera America*, various speakers refuted denunciations published in *North American Review* several weeks earlier. The draftees were told that all New Mexicans despised anyone "who wants to say that we in New Mexico are not patriotic." Then a large crowd accompanied the draftees to the railroad depot. These men were among at least three hundred who departed New Mexico between 26 and 28 August. Trains took them east to Little Rock, Arkansas, and then a final eight miles northwest of the city to Camp Pike. That afternoon's speeches resonated with twenty-three-year-old Geronimo S. Barboa and twenty-eight-year-old Toribio Trujillo, who a month later wrote the newspaper to say that they hoped to leave Camp Pike soon to fight "in order that the Germans will know that Hispano-Americans are there to make them surrender so that peace can triumph."[66]

Camp Pike drew its draftees from all over the nation, and it was organized in the spirit of Americanization, which meant that its development battalion for foreign-language-speaking troops stressed learning English and, for those not citizens, taking classes to qualify. Congress passed legislation in 1918 allowing for naturalization of anyone in the military—including waiving the five-year residency requirement—and three thousand men at Camp Pike became naturalized citizens, including a few New Mexicans. Cleto Enriquez was born in Mexico on 13 May 1895 but had long lived in a village in Union County while working as a farmer, laborer, and clerk in a local mercantile. Enriquez entered Camp Pike as part of the late August draft call and besides his military training "completed citizenship by going before the Federal Court in Little Rock, Arkansas."[67]

Two Nuevomexicano soldiers who served as English-language instructors at Camp Pike reported on how their duties evolved and expanded.

Twenty-five-year-old Pvt. Juan B. Gallegos from Anton Chico in Guadalupe County reported:

> My first occupation was to be interpreter for the Spanish boys (those that could not speak English), and work as clerk (or rather make some office work for about a month). I had to be kept in the office so that the company commander could understand the Spanish boys. After that I had to act as corporal in order to interpret the commands so that the company commander had to teach me first then I had to teach the other boys. I used to teach English about an hour every day in order that those who could not speak English could understand enough to go across.[68]

The other instructor was thirty-year-old Joseph H. Gonzalez of Cerrillos, who had a tenth-grade education and had worked as a clerk and interpreter. Several weeks after leaving for Camp Pike on 28 August, Gonzalez was appointed

> as a School Superintendent, looking over the schools that were established for illiterates and non-English-speaking soldiers. I was supplied with all the necessary material for the schools, and I was quite successful in all the instructions that I was giving to the men. . . . Many of the boys who were unable to write their own names when they first went into the Army, or speak a word of English, they were writing letters by their own hand to their homes before they left the Army, the proudest bunch of soldiers that one ever saw. I still keep a record of the soldiers who attended the schools there.[6]

New Mexican nationalism needs to be understood for its role in sending men into the military. Long maligned as suspect for their loyalty, the state's residents—and especially Nuevomexicanos—seized the opportunity to stand proudly on the world stage as soldiers, sailors, or marines. New Mexicans in uniform were urged to be sentinels. "Valiant sons of New Mexico, touch, and if possible, eclipse the glories of Sparta. March into combat animated by the same emotions that in the Spartan soldier inspired such fervent patriotism. March and fight with valor." With these words distinguished Nuevomexicano public intellectual Benjamin Read opened his farewell address to fifteen Nuevomexicanos departing for Camp Pike in late August 1918. He appealed to their pride in themselves and their loyalty to their home state. Read's lofty ideals animated many men leaving for camp, but soon his words would be confronted by a grinding, grim reality—combat.[7]

GERMANY'S THREAT

The prospect of a victorious Germany carving up the Southwest and returning the area to Mexico came to light through the Zimmermann telegram about five weeks before the United States declared war on 6 April 1917. This political cartoon stoked war fever, and an alarmed American public, including some New Mexicans, occasionally turned patriotism into vigilantism against German Americans. "Hand Carving Up a Map of the Southwestern United States," cartoon by Clifford K. Berryman, *Washington Evening Star*, 4 March 1917.

Image courtesy of Library of Congress, Prints and Photographs Division, LOC no. 2016678747.

PRESIDENT WILSON'S APPEAL

President Woodrow Wilson tirelessly promoted public support for the war. This poster asking Americans to provide Christmas packages to AEF troops appeared before the armistice on 11 November 1918. It resulted in many tons of holiday treats being distributed, and enclosed in each package was a card that read, "Christmas from the folks at home through the Red Cross." "I Summon You to the Comradeship—Woodrow Wilson, Answer the Christmas Red Cross Roll Call," poster by Leo Mielzinger, 1918.

Image courtesy of Library of Congress, Prints and Photographs Division, LOC no. 2002719772.

NEW WOMEN

Euro-American women of means sought greater opportunities for three decades prior to this political cartoon appearing in 1917. Wartime mobilization provided an unparalleled boost to these efforts, allowing women to participate in local, state, and national projects. New Mexico was the first state to heed the federal government's call to organize its women, beginning in early May 1917. "Revised," cartoon by Kenneth R. Chamberlain, *Puck,* 14 April 1917.

Image courtesy of Library of Congress, Prints and Photographs Division, LOC no. 98502833.

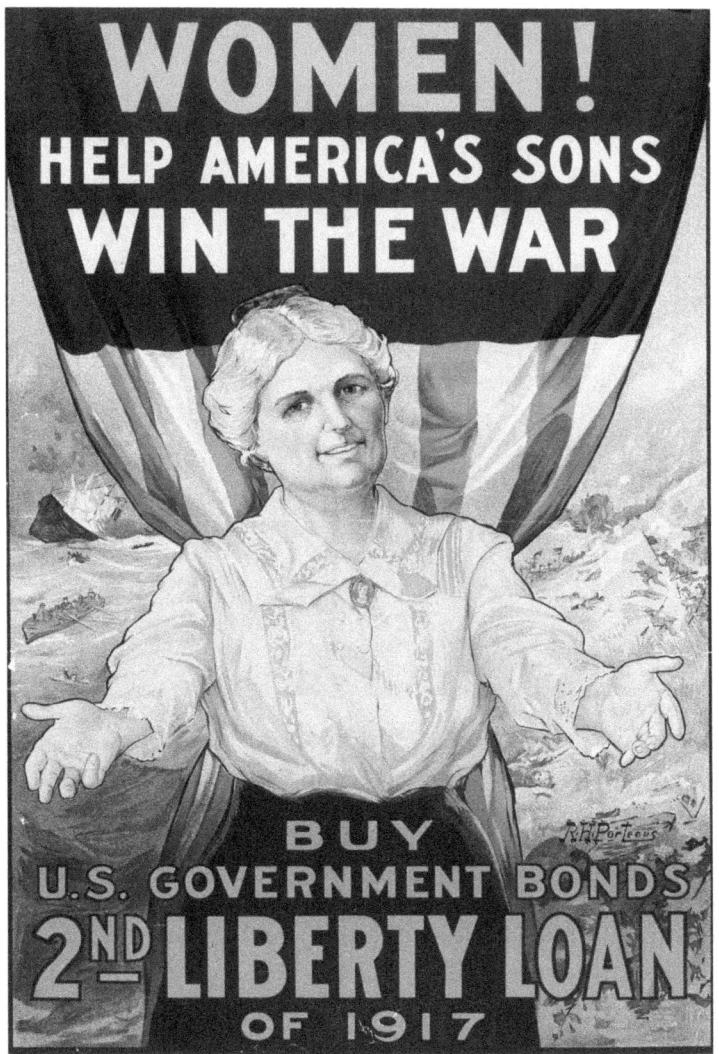

BUY BONDS

The federal government spent $24 million each day fighting the war. Citizens helped fund this unprecedented expense through four Liberty Loans, or bond drives. New Mexico's quota for the second drive in October–November 1917 was $ 3.1 million. The state's total purchases of bonds in 1917–18 paid for about eighteen hours of one day in the war. "Women! Help America's Sons Win the War," poster by R. H. Porteous, 1917.

Image courtesy of Library of Congress, Prints and Photographs Division, LOC no. 93510435.

CHARLES SPRINGER (1858-1932)

Appointed chair of the New Mexico State Council of Defense, Springer—a Colfax County Republican—had more power during the war than any elected New Mexico official, including the governor. The legislature appropriated $750,000 for wartime expenditures in May 1917, turned over control of the state's purse strings to Springer, and adjourned until January 1919. "Charles Springer," from *New Mexico Constitutional Book, 1910* (compiled and printed by C. S. Peterson, Denver, Colorado [1911?]).

Image courtesy of State Archives of New Mexico, collection 1973-001: New Mexico Secretary of State Records, box 7036, folder K-25.

NUEVOMEXICANO MUSICIANS

(Opposite, bottom) Music was a popular pastime that also reinforced camaraderie. The latter consideration took on added importance beginning in May 1918 when two thousand draftees from the state, including these four Nuevomexicanos, began reporting to Camp Cody, the training camp of the National Guard's 34th Division in Deming. Placing National Army soldiers in a National Guard camp created tensions music could help abate.

Courtesy State Archives of New Mexico, collection 1973-019: Records of the Adjutant General, box 10897, folder 4.

DRAFTEES LEAVING AZTEC

The draft was the State Council of Defense's most important mobilization. Conscripted soldiers nationwide began leaving for sixteen National Army training camps early in September 1917. Their journey began on a railroad station platform, and men from Aztec were among the state's 1917 quota of 2,300 draftees who rode about 700 miles east to Camp Funston, Kansas. "Train Depot Departure," 1917, Henry Jackson Collection, no. 1993-0001.

Courtesy of the Aztec Museum and Pioneer Village, Aztec, New Mexico.

155 MM GPF (GRAND PUISSASNCE FILLOUX)

The 130 men of New Mexico's Battery A of the National Guard arrived in France in early January 1918 as part of the 146th Field Artillery. They immediately became the first American artillery unit to receive the 155 mm GPF, a French-made gun capable of launching a 100-pound shell eleven miles. Battery A was on the battlefield continuously from July to the war's end. This never-before fully identified photograph shows the 146th FA moving into their first combat position a few miles west of Château-Thierry during the second week of July 1918.

From American Battle Monuments Commission, American Armies and Battlefields in Europe (Washington, DC: Government Printing Office, 1938), 99.

GAS MASK

(Opposite) Everyone at or near the front was exposed to poisonous gas. Pvt. Tomas Rivera from El Rito, Rio Arriba County, was an infantryman in the 32nd Division who fought in the Meuse-Argonne offensive. His gas mask was a constant companion and prevented serious complications from exposure, although as with most infantrymen in the Meuse-Argonne he suffered somewhat from gas poisoning in the postwar decades. He resumed his position as a schoolteacher upon discharge, but in the 1930s he moved to Albuquerque and took a job selling furniture.

Courtesy State Archives of New Mexico, collection 1973-019: Records of the Adjutant General, box no. 10899, folder 11.

USS *LEVIATHAN*

The largest ship in the world when launched in 1913 as a German passenger liner, the *Leviathan* was confiscated when America entered the war. Soon it was placed into service as a U.S. Navy troop transport. It could carry 14,000 men at a time, and it delivered the most New Mexicans to Brest, France. The painted camouflage pattern, known as dazzle, had several variations, including one New Mexico artists developed. "Coaling the Leviathan, Brest, France, May 30, 1918," photographer unknown.

Image courtesy of Library of Congress, Prints and Photographs Division, LOC no. 20166513781.

VESLE RIVER, 28TH DIVISION

(Opposite, top) Hundreds of New Mexico National Guard infantrymen in the 40th Division became replacements assigned to the 28th Division upon reaching Brest in June 1918. Combat losses earlier in the month had thinned the 28th Division, and replacements, including New Mexicans, fought along the Vesle River between late July and 10 September. New Mexicans in the 28th Division's Vesle River combat incurred nearly half as many deaths as did all troops from the state killed in fourteen divisions during the Meuse-Argonne offensive. From "The Challenge of the Vesle: Raw Troops Became Veterans at the 'Hell-Hole,'"

American Legion Weekly 1, no. 7 (August 15, 1919): 1.

Every move of the Americans started Boche artillery fire

Raw Troops Became Veterans at the "Hell-Hole"

LT. HARRY ROGERS, 77TH DIVISION

Rogers, from Eddy County, was a newly minted lieutenant whose first engagements were in the Meuse-Argonne offensive. In this rare photograph he is on the far right. He had just taken command of a depleted platoon and successfully knocked out a machine gun nest and captured thirty Germans, including two officers, on 2 October. A few hours later he advanced into a draw and became part of the famous "Lost Battalion" of the 77th Division. Five days later he was killed by a sniper.

From J. O. Adler, ed., History of the Seventy-Seventh Division: August 25th 1917—November 11th 1918 (New York: WHC Printers, 1919), 80.

UNKNOWN KILLED IN ACTION, 89TH DIVISION

The most New Mexicans serving together were draftees from Camp Funston's 89th Division. They distinguished themselves in the war's final two offensives: St. Mihiel (12–16 September) and Meuse-Argonne (26 September–11 November). The 89th Division advanced thirty miles in combat, captured 5,061 prisoners, and had 1,433 battle deaths as well as 5,838 wounded. Twenty-two New Mexicans in the 89th Division died in these two offensives. "In the Wire," photograph by Eyre Powell, 1918.

Image courtesy of Library of Congress, Prints and Photographs Division, LOC no. 2016651301

CROCKETT BROTHERS—SAILOR AND SOLDIER

The Crockett brothers of Roswell—Seaman 1st class Paris (b. 1895) and his older brother Private 1st class Oren (b. 1893)—reportedly were distant cousins of David Crockett. They entered the military in 1917. Paris enlisted in December and was assigned to a cargo ship that brought sugar from Hawaii to Philadelphia, offloaded it, and took on new cargo for delivery in France at either St. Nazaire, which received 2.55 million tons of freight during the war, or Bordeaux, which offloaded 2.19 million tons of freight.

Oren was in the state's 1917 draft quota and reported to the 89th Division in October. At the end of the month he was sent along with more than five hundred New Mexicans to the 40th Division at Camp Kearny near San Diego, California. Upon reaching France in June 1918 he became a replacement soldier in the 3rd Division, where his extraordinary valor in combat brought him a Distinguished Service Medal.

In the 1920s both men moved to California, married and pursued successful careers; Paris worked as a plumber in Los Angeles and Oren owed a paint shop in San Diego. They died in California in 1987 and 1980, respectively.

Courtesy State Archives of New Mexico, collection 1973-019: Records of the Adjutant General, box 10896, folder 7.

CHARLES GOOCH IN RUSSIA

When drafted from Santa Fe County in early May 1918, Gooch joined more than one hundred New Mexican conscripts placed in the Regular Army's 8th Division. Their brigade left California's Camp Fremont and sailed to Vladivostok in September 1918 and began a year-long incursion in Russia. The few New Mexicans killed in action accounted for 8 percent of combat deaths in AEFS actions. Gooch embraced his return to civilian life, showing promise for a future in politics as an officer in the American Legion. It was not to be. He died suddenly in 1922 from a wartime injury to his head.

Courtesy State Archives of New Mexico, collection 1973-019: Records of the Adjutant General, box 10897, folder 5.

CONRAD HILTON'S QUESTIONNAIRE

Responses to questions three and ten are revealing in Hilton's reply to a questionnaire mailed all New Mexico servicemen in October 1919. During Hilton's ten months in the Quartermaster's Corp in the AEF, he worked four months in Paris. While there he surely visited the Knights of Columbus's largest AEF center, where the slogan was "Everybody Welcome, Everything Free." Among veterans, membership in the Knights doubled to 800,000 by 1923, making it larger than the American Legion. Hilton changed occupation and residence several months after submitting his questionnaire, moving to Dallas and acquiring a boardinghouse, which soon evolved into owning hotels. He moved to Los Angeles in the 1930s.

Courtesy State Archives of New Mexico, collection 1973-019: Records of the Adjutant General, box 10897, folder 20.

CITIZEN-SOLDIER AND VETERAN DOUBLE

The cartoon "What Will You Tell Her?" appeared in the AEF newspaper *Stars and Stripes* in January 1919. The four dilemmas depicted involved, as a caption noted, "illusions [that] must never be destroyed." The wartime citizen-soldier became two men in one throughout the 1920s and 1930s—a veteran hiding secrets of his life in France, especially of combat, and a civilian trying to reconnect with loved ones. Cartoon by Wallgren, *Stars and Stripes* 1, no. 51 (January 24, 1919): 7.

Image courtesy of Library of Congress, control no. 20001931.

FADE AWAY

Posters in a general store in the village of Chacon in Mora County caught the eye of government photographer John Collier Jr. in 1943. He recorded a visual metaphor of the persistence of World War I in the midst of a new war. Collier noted that idlers—some perhaps veterans from 1917–19—tarried outside the store with horses hitched just beyond them. The overall impression was of a bygone time lingering but fading. "Chacon, Mora County, New Mexico," photograph by John Collier, 1943.

Image courtesy of Library of Congress, Prints and Photographs Division, LOC no. owi2001017417.

CHAPTER 5

"Slept in Mud, Bathed in Blood"

Soldiers and marines from New Mexico stepped off the gangplank and onto the cobblestone streets of St. Nazaire eighty-one days after the United States declared war. They were part of the first contingent of 14,000 "Yanks" to arrive "over there"—between 26 and 29 June 1917. Raw recruits far outnumbered career infantrymen of the Regular Army, and one of their captains admitted the volunteers were a motley lot: "The personnel of the division was not impressive. Many of the men were undersized and a number spoke English with difficulty." Once off the transports, the soldiers passed through the town of about 39,000, their appearance and behavior confirming for all who saw them that "most of them were ignorant of the rudiments of march discipline." But George C. Marshall soon saw beyond the training lapses to admire their mettle and praise them as "remarkably gallant fellows who fought so hard and died so cheerfully [read: willingly] not many months later."[1]

The First AEF Combat Soldiers

The port city of St. Nazaire, situated on the north side of the Loire River five miles inland from its mouth on the Atlantic coast, was about 225 miles southwest of Paris, where on 4 July 1917 the roar of Parisians greeted Pershing, key aides, and the 16th Infantry Battalion—ill-prepared volunteers such as Delfino Gonzales and his cousins, Jose F. and Casiano Trujillo, all from Tucumcari, along with seasoned Regular Army soldiers. They paraded five miles through the city to pay tribute

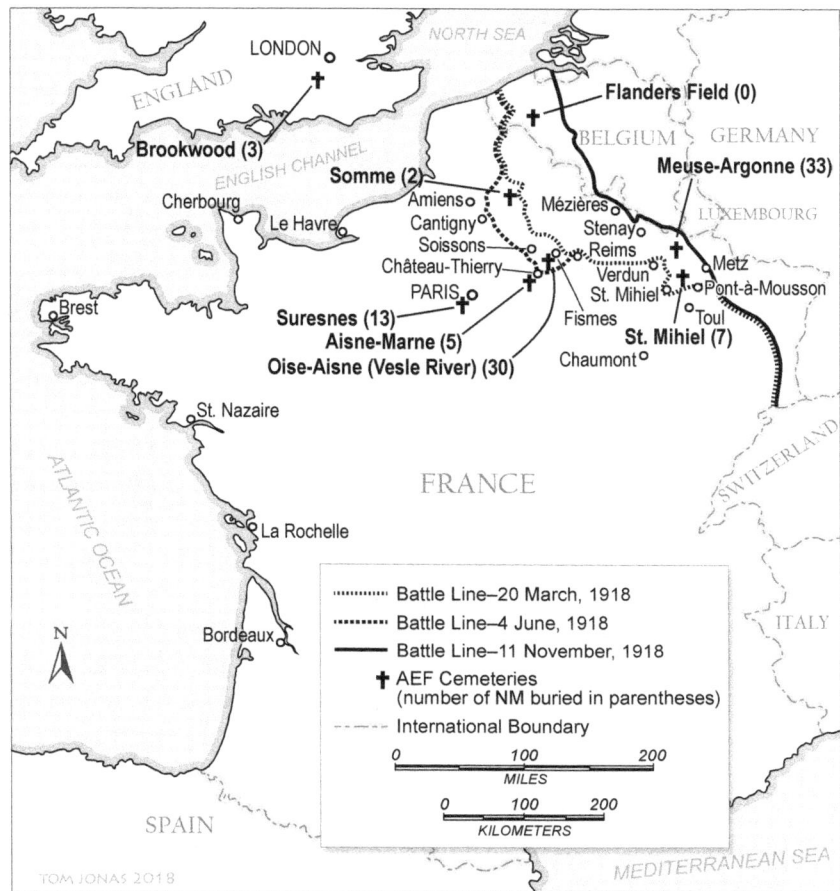

Map 2. France, the western front, and AEF cemeteries.

at several French military memorials, most notably the grave of the Marquis de Lafayette, who fought with colonialists in the American Revolutionary War. A crowd estimated at one million erupted into cheers when Quartermaster Corps captain Charles E. Stanton proclaimed in tribute, "Lafayette, nous voilà" (we are here).[2]

About five weeks later a second contingent of the 1st Division docked in England, including some New Mexicans, and staged their own symbolic public appearance when volunteers and Regular Army troops marched through London and passed in review for King George V at Buckingham Palace. News of these parades was eagerly read in the United States, including in front-page stories in New Mexico newspapers. But for all the cheering that these first American troops heard, perhaps what echoed loudest in Pershing's mind was the awareness that he would command an army-in-drill for many months. So he left Paris in September to get about the business of forging a combat-ready army at his headquarters in Chaumont, a city of 15,000 about 140 miles south of Paris at the western edge of the historic Lorraine sector. Two forests demarked the region's southern and northern extension, the woods in the Vosges Mountains and the Argonne Forest, respectively, with the latter simply the name for the southern portion of the Ardennes, which then and today is an expansive forest covering Belgium and much of Luxembourg. The American, or Lorraine, sector was about 150 miles long and 70 miles wide. Here the AEF settled in and began training, with Toul about 50 miles northeast of Chaumont as the sector's operational command center. Not all AEF divisions trained here, though. Pershing agreed to place some AEF troops with French and British units, with the latter receiving the largest number (ten divisions), and two—the 27th (New York National Guard) and 30th (Carolinas and Tennessee)—were placed for the war's duration with the British Expeditionary Force.[3]

The second contingent of 14,000 embarked for France in intervals over four months, with the first of these departing on 31 July 1917, and each group had a diverse mix of personnel: field artillery, signal corps, more infantry recruits, railroad workers, and a sizeable number of what became the first Services of Supply workers—men such as Hugh C. Fraser of the Quartermaster Corp. These troops went first to England, but Fraser seemed not to have marched through London as did many of the infantry. Upon arriving in northern France he and sixty others were assigned to St. Nazaire, where he spent his two years in France because "a transfer from our organization was not considered then, nor later." In fact, support personnel, indispensable in any war zone, were the majority of soldiers in the AEF, about 60 percent. Frazer oversaw German prisoners of war doing whatever work was needed from them but primarily working in clothing and equipment salvage, and by the end of the war he had risen to sergeant first class responsible for forty enlisted men and 250 German prisoners.[4]

Not until 22 December did the final units of the 1st Division arrive in France. By that time Brest, with a population more than twice that of St. Nazaire and 196 miles due north, had become the principal port of debarkation for AEF troops and, in 1919, for their homebound embarkation. It also served as the U.S. Navy's headquarters. St. Nazaire quickly became a principal port receiving shipments to Services of Supply depots, but it also became embroiled in a dispute that strained

U.S.-Franco relations. At issue was a matter personal to each man in the AEF, of daily concern to General Pershing, and a flashpoint for French officials holding municipal, provincial, or national office: prostitution and the risk of sexually transmitted diseases.[5]

A complex and long-running civil-military dispute began a week after the arrival of the first troops when Pershing issued a general order suspending all soldiers' pay for three months. He believed that the quickest way to cut off men from prostitutes was to withhold pay. What ensued, as French scholar Jean-Yves Le Naour wrote, was that "this question of sex remained open until the departure of the expeditionary body, in spite of repeated, indeed relentless efforts by high French authorities to convince the Americans to use '*les maisons de tolérance.*'" These sites were the network of municipal registered and inspected brothels that had existed since the late nineteenth century.[6]

Pershing's decree did not work, and officials in St. Nazaire reported in early September that each week more than 1,500 U.S. soldiers patronized prostitutes. Moreover, demand had dramatically spurred an increase in illegal or uninspected and unregistered *prostituées clandestines,* who were five times more numerous than legal sex workers. A clash of cultures ensued: the army's Progressive Era morality and proscription of prostitution versus French officials accepting what they called "the reality of human passions," especially in young men. Clashes increased in frequency in the fall of 1917. Colonel Bash, base commander at St. Nazaire, demanded the expulsion of all prostitutes—registered as well as illegal— from the municipality on 31 October. This incident soon came to the attention of French prime minister Georges Clemenceau, who protested to Pershing. A series of exchanges culminated in a formal conference on 8 March 1918 in which the army announced a plan for soldiers to receive a hygienic wash at prophylactic stations immediately after sexual contact. Two weeks later the German spring offensive accelerated the pace of war, and each country's leaders—and the AEF infantrymen—shifted their focus to the battlefield and cases of venereal disease quickly declined. But troops on the move, and especially in rear areas, amused themselves while marching with an act of coarse sublimation accepted by the army: singing risqué, ribald, and raunchy marching songs, the most popular of which were innumerable variations of "Mademoiselle from Armentières."[7]

Many of the two million men of the AEF had feet of clay, and their impulses proved too strong to be curbed by army decrees. In June 1918, Pvt. Leonardo Lucero of Rio Arriba County arrived in Nevers, 225 miles due east of St. Nazaire, for duty with Depot Three of the Intermediate Medical Supply. This town of about

28,000 was tethered to St. Nazaire as a link in the port city's AEF distribution network, but it also was a node in the web of women catering to men's desires. When Lucero and "16 New Mexicans all of our state" were excluded from a local 4th of July parade because "some complaint came along by some dirty fellow" alleging the state's troops were incapable of marching in formation, the men were "all discussed [disgusted] and went out to our barracks, which was a barn." But soon "all the Spanish Americans went like crazy for the cafes and whorehouses for entertainments after being honest [and] clean in mind and deeds [since arriving in France]." The following week Lucero and another unidentified Nuevomexicano were sent to work at an evacuation hospital near Château-Thierry and thereafter to medical facilities supporting Allied offenses for the war's duration. He wrote nothing further about "entertainments," nor were such matters directly mentioned by any other New Mexicans in service questionnaires. Also silent were the voices of innumerable fourteen- and fifteen-year-old French girls recruited, abused, quickly discarded, and replaced in endless cycles during the war years. Long overlooked, too, was Pershing's double standard—his wartime intimacy with Micheline Resco, a twenty-three-year-old Romanian artist he met in Paris in June 1917 and secretly married in 1946.[8]

Cantigny

George C. Marshall, who distinguished himself in World War II as chief of staff, had high praise for the lieutenants who arrived with him in late June 1917: "I have never seen more splendid looking men and it makes me very sad to realize that most of them were left in France." One of these young lieutenants in the 1st Division was Joseph Quesenberry of Las Cruces, whose experiences illustrate the early months of the AEF and activities of the 1st Division. After the parade in Paris, Quesenberry spent several weeks in training and in late July 1917 was assigned to Company K, 18th Infantry. On 3 October his company took first place in a battalion-wide competitive drill, and the next day Quesenberry was promoted to captain. October through December saw his battalion begin training in the Lorraine sector, and then in January they moved north of Toul ten miles or so into the front line on the St. Mihiel salient, relieving a French division. A winter blizzard and enemy artillery made their first weeks in the trenches miserable.

Reportedly these infantrymen were "the first American troops to go against the Germans for purposes other than training." On 11 March, Quesenberry led "the first American raiding party in command of an American Officer to go 'over the top,'" and he personally briefed his commanding general, who in turn reported the results to General Pershing. These raiding sorties were ostensibly to gain intelligence about enemy positions and, if possible, capture prisoners and documents, and both sides regularly launched them under cover of darkness. Probing areas immediately behind enemy lines soon become part of what one did at the front, missions often undertaken to show the mettle of officers and troops whatever the assigned objective. The front occupied by the 1st Division's battalions was dangerous. In mid-March 1918 the unit's casualty report listed 126 killed in action, 134 killed by accident, 475 wounded, 21 captured, and 641 died of disease. A major contributor to this latter figure was the especially severe winter that settled over that part of France.[9]

A dozen days after the German offense of 1918 began on 21 March, the 1st Division was relieved on the St. Mihiel salient by the 26th Division (New England National Guard). A week later they were loaded onto trains and taken northwest of Paris, where they detrained and marched northeast for about seventy miles with packs weighing between seventy and one hundred pounds. On the fifth day they reached a French-held section of the front opposite a bend in the bulge, or salient, below the tiny French village of Cantigny. At their backs sixty miles northeast was the English Channel, and just twenty miles to the northeast was the strategically vital city of Amiens, where five railroad lines serving the French and British forces intersected. Immediately in front of the 1st Division lay the village's remnants on a ridge 650 feet above them, which afforded the dug-in enemy unobstructed vistas of the Allied line. A week later, on 25 April, Captain Quesenberry led Company K into makeshift trenches, shell holes actually, when the 1st Division relieved a French division. Daily the Germans kept up an intense artillery barrage averaging 3,450 shells, including ones filled with mustard gas, which the Americans experienced for the first time at Cantigny. On Saturday, 27 April, thirty-year-old Cpl. August ("Gus") Chretien of Gallup, assigned to Company E, 16th Infantry, died in combat in the improvised line, the first New Mexican killed on the battlefield in France. Corporal Chretien was born in France, and when he was about two years old, in 1890, his parents immigrated to the United States. His grave is in his native France. The next day Capt. Joseph Quesenberry was "killed by the burst of a German shell." His remains were returned to his family after the war.[10]

One month later Cantigny became the first major battle for the AEF. Pershing wanted to make a statement about the resolve and preparedness of his soldiers—as much for the benefit of the Allies as for the enemy, given the dim view many had of his troops after the hapless Punitive Expedition. He ordered the taking and holding of Cantigny no matter the cost in lives. At 4:45 A.M. on Tuesday, 28 May 1918, shelling commenced from 234 pieces of light and heavy artillery positioned every thirty feet along a mile and a third of the front. Two hours later regiments of 1st Division riflemen followed a rolling artillery barrage laid down in front of them and accompanied by French tanks and American flamethrowers. Their steady advance secured complete control of Cantigny within two hours, all with limited American casualties. Total annihilation befell the enemy deeply entrenched in the village. Then the Germans began two and a half days of counterattack in three separate waves preceded and followed by unrelenting artillery barrages. The enemy inflicted just over a thousand casualties on the 1st Division; twice that number of Germans were killed or wounded. Over the next ten weeks an additional 5,200 Americans soldiers of the 1st Division were wounded or died defending Cantigny and the adjacent line. During the seventy-two days they fought at Cantigny, the 1st Division had 6,284 casualties. Killed were 20 percent of the enlisted infantrymen and 14 percent of officers; of the wounded, 47 percent (2,647) were victims of poison gas. Thus two years to the month after Pershing led a fruitless search in northern Mexico, he was now in northern France with a transformed American army. As one general later wrote, Cantigny "was the first cold foreboding to the German that this was not, as he had hoped, a rabble of amateurs approaching."[11]

Two New Mexicans lost their lives at Cantigny on 9 and 10 June: respectively, bugler William H. Goodwin, of Guadalupe County, and Pvt. Delfino Gonzales of Tucumcari, both in the 16th Infantry. Goodwin enlisted in the Regular Army in 1903 at age twenty-two and "from that year on was in the army practically all of the time." He died when "a shell burst directly in front of his dugout, completely destroying it." Delfino Gonzales likewise died when an enemy "high explosive shell" landed near him. Upon bursting, such a shell disintegrated into a high-velocity shower of hot fragments of the projectile's steel exterior. At thirty-five years old, Goodwin was twice as old as Gonzales, who had been in the army just fourteen months when he was killed.[12]

Château-Thierry and Belleau Wood

Commander-in-chief of the French forces Henri-Philippe Pétain sat down with General Pershing on 30 May just as the worth of America's fighting force was being proven at Cantigny. Pershing had eleven divisions in France when they met, but they were strung out along the nearly 500 miles of the western front from Calais on the English Channel to the Vosges Mountains. Pétain confronted a

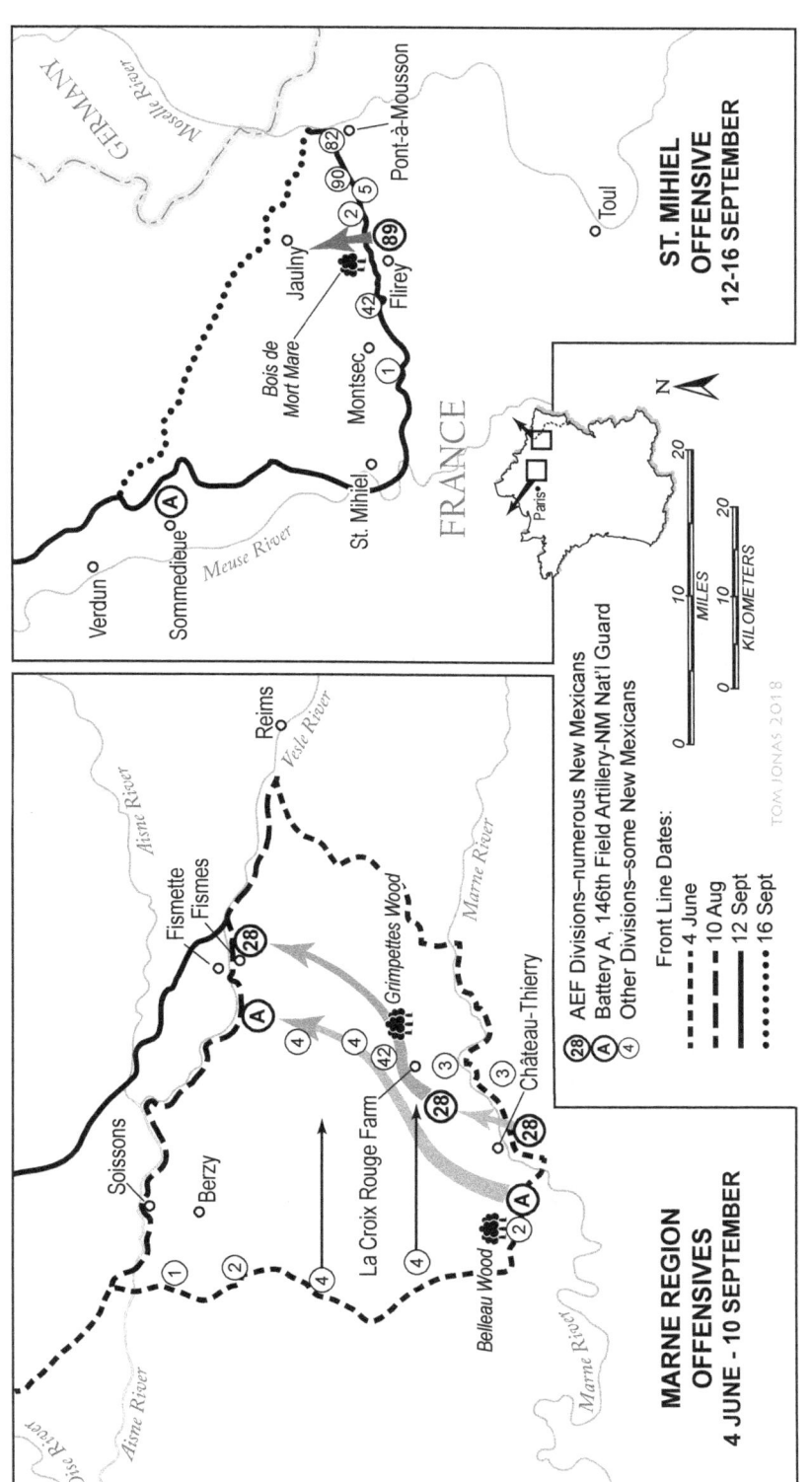

Map 3. AEF summer offensives in northeast France, June to September 1918.

rapidly deteriorating situation. The third wave of the enemy offensive had begun on 27 May. Within three days German soldiers descended out of north-central France, crossed the Aisne and Vesle Rivers, and reached the Marne River, an advance of nearly forty miles. Suddenly Paris was within range of their biggest guns, and both artillery shelling and aerial bombing of the capital occurred. Fearing imminent disaster, Pétain needed to reinforce two main routes to Paris, and he beseeched Pershing to provide him with American divisions to protect the Marne River at Château-Thierry, a town of about 7,500 fifty-six miles east of Paris. Pershing quickly consented, and two nearby Regular Army divisions, the 2nd and 3rd, were ordered to move toward Château-Thierry.

The Americans and Germans faced off at the opposite ends of two bridges in Château-Thierry on Saturday, 1 June. The German troops were part of an elite force, known as storm troopers, whose objective at Château-Thierry was to sweep across the Marne River, take control of its bridges and the railroad running east and west, then move westward and attack Paris. They sought to deliver a crippling blow to the nation's psyche that would result in France's capitulation. None of that happened, because the enemy was stopped at Château-Thierry, and for the second time in a week the Germans realized that the Americans were a formidable foe.[13]

The 8th Machine Gun Battalion of the 3rd Division arrived in relief at Château-Thierry on 6 June, and among these incoming soldiers was Cpl. Frank McCrarey of Union County, who had turned twenty-eight the day the battle began. McCrarey had been drafted into the 89th Division in September 1917 and assigned to a machine gun battalion, but at the end of March he was sent to France and placed in the 3rd Division. At the same time that his battalion took up its defensive position at Château-Thierry, a battle intensified seven miles west that for the next three weeks would engage the 2nd Division, including its marine regiments.[14]

At the Battle of Belleau Wood on Thursday, 6 June, the marine corps suffered its bloodiest day until the landing on Tarawa Atoll in November 1943. Thirty-one officers and 1,056 enlisted men died or were wounded in four assaults that Thursday. Rightfully the battle remains a hallowed memory in the marine corps, but it is also, and equally rightfully, the subject of intense scrutiny among many military historians. The criticisms are threefold: reliance on consistently faulty intelligence; minimal strategic value of the target; and the folly of marines marching side by side in a straight line across wheat fields without any artillery support and into the line of fire of German machine guns.[15]

The 2nd Division faced one of Germany's premier units, the Prussian Guards, well equipped and entrenched in a mile-square dense forest "on high, rocky ground [that] hid innumerable gullies and boulder heaps." The 5th and 6th Marine Regiments finally gained a firm hold in the woods on Tuesday, 11 June. On 16 June the 6th Marines were relieved from their position in the southern part of Belleau Wood, "where they had been badly hurt from artillery, and especially gas, which knocked down many men." One among the survivors of Belleau Wood from the 6th Marines was twenty-year-old Pvt. John W. Barr, who had settled in Las Vegas, San Miguel County, in 1916. He had four years' training in a military prep school and upon enlisting in January 1918 was offered first a captaincy and then a lieutenancy but "refused both because of the responsibility in men's lives attached to such commissions." For Palmer Ketner of Gallup, transported to France in June 1917 and initially assigned as a stevedore at St. Nazaire, manual labor quickly yielded to placement in a marine regiment within the newly formed 2nd Division. At Belleau Wood Ketner distinguished himself for bravery and was awarded a battlefield promotion to second lieutenant. He briefly attended an officer training school before being assigned to the 6th Regiment. He died in combat on 2 November.[16]

What Barr, Keltner, and all fighting at Belleau Wood endured was succinctly described by a fellow marine: "Been in this blazing inferno for almost ten days with little food, and very little sleep, to say nothing of the shortage of water [and] the shell fire was nerve-racking and every man was more or less shell-shocked." The AEF was unprepared to deal with a psychological disorder described as "shell-shocked," which is known as post-traumatic stress disorder today. The condition became the war's signature psychological wound, and among veterans in the interwar years the most common reason for hospitalization. All that was ahead, and the soldiers staggered forward in combat in Belleau Wood until finally after twenty days the 2nd Division and remaining marines prevailed, but only after artillery barrages denuded the eastern quarter of the former hunting preserve and widespread hand-to-hand combat enervated the enemy. If Cantigny had been Pershing's declaration that the Americans were a determined fighting force, then Belleau Wood was the exclamation point to that statement.[17]

Besides the marine casualties, nearly a thousand Regular Army soldiers fell in the three weeks' fight, including two New Mexicans. Homer E. Weathers of Curry County enlisted in the Regular Army in July 1916 and spent time on the Mexican border before sailing to France in early September 1917. Upon arrival he was assigned as a corporal to the 23rd Infantry Regiment, 2nd Division. He had been in the army twenty-three months when he died at Belleau Wood on 6 June, four months before his eighteenth birthday. Twenty-six-year-old medic Pvt. Frank C. McDermott of Portales "died in action on June 16, 1918 while engaged in caring for the wounded in Belleau Wood. It was while a heavy enemy barrage was on, and at the exploding of a shell near him, that a comrade saw him fall. He was dead when the comrade reached him."[18]

The high casualty rates from Cantigny, Château-Thierry, and Belleau Wood were a prelude to sanguinary battles to follow. Combat division strength had to be maintained, and the solution was the replacement system. Divisions arriving in France beginning in April 1918 went first to a replacement depot from which infantrymen were dispatched as needed to fill in the ranks at divisions depleted in recent fighting. Combat infantrymen usually went in increments of platoons or companies as replacements, which is why New Mexicans ended up in all twenty-nine combat divisions in the AEF. New Mexicans sent as replacement troops to the 28th Division (Pennsylvania National Guard) in June and July suffered the highest casualties among the state's replacements. Services of Supply units likewise received replacements, but typically as squads or platoons.

Defense of the Marne and the Aisne-Marne Offensive

In early July attention turned toward celebrating the upcoming French national holiday, *La fête nationale* (Bastille Day), on the 14th, but concern also grew that on or about the same day the enemy would launch another offensive to break through the front and attempt to capture Paris. To help stem such assaults, heavy artillery manned by Americans, including 126 New Mexicans in Battery A, 146th Field Artillery, arrived just west of Château-Thierry after five months of training. These men had been reassigned to the 66th FA Brigade, a move precipitated by the 41st becoming the first designated depot, or replacement, division. All of its infantrymen were disbursed as needed to combat divisions or placed in support positions. The 66th FA had two battalions—the 146th and 148th, each with six batteries—and Pershing designated these as corps or army artillery, which meant they were positioned as Pershing decided. As a result, the 66th FA was nearly continuously in combat from mid-July to 11 November 1918.

As soon as Capt. Charles de Bremond of Roswell and the 126 New Mexico enlisted men in Battery A arrived in France, they were sent from Le Havre to the southwestern port city of Bordeaux, a sixty-hour train trip. The men were ushered into French troop transports that had also served as freight boxcars and were labeled "8 Chevaux, 40 Hommes"; the phrase "8 Horses, 40 Men" became one of the most repeated in postwar recollections, a shared memory of misery endured. Upon arrival in Bordeaux they marched ten miles southwest to an artillery training facility at Camp de Souge. De Bremond, fluent in French and an experienced artillery officer, quickly distinguished himself, was promoted to major and soon to lieutenant colonel, and commanded the 146th FA Batteries A and B until debilitated by gas in August.[19]

Upon arriving at Camp de Souge the 146th FA became the first heavy artillery unit in the AEF. The New Mexicans' previous experience and training had been with 75 mm artillery, but now they were assigned the 155 mm Grande Puissance Filloux, or GPF. These guns were French designed and manufactured, weighed fourteen tons, and fired a projectile slightly more than six inches in diameter, weighing a hundred pounds, with a range of eleven miles. The GPF had been used on the battlefield only since the summer of 1917. Moving them required a ten-ton tractor, and so the 146th FA switched from being dependent on horses and became a motorized unit. Under optimum conditions, which were nonexistent in combat, the guns could travel six miles in an hour. When the twelve batteries of the 66th FA Brigade moved their personnel, ordnance, supplies, and kitchen as a column, it stretched for more than six miles. Each battery had four GPFs. The unit's official history reported that "the 66th F.A. Brigade fired over half of the entire amount of the G.P.F. high-power ammunition used by the United States in the war with Germany," or more than 132,000 rounds, and of this amount the 146th fired 70,895 rounds (52.7 percent), and the estimated total cost of the ammunition fired was more than $6.5 million dollars ($105 million in 2017).[20]

Their first combat shelling came on 13 July near Vaux, three and a half miles west of Château-Thierry and once a village of eighty-two stone houses occupied by the enemy. Artillery had reduced it to rubble in the first ten days of July. Enemy troops, though, remained concentrated in the area in advance of their expected assault to gain access to the road to Paris. As Sunday yielded to Monday, 15 July, the enemy initiated their offensive with an artillery barrage of three and a half hours along fifty-plus miles of the Marne River. The Germans timed their offensive based on what turned out to be a major miscalculation—that the French troops would be impaired after celebrating their national holiday.

The heaviest fighting involving New Mexicans between 15 and 17 July was along a front between Château-Thierry eastward about a dozen miles. Various French divisions together with the American 3rd and 28th Divisions held this crucial area. Between 250 and 350 New Mexicans had been sent to these two divisions as replacement troops only weeks earlier, with the majority assigned to the 28th

Division. About twenty-four miles farther east at Reims fighting intensified as the enemy sought unsuccessfully to capture this major railroad interchange, but the most intense fighting occurred east of Reims. There the 42nd Division and French divisions fought off an enemy advance heading west after crossing the Marne. Fewer than two dozen New Mexicans were in the 42nd Division in their first major engagement, and none from the state died. The unit's national guardsmen were selected from twenty-six states and the District of Columbia, resulting in a force that one of its officers, Maj. Douglas MacArthur, described as spanning the country "like a rainbow." The appellation "Rainbow Division" soon stuck.

Three New Mexicans were killed in three days of fighting east of Château-Thierry. Two from the 3rd Division died: Pvt. George Hall of Quay County and Pvt. Verdie J. McReynolds of Curry County, who had married on 9 June 1917, never saw his daughter Ida Belle born just before he sailed for France in April 1918, and died six days after his first wedding anniversary. In the 28th Division the one fatality among New Mexicans was Aparicio Rael, a twenty-three-year-old private from Guadalupe County and a replacement soldier from the 40th Division. His mother remembered him with a mix of patriotic pride and resignation: "He served his country to the full extent[,] gave his life[,] all any man can do."[21]

To the west of Château-Thierry the enemy had fewer troops after being battered for three weeks in Belleau Wood. The targets assigned Batteries A and B were in support of the 26th Division and especially the 2nd Regular Army in and around the destroyed village of Vaux. An American participant succinctly described the batteries' role: "The Germans made a small demonstration on the front of the 26th Division at Vaux, and made somewhat of a penetration by infiltration. A barrage [from 146th FA] was brought down which stopped all further attempts, and counter attacks drove the Germans out of the part of the line they had captured." On 17 July the 146th FA prepared to move toward the northeast.[22]

The Allies launched the Aisne-Marne offensive on 18 July. The general-in-chief of the Allied armies in France, Généralissime Ferdinand Foch, had been planning to seize the initiative since 14 June 1918. With great secrecy he mapped the Aisne-Marne offensive with a few French generals and Pershing, plotting a counterattack that not only removed the immediate threat to Paris but forced the enemy's retreat, first from territory overrun since 21 March and ultimately from all of northeastern France. The initial success of the offensive had much to do with Foch being able to send the Americans, and their French allies, into battle employing on a grand scale what the 1st Division had seen in its assault on Cantigny: artillery in rolling barrages, tanks, airplanes, and masses of infantrymen to overwhelm the stunned foe. Sustaining the first morning's level of mechanized warfare proved impossible on a front nearly seventy-five miles long. Moreover, unusually heavy rain soon turned the battlefield into a muddy quagmire, but in the opening hours the Allies' offensive surprised the enemy and the claw-back of French territory began.[23]

At 4:35 A.M. on Thursday, 18 July, with no advance artillery bombardment, nearly half a million French and American soldiers "went over the top" and caught the enemy largely by surprise. Among American infantrymen the battle was usually considered a continuation of the fight at Château-Thierry; however, it soon became known as both the Second Battle of the Marne and the Aisne-Marne offensive. The latter designation referred to the two rivers flowing westward through key cities Soissons, held by the Germans, and Château-Thierry, largely in Allied control and twenty-five miles to the south. These two cities, together with Reims, at thirty-six miles to the east and equidistant from both Soissons and Château-Thierry, formed an isosceles triangle framing a valley of gentling rolling hills slit by ravines. This bucolic setting of 450 square miles (288,000 acres) was an agricultural basin in which wheat predominated. Throughout the fields were splashes of crimson from the ubiquitous poppy, portending in its color a bloody summer in 1918 and thereafter adopted as the symbolic flower of remembrance each Memorial Day.

The Allies' Aisne-Marne offensive would eliminate the curving bulge encompassing approximately seventy-five miles of front created four months earlier and retake Soissons. To remove this salient, its west and south extensions were simultaneously attacked beginning on Thursday, 18 July. The strategy was to push back the western edge of the salient quickly and retake the road connecting Soissons to Château-Thierry, which was accomplished within four days. Once the main western supply route was severed, the southern edge of the salient could be squeezed on two sides. The enemy realized their predicament on 21 July and began an orderly withdrawal from the Marne, defending the relocation of their artillery and supplies by fighting to delay and disrupt the Allies advancing eastward and northward. The topography between the Marne and Aisne aided them. Scattered throughout this region were what the Americans came to call islettes—small, dense woods surrounded by large expanses of open fields stabbed with ravines. Belleau Wood had all these features, and many more such defensive islettes existed. As the enemy retreated into islettes, their machine guns and artillery killed and slowed the advancing Allies.[24]

New Mexicans were present in all the attacking divisions—the 3rd and 28th Divisions from the south, which were embedded within French units, and the 1st and 2nd Divisions from the west, which fought as self-contained divisions alongside French divisions. At the pivot point between the attacking forces from the west and south were two other divisions—4th and 26th—each initially supported by the 146th FA. The 42nd Division was in reserve, fifteen miles behind the front line of the 4th Division. Batteries A and B soon moved diagonally to the northeast. The battle to regain Soissons took two weeks, but the 1st and 2nd Divisions were in combat the opening four days and then relieved. The remaining American troops in the 3rd, 4th, 26th, 28th, and 42nd Divisions were on the battlefield longer—some for nearly seven weeks.[25]

The 1st Division lost a New Mexican in the each of the first three days of the Aisne-Marne offensive. Immediately after fighting commenced, Sgt. Kenneth K. Burns of Grant County led a three-man team into the fray to string "multiplexed wire, allowing them to carry simultaneously telephone and telegraph traffic." Sergeant Burns had turned seventeen just two weeks previously. He entered college at age fourteen, but when his country declared war his mother consented to his desire to enlist, and he sailed with the first contingent of troops in June 1917. In the army he quickly set himself apart. By mid-July 1918 he already had received three citations for bravery and was to go to officer training school at the end of month. He stood six foot two inches, weighed 165 pounds, and was a born leader. His three-man team was unable to use pack horses to carry the "great reels of wire" because the horses had not yet arrived due to the haste with which the 1st Division had been dispatched. So the signal corps' "tireless workers converted themselves into pack horses" and hauled "wire for miles" to set up communications. Although the element of surprise was with the 1st Division, they covered just over two miles that first day, and most of that gain came in the morning. Sergeant Burns and his squad came under heavy artillery shelling as they strung wire to the front. When a shell landed near them, killing all three, Burns died instantly, "a piece of enemy shell passing through [his] forehead."[26]

On 19 July at 4:00 A.M.—first light—the Allies began day two of the battle for Soissons and immediately encountered redoubled resistance: "The enemy, alarmed by the overwhelming of his chosen troops and the rapid Allied advance ... reinforced his line, strengthened his artillery, and thickened his machine guns." Casualties soon mounted in the 1st Division, 26th Infantry, including thirty-one-year-old Pvt. Earl Elliott, single and a rancher from Union County. He had enlisted in May 1917 and was among soldiers in the first contingent to arrive in France. His mother remembered him for his steadfastness: "I never knew him to shirk no matter how hard the job was." On the second day of the battle for Soissons, his battalion's mission was to push ahead at least three miles across corn fields and take control of the road connecting Soissons to Paris. Private Elliott—and hundreds more like him in the 26th Infantry—went forward unreservedly that day:

> The echelon ranks rose and followed the protective barrage that beat the ground ahead of them. Almost instantly came the German reply. From what seemed like hundreds of machine guns was heard the rat-tat-tat-tat-tat that was so deadly in its significance and the air was torn by the shrieks of bullets. The losses came so rapidly that for a moment the forward echelon seemed to be withered. The officers dashed to the front of their men, and with shouts and gestures they led their units straight into the successive lines of machine guns. The enemy machine guns continued to fire until the gunners were killed. The remnants of the troops charged over the crest . . . and came under direct fire of batteries posted beyond. Here the one officer and the handful of men who remained dug in to hold what they had gained at such a heavy cost. In spite of heavy losses, the regiment reached a position across the Paris-Soissons road [and held it].

Private Elliott was among the "heavy losses" incurred that day. Several days later a Scottish division relieved the 1st Division, and "the first task of the [relief] division was to bury the many American dead still lying in swathes in the cornfields where they had fallen." The 1st Division's official report stated that its "losses were staggering."[27]

Pvt. Jose Felipe Archuleta, also from Union Country and in the 26th Infantry, survived the first two days but not the third. Born in mid-February 1891, he had been working in Wyoming as a sheepherder prior to the war. He was one of several thousand replacement troops the 1st Division received earlier in July to fill in for the losses at Cantigny. On Saturday, 20 July, the day's mission was every bit as formidable as on the previous two days. The infantrymen of the 26th were to capture the town of Berzy-le-Sec, which "stood on a prominent knoll almost surrounded by ravines" with thick brush and sloughs. Soissons was three miles to the northeast. At noon on a sunny, hot Saturday the Allies' heavy artillery bombarded Berzy-le-Sec for two hours before the 26th Infantry's assault began behind a rolling barrage at 2:00 P.M. The infantrymen moved unchecked at first. But as they approached the hill leading to the town the enemy's artillery and machine guns proved too much and stopped the advance at a point several hundred yards below the town, having inflicted heavy casualties, including Private Archuleta. The next day, after an intensive three-hour Allied artillery barrage, the infantry was finally able to overrun the town and control the road between Soissons and Château-Thierry. The following day the enemy began a measured retreat from the Marne front, and the next night the 1st Division was relieved. Late in the afternoon of 2 August, Soissons was once again under French control. In four days of fighting the 1st Division had lost 1,714 killed, 5,492 wounded, 76 missing, and 35 taken prisoners—a total of 7,317 casualties.[28]

Vesle River in the Oise-Aisne Offensive

On 24 July 1918—the first full day the 1st and 2nd Divisions began a period of rest and reorganization—Généralissime Ferdinand Foch outlined an offensive that would ultimately defeat the enemy, a victory all Allied military leaders assumed would come in 1919. Foch's plan turned into what his countrymen called the Battle of France or, for the British, the Hundred Days Battle. Ninety-three miles northeast of Soissons was the city of Mézières, the linchpin in the enemy's railroad supply line because through it passed hundreds of trains daily carrying all that sustained its troops in France and Belgium. Its capture—and the taking of cities such as Stenay along its rail line to the east—would fatally disrupt German logistics, and so Foch needed the Americans to commit to an inexorable fight—a war of attrition. What the American soldiers in the coming offensives never knew was that they were caught in a doubly deadly set of doctrines, one French and one American. Foch's war of attrition would be accelerated for them because of Pershing's insistence on a policy of open warfare—the soldier with a rifle and bayonet charging the enemy—which in the blistering critique of one distinguished military historian amounted to "smothering German machine guns with American flesh." It is also an apt epitaph for many of the casualties incurred during all AEF offensives because "infantry advanced in long lines or bunched together, machine-gun nests were rushed rather than outflanked, and units failed to maintain coordinated attacks and had great difficulty arranging adequate artillery support."[29]

Généralissime Foch's plan designated Thursday, 8 August 1918, as the first stage in his campaign of attrition with the launch of the Oise-Aisne offensive, but in fact for New Mexican soldiers it had begun on 24 July. One of the newly arrived soldiers to the Aisne-Marne offensive was twenty-seven-year-old Pvt. Benjamin W. Kemp, a rancher from Magdalena in Socorro County. His experience was representative of the intensity and danger faced by New Mexicans assigned to the 28th Division in the final weeks of the Aisne-Marne offensive and the beginning of the Oise-Aisne offensive on 8 August. Private Kemp was part of the September 1917 draft call-up from Socorro County, and he went briefly to Camp Funston but on 24 October was sent to Camp Kearny. He arrived at Le Havre in mid-July and nine days later stepped off a crowded troop transport train near Château-Thierry.

> [I was] then assigned to Co[mpany] A 109the Infantry July 27. Marched through Chateau-Thierry morning of 27 July. Came under shell fire evening 27th. Advanced to position just west of Courmont [a village almost midway between Château-Thierry and Fismes, twenty-three miles northeast]. Three men killed, four wounded from shell fire out of Co. A evening 28th. Advanced in to Courmont morning 29th, two men killed three wounded out of first platoon A Co., was covered with dirt from explosion [of a] shell myself. Moved to wheat field evening of 29th. Shelled and shot at by German aviators.[30]

Several days ahead of the 28th Division and moving about twenty miles northeast from Château-Thierry was the 42nd Rainbow Division. Late on Friday afternoon, 26 July, they waded into wheat fields and attacked a stone farmhouse and outbuildings, which the enemy used as an antiaircraft artillery site. The ensuing combat became known as the Battle of La Croix Rouge farm, which locals understood not in the literal sense—Red Cross farm—but in its connotation—Mercy farm. On a Friday afternoon and night in July 1918, the site showed no one mercy.

Wave upon wave of 42nd infantrymen attacked a well-defended position without artillery support before finally overwhelming the enemy. The battalion principally involved was drawn from Alabama and Iowa national guardsmen, and among these were one soldier each from New Mexico—Pvt. Jack Martin, Sierra County, and Pvt. Ernest O. Emerson of Roswell. It is not known what became of these two soldiers, but sanguinary fighting at La Croix Rouge farm lasted four hours. Soldiers ran a gauntlet of artillery and machine guns that inflicted 65 percent casualties, and the survivors' final charge was followed by hand-to-hand fighting. A commanding officer reported on the carnage: "The ground was literally covered with the killed and wounded, both American and German. For some distance you could actually walk on dead men."[31]

On 27 July the Rainbow Division's surviving troops pushed ahead to where the American offensive had stalled, about four miles to the north in a small wooded area. Here Germans redoubled their resistance atop a hill known as

Grimpettes Wood. The enemy troops were ordered to hold the Americans at bay for as long as possible to allow their retreating artillery and supplies to cross the Vesle River five and a half miles to the north. Rain had resumed for two days as the first companies of the 28th Division moved into position on 24 July to attack Grimpettes Wood, fronted for over five hundred yards by a gently rising open field. The 28th's infantry trudged to their position, but the division's 75 mm guns encountered "a sea of mud. Heavy artillery and transports sunk in the mud up to the hubs." As a result, the 146th FA could provide only lateral artillery fire from the west when they arrived nearby on the 27th, the third day of assaults. Six frontal attacks in open warfare fashion resulted in over 1,100 American casualties at Grimpettes Wood between 24 and 29 July.[32]

Finally, late on Monday, 29 July, all artillery came into position near Grimpettes Wood and intense shelling began. A coordinated "sweeping artillery fire had almost completely destroyed the woods" when the infantry entered it at 2:30 in the afternoon on 30 July. Soldiers from the 42nd Division (replacing a French division) augmented the 28th and a newly arrived 32nd Division (Michigan and Wisconsin National Guard) to overwhelm the remaining enemy. Private Kemp reported on the final attack:

> On the evening of July 30th at 8:00 o'clock the first battalion charged up Hill 204 [at Grimpettes Wood]. A company captured 15 or 20 Germans in a wheat field the other side of hill[;] after[ward] we had orders to fall back to the woods on the hill. Germans laid down a barrage. Lieutenant called for volunteers to carry in wounded, [I] helped pack wounded back to first aid station until after dark, got separated from company, reported missing in action, made acting sergeant of stretcher bearers. Fell back to trenches on morning August 1st.[33]

Grimpettes Wood claimed two Nuevomexicanos: on 28 July, Pvt. Liberato Jaramillo (109th Infantry, 28th Division) of Valencia County; on the 29th, Pvt. Jose Leon Madrid (109th Infantry) of San Miguel County. Privates Jaramillo and Madrid were draftees who went first to Camp Funston in early October but after several weeks were sent to Camp Kearny, where they spent some time in the 164th Developmental Battalion. They had been in France less than a month when they were killed. Both men had worked herding cattle before being drafted. Private Jaramillo was twenty-six and Private Madrid twenty-two when they died.[34]

Cpl. Andres S. Ribera of Santa Fe participated in the assaults carried out by the 109th Infantry at Grimpettes Wood. He wrote his eyewitness account upon returning home in mid-June 1919. As with so many of the New Mexicans in the 28th Division, Corporal Ribera enlisted in the New Mexico National Guard, trained briefly in Albuquerque, and arrived at Camp Kearny in mid-October 1917. Prior to his military service he had worked as a laborer at a hotel in Santa Fe, had completed the eighth grade, and was twenty-years old when he arrived in France as a replacement troop on 14 July 1918. Seven days later he was placed in the 28th Division near the front at Château-Thierry, just as the enemy began retreating from the Marne River. Six days after that he first saw Grimpettes Wood:

> Next morning we marched to the front line without eating and hiked all day and it was raining all day, too, and we went through a plow[ed] field, which [left us] surly since there we started our hardships, [which lasted] until we got near the front line where [things] were worse. We were about three or four miles [from the fighting] when we went near the woods on which since [from] these we started to lose some of our men, because the enemy shelled us all morning. Next day in the morning between 6 and 8 o'clock we went over the top, that was on July 28, 1918, but when we went over the top the enemy open[ed] fire at us from both sides, left and right and on the center, which caused heavy casualties, losing both of our officers because they did not even last half an hour after the battle had started and we were without officers since that very hour on which we were left under machine gun fire and also under shell fire, too, and not even that [was the worst of it] but our own artillery was firing short and we were even suffering our own artillery fire, but that same evening about seven o'clock they brought us back of the front line. . . . Next morning when I awaked I felt my gas burns of mustard gas on my arm, legs, hips and other different parts of my body.

Corporal Ribera spent two months in an AEF hospital recovering from the effects of mustard gas and returned to the 28th Division in mid-October.[35]

After Pvt. Benjamin W. Kemp rejoined Company A, 109th Infantry, 28th Division, and rested a few days from the fighting in Grimpettes Wood, the division "started [to] march for Fismes [on] Aug. 5th, breathed gas on night of Aug. 9th, knocked out by exploding shell on evening of Aug. 11th while company was taking over front line. Sent to Base Hospital No. 7 [near Tours, 190 miles southwest of Fismes]" and to two other hospitals in France and the United States. The town of Fismes and the village of Fismette opposite it across the Vesle River and the nearby areas on both sides of the river were the last part of the salient to be retaken in the Aisne-Marne offensive. Fighting to control Fismes and Fismette occasioned one of the most controversial engagements of the war for the Americans. The French general in command ordered taking and holding a bridgehead in Fismette while supporting the attack from Fismes. It was a foolhardy decision fully recognized as untenable by the Americans, but they dutifully obeyed the order. Hundreds of soldiers in the 28th Division's 112th and 109th Infantry died in fighting at Fismette and Fismes, including one New Mexican killed on the Vesle River near Fismes several days before the main assault, likely sent as part of a reconnaissance patrol. Max Delgar of Socorro County died on 3 August, two months before his twenty-first birthday. He had joined the New Mexico National Guard in June 1917, went to France a year later, and served in Company L of the 109th Infantry. His death seemed like abandonment to his mother, his only surviving parent, a loss made the more painful because more than two years after the war ended she had not received the insurance money she claimed was due her.[36]

The tragedy at Fismette was actually an opening salvo in Généralissime Foch's next stage of the offensive, which folded seamlessly into the Oise-Aisne offensive from 8 August to 10 September. Americans, in concert with French divisions, were to continue pressing the enemy north along the front from Soissons to Reims. The aim was not to make a breakthrough at any single point; instead, the goal was to keep the enemy in steady retreat everywhere. This meant that the 28th Division, joined by the 4th Regular Army Division and the 32nd Division, fought along the Vesle west and east of Fismes and pushed the enemy between five and seven miles north of the river. In these attacks and counterattacks, no one in New Mexico knew that the thirty-three New Mexicans killed in combat along the river were the highest number of combat deaths from the state that summer.[37]

One survivor's battlefield account is representative of what the several hundred New Mexicans endured along the Vesle River. Pvt. Delfin Sabedra was twenty-five years old, claimed he had "no education," had lived in a village in Valencia County, and was a draftee sent as a replacement troop. His first day in combat with the 109th Infantry, 28th Division, occurred on 31 July, and five days later he was in a makeshift trench a short distance south of Fismes. Upon being picked to locate the company's rolling kitchen and carry food back to his squad, Private Sabedra set about finding another soldier to accompany him: "I wanted him to go with me as I was terribly scared because the enemy's artillery was hitting us in this place." His concern was well founded. Anyone heading to the rear, whether in an ambulance or on foot as a messenger or retrieving food, could expect to be targeted by the enemy's artillery batteries. Private Sabedra successfully completed this mission, but "when we arrived with the food another order arrived that our squad was to leave."[38]

Shortly afterward his squad began "working until two in the morning making a trench for a machine gun and waited for an attack by the enemy like on another day. About ten in the morning when I was falling asleep [was] when a gas shell drenched me that hit above my trench." He was likely the victim of the poison liquid diphosgene, a lethal lung irritant. Though his gas mask saved his life, it did not fully protect him. Private Sabedra returned home and a week before Thanksgiving day 1919, when he reported "feel[ing] yet the consequences" of being gassed, he wrote about his wartime experiences. At the end of his account, he expressed regrets about his conduct during the war. Whether it was so-called survivor's guilt or anxiety from another source, few admitted to it so soon after the war's end. Sabedra concluded his statement with this lament: "On occasion, I have not been man enough, forgive me." Whatever the inner turmoil he alluded to, he went on with his life and in the 1930 census was listed as working as a farm laborer in Valencia County, was married, and had three children. A forgiving assessment of combat veterans came from wartime secretary of the navy Josephus Daniels in 1932. He lauded veterans in a rhyming couplet—"Slept in mud, Bathed in blood"—and praised them for creating productive lives after their discharge.[39]

St. Mihiel Offensive

The Oise-Aisne offensive ended on 10 September, and on Thursday, 12 September, another major offensive began at the St. Mihiel salient on the Toul front, 110 miles southeast of Fismes (see map 3). It ended the following Monday (16th) with the front line pushed about thirty miles north of Toul. In the run-up to this battle, the largest contingents of New Mexicans were in the 89th Division of the National Army and Battery A of the 146th Field Artillery. The 28th Division of the National Guard did not participate in this offensive since they had no time to replenish their losses from the Oise-Aisne offensive.

The National Army soldiers from New Mexico had never been so wet and cold as in late summer 1918. They dutifully endured ankle-deep mud during eight-day rotations in trenches. Assigned to the 89th Division, the New Mexicans came from throughout the state, and since mid-July they had been posted about 160 miles east of Paris and a dozen miles northwest of Toul. This town of about 13,000 anchored the southern end of the Meuse River valley, and some forty miles distant was Verdun, where ten months of fighting between February and

December 1916 resulted in more than 300,000 French and German soldiers killed and at least 450,000 wounded—all to produce a stalemate.[40]

In early September 1918, New Mexicans near Toul were a mere speck in an army that soon swelled to 1.2 million Americans in the region. But their presence made a lasting impression on Ashley Pond, a Red Cross Canteen volunteer from central New Mexico who spent several months with them. He especially noted encounters with Spanish-speaking natives, the Nuevomexicano "boys from Mora, Las Vegas, Santa Fe, Las Cruces—every place in New Mexico seemingly represented," and each incident "gave a little stronger tug at my heart strings than the sight of our other American boys." Pond did not enter frontline trenches, but he would come across New Mexicans patrolling "a lonesome dark road in the beating rain" and delighted in seeing "those faces light up at the familiar sound of '¿Cómo está, amigo?' sprung unawares at them." Whenever troops moved from the front trenches to the rear, Pond was there to offer them coffee and donuts and was always touched by the willingness of Nuevomexicanos to serve so far from home—more than 5,300 miles from Santa Fe—"in this land of chilling rain—a desperate contrast to our almost perpetual sunshine." Pond's account conflates encounters during at least ten weeks, and he omits mention of drinks stronger than coffee. But reports from Companies B and F of the 356th Infantry for August mentioned that their troops in the rear "made the acquaintance of those famous French sisters 'Vin Blanche' and 'Vin Rouge,'" and the orders to move into position for the St. Mihiel offensive came "just before the men had completed their task of enforcing prohibition by drinking the town dry."[41]

The 89th Division's trenches were on the lower slope of a drainage that rose to 500 feet above them just half a mile to their northwest at Montsec, a promontory doubly mocking them. For four years German soldiers held it and monitored every move across a wide horizon. But the cruelest affront came in the name: Dry Mountain. When it rained—as it did often from August through November—it shed water onto the marshes below and turned trenches into bogs. The Germans had seized and held a triangle of land encompassing about 200 square miles since the war's first months, and at its eastern tip was the German-occupied town of St. Mihiel, where their advance had stalled. For four years this area was a conspicuous bulge in a nearly 500-mile western front. For several years both the German and French military considered this portion of the front a quiet zone that provided a brief respite to fatigued troops.

Although the fight at St. Mihiel lasted only four days, preparation for this offensive had been under way for eight months. The 21st Engineers began working in January to provide railroads vital to the transport of troops, ammunition, and food. Divisions had been gradually entering the Toul sector for training since early spring, activity a wary enemy monitored from heavily fortified Montsec. As new units arrived, the enemy regularly directed artillery barrages against them, shelling that also fell onto nearby railroad construction crews. Pvt. Adolph Abeyta, a volunteer out of Las Vegas assigned to the 21st Engineers, summarized events from April into September:

> On April 5th the Germans, no doubt having learned that the 26th, then a new division, had just taken over the [front] lines, heavily shelled the Sector with H.E. [high explosives] and gas. A detachment of Company A men, working on the grade near Raulecourt [about five miles due south of Montsec] was caught in shell fire directed at a battery that was located nearby. Owing to the fact, no doubt, that one of the members of the party was carrying a horseshoe, no one was injured although all were covered with mud from head to foot. During the spring and on into summer we continued to send off detachments on new construction . . . each with varying experiences.[42]

As more divisions entered the Toul sector between June and August, the enemy targeted each with artillery barrages on their first day or two in the trenches. Likely a casualty of such shelling was Pvt. Pedro S. Romero of the 1st Division. After his unit's relief on 24 July, they had moved 150 miles from near Soissons to the far east side of the Toul sector around Pont-à-Mousson, on the Moselle River twenty miles northeast of Toul at the point where the salient had been pushed southwest from the front line in 1914. There the 1st Division entered the trenches on the night of 4–5 August. On 6 August, Private Romero of Tucumcari—who enlisted in early October 1917, went to France as a replacement troop from Camp Kearny, and turned sixteen on 1 August—died in what the AEF called "local actions."[43]

The enemy's artillery attack on newly arrived troops took a decidedly aggressive turn when the 89th Division began its frontline duty in early August adjacent to the 1st Division on its east. The enemy's poison gas attack began "just hours after the last of [the 89th's] regiments had taken its place in the trenches." On the night of 7 August and early morning of the 8th, companies of the 354th and 355th Infantries became the target of the war's most deadly gas attack on an AEF division as it arrived at the front. In two bombardments of ninety minutes each separated by several hours, Companies B and D of the 354th and Companies A, C, and D of the 355th Infantry suffered a total of 598 casualties among 1,250 soldiers (48 percent). A contemporary account stated that 376 gas shells exploded on the three companies of the 355th. Based on the rosters of these two regiments, forty-one New Mexicans served in them, with thirty-five (85 percent) assigned to the 355th. From among the five companies affected in the mustard gas attack, eyewitness Ashley Pond said that "many New Mexico boys" were among the victims.[44]

In 1917 the Germans had introduced two chemical weapons of mass destruction: diphenylchlorarsine (also known simply as arsine), a powder that caused uncontrollable sneezing as well as vomiting and headaches; and, most pernicious of all, mustard gas, or dichloroethyl sulfide, first used in July 1917. Mustard gas could remain on clothing or in the soil for several days or weeks (depending on the weather), maximizing its delayed release and enabling it to continue blistering skin, destroying body tissue, blinding, and if breathed causing internal bleeding. These two types of poison gas shells were particularly effective when combined in an artillery barrage, a tactic employed on 7–8 August. As one observer wrote: "Starting with just a little arsine so you couldn't keep a [gas] mask on for sneezing, they shot over [a] very high concentration of mustard gas."[45]

Fortuitous positioning of many other New Mexicans in the 355th saved them from becoming casualties in the arsine/mustard gas attack. Had the wind blown out of the northeast rather than the northwest, the mustard gas would have carried onto Company B, which was immediately west of the affected area and had fourteen New Mexicans assigned it. No subsequent gas attack along the Toul sector wounded and killed on the scale of the bombardment on 7–8 August, but the enemy's poisonous gas shelling yielded a steady number of casualties on this front throughout August.[46]

When the 89th entered the trenches in early August, the standing orders for holding the Toul front stated unequivocally that "combat groups would not leave their position but would hold to the last [i.e., capture or death]. No modification was mentioned in the case of mustard gas." Two weeks after the attack the division's inspector reported that "the enlisted men did as ordered" and for forty hours maintained their discipline "in an exemplary manner" while occupying gassed trenches. The report found that the chief "reasons for heavy list of casualties" were inadequate training and lapses in leadership. A 1960 study harshly criticized division leaders at all levels for failing to assess the danger:

> The 89th Division, from its commanders down to its company officers, would not believe, in their first encounter with German yellow cross gas

[mustard gas] in August, that contaminated ground could not be occupied. The division suffered over 600 gas cases before its French superiors arrived on the scene and ordered the gassed area evacuated. . . . It would be interesting to speculate on the number of companies and battalions that might have been used up through continuous replacement of gassed units on that occasion before the division finally came to realize its folly.[47]

In the immediate aftermath of the gas attack the 89th instituted new training in the use of gas masks and enforced regular inspections for the masks' serviceability. Another response to the attack was stepped-up intelligence gathering through nighttime patrols and raids. This increased activity had fatal consequences for Pvt. Jesse R. Cross, assigned to Company E of the 356th Infantry. His good friend, Damiano C. de Baca, laconically recorded his death: "First man killed [in Company E] was sniper Jesse P. [R.] Cross, [who] was killed by our own men taking him for German on August 15." Thirty-year-old Private Cross, a rancher from Chaves County, spent one month training at Camp Funston and had qualified as a marksman, hitting small targets at 100, 200, 300, and 600 yards with at least eighty-five out of one hundred shots. In late July he rejoined the nine other New Mexicans in his company after a three-week quarantine because of exposure to measles. When killed, Private Cross was either in no-man's-land or behind enemy lines when felled by friendly fire. His parents and eight brothers and sisters reportedly found solace in the words of his company captain: "Although your son was killed by accident, he was doing his duty in the front lines. . . . He died an honorable death."[48]

The first time the 146th FA used poisonous gas was during the St. Mihiel offensive. These artillery shells were filled with yperite, a form of mustard gas. Battery A arrived at the Toul sector during the night of 28–29 August and the next day positioned its guns five miles northeast of the town of Sommedieue, which became the brigade headquarters and was located fourteen miles north of St. Mihiel near the point where the western bulge in the front line began and just six miles due west of Verdun. They hauled their 155 mm GFPs and an ammunition inventory of 3,806 artillery shells into position for their third frontline combat shelling. Thus two of the state's three concentrations of soldiers were on the western and southern sections of the St. Mihiel salient. The 28th Division continued to fight along the Vesle River until moving due east beginning 10 September toward their next staging area at Chermont-en-Argonne, located twenty-two miles due west of the 146th FA headquarters in Sommedieue.[49]

Batteries A and B found their new position "heavily wooded and very rolling and rugged" but also "a welcome change from the fields [of the summer offensives] filled with innumerable dead horses and men and plowed up with the intensive artillery fire." They also embraced receipt of yperite shells. The brigade's official history reported that "it was with a quiet satisfaction that the men rammed these projectiles filled with poisonous gas" into their guns' firing chambers. On the evening of 11 September the battery received orders to "cut the trees in front of the guns in order to commence firing on the following morning." At 1:00 A.M. on Thursday, 12 September, they began a seven-hour artillery barrage that "belched forth a fusillade of shells until it seemed that the woods were alive with nothing but artillery of all calibers." Batteries A and B expended 1,530 shells (an undetermined number of which were gas) during the four days of the offensive, with 37 percent (564) launched on 12 September. The 146th FA's primary objective was to "cut off the retreat of the enemy from the southern portion of the salient through constant artillery fire." Their success was evident in the estimates of 13,000–17,000 prisoners rounded up.[50]

The infantrymen of the 89th Division occupied a ten-mile stretch of trenches from 7 August until 9–10 September, with the 355th and 356th—in which the majority of the division's New Mexicans served—positioned in the trenches from just west of Montsec to about five miles to the east where they faced Bois de Mort Mare (Dead Pond Forest). The 146th FA found their wooded area ideal cover for their guns, but the soldiers in the 355th and 356th realized that the area above them was a death trap akin to Belleau Wood. Poppies blooming on the hillside facing them belied the dangers beyond. Three sets of hills lay ahead, divided by marshy valleys, and "running diagonally across these and valleys [was] a continuous belt of dense forest." Bois de Mort Mare was an amply appointed devil's butcher shop.

> Across from Flirey was that tower of defense in the German line—the Mort Mare Wood. All that could be seen of it from our lines was a confusion of wire and gnarled trees. But the enemy had dug and cut and tunneled and wired and built until he made the wood a more impregnable fortress than the strongest castle of old. In its strong dugouts large numbers could be held ready to repel an attack. . . . Its concrete pill boxes were carefully made, its wire high and wide.[51]

After dark on 9 September the 89th Division began to shrink its presence from ten miles of front line to about two and a half miles. Filling in to their west and facing Montsec were the 1st Division, with the 42nd Division on its east, then the 89th Division poised to attack Bois de Mort Mare. Bordering the 89th on the east was the 2nd Division. The 89th was assigned a significant objective—the defeat of two enemy divisions lodged in front of them in Bois de Mort Mare.

It began raining early in the evening of 11 September and continued for more than thirty-six hours, sometimes as a torrent. The march into the trenches and the hours preceding the assault were vividly recalled by New Mexicans in several different companies of the 356th Infantry. Pvt. Manuel Rodriguez, a twenty-four-year-old railway worker from Española in Rio Arriba County assigned to Company I, had a limited grammar school education and drew liberally from the company's official history:

> The morning of September 12th, 1918, probably marks the beginning of the most notable and exciting day in the experiences of the men of Co. "I," 356th Infantry. On the night of Sept 11th we had moved out of Hazel Wood [the forest behind Flirey] up into dugouts, located on the reverse side of a hill in what had been dubbed by the French as "Gas Hollow" [site of the bombardment on 7–8 August]. The next morning about 12:30 AM, stripped of all excess equipment, we filed out thru a long and muddy communication trench to our position facing the enemy. The night was so dark and the footing so uncertain that it was imperative that the boys take hold of each other and form a continuous chain to keep from becoming separated and lost. After about two hours of this we reached our position. From that time on to zero hour [5:00 A.M.] was perhaps the most trying time for all.[52]

Pvt. Jack D. Trainor, thirty years old from Santa Fe and in Company L of the 356th Infantry, recounted in his own words the night of 11 September and early morning of the 12th, an experience shared by all New Mexicans at St. Mihiel:

> In the evening it started to rain as usual and it just seemed to pour that night. Our men were all standing in groups under the large trees [at Hazel Wood] and getting such shelter as they could and about midnight orders came for us to move into the front line trenches at Flirey. We moved through the trenches in mud and water the best we could until we got to our respective places and then waited for music. At one o'clock in the A.M. of Sept 12th the allied barrage opened up, their artillery included every size from the one pounder [37 mm mortar shells] up to the big 16 inch naval guns [mounted on specially adapted railroad cars] and were placed about 40 meters apart. From 1 A.M. until 5 A.M. the artillery kept up a steady roar, the flashes of the big guns kept it lighted up as if it were day, and it was so

noisy that it was nearly impossible to make the man that was next to you to be heard no matter how loud he shouted.[53]

Then, as suddenly as it had begun, the artillery barrage ceased at 4:55 A.M., followed immediately by divisional machine gun fire arched over the Americans' heads to suppress enemy gunfire. The shout to "Go over the top" came "at 5:00 A.M. sharp." Private Trainor described the first hour of the St. Mihiel ground offensive:

> Fritz was laying over a heavy barrage and shrapnel was whistling through the air everywhere. We had just started over when two of our officers—Lieut Schinn and Lieut Macatee—were wounded but they refused to be evacuated and kept with us until later when their condition necessitated their removal and they were sent back. With no officers the non-commissioned officers [sergeants] were compelled to take their men on [the offensive]. We crossed the shattered [enemy] trenches and pressed on through heavy belts of barbed wire entanglements.[54]

Three noteworthy tactical maneuvers occurred during the St. Mihiel offensive. One of these was entirely spontaneous. The American infantrymen did not wait for the engineers and others assigned to cut the barbed wire barricades. They got atop them and walked across, an act that amazed French officials when they learned of what happened and insisted it be re-created to verify they did so. The other two tactical innovations represented lessons learned since early June. One was to not attempt a frontal assault against heavily fortified positions, which in this offensive meant Montsec and Bois de Mort Mare. Instead the divisions outflanked each fortified area, fought their way to encircle it, and while troops held firm at the front the infantry troops squeezed the enemy's position from the sides and the rear. This maneuver had never been rehearsed by the AEF. Employing it was fraught with the possibility of friendly-fire accidents, but no reports of such losses are in the official records or in accounts by New Mexicans. Another lesson learned represented an abandonment of open warfare's use of tightly massed troops. Instead the infantrymen were well spaced, often twenty feet apart, at staggered intervals, and led by a rolling artillery barrage. But unquestionably the greatest advantage for the American troops was a decision by the German high command just prior to the battle to abandon the St. Mihiel salient. The date set for their full pullout was 15 September, but the departure of artillery had begun on 11 September. The decision to withdraw demoralized the enemy in the salient and, though resistance was at times fierce, it was nothing like what might have occurred had the enemy's troops fought a sustained, pitched battle.[55]

Among the seven thousand casualties at St. Mihiel were some New Mexicans. From Company I, Pvt. Manuel Salazar, a miner from Rio Arriba County who had his twenty-second birthday just three days before the offensive began, was wounded shortly after going over the top but continued to fight until later in the day, when his wounds required attention. His squad leader, a corporal from Missouri, reported that while Private Salazar was on his way to a field hospital an enemy artillery shell exploded near him, killing him instantly. Among the wounded at St. Mihiel were Robert S. Smith and brothers Robert and John Keller. Little is known about Smith except that on 13 September he was hit by shrapnel so severely in his left arm that it had to be amputated. The Keller brothers from Lincoln County were in Company K of the 356th Infantry. At St. Mihiel both were hit by machine gun fire in the lower body, an area targeted by the enemy to cripple soldiers and drain resources by requiring extensive treatment. Twenty-seven-year-old Robert was hit in the hip and "was through four hospitals in France and two since coming to the U.S." He was treated at an army hospital near Ft. Worth, Texas, in late May 1919. At the same time, his brother John, who "was shot in the left thigh by machine gun," was at an army hospital in Houston. The state's Historical Service office was never able to determine the number of New Mexicans wounded during the St. Mihiel offensive.[56]

Within thirty-six hours of the 89th Division's infantrymen going over the top, they had rolled up all of their objectives and thoroughly routed the enemy. On 16 September divisions on the 89th's flanks were being prepared to redeploy northwest in advance of the Meuse-Argonne offensive, which began ten days later on 26 September. The 89th took over responsibility for holding most of the new front in the St. Mihiel salient. Assisting them on their southeast flank was the 90th Division (from Texas and Oklahoma, including twenty-seven New Mexicans). The 89th Division was centered in and around Beney, and Verdun was twenty-four miles to its northwest. The 90th occupied the southeastern portion of the new front, which put their 220 mm artillery within range of a major resupply railroad line passing through Metz less than fifteen miles to their northeast. The 89th would remain on the Beney front until relived on 7 October when it began heading to the Meuse-Argonne.[57]

Their ultimate objective was twenty-nine miles northwest of Verdun at Stenay, a railroad junction on the Meuse River that the 89th Division entered during the early morning of Monday 11 November.

CHAPTER 6

"Terror by Day and by Night"

The 28th Division moved in a northeasterly direction to the Argonne Forest after the St. Mihiel offensive. Upon arriving, they were positioned along the forest's southeastern edge parallel to the Aire River. Glimpsed from afar, the Argonne Forest presented a benign canopy. Beyond it the Aire tumbled along nearby, and though no bridges remained standing, it was generally fordable at depths of two to four feet. Coming nearer to the forest, though, proximity allowed the soldiers a frightening inspection. Upon entering the Argonne, one soldier in the division adjacent to the 28th described it as "a bleak, cruel country of white clay and rock and blasted skeletons of trees, gashed into innumerable trenches and scarred with rusted acres of [barbed] wire, rising steeply into claw-like ridges and descending into haunted ravines, white as leprosy in the midst of that green forest, a country that had died long ago, and in pain."[1]

28th Division in the Argonne Forest

The 28th Division, together with eight other AEF divisions, began its assault in the Meuse-Argonne offensive on Thursday, 26 September, at 5:30 A.M. French divisions bracketed the west and east flanks of the AEF. The 28th Division moved relentlessly north nearly six miles during the first two days of the offensive, all while enemy artillery bombarded them until they finally retook the village of Apremont, which was at the forest's edge a short distance from the Aire. Over the next ten days the 28th moved about four miles northwest toward the village of

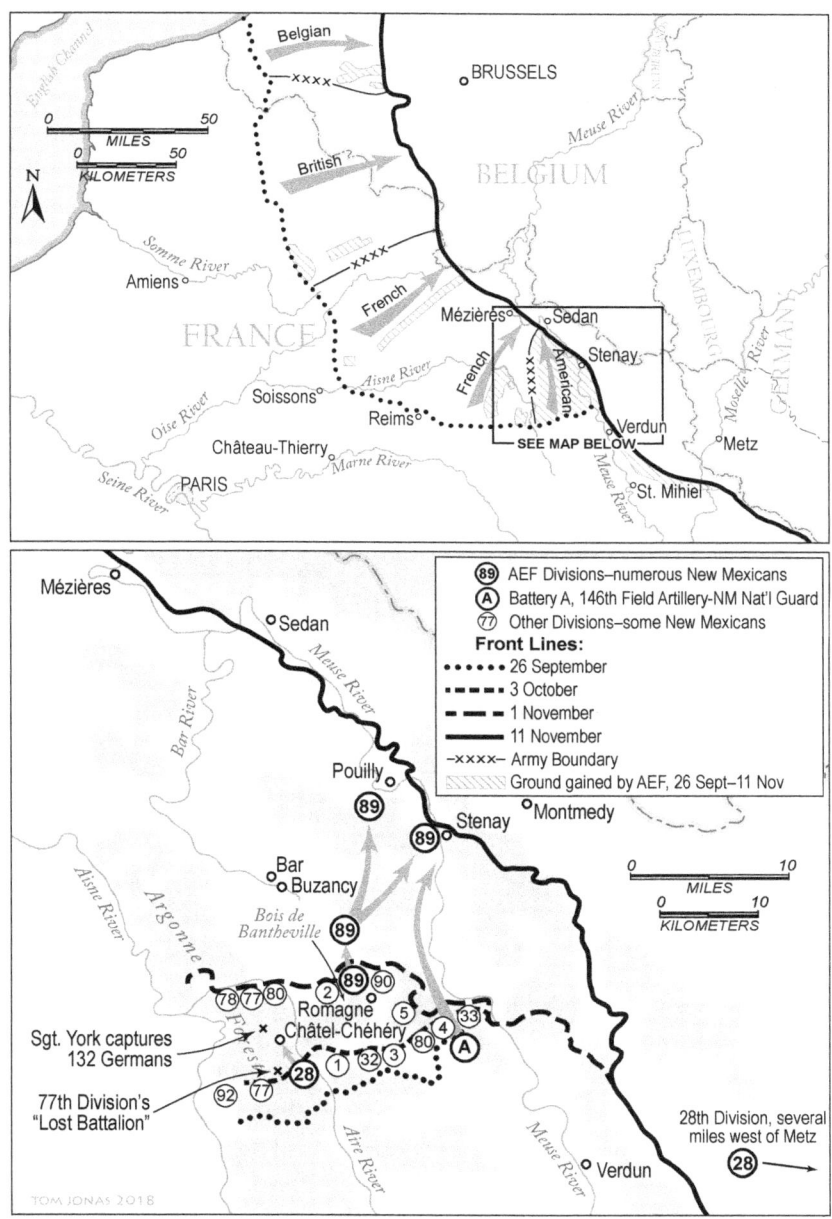

Map 4. The Meuse-Argonne offensive, 26 September to 11 November 1918.

Châtel-Chéhéry and prevailed against grueling counterattacks to finally capture it on 7 October. German resistance was accomplished through superiority in the air, artillery positioning, and machine gun placement—all of which greatly slowed AEF divisions in the Argonne for several weeks after 28 September. But delays such as the 28th Division encountered agitated Pershing. He demanded advances at whatever the cost, admonishing everyone to heed his tactical mandate that "energetic measures" be employed to carry out an "aggressive attack."[2]

Pfc. William N. Sibley of Deming, with Company B of the 109th Infantry of the 28th Division, lived through what Pershing described as "a direct frontal attack against strong, hostile positions." Sibley wrote a journal recounting his experiences in 1919. His episodic narrative mixed combat descriptions with recollections of the toll battles took on soldiers' minds and bodies. He quickly passed over the first day and a half of the Meuse-Argonne offensive to focus on seven incidents that occurred during the next ten days. His telegraphic account re-created the war's unpredictable oscillation between terror and exhilaration, where the soldier's battlefield horizon was reduced to steeling himself against the sights and sounds of the dying and wounded while besieged by hunger, cold and rain, exhaustion, diarrhea, and the enemy's artillery and machine guns.[3]

Sibley's account is his own story, but it is also typical of what New Mexicans—and all soldiers—went through in the first weeks of the offensive:

> Then we moved up to a creek bottom that had a high bluff on the north side, so we dug in. The town of Apremont was a short distance ahead. After a short rest we moved out of the creek into an open field and ahead of us [were] some trees and bushes, where the Germans opened up machine guns and we all dropped to the ground. A man back of me got a bullet through him just above the hips. He kept hollering for help.... I crawled back to him.

Upon reaching the wounded man, Sibley was pinned down again as machine gun fire killed two men nearby and wounded one behind him. Fearing the next burst of fire, Sibley suddenly heard movement from behind. "A baby tank [a French-made Renault FT] rolled up from the creek and drove right up to the bushes and opened up a one-pounder [37 mm shell] on him. That was it. The Sgt. said get someone to help and take him back to first aid."[4]

The Meuse-Argonne marked the first extensive use of tanks. None from U.S. factories were available for this offensive, but the French provided the AEF 355 Renault FTs. Lt. Col. George S. Patton commanded the first American tank battalion, but he was wounded early in the Meuse-Argonne offensive. The tanks lumbered on, although most of them never reached their maximum speed of just under five miles per hour. One scholar succinctly noted their significance for military history: "There were no grand drives in 1918 for the Renaults, only a monotonous string of brutish little engagements between Renaults and German defensive positions [primarily machine gun nests]. These skirmishes may not have represented the birth of the blitzkrieg, but they certainly heralded the end of trench warfare." Sibley saw one of these "brutish little engagements" and survived because of it.[5]

An all-night trek ensued to carry the wounded man to the first-aid station in a shelled-out village three miles in the rear. With each step mud oozed above their ankles, and a heavy downpour continued. Once there Sibley had to force overwhelmed aid station attendants to accept the wounded soldier. Next Sibley scrounged for something to eat. He could find only "a head of cabbage, I still had a little piece of corn beef and 2 hardtacks in my mess kit." Upon returning he reported to his first sergeant, who announced, "I've got some good news. We have been relieved for a few days, and got some chow. I didn't know which was the be[tter] news. That was the fourth day since we got a meal."

The next incident Sibley narrated involved the company's mess sergeant seeking answers to why no hot food had reached them for nearly ninety-six hours. What he uncovered was a mini-lesson in battlefield logistics. "The man that was supposed to bring the food up to us in a cart pulled by a horse would come up to where a few shells [were] falling, dump the food and go back. I never heard what happened to him." No doubt some food deliverers did flee at the first sign of danger, but more often their horses bolted when shells exploded nearby. Moreover, a general paralysis existed on byways caused by excessive traffic and mud that mired everything, which meant that the kitchen train (as it was called), typically pulled by horses (and mules sometimes), could not get anywhere near the front for days. But perhaps the most basic reason for delays in receiving food was a matter of priorities. All supplies came by rail from Bordeaux, and ammunition preceded food during offensives.

Sibley's fourth incident describes his return to combat in Apremont:

> In about 3 days we moved up to the front, pulled into Apremont. The road made a bend to the left, then on the north side was a block wall. We got orders to get against the wall. The Germans started to shell us as soon as we got to the town. . . . Casualties were being brought into Apremont, laid on the ground, some wounded some dead. As we slumped down against the wall a small German plane swooped down low, tilted his left wing, opened

up a machine gun, hit several men and disappeared. As I picked up my rifle leaning right in front of me, a piece had been knocked out of the stock.

Enemy aircraft controlled the skies during almost the entire offensive, allowing them to direct fire against AEF troops. The casualness with which Sibley realized how close he came to taking a bullet is characteristic of the "my number was not up" attitude adopted by most soldiers.

The regiment's next objective was to capture the village of Châtel-Chéhéry, which though only about three miles northwest of Apremont nevertheless required a week of intense fighting to reach. During that time,

> the Germans shelled us pretty heavy. Many of their shells were shrapnel shells [along] with mustard gas. Mustard gas was used mostly.... At one time a shell landed a few yards from where I was. I noticed a cloud of smoke spreading out just as I scooped my mask on. I got a whiff of the gas and was positive it was chlorine.... In about two days we moved on up to village called Chatel Chery. It was a hilly area and forest to the west and north.

The kitchen train had finally made it to Apremont, and Sibley and three others were sent on a six-mile round-trip mission to carry the food forward. "The question was how we would carry it. We lost one man on the way down, one fellow looked around and found a little cart. We put the big iron pot of stew on it, had some French bread and rice, started back." Sibley's cryptic reference to a "lost man" is likely not attrition due to casualty but rather a straggler. A week after this incident Lt. Gen. Hunter Liggett took command of the First Army, and a pressing issue was that an estimated 100,000 men—one-tenth of the troops then in the offensive—had drifted away from their assigned units to become a floating population at the rear. Just over 4 percent, about four thousand, of these stragglers were changed with desertion, but only 3.3 percent (132) were convicted. Some authorities believe the majority of stragglers were either lost after being separated from their units, sick, or shell-shocked and unable to function.[6]

When the chow detail arrived at Châtel-Chéhéry, B Company was in the woods west of town. Sibley's fatigue at this point was palpable: "It had rained all day, I slumped down in the bushes beside the road." Presently a sergeant came by and designated Sibley to join a reconnaissance squad drawn from various companies and led by a lieutenant. Sibley tried unsuccessfully to beg off: "I told him I couldn't walk very good, but he said this wouldn't be bad, he didn't think we were going very far." In fact they hiked miles farther into the woods. As nightfall approached, Sibley and several others were told to follow a corporal across an open field to make contact with another reconnaissance group from the division's 110th Infantry. That route brought them under repeated machine gun fire. "We would hit the ground for a few minutes then start again, run and drop." In returning they minimized risk by moving "below the open field where we were not seen by the Germans."

The seventh and final incident began "well after midnight Oct 8th" when the reconnoiterers rejoined their companies and learned that "the 82nd Division was relieving us. We hiked back quite a ways in the woods, camped and got a little sleep, then our regiment hiked all day, [and I was] dragging my right foot and nearly all of us had diarrhea." Sibley had endured much adversity and survived two grueling weeks of combat, but more than a thousand infantrymen in his division had fallen on the battlefield. Included among the dead were ten New Mexicans killed in action, four from the 109th and six from the 110th Infantry, and eight of them Nuevomexicanos.[7]

On 8 October 1918 the 28th Division passed within a few miles of the two most famous incidents for the AEF in World War I, both of which occurred on that day: Cpl. (later Sgt.) Alvin C. York killed twenty-one enemies and, together with a small squad, captured 132 prisoners; and the so-called Lost Battalion was rescued—an evacuation of the 194 AEF officers and infantrymen who survived from among 454 encircled and besieged for five days. New Mexicans had links to both events—tangentially to the first and as participant in the second. Private Sibley reflected on that day seven decades later (in 1981) and said that "the word came to us that they [82nd Division] captured all manner of prisoners." Although specific information about York's accomplishment did not come until later, Sibley clearly read books about York published in the 1920s. Surprisingly, though, he never mentioned that York's patrol traversed the same wooded area about a mile northwest of Châtel-Chéhéry that he had reconnoitered the previous night. Widespread and lasting public awareness of York's exploits came only after release of a major motion picture in 1941—starring Gary Cooper as the backwoods sharpshooter Alvin York, directed by the incomparable Howard Hawks and released ten weeks before the United States entered World War II.[8]

A New Mexican in the Lost Battalion

By the time *Sergeant York* drew audiences to theaters, World War I was receding in most Americans' consciousness and along with it the 1919 silent film *The Lost Battalion* directed by Burton L. King, a prolific silent-era movie maker. The cast included many of the participants playing themselves. Likewise completely forgotten is the significant participation of a New Mexican—twenty-seven-year-old Lt. Harry Rogers from Lakewood, a small community ten miles south of Artesia in Eddy County. He arrived in France in May 1918 but did not get his commission until 13 July. His assignment for the next two months was to the 367th Infantry, 92nd Division. This segregated division of black infantrymen elicited favorable comments from Rogers, and after a month they moved to the Vosges Mountains and took up positions in a quiet part of the front under the supervision of the French 87th Division. The 92nd began to move northwest to join the First Army in the Argonne Forest on 20 September. Rogers accompanied them but upon arrival about 29 September was assigned to the 77th Division, which he joined the next day and was placed in charge of depleted Company B of the 308th Infantry, with fifty-four men. He was the only officer in that company. Rogers arrived just as troops of the 308th Infantry broke free after a two-day enemy encirclement on a hill just beyond a cemetery in the Argonne. Neither Rogers nor anyone in the 308th realized that incident was a foretaste of impending combat, with the graveyard a harbinger of the killing field awaiting them.[9]

The 308th Infantry was under the command of Maj. Charles Whittlesey, a thirty-four-year-old National Army officer and Harvard-trained lawyer with a practice in New York City. Designated as the attack battalion on 2 October, the 308th would be the only unit in the entire First Army to take its objective that day. The orders of the division's commanding general, Maj. Gen. Robert Alexander, showed him to be a committed disciple of Pershing's dictum to push ahead on the battlefield regardless of casualties. He later characterized his orders that day as "quite positive and precise: the objective [Charlevaux Mill] was to be gained without regard to losses and without regard to the exposed conditions of flanks." Major Whittlesey's six depleted companies of the 308th and an additional company from the 307th had a total of 438 infantrymen and sixteen officers, which as manpower was less than the strength of two full companies. This force was expected to take their objective without knowing what they might encounter, absent any artillery support or nearby reinforcements, insufficiently supplied, and without regard for soldiers' lives. Disaster awaited on a nearby hillside.[10]

In the early afternoon they came upon unoccupied trenches defended solely by three machine guns clustered in a single nest. Major Whittlesey assigned Lieutenant Rogers to eliminate their fire, and at about 2:00 P.M. he judiciously deployed a twenty-man squad to outflank it, surround it from behind, and rush it while the rest of the company provided diversionary fire. Twenty-eight enemy infantrymen and two officers, one of whom spoke English, were captured in a fifty-minute engagement. It can only be speculated, but the tactic Rogers used may well have been learned from the French division that trained the 92nd Division. In any event, Rogers wisely pursued a cautious approach, one lauded by an authority on the AEF, who contrasted "Alexander's callous orders that 'objectives were to be gained without regard to losses'" with the fact that "the men of that division had learned better than to impetuously run headlong into machine-gun fire." Alexander had spent his first six months in France in charge of training newly arrived troops to be sent as replacements. In that capacity he had rigidly adhered to Pershing's doctrine of open warfare; he wrote after the war that "one principle was insisted upon—that training *for the open* was of primary value and that of that training the utilization of the rifle as a *firearm* was indispensable to success." Fortunately Lieutenant Rogers had trained under the French and learned combat tactics appropriate to the war's battlefields, lessons Alexander never imparted to the tens of thousands of AEF soldiers who passed through his base.[11]

A brief wire service dispatch appeared in the *Albuquerque Morning Journal* on 9 October that summarized events during the late afternoon and night of 2–3 October: "After a system of trenches running east and west had been captured near the [western] edge of the Argonne the Americans passed these trenches and gained ground [five-eighths of a mile] to the north. During the night German troops slipped to the rear and into the trenches captured earlier by the advancing forces. Meanwhile the Germans had closed in on the east and west, completing the circle."[12]

After the enemy closed the gap breached by Whittlesey's troops, the next five days would forever link the Argonne Forest combat with a group of soldiers from the 308th Infantry who came to be know, erroneously, as the Lost Battalion. They were neither a battalion nor lost; rather, they were seven weary, depleted companies holding a hillside about three-eighths of a mile east of their designated objective and awaiting reinforcement. Lieutenant Rogers's Company B positioned themselves closest to the muddy Charlevaux Brook sixty-five feet below them in the draw. It rained nearly continuously after 27 September until mid-October, so drinking water was not an immediate need. All other necessities, though, were lacking—food, tents, warm clothing, blankets, ammunition, mortars, and liaison with troops on their flanks. An assessment of their circumstances occasioned a long discussion that first night between the executive officer, forty-one-year-old Regular Army captain George G. McMurtry, and Major Whittlesey. The latter had stated his concerns to his superior prior to the mission. Both men, as the executive officer later recalled, "had thought this whole Meuse-Argonne offensive smacked of the costly and ignorant optimism of 1914." They realized headquarters' assumptions about battlefield conditions and the preparations and support provided were not aligned with what the 308th actually faced. To Whittlesey and McMurtry, "it was equally obvious that the mission of their own division . . . had been that of a containing force, expected to advance rapidly. . . . The rub was that they were now being asked to assault the strongest German positions of the whole front without any of the usual equipment and preparation for such assault except some not very effective artillery protection." Rather than rolling through the Argonne Forest, the 77th encountered five enemy divisions, and about 125 of these troops had a noose around Whittlesey's unit.[13]

The full weight of their predicament emerged in the predawn gray on Thursday, 3 October, when the enemy unleashed artillery, machine guns, snipers, and mortars. Whittlesey's men were encircled and pinned to their hillside encampment with its shallow funk holes (the World War I term for a foxhole). This second time to be surrounded in a week would play out much differently, not least being that all of America quickly learned of the "Lost Battalion." Within a day American journalists near the front, ever eager for a galvanizing story, seized on the standoff along Charlevaux Brook as a way to parse from the inchoateness of the offensive a single incident of consequential human drama and frame it as a heroic life-and-death conflict. Ironically, troops from the 77th Division as nearby as two miles to the east knew nothing of the siege along Charlelvaux Brook until days after it ended.[14]

Courage and resilience were evident throughout the seven assaults Whittlesey's men rebuffed. The leadership of officers such as Lieutenant Rogers was singularly exceptional. Whittlesey praised him for how he "held his men together during those hard days with a fearlessness and ability that I can never forget." Among the hardships was the absence of any food after the second day, and gnawing on morale was an inability to bury or reduce the stench from the dead. Then on the fifth day an assault by flamethrowers came directly at Company B, launched from about 250 yards away and up a hillside with a 17 degree slope. Two soldiers were burned to death, but the charge was repulsed. General Pershing awarding Lieutenant Rogers the Distinguished Service Cross, and part of the citation read, "By his personal example of calmness he kept his men in order and helped repel counter attacks." The last of these attacks was the flamethrowers, and almost immediately afterward Rogers "was shot through the body by a sniper's bullet, and was killed instantly." The next day rescue efforts intensified as units of the 82nd Division supported by corps artillery threatened to overrun the east flank of the enemy, forcing them to withdraw north. At 3:00 P.M. on Sunday, 8 October, Whittlesey and 193 infantrymen and officers walked out of their "fiery trial." The next morning's headline in the *Albuquerque Morning Journal* summarized their saga: "Lost in Forest, Surrounded by Foe, Hungry and Cold, Yankee Battalion Holds Out Five Days." Unreported at the time was that nearly half of the men—43 percent—were casualties.[15]

The Meuse-Argonne offensive became the deadliest battle in American history. Killed during its forty-seven days were 26,277 Americans. As one distinguished scholar observed, "Twice as many died in Meuse-Argonne as in the next most costly battle, Okinawa in 1945." New Mexicans were present in the Regular Army, the National Guard, the National Army, as well as organizations not assigned to divisions, principally railroad and forestry units and the 66th Field Artillery. The total number of New Mexicans in the AEF was not determined by state officials, but an informed guesstimate would be 6,250 (45 percent of all New Mexicans in uniform). Given that about 60 percent of AEF personnel were in auxiliary or support positions, the Services of Supply would likely have had about 3,750 New Mexicans. Twenty-nine combat divisions incurred casualties in France, and about 2,500 New Mexicans served in all of them. But three divisions—the 89th (National Army), 28th (National Guard), and 1st Division (Regular Army)—had the largest number of the state's men and recorded the most casualties.[16]

New Mexicans and the AEF's Way of War

Fifty-eight New Mexicans were killed and hundreds wounded during the Meuse-Argonne offensive. These casualty figures are miniscule in the vast unleashing of a million–plus American soldiers in that offensive, but the combat that sowed sorrow statewide in the fall of 1918 illuminates the AEF's way of war. The Meuse-Argonne offensive was a replay of three conditions that the state's soldiers had faced on other battlefields in France. First, the geography of the Argonne Forest was Belleau Wood writ large. The forest was more than four hundred square miles, whereas Belleau Wood, site of sanguinary fighting during three weeks in June, was one square mile. Moreover, the Argonne Forest was likewise thickly wooded and laced with ravines and steep hillsides, but because it had been occupied for four years rather than simply the three months of Belleau Wood it was fortified with concrete bunkers and pillboxes, barbed wire barriers twenty to thirty feet deep in open areas and on the perimeter, and artillery on its heights that covered every angle of attack. Second, the enemy launched many more poison gas attacks in the Meuse-Argonne offensive than in previous battles. The 89th Division endured costly gas assaults in October, attacks almost unknown today—at Jaulny on the 6th and in Bois de Bantheville at the end of October. Third, New Mexicans were victimized by the recklessness of senior AEF commanders as epitomized by forgotten assaults across the Meuse River on the last days of the war. The final days of the war were consistent with the AEF's prevailing philosophy of warfare, one George Marshall succinctly described in 1919:

> War is a ruthless taskmaster, demanding success regardless of confusion, shortness of time, and paucity of tools. . . . [Commanders] must demand results, close their ears to excuses, and drive subordinates beyond what would ordinarily be considered the limits of human capacity. Wars are won by the side that accomplishes the impossible. . . . The army with the higher breaking point wins the decision.[17]

The commander of the 89th Division, Maj. Gen. William M. Wright, knew orders received on 3 October to take over several miles of the line to his east on the St. Mihiel front endangered the men of the 356th Infantry, the unit assigned that task. Wright and his aides had repeatedly inspected the area and found that it had "much gas and poor shelter [trenches] for the men." When the 356th Infantry relieved a counterpart in the 78th Division (New Jersey, Delaware, and northern New York), which was sent forward to the Meuse-Argonne, defenses against bombardment by poison gas shells remained inadequate.[18]

When Company I of the 356th entered the line at Jaulny, about thirty-two miles southeast of Verdun, on 4 October, they immediately began "working hard on the trenches" to deepen them (see map 3). At least forty-seven New Mexicans were in this company, and their task was formidable. They had not created adequate shelter when on the night of Saturday, 5 October, at about 9:00 and continuing into the early hours of Sunday they were heavily shelled with arsine and mustard gas. Cpl. Elbert R. Brown of Lincoln County reported that when "I Company got gassed about 185 men were gassed and sent to hospitals. Only 21 men were left for duty." Another observer reported that on 9 October I Company had only sixteen members when they were loaded onto a truck bound for the Meuse-Argonne. Among those unaffected by the attack, cooks were the most numerous according to Pvt. Isaac Quintana of Rio Arriba County, likely because their worksite was separated from the infantrymen in the trenches. Brown was among only a handful of New Mexicans gassed who returned to the company after a two-week hospitalization. Also lightly gassed was Biterbo Gallegos of Grant County, who returned to duty on 31 October but was killed in action on 3 November. Ten weeks earlier his brother, Manuel, of the 28th Division, had died in the fight along the Vesle River. Of the forty-seven New Mexicans on the Company I roster at the war's end, only fifteen completed the state's service questionnaire, and five of these men had been assigned to the company after 6 October. Several New Mexicans in Company I were so severely wounded that they were returned to the states in 1919 after three or more months in hospitals. Among the severely gassed were Pvt. Pedro Fresquez of Tularosa, Pvt. Abe Cawyer of Grant County, and Pvt. Isaac Quintana from a village in Rio Arriba County. The latter two reported lung problems leading to disability in 1919, and Fresquez said he had developed tuberculosis.[19]

Perhaps the luckiest member of Company I was Sgt. Rudolph A. Forderhase from Missouri, who had such a debilitating attack of dysentery that he was hospitalized on 30 September and returned to his company a few days after the gas attack, rejoining the fifteen soldiers left in the company. An investigation after the incident revealed details that explain what happened to I Company. The enemy's attack mimicked that of 7 August: it began with arsine shells followed by mustard gas, and the investigator reported that "practically all of its men [were] gassed owing to the company commander ordering off the masks," an irresponsible decision coming less than two hours after the shelling stopped. Two other companies—L, which was adjacent to I in the trench, and E—also suffered casualties, though early reports had their numbers significantly lower than for I Company: eleven for L, twenty-three for E, and 168 for I. Data from area hospitalizations between 5 and 7 October, though, show higher numbers for gas victims, which suggests that underestimating occurred for companies L and E. One New Mexican in L Company reported that he was part of a work party that "received orders to proceed to the trenches which were occupied by I Company and bring back their equipment." Doing so brought renewed enemy shelling, which lasted all night, and it took five trips to gather all of I Company's belongings. No statements were found about this incident from New Mexicans present in E Company.[20]

The skeletal crew of I Company along with both infantry brigades of the 89th Division began moving forward on 9 October. Company I was part of a convoy of small trucks—each about the size of a three-quarter-ton pickup—used to transport the troops to Verdun, their first stop on the way to the front lines. The journey was uncomfortable in the extreme—no room whatsoever to move, potholes hit with solid tires jarring the truck and all in it with unrelenting regularity, prompting one rider's wry observation that "no doubt our posteriors were imprinted on the floor boards for several days." Finally the 356th began arriving at their destination, the village of Recicourt, ten miles due west of Verdun. Once there they marched for two nights in the rain and mud ten miles to the northwest to the villages of Eclisfontaine and Epinonville. It took nearly a week for the entire 89th Division to be assembled, and supplementing them were two thousand replacements. Between 15 and 19 October training and regrouping occurred before the division starting what would become their final push of the war—twenty-five miles northeast to Stenay and five miles farther upriver to Pouilly and decisive control over the enemy's rail lines.[21]

Pershing's superior, Généralissime Foch, personified war as a ruthless taskmaster. "When [on 13 October 1918] the American commander started to describe the difficult, heavily defended terrain his men were facing, the French generalissimo stopped him cold. 'Results are the only thing to judge by,' he said." Inevitably results exacted high battlefield casualties, which proved unacceptable to the American public and served as background to growing resentment toward the army, a turn of events that would roil Congress between November 1919 and February 1920 and diminish public support for the military in the interwar years.[22]

Early in the evening of 15 October, General Pershing visited General Wright to prepare the 89th Division's commander for the message he would hear the next day from Wright's newly appointed immediate superior, Maj. Gen. Charles P. Summerall—either produce results or be replaced. Pershing and Wright had known each other since preparing to enter West Point and had been roommates, but the only observer of their meeting reported that "Pershing [was] grim and severe, Wright really sweating from every pore." An animated Pershing pounded the table and insisted, "What we need are two-fisted fighters who will push their way through regardless of cost." The next morning Wright relayed Pershing's message in talks to each regiment. He called together the officers and noncommissioned officers down to corporals and set forth Pershing's insistence that the division succeed in taking their objectives and crush the enemy. Wright brought all corporals to the front of the gathering and beseeched each of them to lead their squads in an aggressive fight, "to put it across," and they responded with a lusty "We will!" Summerall arrived to address the division's officers beginning at about 11:00 A.M. He delivered the same message but with sharper edges. After two perfunctory sentences acknowledging the division's contributions to date, Summerall launched into a thirty-minute harangue about a number of "things that I have found in my experience must be done, and more things which must not be done." Heading the list of necessities was the insistence that "lieutenants and captains . . . be well to the front during the attack . . . [to] inspire and encourage their men to press forward." The main thing to be avoided was fear of the enemy's machine guns. He ordered aggressive action to crush machine gun nests, which ultimately came down to them being "destroyed by the use of the bayonet or the threat of the bayonet." Summerall's commands upon dismissing the officers were iron-fisted dictates: "It must be done whatever the cost" and "You are being watched." Col. Conrad S. Babcock, commander of the 354th Infantry, called Summerall's speech "the poorest exhibition of battle leadership possible to make." Echoing this sentiment was a bistering assessment from a distinguished scholar of the AEF, historian Robert H. Ferrell: "Summerall contributed only blather" to efforts in winning the war.[23]

The 89th Division's first test in the Meuse-Argonne offensive lay several miles to their north and slightly west in Bois de Bantheville. This kidney-shaped dense forest covering about five square miles (3,200 acres) was one of innumerable "wooded islands" that collectively were known as the Argonne Forest. The 89th Division was to clear the Bantheville woods, a task vastly more difficult and costly in casualties than Major General Summerall expected. The enemy continuously infiltrated at night, which required repeated sweeps to clear previously "secured" areas. But the greatest obstacle was bombardment by poison gas shells, principally filled with mustard gas, which rained down on them at night and in the middle portion of the forest. The 353rd and 354th Infantries suffered the most casualties, estimated at four hundred, but none seem to have been New Mexicans. Colonel Babcock succinctly described the pervasiveness of poison gas after an inspection on 27 October: "The woods seem to be saturated with gas . . . not so much the result of a single attack on specific areas as the continued gas spread for several days over a wide area." Years later he summarized the effect of the "enemy shell[ing] the entire area systematically," which resulted in "severe casualties almost daily."[24]

Two detailed accounts describe events in Bois de Bantheville. One is from Pvt. Conrado Lucero, who was twenty-five years old when he was drafted from Las Vegas in October 1917. A year later he was with a mortar unit of the 356th Infantry that entered Bois de Bantheville just after midnight Sunday, 20 October, in support of B Company. They went only a few miles

> after which the enemy put up very strong resistance and in addition it was a very rainy, dark night and very difficult for fighting. Well, I, Conrado Lucero, together with 90 or 100 other men had the bad luck after the

advance began that the lieutenant commanding us got lost and did not know our whereabouts. He gave us orders to continue advancing forward [even though] we were lost and were behind the enemy's line causing me and a quarter of the rest of the American soldiers to enter into a place where we were completely surrounded by the enemy. It was not possible for us to get out of there from 20 October to [Thursday] night the 24th and while there we almost wanted to die for lack of food and water. Well, besides all that during these [five] days and [four] nights we had to withstand various assaults by infantry and machine guns and one gas attack. We lost almost half of those that entered there, some died and others very badly wounded, among those who died was a young Hispano American named [Pvt.] Atanacio Garcia from Albuquerque [Los Duranes].

Private Garcia was killed in action on Tuesday, 22 October. He was twenty-four years old when inducted as part of the draft in late March from Bernalillo County, was a laborer with limited formal education, and trained eight weeks at Camp Funston.[25]

A second statement recounting events in Bois de Bantheville is from I Company, which was in the woods 20–31 October, and it is extracted from the memoir of Sgt. Rudolph Forderhase. I Company received nine replacements before entering Bois de Bantheville, sufficient for it to be a half-platoon of twenty-five men but still too small to operate alone, so they were attached to a machine gun company in the 356th and assigned to carry ammunition. In some ways I Company's twelve days there were a completely different story from the costly bungling B Company endured. Bois de Bantheville had numerous huts left by the enemy, and these structures afforded Sergeant Forderhase, Corporal Martinez, and the men of I Company a dry place to eat and sleep and a hiding place from snipers. But dangers abounded and almost daily they engaged the enemy and absorbed casualties, which hardened them to normal instincts. After one skirmish they had to move

> across an open area. We heard a single cannon shot from our left rear, then heard the shell pass across our front and hit the ground and explode near the column of our infantry. A fragment struck a man, who fell, and whose cries of anguish we heard for some time. The column continued without paying any attention to their fallen comrade and made their way into the cover of the nearby forest. On the surface, this seemed cruel and inhuman.... There was always the possibility that the enemy had the range

and was prepared to saturate the area with fire from an entire battery. . . .
I have no doubt the single casualty was shortly found and attended to by
the Medics. This was the regulation practice.

Other incidents inured soldiers to battlefield carnage. One common sight took a while to make sense of—dead men heaped along paths in the woods. Rather quickly, though, "it became clear that when stretcher bearers, on finding their burden had become lifeless, would deposit the body by the side of the path and go back for another casualty."[26]

146th FA and Battery A

Relocating the four 155 mm GPFs of Battery A after the St. Mihiel offensive typified the difficulties in bringing artillery forward. Beginning on 15 September they slowly moved northeast of Sommedieue about seven miles to Verdun and then another twelve miles northwest to the destroyed village of Marre. Though the distance traversed was not very far, they had to overcome three conditions that slowed all travel: traffic moved only at night in an attempt to maintain secrecy of the buildup; the few roads available were an unending series of shell holes requiring extensive filling with the rubble from ruined villages; and rain deepened the ubiquitous mud, which bogged down all movement.[27]

Finally settling into a ravine outside the village of Marre about 20 September, Battery A joined the six-hour artillery barrage that preceded the Meuse-Argonne offensive on 25–26 September: "All of the guns spoke with one acclaim until the earth fairly shook with the jar of explosions." Their targets were to the north in the long, wide valley bordered on the east by the Meuse River and on the west by the Aire River and the Argonne Forest. Into this area they poured "constant harassing and interdictory fire on all of the back areas, main highways, towns and other places where enemy troops were likely to be concentrated or where they could be seen." By the night of 27 September the initial wave of troops had outdistanced the range of their 155s, so the six batteries were silenced for nearly five days. On 2 October, Batteries C through F were sent about a dozen miles northwest to the village of Cuisy, "a difficult passage with guns and trucks on the almost obliterated roads through the old No Man's Land."

Batteries A and B remained outside Marre, on the southern flank of the offensive and less than two miles due west of the Meuse. For ten days they supported a French division that had crossed the river and was fighting its way northeast. On 12 October they began a push northwest about a dozen miles to positions on the road heading from Cuisy toward Denneveaux, a village about two miles west of the Meuse. Along the road's seven miles were placed the regiment's batteries, although Battery A remained near Cuisy and fired north and northeast upon the enemy's rearward areas for a dozen days. Between 12 and 31 October the batteries of the 146th FA expended a total of 1,354 155 mm shells. Their guns were silent for six days and active on fourteen days, with each battery of four guns firing, on average, a total of 257 shells during their active days.

When the final stage of the offensive began on Friday, 1 November, Battery A solidified its importance in the final push eastward toward the vital railway center of Stenay, which became a principal military objective of the First Army. Battery A worked in support of the 2nd and 89th Divisions as they moved relentlessly north. But on 7 November and about six miles into this campaign they reached a fully exposed valley "hemmed in on either side by high hills, and such a contour did not permit of any further advance." From there they continued their bombardment, which increasingly involved the use of gas shells. During the final eleven days of the war, the batteries of the 146th FA expended a total of 1,841 shells, for an average of 307 shells daily per battery. The AEF's increased use of poison gas is evident in the report of 648 gas shells fired between 4 and 8 November by the 146th FA, for a total of 108 gas shells on average for each battery.

The Last Push

Company I was reassembled on Friday, 25 October, drawing to it men from various other companies in the 356th. Beginning on 3 November the 356th rotated to a frontline combat force and remained on the attack until the war's end. Two soldiers from New Mexico in that regiment left sufficiently detailed accounts to reconstruct their final few weeks of the war: Cpl. Augustine Martinez, I Company, and Pvt. Jack D. Trainor, L Company. In their experiences are glimpsed the war as they knew it. A few months after the war ended a New Mexico legislator struggled to find words to describe the Meuse-Argonnne offensive to his colleagues: "God—how can I paint a word picture to bring home to you, to make you sense the agony, to feel something of the terror by day and by night which these our own boys faced in far-away France?" Martinez and Trainor's accounts are such a wartime canvas.[28]

When the final campaign of the offensive began on 1 November at 3:00 A.M., Private Trainor thought the AEF's artillery shelling "was even heavier than the barrage at St. Mihiel, as there was a greater mobilization of artillery and they were only ten meters apart." At 5:30 A.M. the firing lifted and moved forward to protect the troops. I and L Companies were in reserve, but all troops "moved forward all day." Their final weeks in the offensive were not a triumphalist march but rather a mud-encrusted slog in pursuit of a slowly retreating enemy who bedeviled the 89th Division with intense shelling, air attacks with machine guns and bombs, and extensive use of land mines. Day and night the 89th kept pushing ahead, stopping only for a few hours several times in daylight and darkness. Death stalked everyone, selecting some, skipping over others, including Private Trainor. Just after "midnight [4 November] when we stopped for a rest I had a very narrow escape while I was on outpost duty with my automatic Chauchat rifle. A large shell broke about 10 feet from me and covered me with mud and stones, but it did not hurt me a bit. I shall never forget the blinding flash of that shell as it burst."[29]

The next day, 5 November, the 89th Division reached the Meuse River along a four-mile front. The 355th and 356th Infantries were opposite the village of Pouilly-sur-Meuse. Four miles to their south the 353rd and 354th Infantries fronted the village of Laneuville-sur-Meuse, which was a mile and an eighth west of the city of Stenay on the far, or east, bank of the Meuse. After leaving Bois de Bantheville the division had pushed north nearly eighteen miles. Between 5 and 9 November the regiments reinforced and organized their positions, allowed artillery to catch up with them, and prepared to cross the Meuse. Reconnoitering became especially active during these days, and Capt. Arthur Y. Wear of I Company received an order to send volunteers

> to swim across the river and attempt to get information as to the strength and disposition of the German troops. The stream was near bank-full [the high water the result of intentional damming to flood the area]. . . . The water was cold and deep. Only about half of those who volunteered were selected. Of these, only a few succeeded in getting across. About half were killed by the enemy or drowned in the cold water. Only about half of those who got back were able to give information of any value. . . . When the surviving swimmers returned and informed Captain Wear of what had been accomplished, he walked a short distance into the dark and somber woods and shot himself in the head. . . . He was a very conscientious man and, doubtless, felt guilty about sending these men on such an unpromising mission. . . . The news of his suicide, and the fate of the swimmers, was promptly transmitted to Division Headquarters and there were no more efforts to swim the river.[30]

During the night of 10–11 November, I Company was ferried across the north-flowing Meuse without incident in pontoons that carried seventy-five men and took twenty minutes for a round-trip. The river near Pouilly-sur-Meuse was 100–200 feet wide and because of the flooding more than eight feet deep almost immediately off the shore. In addition, irrigation canals on the east side were likewise blocked and their waters spread eastward, creating marshes. The 356th Infantry's 2nd Battalion Companies E, F, G, and H encountered the most resistance. Their pontoons reached the east shore amid artillery fire that followed them inland. Pvt. Adolfo Ortiz of Santa Fe gave a capsule summary of the toll: "losing over 300 men . . . the [regiment's] heaviest casualties."[31]

From E Company, Pvt. Damiano C. de Baca of Bernalillo was hit by shrapnel in the right leg as he climbed ashore, and twenty others in his company were also wounded in that attack. He was hospitalized until 20 December and then returned to his company. Two Euro-American privates from F Company, twenty-nine-year-old Reginald E. Baird of Eddy County and twenty-six-year-old Hugh Calvin Wharton of Otero County, died in the heavy shelling. Shrapnel likewise perforated the bodies of an officer and twelve men in G Company, including two Nuevomexicano privates—Jose Eligio Madrid from Rio Arriba County, one of only twenty-five original members of the company from Camp Funston, three weeks away from his twenty-eighth birthday, and leaving a wife and two children under the age six; and Arturo Montoya of Roy in what was then eastern Mora County. Montoya had joined G Company sometime after arriving in France in early July. For the next two months he wrote weekly to his aged father and mother (none of the letters were found). Soon after the St. Mihiel offensive Jose Maria Montoya received his son's final letter informing him that G Company was "going to continue pushing forward." Among H Company's losses were twenty-two-year-old Pvt. Leon B. Vaughan of Union County and twenty-six-year-old Pfc. Royal C. Boehrig of Grant County. All but Private Madrid had been called in the draft of late April 1918. Five of the men were killed in action as the war's end was in sight, but Private Boehrig died of his wounds three months later in a hospital on 12 February.[32]

Once I Company reached the east shore, they began to work their way a short distance south toward Pouilly-sur-Meuse. Cpl. Augustine Martinez of San Juan County, who had turned twenty-three three weeks earlier, recalled that day a year to the week later and told of his participation in a five-man squad:

> At 9 A.M. [11 November] we had orders to clean up a certain woods for there [were] some machine gun nests where we met strong resistance. Finally we reached our objective losing four men [three privates and a lieutenant]. . . . So I was the only one left out of the five. I killed 2 Germans[—]one officer

and one private[—]and four more got away but I killed those, too, after my 3 men were killed and my officer wounded [he died later that morning]. On the 18th of Nov I was recommended for the Distinguished Service Cross.[33]

Unbeknownst to Martinez, the war had officially ended about the time he eliminated the machine gun nest. I Company had not been notified of the 11:00 A.M. armistice, although German prisoners taken about mid-morning had told them, information the American soldiers had no way to verify. Finally I Company received official confirmation at 11:30 that morning, although at the armistice's appointed hour I Company and all AEF troops at the front noticed a sudden silence.[34]

The two hours preceding the armistice had been as intense an artillery barrage as any coming before a major offensive. Some artillery units in the AEF responded to divisional commands to use all their remaining shells or face court-martial. Other units likely unleashed their fire power because it was happening all around them. The 146th FA was unrestrained in its firing activity on 11 November. Their mean number of expended shells was 396 daily between 1 and 9 November in support of the 89th Division. Between noon on 10 November and 11:00 A.M. the next day, they launched 494 shells—a 25 percent increase over the mean number fired earlier.[35]

Fifty-eight New Mexicans died during the Meuse-Argonne offensive: seven lost their lives between 26 and 30 September; thirty-four died in October, nearly half from disease; and seventeen succumbed between 1 and 11 November. During the war's final twenty-four hours, seven New Mexicans were killed in action—six in the 89th Division, and five in the 356th Infantry. Other statistics show just how fateful the war's final twenty-four hours were for New Mexicans: the final seven soldiers killed in action were 12 percent of all from the state who died during the whole offensive, but these seven were also 41 percent of the New Mexicans who died between 1 and 11 November.[36]

Joseph E. Garcia of Bernalillo County observed the final barrage near Stenay, which the 89th Division had liberated that morning. It "seemed that both sides were trying to use up every last piece of ammunition on each other." Garcia was a First Army driver who had been given that assignment after being wounded and gassed serving in the 42nd Rainbow Division. Early that morning he had taken some officers "to an overlooking site above Stenay to observe the end of the fighting." Casualties were inevitable in such an onslaught of shells, but amid a history-making moment no one thought about it until it happened just before 11:00 A.M. A shell suddenly exploded nearby and a piece of shrapnel hit a soldier standing next to Garcia and "killed him instantly." For the rest of his life Garcia attended mass on 11 November "to remember the story and the soul of that soldier who passed away that morning," just one of 3,300 AEF soldiers killed that day—all of whose deaths Garcia considered "utterly useless."[37]

After 1,559 days of war, the fighting ended. Joseph Garcia's profound awareness of the senselessness of a death so close to the end was one of a variety of reactions New Mexicans had that day. Pvt. Frank Alarid from Albuquerque, assigned to the 89th Division's engineers, described for his father the impact of the armistice: "I will never forget November 11th. At 11:00 A.M. when they told us to stop firing, it got so quiet that it seems like it was a fantasy. Then we let loose with our shouts of joy." Alarid had expected to die in the war, so his emotional release was a survivor's relief.[38]

Physical exhaustion gripped many infantrymen. Pvt. Jack D. Trainor and comrades in L Company were enervated. Their day began around midnight when they set out for the pontoons. Upon reaching the far shore "we started our advance through a swamp wading knee deep in mud and water and as the night was very cold several of the boys had their toes frozen. I believe this night was the most miserable one I ever passed as I did not care then whether I lived or died and all the boys I talked to felt the same way." They came under continuous machine gun fire, "but on account of the heavy fog they were unable to do much damage to us. . . . only one man killed and one captured." At 11:00 A.M. they had no idea why enemy firing ceased, and when German soldiers began walking toward them announcing the war's end they took them prisoners. Not until 1:00 P.M. did they receive official notification of the armistice. Trainor noted laconically, "The boys did not give vent to any expressions of gladness but finished building their dug outs [foxholes] and laid down for a much needed rest as we had not had a good nap for over a week."[39]

For the nearly one hundred New Mexicans in the 28th Division, survivors of three major offenses, 11 November was bittersweet and anticlimactic. They had been in reserve about fifty miles to the southwest, positioned on the eastern edge of the former St. Mihiel front. They were poised to advance on Metz, but their commander elected to hold them in place, interpreting the message that accompanied confirmation of the pending armistice as giving division commanders the discretion to engage the enemy actively or put on hold further hostilities unless provoked. The commander of the 110th Infantry received and complied with this message at 8:35 A.M.: "Do not advance. Take defensive position. Organize for defense. All firing to stop at 11:00 A.M." These men watched and waited, marking the end of their combat days with their own thoughts. For

Pvt. Adolfo Abeyta from Tucumcari, one of the several hundred New Mexicans assigned to the 21st (Railroad) Engineers, the Meuse-Argonne offensive had been unending, backbreaking, and exceedingly dangerous work. On 1 November the 21st Engineers had left Bois de Bantheville along with the 89th Division and begun to restore an abandoned railroad line. During their work, "the artillery fire was the heaviest we had experienced. Every man escaped death by a hair's-breath a hundred times these days.... The armistice came on the 11th, but still our work continued." They labored until 25 November, when the rail line became usable and train cars began "hauling ammunition in large quantities" reclaimed from the AEF as well as confiscated from the enemy.[40]

The 2nd Division, paired with the 89th Division in V Corps, had moved several miles north of the 89th on the night of 10–11 November. They swept south toward Pouilly-sur-Meuse in the war's final hour. Soon their men, both Regular Army and marines, mingled with the 89th. The respect the 2nd Division showed their National Army comrades, especially their complete lack of braggadocio, deeply impressed Sergeant Forderhase of I Company. A marine in the 2nd Division, 3rd Brigade, Ray DeWitt Herring, later recalled the same sense of quiet, dignified comportment and put on paper one of the most poignant statements about the war's end:

> No hilarity, no singing paeans of victory. Too rapid had been the change from the threshold of death on this broken battlefield now promising life to the fortunate buddies of the unrequited slain. An aloofness was upon all, and a silence as of the great unaccustomed shadows thrown by the first camp fires known to this generation of soldiers. The pageantry of the storied camping ground was lacking. The camaraderie about the beacons flaring fitfully along the horizon was of the fellowship of the disconsolate and lonely. Nothing could be so empty as victory.

Herring's elegy gave voice to a final reaction—putting aside "the world of woe encompassed in that tragic quadrennium beginning in 1914" and moving forward, however haltingly: "Many days must pass before life could be cherished. Never again could it be embraced with rapture."[41]

Waiting to Go Home

After the armistice the AEF imposed up to nine months of waiting on soldiers eager to be sent home. The majority of troops, twenty-one divisions in all, remained in France until ships were available for the voyage home. First in line to return were the wounded and sick. Most of the AEF's infantrymen in France had left by July 1919, followed by Services of Supply soldiers throughout the summer. Eight other divisions, organized as the Third Army and an occupation force in Germany's Rhineland, departed between mid-May and late August. New Mexicans were present in each of the occupying divisions—1st, 2nd, 3rd, and 4th Regular Army, the 32nd and 42nd Divisions of the National Guard, and the 89th and 90th from the National Army. General Pershing selected these divisions as a reward for distinguished effort during the Meuse-Argonne offensive.

Among New Mexicans in France after the armistice, the largest number were in the state's National Guard in the 40th Division. Beginning in late December they started welcoming back comrades who had been sent as replacement troops during the summer and early fall. The 40th Division slowly gathered in its widely dispersed troops at their new camps in the Bordeaux district, where surely many accounts of their combat and Services of Supply experiences were shared. But none of what was recounted rivaled stories of New Mexicans in the division's military police.

The approximately four hundred New Mexican MPs had been entangled in the AEF's biggest scandal—abuse of prisoners at Prison Camp Number 2 on the eastern edge of Paris in the town of Chelles. There the army established a prison camp in September 1918 to handle men who had drifted into Paris from their frontline units, were absent without leave, and in the words of General Pershing "were among the hardest characters in the American Expeditionary Forces." The events at the camp had an unfortunate connection with New Mexico's 40th Division, as outlined by 1st Sgt. William A. Poe of Deming:

> [I] was appointed First Sergeant on September 5, 1918. The 79th Brigade [40th Division, with Infantry Regiments 157th and 158th] of which my organization was a unit was sent to Chelles, France, to take charge of Replacement Camp. The 158th Infantry taking charge of Prison Farm No. 2, with Lt. "Hard boiled" Smith [32nd Division] in immediate charge as prison officer and Colonel E. P. Grimsted [Edgar B. Grimstead, 158th Infantry] in command of the area. They being directly responsible for the terrible conditions at that prison, in my personal estimation.[42]

The reference to terrible conditions may seem cryptic today, but the army and Congress investigated the prison camp in 1919, with newspapers reporting on the inquiries into abuses inflicted by MPs there in November and December 1918. Lieutenant Smith and two other second lieutenants from the 158th Infantry were convicted at courts-martial along with a sergeant from the 110th Infantry,

28th Division. All were charged with beating, abusing (including denying food), and robbing imprisoned men, and Smith received the longest sentence: eighteen months confinement and hard labor. The army shut down the prison camp in mid-December 1918 and promptly ordered the 40th Division to the Bordeaux district, 310 miles southwest of Paris.[43]

Accompanying the 40th Division was Alfred M. Bergere, New Mexico's only Knights of Columbus representative in the AEF. He had been appointed overseas secretary in August and arrived in France in September. "He was first appointed to the 27th Division of New York [on loan to the British and serving near the Belgian border] until he could find the whereabouts of the 40th Division." In late October he relocated to Amiens and joined vestiges of the 40th Division in far north-central France near the English Channel. In the Bordeaux district Bergere and assistants under him opened canteens, or huts, in seven towns. At these facilities the Knights provided free to 18,000 troops "several million cigarettes, and several tons of chocolate, hard candy, gum drops, chewing tobacco, toilet soap, shaving material, playing cards, dominoes, and thousands of magazines." Each canteen had a large room used variously for writing letters home, weekly musical entertainment, and Sunday masses. The 40th Division also received KOC-supplied baseball equipment. Throughout the AEF after the armistice, teams organized and competed—weather permitting. Baseball proved immensely popular among troops because it allowed for far more participation than did football, which the army officially sponsored.[44]

Other Stories of the AEF: Siberia and North Russia

President Wilson called the nation to arms in a very public way in April 1917, but fifteen months later he quietly extended the AEF's mission three times. In executive orders he directed Pershing to move troops into Italy and Russia, with the latter being a choice that was "the clear and fixed judgment of the Government of the United States [i.e., the president], arrived at after repeated and very searching reconsiderations." Wilson authorized these interventions after the Allies, and in particular Britain, pressured him to send American support. Pershing in turn dispatched the 332nd Infantry Regiment and the 331st Field Hospital from the 83rd Division (Ohio and West Virginia) to northern Italy to reinforce their front against Austrian and German troops at the end of July. Few and perhaps only one New Mexican participated in this incursion. Pvt. Felipe P. Barela, twenty-three years old from Sierra County, served in an ambulance unit with the 331st Field Hospital.[45]

A more consequential act for New Mexicans began when Wilson instructed Pershing to place the 339th Infantry Regiment of the 85th Division (Michigan), with at least four New Mexicans, into northwest Russia. Then on 3 August he directed that five thousand infantrymen and one hundred officers from the 8th Division, training at Camp Fremont, along with fifty-three officers and 1,537 Regular Army soldiers in the Philippines, become garrison forces at Vladivostok on the Pacific coast of Russia in what the military referred to as Siberia. Actually the troops from the Philippines were disbursed at outposts along more than 200 miles of the Trans-Siberian Railroad west of Vladivostok. Among the infantrymen shipped out of San Francisco were about one hundred New Mexicans.[46]

Just as a murder in Sarajevo on 28 June 1914 started World War I, so, too, did a murder in Chelyabinsk, Russia, on 14 May 1918, "spark a chain of events that eventually led to US military intervention in both north Russia and Siberia." Chelyabinsk, 1,500 miles east of Moscow and just across the Ural Mountains, was a six-day train ride of more than 5,200 miles east along the famous Trans-Siberian Railway to Vladivostok. At the rail yard in Chelyabinsk sat a train headed west that carried captured Hungarian soldiers being sent home after the Russians withdrew from the war in February 1918. Soon pulling in opposite them was a train carrying Czech and Slovaks soldiers heading east, men the Russians had mobilized when war broke out but now were allowed to board ships in Vladivostok to be transported to France and fight for the Allies. Proximity of the trains brought long-standing national enmity to a boil, and a Hungarian soldier killed a Czech soldier. Quickly the local incident escalated, and its bloodshed became part of a great conflagration that took the lives of tens of millions between 1918 and 1922 in what is known as the Russian Civil War. By summer that national conflict became an international one when a dozen Allied nations, principally Great Britain, France, Japan, and the United States, intervened militarily. The British sought to save Russia from the grip of the Bolsheviks by aiding dissident forces and reopening the eastern front. Wilson never acceded to those expectations and instead said U.S. intervention was "to guard military stores and help the Czechs embark for France." In fact each of the countries intervened for its own reasons, but the unifying pretexts were to prevent Germany from hauling away large quantities of military supplies from northern Russia and to aid Czech-Slovak soldiers, numbering 30,000–60,000 and regarded as Allies stranded and under attack in and near Vladivostok.[47]

The 8th Division soldiers wore a shoulder patch that read "AEFS," for American Expeditionary Force Siberia. If mud characterized the AEF in France, then ice was the counterpart in Russia. To the men sent to Siberia, the winter was not as severe as most feared, but during December and January the mean temperature was about five degrees above zero. Though little snow fell in Vladivostok, ice covered the harbor and frostbite was a constant possibility for anyone outside for more than a few hours. Nevertheless, the commander claimed that almost no cases occurred because of the care taken with providing the troops explorer's clothing, which navy officer Robert Peary had used (with fur exterior over layers of canvas and wool) during Arctic trips between 1886 and 1909.[48]

Pfc. Charles Gooch, son of a Euro-American father and Nuevomexicana mother, was twenty-seven years old when he arrived in Vladivostok, had taught school for eight years, and served in the New Mexico National Guard from 1911 to 1915. The May 1918 draft claimed him, and he left his native Santa Fe to train at California's Camp Fremont near Palo Alto. His year in Siberia was representative in many respects of the experiences of New Mexicans sent there. He matter-of-factly summarized his duties:

> In August 1918, after having been trained, I was selected with several thousand others for overseas service in Siberia. Sailed from San Francisco, Calif., on the U.S.A.T[ransport] Sheridan on Sept. 2, 1918. . . . We arrived in the harbor of Vladivostok, Siberia, Sept. 30th, 1918 and disembarked Oct. 1st 1918. . . . From November till March I was clerk in the American Red Cross Hospital on Russia Island out in the bay from Vladivostok. In March 1919 I was ordered back to my company [I Company, 31st Infantry], and shortly after was made a Special Military Police at the Vladivostok Railroad Stations. Each allied nation had a special police here. In May 1919, my company was ordered out to protect the railroad along the Souchan [Suchan coal field] Sector [about seventy-five miles northeast]. For five months we were along this line during which I took part in several skirmishes against the Red Guards [Bolshevik soldiers]. . . . We would go out in search of [Cossack] bandits and Red Guards. Ordered back to the U.S. Sept. 25, 1919 and sailed from Vladivostok Oct. 7, 1919 [arriving San Francisco 1 Nov. 1919].[49]

Gooch's first two assignments were no doubt a result of his four years in the New Mexico National Guard. Duty as special police was one of the most challenging assignments. A twelve-nation international force was responsible for maintaining order in Vladivostok, whose population during the intervention swelled to 350,000 inhabitants, twice its normal size. It had also become a magnet for violent criminals released from Russian prisons during the Russian

Civil War, and in Vladivostok they sought to steal ammunition and military supplies. Military warehouses were also priority targets for many local Cossacks, who were of doubtful loyalty as anti-Bolshevik fighters and often were merely opportunistic thieves.⁵⁰

Though Gooch worked mostly indoors, most of the 8th Division served outdoors. Pvt. Frank Beaman of Albuquerque, who turned thirty-two just two weeks after arriving in Vladivostok, spent hours on "the drill ground[, which] was the ice in the bay most of the time," and the drudgery of the parade field was punctuated only by "regular guard around quarters . . . some guard duty around magazines of Russian supplies . . . and K.P." He also went with the contingent of companies sent in early spring to guard the Suchan coal fields. This area's coal supplied the Trans-Siberian trains for 2,000 miles of their route. The miners were Bolsheviks, but they nonetheless were friendly toward the Americans. But the Red Guard and especially Cossack bandits sought to disrupt the troops assigned there, and skirmishes and casualties occurred.⁵¹

At daybreak on Wednesday, 25 June 1919, about seventy-two Americans at an outpost guard camp were asleep in tents just outside Romanovka when ambushed "by four or five times their number" of Red Guard troops. Eighteen AEFS soldiers died almost immediately, but the surviving troops responded with their new Browning automatic rifles, which could fire twenty shots at a burst. Both sides stood their ground until the attackers fled when a relief force of AEFS troops arrived about noon. Two New Mexicans died in this attack: twenty-five-year-old Pfc. Brooks Lee, of medium height and stout frame who had worked on a cattle ranch in Grant County prior to being drafted and sent to Camp Fremont, and Pvt. Nestor Lopez of Socorro County, a tall and slender twenty-eight-year-old sheepherder from near Datil, whom a draft official noted "does not speak English." Both men were single. In retaliation the AEFS "made a number of punitive expeditions into the surrounding country and suffered a few casualties." Sgt. Anastasio Montoya of Santa Fe, who had served in the New Mexico National Guard for seven years, including during 1916–17, and was a popular waiter in Santa Fe prior to being drafted, was severely wounded by gunfire in a raid on the nearby town of Novitskaya on Wednesday, 2 July, and died three days later.⁵²

The three New Mexicans killed in late June and early July 1919 were among only thirty-five AEFS soldiers who died in combat in far east Russia, which meant that New Mexicans were 8.57 percent of all American soldiers who died there. The facts could not be crueler: seven and one-half months after the armistice suspended hostilities in France, and the same week the Treaty of Versailles was signed ending the war, three New Mexicans died in the AEFS. The possibility of dying in Russia was very much on the mind of Pfc. Gooch before he went on patrol in the Suchan coal region. It became the theme of a poem, "Saving Russia," he published in the AEFS newspaper, *Here and There with the 31st,* and it was reprinted in the *Santa Fe New Mexican* in early April 1919. He presented an imaginary conversation with his mother, who told him "Most patriotic you must be / . . . / But what she never said to me / Is that she'd send me overseas to die for Russia." He ponders a question for her: "To ask her if with joy she'd yell / Should I return all shot to 'ell / Thru savin' Russia."[53]

The misplaced patriotism Gooch challenged would have resonated with the five thousand American soldiers sent to northwest Russia, an expedition that included three volunteers from New Mexico: Terrell D. Thompson of East Las Vegas, twenty-nine years old; also twenty-nine years old was Emil H. Willmunger, born in Gallup; and twenty-eight-year-old Ralph Voylles of Portales in Roosevelt County, who had been in the New Mexico National Guard along the border in 1916–17. The three had worked on railroads and were among 720 noncombatant volunteers assigned to the 167th Transportation Corps and under the command of the AEF North Russia (AEFNR). Their arrival at Murmansk, an ice-free port 370 miles northwest of Arkhangelsk and within the Arctic Circle, in March–April 1919 brought much needed expertise to maintain and operate a single-track line vital to communication and transportation. Though no railroad connected the two cities directly, each had a railroad link to the south. The route to Murmansk was the newer of the two, completed in 1917. Keeping it operational for hundreds of miles through thick forests and expanses of bogs became the 167th's chief duty.[54]

A fourth New Mexican was with the 85th Division, 339th Infantry—Pvt. Antonio Archibeque of Las Vegas, who turned twenty in May 1919. How he became a part of troops primarily from Michigan and Wisconsin is unclear. Private Archibeque's experiences in the AEFNR were unlike any faced by soldiers in either Siberia or France. The 339th Infantry had fewer than six weeks of training before being shipped overseas. They arrived in England in early August 1918, were placed under British control, and set sail for Arkhangelsk. This anti-Bolshevik town had severe winters with temperatures sometimes dropping to fifty below zero, and snow settled in from late October to March. The British provided the Americans with winter uniforms designed by the Antarctic explorer Sir Ernest Shackleton, who served about six months with the AEFNR forces.[55]

Snow began falling in mid-October just as the AEFNR increasingly clashed with Red Guard troops pushing north. The 339th Infantry's most violent engagement came on the very day the armistice was signed. Suddenly they were frontline troops pitted against a foe their president did not want them fighting. The inexperienced troops lost scores of men killed and wounded on 11 November, contributing significantly toward the total of 144 soldiers killed in action or who died of combat wounds in northwest Russia. Private Archibeque survived ten months there, but somewhere in his return crossing he took ill and died on 9 July 1919, just after his troop transport arrived in New York. His death underscored the futility of the AEFNR, an opinion the 339th Infantry's official history stated bluntly in 1920: "President Wilson erred badly in judgment" in approving intervention in Russia. That assessment remains valid a century later.[56]

Honored

On a crisp Wednesday morning, 23 April 1919, nearly 25,000 soldiers of the 89th Division marched onto the airfield at Trier, Germany, to await inspection and medal decorations. A sergeant from I Company, 356th Infantry, described the ceremony:

> The General [John J. Pershing] has an excellent sorrel saddle horse which is trucked to all these functions. It would be too exhausting for the no-longer-young-General to inspect these men afoot. He rides the sorrel like the old cavalryman he is. After he looks the entire Division over from horseback, he appears afoot at the center front of the four Infantry Regiments to bestow the decorations on the men and Officers who have won special honors and are assembled there for the occasion. Among those honorees are two men from my own company who received the Distinguished Service Cross for bravery under fire.

One of those two honorees was Pvt. Augustin Martinez of Turley in San Juan County, who single-handedly overpowered and killed six Germans in the war's final two hours.[57]

The Congressional Medal of Honor went to only ninety-one individuals in World War I, most awarded posthumously, and no one from New Mexico received it. The Silver Star and Bronze Star were not authorized by Congress until 1932 and 1944, respectively. The second-highest decoration given during World War I was the Distinguished Service Cross. It had been authorized by Congress in the summer of 1918 and was awarded for extraordinary heroism and bravery during combat. Eleven men besides Martinez received it, some posthumously, including Lt. Harry Rogers, who died in the 77th Division's so-called Lost Battalion. Of the ten other New Mexicans awarded the Distinguished Service Cross, seven were Euro-Americans, two Nuevomexicanos, and one an Acoma Pueblo Indian.[58]

Pfc. Amado Garcia of the Pueblo of Acoma and Pvt. Lauriano Martinez of Colmor, Colfax County, sneaked across no-man's land near Fismes to attack German machine gunners on 28 August 1918. The two New Mexicans and another unidentified soldier—all in the 28th Division—eliminated the threat, which ended in hand-to-hand combat against numerous defenders. Both men returned to their communities, married, and were working, respectively, as a farmer and a laborer in the 1930s. Two soldiers' heroism occurred in the opening days of the Meuse-Argonne offensive and entailed helping men in distress: Pvt. Ivory H. Chaplin from Hurley, Grant County, was assigned to an ambulance company with the 26th Division. He helped improvise an aid station to dress wounds near the front line, a site soon hit with artillery. Chaplin continued to work unceasingly to care for wounded soldiers for several hours while "in the open under fire from enemy machine guns and snipers." Sgt. Henry Melvin Woods of Farmington was part of the 1st Gas Regiment in the opening days of the Meuse-Argonne offensive. Nine men in his company had no gas masks when a gas and artillery bombardment began. Woods ran a gauntlet of enemy fire to deliver eight gas masks and gave his own to the ninth man, then assisted wounded men until overcome by gas and his eyes swelled shut. On the first day of the Meuse-Argonne offensive, assigned to the 91st Division, Pvt. Leo L. Ross from Solano, at that time in Mora County, made his way into the enemy line and in two separate actions captured a total of twenty-seven prisoners and commandeered five machine guns. All three men survived the war, but no postwar records were discovered for Ross, Woods, or Chaplin.[59]

Five other recipients of the Distinguished Service Cross are included in the state's records from World War I. All exhibited selflessness to aid others in the face of overwhelming odds. Lt. Leonard G. Hoskins from East Las Vegas was killed in action in the so-called quiet zone of the Vosges Forest on 28 June 1918. He went into a shell-swept area to rescue wounded men under his command and while bringing several to safety suffered fatal shrapnel wounds. Also honored posthumously were two other officers: Lt. Bryan Mudgett of Carlsbad was one of the nearly two dozen New Mexicans who graduated from the first class of the army's officer training school in Monterey, California, in August 1917. He served with the 90th Division and just a day before the Meuse-Argonne offensive died of shrapnel wounds when the enemy intensified artillery shelling as AEF troops took positions for their attack. Mudgett had refused medical attention earlier in the day and insisted that he remain with the men he commanded. Lt. Benjamin I. Berry from Carrizozo had enlisted in the Regular Army when nineteen years old in 1901. In the Meuse-Argonne offensive he was a newly appointed lieutenant who soon found himself the only officer in his company not killed in the assaults of early November 1918. But he suffered a serious head wound, which a medical officer deemed required his immediate evacuation and tagged him for an ambulance. "As soon as the surgeon had passed on Lt. Berry tore off and destroyed the tag, and returned to his company. In the front line for twenty-four hours, he commanded the defense, then, when relief came, guided his company back from the trenches, and when his self-appointed task was completed—died."[60]

Two enlisted men from Roswell survived the war and left brief accounts of the actions recognized by their Distinguished Service Cross. Twenty-six-year-old Pfc. Oren Overton Crockett, who said he was a distant cousin of famous frontiersman Davey Crockett, served as a runner in the 3rd Division. Early in the second week of the Meuse-Argonne offensive, "under terrific shell and machine gun fire, [he] carried messages from company to platoon headquarters, thus maintaining the necessary communication required for a successful operation." Cpl. Floyd H. Wells, twenty-eight years old, served with the 32nd Division. "On October 16th 1918, I was in an outpost ahead of our lines when a man in my squad was wounded by a machine gun bullet. Another soldier and myself carried him back to our lines under heavy machine gun fire as well as artillery." Crockett returned briefly to Roswell but soon moved to San Diego, California, where he married and was proprietor of a paint business in 1930. Wells never returned to New Mexico. He went to Deaver, Wyoming, and took up farming, married, and had four children by 1930.[61]

The twelve New Mexicans decorated with a Distinguished Service Cross had numerous counterparts from across the state, men who distinguished themselves on the battlefield and whose sacrifices—including death—were unheralded. All among the state's combat soldiers beheld the ancient face of war. Most survived the confrontation, but these men lost a part of their essence in the encounter.

CHAPTER 7

Living and Dying

Transport vessels gave New Mexicans in the army an opportunity to see what sailors did and how they lived aboard ships. Many servicemen's questionnaires include comments about their trips over and back. Most infantrymen agreed with Pvt. Pecho A. Mondragon of Raton that the voyage to France was "a long time of ducking submarines and feeding the fish [seasickness]." He was aboard the RMS *Carpatha* along with several hundred other New Mexicans from the 89th Division during a June 1918 voyage. The *Carpatha,* an English passenger liner in the Cunard fleet, was hit by three German torpedoes and sank on its return trip to the United States, just a month after depositing Mondragon and others in France. The *Carpatha* illustrates three intertwined themes that shaped the navy's role in war: ferrying troops, acquiring transport ships, and being stalked by German U-boats.[1]

Aboard Ship and Afterward

Just as no planning had occurred to guide an American army strategically, tactically, or logistically to fight in Europe, the U.S. Navy was equally unprepared to fulfill its primary role in the war—transporting troops safely. Although the navy had long dominated American military strategy, its sea power was immediately found wanting when an inventory of troop transports revealed that all "were totally unfit for service in the war zone." General Pershing, in his memoirs, acerbically described the navy's status in 1917: "The War Department was faced with the question of sending an army to Europe and found that the General Staff had never considered such a thing. No one in authority had any definite idea . . . where the tonnage to transport and supply them was to come from." The navy had only two seaworthy transport ships, each reserved for the marines and able to carry about 1,500 men. Soon, though, the navy assembled a transport fleet of thirty-five ships to supplement the marine transports. They leased fifteen passenger ships, primarily from American-owned lines, but also seized twenty German passenger and merchant ships docked at American ports when the war began.[2]

Confiscation netted the navy some of its largest transport ships, with the biggest being the German passenger liner *Vaterland* (Fatherland or Homeland), which at its launch in 1911 was the largest ship in the world. After the navy confiscated it on 6 April 1917, its size prompted a renaming—USS *Leviathan*. It carried 11,000–14,000 troops and sailors on each trip and transported nearly 120,000 troops in its two-year service, more than any other ship. It also took more New Mexicans to and from the AEF than any other ship, and a few from the state were among its crew.

One such sailor was Arthur C. Edwards of Santa Fe, who enlisted at age seventeen, having just graduated from high school. He served on the *Leviathan* as seaman 2nd class and gunner's mate, assigned upon completing just over a month at each of two naval training stations: Newport, Rhode Island, and Portsmouth, New Hampshire. At the exact time that Edwards was reassigned to a destroyer and promoted to seaman 1st class in early May 1918, another sailor who was six weeks younger than Edwards was posted to the *Leviathan*—future Hollywood movie star Humphrey Bogart. Edwards, too, would migrate to California in the 1920s and in the 1930 census was living with his wife of five years in Oakland and working as a "train man."[3]

In the final months of the war German submarine activity intensified in a frenzied effort to stem the arrival of American troops. This stepped-up submarine activity had consequences for ships carrying New Mexicans. Not all encounters between troop transports and submarines ended well, as chief commissary steward William A. Ott related. The twenty-one-year-old enlisted in the navy on 2 July 1917, leaving his job with the El Paso and Southern Railroad in Tucumcari to begin training at Mare Island, San Francisco, and then Brooklyn, New York. On 4 February 1918 he went onto the troop transport USS *Mount Vernon* as a cook 2nd class. He was serving "on same [ship] when she was torpedoed off the coast of Brest, France, 260 miles out-to-sea on Sept 5th, 1918. Reaching port all safe under our own steam with 500 wounded on board." Ott was transferred to the USS *Dakotan,* where he received two promotions in ten months and made sixteen round-trip transport voyages during and after the war. In July 1919 the *Dakotan* was put out of commission. Ott boarded the USS *McCawley,* a newly commissioned destroyer with a home port at Boston, and extended his enlistment two years to July 1921. In the 1930 census he was working as a chef in a coffee shop in Boston and had married a local woman. Ott's residence and occupation were clearly altered by his time in the navy.[4]

An eyewitness to one of the navy's concerted efforts to curb German submarine activity was twenty-two-year-old Alfred T. Hubbard of Aztec, San Juan County. Completing a "common school" education as a young teenager, Hubbard worked "farming and stock raising" for nearly ten years until enlisting in the navy on 4 January 1918. After training in San Diego for four months he was transferred to Hampton Roads, Virginia, one of the world's largest natural harbors and serving Norfolk and Newport News. Here he boarded the battleship USS *Nevada* and spent May through July on coastal patrol until ordered overseas 1 August 1918. Then, "sunk submarine on Aug 6th, 1918 at 5 p.m. . . . Was eleven day's crossing. Anchored at Bere Haven Bay, Ireland, near [Cork] where the *Lusitania* was sunk. This was the locality where the [German] submarines were doing their work. . . . stayed there until after the Armistice." Seaman Hubbard received an honorable discharge 25 January 1919 and arrived home on 30 January. Nine weeks later he married, had a son and daughter born in the 1920s, and remained in Aztec as a sheep raiser.[5]

Although the Atlantic crossing occupied an oversized role in the navy's dual duties to deliver troops and war supplies safely to France and to project American naval power, other areas also required its presence, especially for the latter purpose: in Europe, the Mediterranean and North Sea; along the Atlantic coastlines of the Americas; and in the Pacific Ocean. New Mexicans participated in all these naval missions.

Clarence W. Thorne, twenty-two years old from Albuquerque, had worked five and a half years as a machinist in the local railroad yard before enlisting in the navy in mid-November 1917. The navy likewise made him a machinist, and he rose to chief machinist mate before his discharge in September 1919. After a month's stay at Mare Island Naval Training Station in San Francisco, he and seven other machinists entrained to Norfolk for further training. In late March the U.S. government took over all of Holland's ships in American ports, and Thorne was placed on a 7,500-ton Dutch freighter, *Ternate.* For the next thirteen months the USS *Ternate* loaded cargo in New Orleans, sailed to New York, and joined whatever convoy was prepared to go to France. When the war ended, the cargo's destination changed to Italy, where that ally needed food for its citizens and the U.S. Army wanted to resupply the 332nd Infantry and prepare to bring it home. Upon returning to Albuquerque, Thorne resumed work as a machinist for the railroad, married several years later, and had two sons in 1930.[6]

Ten days after President Wilson declared war, seventeen-year-old Joseph D. Paiz Jr. of Logan, Quay County, a high school graduate, enlisted in the U.S. Navy in El Paso. Sent first to San Diego and then to Mare Island for training, he arrived in the Philippines in early December. After serving briefly on ships in waters off the Philippines and sailing to Shanghai, China, where he stayed a week, he returned to the Philippines and spent all of 1918 and half of 1919 aboard ships patrolling its coastal waters. In July he departed for Vladivostok, where he stayed fifteen days until 6 August 1919, collecting equipment for the pending departure of the 8th Division. The return trip included brief stops in Japan and China before arriving in Manila on 28 August. Ten days later he departed for San Francisco and upon arrival was discharged on 6 October, having progressed in ratings from apprentice seaman to boatswain's mate 2nd class. He returned to Logan and resumed work as a motion picture operator but moved to Albuquerque, married in 1927 and became father to a son in 1928, and managed a service station in Albuquerque in 1930.[7]

Also serving in the Philippines at the same time but never on the same ships as Paiz was Reyes A. Sanchez of Socorro, who likewise enlisted in the navy in El Paso in May 1917 at age seventeen. After training at Mare Island, he was transferred to the Philippines in November 1917. In late December, Seaman Sanchez was assigned to the cruiser USS *Brooklyn*, the flagship of the commander-in-chief of the Asiatic fleet. With this duty, Sanchez sailed on numerous military and diplomatic trips to ports in China, Japan, and Russia. He never rose in rank, and after his discharge in December 1919 he reported "total service two years six and one-half months with no furlough." Eleven years after his discharge, and using the Anglicized first name Ray, he lived in Albuquerque with his wife and three young children and was a metal worker for the railroad.[8]

Also serving in the Pacific was twenty-three-year-old Charles L. Johnson from the village of Pastura, Guadalupe County. Enlisting in mid-June 1917, he trained for three weeks at Goat Island, Newport, Rhode Island, before being transferred to San Diego for four additional weeks of training. A machinist before the war, Johnson was assigned for three months "to the USS *Alert* then stationed at

Honolulu, HI, as tender [supply and communication] to a flotilla of (4) K-type submarines." From 30 October 1917 to 26 July 1919 Johnson was a machinist mate 2nd class and later 1st class on the K-3 submarine, which carried twenty-eight officers and enlisted men within its 153 by 16 feet and had four torpedo tubes. Not long after being assigned to the K-3, the submarine was shifted eastward, and it exited the Panama Canal on 1 January 1918. For the duration of the war the K-3 conducted patrol duty in the Gulf of Mexico and South Atlantic. Johnson returned home but sometime in the 1920s moved to Wolf, Oklahoma, worked as a machinist, married, and had a daughter.[9]

The cessation of hostilities brought a few New Mexicans in the U.S. Navy to the periphery of major events marking the war's end. Seaman 2nd class Alfred T. Hubbard of Aztec, who served on the USS *Nevada,* became an eyewitness to history beginning at the end of November 1918.

> We were ordered to Weymouth, Eng[land, about midway along the English Channel coast] where all the overseas American fleet gathered to sail to meet our President [aboard the USS *George Washington*]. We went out about 700 miles [southwest] and escorted him to Brest, France. Every ship fired a 21 [gun] salute in honor of the President. We sailed from Brest that evening [Friday 13 December] at 6 P.M. for the States. Came by way of the Azores.[10]

President Woodrow Wilson and first lady Edith Wilson likewise passed through the Azores on their way to France, where they spent mid-December to mid-February, interrupted by brief trips to Great Britain and Italy. They returned to the United States for several weeks and in mid-March were back in France for three and a half months. On the afternoon of Saturday, 28 June 1919, President Wilson signed the Treaty of Versailles. He and Edith Wilson were on a train that evening to Brest and departed on Sunday. The return journey was ten days, and one of the ships escorting the president's party was the recently commissioned destroyer USS *New Mexico,* which had entered the fleet in September 1918.

The maiden voyage of the *New Mexico* across the Atlantic had been in December when it escorted the USS *George Washington* and its presidential party to Brest. Construction of the *New Mexico* had been approved by Congress on 30 June 1914. When completed in 1918 its hull was 624 feet, sixteen feet longer than any previous battleship in the navy. It was also the first turbo-electric battleship and able to sustain a top speed of twenty-one knots for long periods. "Nine oil-burning boilers delivered steam to two giant turbine-generators, which powered four electric motors, one for each propeller shaft.... [The ship] possessed formidable firepower with 14-inch guns mounted in four massive 3-barrel turrets."[11]

Upon its return the *New Mexico* became the flagship of the Pacific Fleet and soon departed for San Francisco and eventually sailed to Hawaii. Joining the destroyer briefly in California was twenty-year-old Seaman Meliton F. Otero of Albuquerque, a hospital corpsman. Otero reported that he "experienced a fire aboard the USS *New Mexico* while anchored at the San Francisco dock. Three died and forty were knocked out by the fumes." Several months after this accident, nineteen-year-old Yeoman Edward R. Selover was reassigned from the Navy Department in Washington, D.C., to the *New Mexico* and attached to the office of the commander-in-chief, Pacific Fleet. A native of Las Vegas, Selover had enlisted in the navy in July 1916 at age seventeen, having completed the eighth grade and one year at a business school. He worked as a clerk in an Albuquerque candy store before enlisting and returned to that position upon discharge. A few years later he married. They had two sons and a daughter by 1930, when he was an assistant cashier at a local bank.[12]

In addition to transporting the president, the navy had several other essential missions in 1919, principally transporting returning troops, a duty that continued into September. Seaman Lino Gonzales, twenty-one years old from Lemitar, Socorro County, had served a year in the navy, was stationed in Philadelphia, and "on the 12th day of November 1918 [transferred] to a transport service ship USS *Santa Teresa*. [He] served on that transport nine months and twenty days bringing our soldier boys [home] from France." The *Santa Teresa* was a newly built passenger liner the navy chartered and commissioned in mid-November 1918 in Philadelphia. On 3 December it departed for what would be the first of eight round-trip voyages to France. Seaman Gonzales was on board during the ship's entire service as a U.S. Navy transport vessel. Its final voyage was to Brest, and shortly after arriving Seaman Gonzales received a five-day liberty pass and went to Paris. He made no mention of what he saw or did. The return trip brought some men from the 1st Division—the last large contingent to arrive home—to New York on 4 September. The *Santa Teresa* returned to Philadelphia, was decommissioned, and Seaman Gonzales was discharged and returned to New Mexico at the end of September. He lived with his parents for a while and worked on the family farm but was not listed in either the 1930 or 1940 census. Two threads of his World War I service finally reconnected him to public records. He reenlisted in the navy for the duration of World War II in September 1942. He did so while living in Philadelphia and returned there in August 1945 and died in 1952.[13]

A second critical navy mission a few New Mexicans participated in involved minesweeping activity in the North Sea in 1919. When the United States entered the war, German submarines had been traveling at will in the North Sea, around the tip of Scotland and on to wherever they were to be positioned. The British had laid mines from Dover to Belgium to shut off access in the south of England at the Straits of Dover, but the northern route remained open. The U.S. Navy closed it with a mine barrage extending from northern Scotland's Orkney Islands due west 240 miles to Norway, at a width of about twenty-five miles. Laid in more than 6,000 square miles of sea were a total of 70,263 mines, each filled with three hundred pounds of TNT. The U.S. Navy put down 56,611 mines, and the British placed 13,652. To remove the mines after the war, both navies contributed minesweepers, and two New Mexicans were part of the effort from early spring through early fall 1919.[14]

Seventeen-year-old Justus C. Adams from Doña Ana County joined the navy in June 1917. In the spring of 1919 he was assigned to the USS *Grebe,* Minesweeper no. 43. The process he followed for detonating mines had been designed in part by a New Mexican who graduated from the U.S. Naval Academy in June 1918, Lt. (j.g.) Morton Seligman, twenty-three years old upon being commissioned, and son of Santa Fe's postmaster. After serving three and a half months on the flagship of the minesweeping detachment, Seligman spent from April to June conducting experimental work and making preparations for removal of the North Sea mines. He remained in the navy after the war and continued to do experimental work, but he shifted to aviation, participating in early tests of catapults to launch planes from the desk of the USS *Oklahoma* in 1922. He remained assigned to the naval air station in San Diego where he was a lieutenant s.g. in the aviation unit in 1928.[15]

Adams took great pride in the work of the minesweepers:

> Many New Mexico papers and magazines are received aboard this vessel, and are eagerly read by the entire crew [seventy-five enlisted men and five officers]. But there is at present one part of the Navy, and its work, that is scarcely more than mentioned in any newspaper or periodical that has come to our attention.... I refer to the greatest feat that has ever been undertaken... removing the North Sea Mine Barrage with precision and dispatch.[16]

The USS *Grebe,* one of thirty-six U.S. Navy minesweepers in the North Sea (all named for birds), spent sixty-six days at sea and seventeen in port, mostly devoted to repairs after being severely damaged by mine explosions under its stern in early August 1919. About half of the minesweepers incurred damage from explosions. Adams was discharged from the navy in September 1920, and the first record of him thereafter is from 1935 (from data collected in the 1940 census). He was married, had a daughter, and was living on a farm in Colfax County. Five years later he was manager of an oil field in Texas.[17]

Artists and Archaeologists Aiding the Navy

When the United States entered World War I, New Mexico had a well-established international reputation for its art colonies in Taos and Santa Fe. The state's art community quickly stepped forward to assist with fund-raising events by donating art for raffles to aid war relief efforts as well as creating posters to promote events with the original work donated for auction to support charities such as the Red Cross. Typical of early initiatives was work by Santa Fe artists in July 1917 in support of the city's chapter of the Navy League in their efforts "to swell funds for war purposes." The Santa Fe art colony became a "poster squad . . . expected to contribute striking poster designs . . . advertising the patriotic work of the league and its undertakings."[18]

A long-term project involving New Mexico civilian artists gave new meaning to the description "large canvas"—ships. Marine camouflage during World War I deceived German submarine torpedo launchers and saved countless lives of American soldiers and sailors on troop transports, many navy ships, and tons of food merchant ships carried to Allies. Artists used colors and patterns painted on the sides of ships to confuse calculations of distance, speed, direction, and size of vessel. New Mexico's contributors to camouflage painting were two Santa Fe artists—Bror Julius Olsson (B.J.O.) Nordfeldt (1878–1955) and William Penhallow Henderson (1877–1943).[19]

Nordfeldt had been in San Francisco when the United States declared war. Ten days later, on 16 April 1917, the U.S. Shipping Board, Emergency Fleet Corporation, was established. Shortly thereafter Nordfeldt became a supervisor of camouflage painting on merchant vessels in the Fleet Corporation's Steel Ship Division. Henderson arrived in San Francisco in August 1917 to work for the Shipping Board in the same division as Nordfeldt. Together the men are credited with developing "the Pacific Coast 'camouflage' to such an extent that it became a standard with which Atlantic Coast inspectors compared the work done in the eastern shipyards." Henderson took pride in the camouflage painting, telling his wife about the "fine work done in the yards here." He also found time to work in his own studio in San Francisco on paintings, some of which had been in a recent exhibition in the city. When the war ended he submitted his letter of resignation on 15 December 1918 and soon returned to Santa Fe.[20]

Edgar Lee Hewett and the two institutions he directed concurrently—the School for American Archaeology (1907–46) and the Museum of New Mexico (1909–46)—each had important roles in New Mexico's support for the war. The museum's promotion of range finder art (see chapter 4) has slipped into obscurity. But another activity largely unknown during and after the war resurfaced in the early twenty-first century—the spying done by a member of the School for American Archaeology, which had been renamed the School of American Research in 1917. Hewett allowed the school's leading Maya archaeologist, Sylvanus G. Morley (1883–1948), to use his professional research as a cover for covert intelligence gathering in Mexico and Central America on behalf of the Office of Naval Intelligence.[21]

When Germany resumed submarine warfare early in 1917, the U.S. Navy immediately became concerned that the Germans would attempt to target American commercial and naval ships coming through the Panama Canal (opened in 1915) and crossing the Caribbean Sea. Casting about for espionage agents who could provide detailed reports of German activities along the coastal regions of eastern Mexico, the Yucatán, and the western Caribbean coast of Central America, the government settled upon Maya archaeologists as a potential pool of spies. Chief among them was Santa Fe's Sylvanus Morley.[22]

When approached by Naval Intelligence officers in March 1917, Morley quickly accepted, became Agent 53, and set to work on the navy's two priorities: determining whether German submarines were operating out of clandestine bases along the more than 1,200 miles of Mexican and Central American coastline, and assessing the sources and extent of anti-Americanism in the same regions. Morley stood five feet, two inches and weighed just over one hundred pounds, but his hyperactive disposition is evident in his several thousand miles of reconnaissance on foot and horseback between April 1917 and March 1919 and the thirty-two lengthy intelligence reports he sent to Naval Intelligence during these years. He became, arguably, one the most important American spies of World War I and was at the center of a web of agent-cum-academics in regions of ancient Maya ruins. The intelligence network he set up repaid the time and expense of its creation by allowing the U.S. government to exert precisely what Morley believed essential—political and economic influence during Mexico's instability in the 1920s.[23]

The 9 Percent

Approximately 1,250 New Mexicans served in the U.S. Navy during World War I. They were 9 percent of the state's men in uniform, and more than a hundred of them completed postwar service questionnaires for the Board of Historical Service. The casualty files also include data on the few men who died while in the navy—mostly from the influenza, some in accidents, but several when ships sank. The accounts from sailors—and a few naval officers—are in many ways a counterpoint to the background and experiences of soldiers, especially draftees. The amount of schooling was the most obvious difference. New Mexicans in the National Army generally had three or four years of education, whereas almost all the state's enlistees in the navy had graduated from high school. Absent in their narratives are scenes of the maw of war. Instead the sailors' wartime assignments almost always afforded them an opportunity to broaden their understanding of themselves and the world in visits to foreign countries. Although their duties were arduous and even dangerous, they frequently gained a new perspective on their abilities and interests. Some left the navy optimistic about their future.

Representative of sailors who were conscientious though not noteworthy during their enlistment, but eager to shake hands with the future upon discharge, was Yeoman 1st class Herman G. Baca of Belen. He had enlisted in the navy in May 1917 at age twenty. Before the war he had been a schoolteacher in a village near Grants, but his time in the navy greatly expanded his horizons. He reported that while serving on the freighter USS *Major Wheeler* he "was in Peru, Chile, Panama, Cuba, Haiti, England and France and all along the eastern coast of the U.S." Upon his return to New Mexico he seized the opportunity to get in on the ground floor of the growth of the American Legion and quickly became the state's leading recruiter. That success catapulted him into becoming the American Legion's first elected state post commander in October 1919. Baca worked on behalf of the state's veterans throughout the interwar decades.[24]

Influenza Pandemic

The influenza pandemic of 1918–19 occurred when a virus opportunistically intertwined with the carnage of World War I. The result was a rapacious agent of death, exceeded in human history only by smallpox. The influenza pandemic took the lives of millions of people from every continent except Antarctica, and estimates of the toll range from 62 million to about 112 million—civilians and combatants alike. The war's global scale was paralleled by the scope of the influenza pandemic, but the virus's fatalities were at least four times more numerous than the war's deaths. Most vulnerable to the flu were children, young adults from their late teens into their thirties, and those sixty or more years old. Men in the military faced a double exposure in the fall of 1918. The deadliest battle for the AEF—the Meuse-Argonne offensive between 26 September and 11 November of that year—was fought as the influenza pandemic peaked.

For the U.S. Army the origins of the influenza pandemic were in Kansas. More than a thousand laborers imported from China arrived at Camp Funston to do scut work at the end of February 1918. Within a week influenza swept through the camp. Some scholars have speculated that these Chinese laborers were a vector for the influenza virus because of that country's concentration of pigs sharing space with humans. Other writers have drawn attention to thick smoke blanketing the camp at the exact time of the flu outbreak, a product of burning a winter's accumulation of manure from more than 10,000 horses and mules and releasing into the air a microbial cocktail that had brewed in dung for months and was now breathed by soldiers.[25]

At even greater remove and a year earlier, influenza swept through a British base camp in northern France in early 1917. This outbreak has been postulated as evidence that a mix of "[poisonous] gas [and excrement from] pigs, ducks, geese, and horses . . . provided the conditions for the emergence of the 'Spanish' influenza." A path by which a virus from that camp made its way to Spain has not been charted, but the origin of the erroneous name is clear. Spain, a neutral country, imposed no blackout on newspaper coverage of events that could have intelligence value if reported in a belligerent country. "As a result news about the epidemic would appear in Spanish papers, giving the impression that it was the only country affected by the illness." On Sunday, 26 May 1918, the Madrid daily *El Sol* used the headline "The Epidemic Continues" to describe widespread incidents that began appearing at the end of the previous week. The paper reported outbreaks in the capital but especially in areas near the French border, particularly in Barcelona. The rector of the city's university, a medical doctor, reported that the flu was "something more severe" than typically encountered seasonally with *la gripe*. In the northern ports of La Coruña and El Ferrol flu was widespread, and soon *El Sol* reported that "the flu fever has invaded all of Spain and, within days, has spread incredibly fast." In Madrid an estimated 80,000 were stricken, and even King Alfonso XIII was bedridden. Fortunately, though, death rates remained low.[26]

A month later this first wave of the epidemic had subsided on the Iberian Peninsula, but we now know that the influenza moved about freely. It appeared in Portugal, Greece, and Paris in April; in England, Scotland, and Wales in June and July and among German soldiers on the western front in the same months; in Denmark and Norway in July; and in Switzerland and Holland in August. Each of these incidents in Europe and the United States is a reminder that the influenza virus is different from almost all other viruses. It mutates rapidly, becoming more resistant and able to survive in many settings. Thus it was that in eighteen months between 1918 and 1919 the influenza virus became virulent and voracious, sickening 500 million people and taking the lives of as many as one-fifth of those stricken. Thus did the first appearance of the H1N1 virus bring its havoc to modern civilization, ratcheting up both morbidity and mortality rates for influenza, with deaths skyrocketing from 0.1 percent to an unprecedented 2.5 percent of the population worldwide.[27]

Influenza in the Military

The published reports of influenza's presence between January 1917 and August 1918 yield two conclusions. First, just as the war drew soldiers to France from across the globe, so too did viruses from at least four continents—fresh from their first skirmishes with men, women, and children in Asia, North and South America, and Europe—recombine in France during the summer of 1918 and unleash a new, virulent offensive in September. This second-wave virus coincided with the mobilization of millions of American soldiers for the Meuse-Argonne offensive. The influenza struck hundreds of thousands of these soldiers, killing among the Americans almost 15,900 in the AEF and nearly 30,000 in stateside camps.

Second, the first wave of influenza hit hardest in the United States at Camp Funston, Kansas. Beginning on Monday, 4 March 1918, when a cook reported to sick call, an unprecedented degree of sickness enveloped the camp: "Between March 4 and March 29, 1,127 men in a camp of 29,000 were sent to the [Fort Riley] base hospital with a disease clinically diagnosed as influenza. 'Many more' were said to have been cared for in the infirmaries of the camp. There were 237 cases of pneumonia in March, with a mortality of 20 per cent [forty-eight soldiers]." To put these forty-eight deaths in three weeks into statistical perspective, in all thirty-two training camps during the final four months of 1917, fewer than one hundred soldiers died from pneumonia.[28]

One of the forty-eight succumbing to pneumonia at Camp Funston was twenty-five-year-old Raymond C. Bloom of Magdalena in Socorro County. He was part of the 89th Division and assigned to its medical corps officer candidate school adjacent to the Fort Riley hospital several miles west of Camp Funston.

Bloom died at 6:10 A.M. on Friday, 22 March 1918, sixteen days after arriving at the Army Medical Department Training Corps and three days after being admitted to the base hospital. His final two weeks began with the quick onset of symptoms: "a severe headache, chills or chilliness, pains in the back or legs, temperature sometimes as high as 104, great prostration, and drowsiness." Bloom's death followed a trajectory where "influenza paves the way for the pneumonia," which set in about seven days after he contracted the flu, and three and a half days later fluid in the lungs took his life.[29]

Raymond Bloom boarded a train to go to Camp Funston on the afternoon of Tuesday, 5 March. His status as an officer candidate meant he left ahead of the thirty-one men Socorro County sent to Camp Funston as draftees on 8 March. That night he rode through northeast New Mexico, over Raton Pass, and into Trinidad, Colorado. The train stopped there for breakfast, and he wrote a short note to his mother and mentioned having a "good night's rest, thanks to blanket." This note of gratitude was his last communication with his family. Bloom was single and had resided in Magdalena for three years, staying on property his family owned after completing his studies at Williams College, Massachusetts, in 1915. He worked as a clerk at Becker & McTavish, a successful general mercantile business that also sold farm implements as well as Studebaker cars and Goodyear tires. Bloom found his niche in the automotive department, and his employer described him as "likeable, true, and reliable." A military escort accompanied Bloom's coffin on its train trip to Santa Fe—exactly three weeks after he left for camp. He was the state's first casualty of World War I to be buried in Santa Fe's National Cemetery, and Governor Lindsey, state officials, and city leaders from Santa Fe and Magdalena attended his funeral.[30]

World War I continued a pattern spanning millennia: disease killed more soldiers than did combat. The second wave of influenza, beginning in mid-September and continuing through the winter, was borne by a particularly lethal virus. Among American troops stateside it erupted first at a National Army facility near Boston, Camp Devens, on 12 September 1918. Its two-month run stateside produced "306,719 cases of influenza reported among the troops in America. During the same time there were 48,079 cases of pneumonia and 19,429 deaths. About one in every five had influenza, that of those about one in six developed pneumonia and that of the pneumonia patients about two out of five died." The following is a list of the four training camps to which New Mexicans had been sent in largest numbers, the date the influenza outbreak began, and the order of infection among the thirty-two camps: Camp Funston, 20 September, sixth among the the thirty-two National Guard and National Army camps for first flu cases; Camp Pike, 24 September, ninth among camps for first flu cases; Camp Kearny, 27 September, twelfth; and Camp Cody, 3 October, seventeenth. The navy had fewer than one-quarter the number of men in uniform compared to the army, but the influenza pandemic overwhelmed its thirty hospitals worldwide. The navy's total number of deaths from the virus was 4,158, excluding an unknown number of at-sea deaths. Four New Mexico sailors were reported as dying from influenza stateside in 1918–19.[31]

A total of 127 soldiers and three sailors from New Mexico died stateside from influenza between September and December 1918. These deaths occurred at thirty-eight sites, including training camps, forts, naval facilities, and civilian hospitals. Sites recording five or more deaths of New Mexican soldiers in these four months were as follows: Camp Dix, New Jersey, twenty-two; Camp Pike, Arkansas, fifteen; Camp Mills, Long Island, New York, twelve; Camp Cody, New Mexico, nine; Camp Kearny, California, six; Camp McArthur, Texas, six; Camp Travis, Texas, six; and Camp Logan, five. These eight camps accounted for 58 percent of the stateside deaths of New Mexico men in uniform. Very few enlistees from New Mexico were at Camp Funston/Fort Riley in the fall of 1918, and only two deaths were reported from among the state's new recruits at the Kansas facilities. One of these was eighteen-year-old Kipling Wade, who entered the army on 5 July 1918 at Farmington after graduating from Mancos (Colorado) High School. He was sent for signal corps training at Fort Riley, but fourteen weeks later he died from flu-related pneumonia. His body, accompanied by a soldier and his father, "was met at the [Mancos train] station by a number of local citizens and at 2:30 in the afternoon all the business houses closed, a long line of automobiles, displaying the national colors, gathered at the undertaking parlor on North Main Street and slowly followed the corpse out to its final resting place." This public display of a small town's support in tribute to a young soldier may have provided some in the community a way to grieve all lives lost to the flu and war.[32]

Beginning in midsummer draftees were primarily sent to Camp Pike and three camps in Texas, and twenty-six New Mexico soldiers died of influenza in these four camps, or 20 percent of the total. The nine deaths among New Mexicans at Camp Cody represented 7 percent of the total of 128 soldiers who died there in the six weeks prior to the armistice, with 94 percent of all the camp's fatalities occurring between 23 October and 6 November. No new draftees from the state were inducted during the final seven weeks of the war. The state's draft boards were preparing to call up more than two thousand new soldiers at the end of October when telegrams began reaching Governor Lindsey that medical examinations were suspended in numerous communities. Representative of the messages received in Santa Fe were comments from Clayton—"lots of flu . . . quite fatal . . . examine as soon as safe"—and Silver City—"influenza worse than at any time . . . can't do [physical] examinations."[33]

But it was at two embarkation sites—Camp Dix and Camp Mills, where tens of thousands of soldiers were collected before going to France—that the highest number of New Mexicans died: thirty-five, or 27 percent of the total number of stateside deaths among the state's soldiers. In addition, ten New Mexicans died of influenza on ships while crossing the Atlantic Ocean. If a transport ship could dock in France within three days of the death, the deceased were interred there; if not, they were buried at sea—except for those on the *Leviathan*, which had refrigeration, caskets, and storage space sufficient to handle nearly a hundred corpses. Among New Mexicans in the AEF, sixty-three succumbed to disease between September and December. Disease accounted for 54 percent (270 victims) of the state's 502 fatalities of servicemen, whereas only 26 percent (131 men) were killed in action and an additional 13 percent (sixty-four soldiers) died from their wounds. A grim statistic encapsulating that disease trumped combat in its death rate was a ratio reported by the University of New Mexico. Among its students in uniform, four died; three were taken by influenza-induced pneumonia, only one fell in battle.[34]

A few recollections from among those closest touched by influenza deaths recover their lives from obscurity, if only momentarily. Twenty-eight-year-old Pvt. Hugh C. Carlisle, a UNM student who had worked previously as a traveling salesman, was drafted and sent to Camp Travis on 25 July 1918 but was quickly transferred to the 81st Division at Camp Wheeler, Georgia, where he was assigned as a medic to the 106th Field Signal Battalion. His division began departing for France on 16 September but was divided among several different convoys. Carlisle boarded his troop transport on 7 October. A statement from his commanding officer to his wife of sixteen months and his mother reads as follows: "When the influenza started on the Transport, Private Carlisle worked day and night with the sick, when he contracted the disease. He was given all medical attention but passed away October 18, 1918." He was buried at the Suresnes American Cemetery near Paris.[35]

Troop ships in the fall of 1918 became floating incubators for influenza. The statement of physician and surgeon Lewis B. Robinson of Pinos Altos in Grant County, commissioned a lieutenant in the medical corps, is a representative account of influenza's toll during the Atlantic crossing. He accompanied the

African American 813th Pioneer Labor Battalion to France and briefly mentioned their treatment, then was reassigned to the 33rd Division at the front in the Meuse-Argonne offensive.

> We set sail on the 15th of September with 13 vessels and 50,000 troops convoyed by 5 torpedo boat destroyers, the battleship New Hampshire and a cruiser. . . . We had 1,000 cases of Spanish Flu on the ship with 4 deaths on the voyage. [Arriving at Brest on 28 September, we] marched four miles out to fields surrounded by high hedge fences. Men slept on the damp ground and sent 6 to the hospital with pneumonia. Rain and mud everywhere.

Lt. Howard H. Edwards, twenty-four years old from Las Cruces, served in the Signal Corps: "In Sept 1918 [I] sailed for France on the USS *Leviathan* during 'flu' epidemic. Numerous cases on board and of the 13,000 on board a third were affected, including myself. Was taken off ship at Brest and spent a week at Kerhoun hospital near that point." Edwards never fully recovered and after spending two days at the front was "put before [a medical fitness] board which classified me a disability case." Ninety-six soldiers died of the flu on the *Leviathan* during that voyage, with thirty-one succumbing on the final day at sea. Only six of the deceased had to be buried at sea.[36]

Among the more than 1,200 New Mexicans sent to Camp Cody in June 1918 was twenty-four-year-old Candido Montoya, single and a sheepherder and farmer from San Patricio in Lincoln County. He was assigned to a development battalion and remained in camp when the 34th Division went overseas. In Private Montoya's two-and-a-half-page letter home to his parents, Estanislao and Socorra Montoya, written 16 September 1918, a premonition of death overshadowed everything he said. News of the death of his godfather left him "still feeling in my sad heart a great sorrow," and though he knew his godfather "rests with my Lord," a foreboding, contemplative mood filled the letter. In a long final paragraph he bid a fond farewell to all in his extended and immediate family and ended by saying "good-bye, good-bye, my beloved parents." A terse annotation on his service record noted, "Died of influenza November 5, 1918, at Camp Cody after a short illness. Buried at San Patricio." Situating Private Montoya's passing within the trajectory of influenza at Camp Cody, he succumbed in the period of greatest loss. The first victim died on 3 October, with six more passing over the next two weeks, but then between 24 October and 7 November a total of 107 died, or nearly eight men every day.[37]

Another June draftee at Camp Cody was twenty-three-year-old Pvt. Onofre N. Candelaria of Old Town in Albuquerque. A machinist with the AT&SF Railway, Candelaria left for camp when his wife, Juanita, was one month pregnant with their daughter, Clementina (born 27 February 1919). He spent two months at Camp Cody before leaving with the 34th Division for their embarkation camp at the end of August. Arriving at Camp Dix, New Jersey, most of the infantrymen were quarantined from 16 September to 12 October because of influenza. During the twenty-six days spent in quarantine at Camp Dix, a New Mexican soldier died on average every twenty-eight hours. A total of twenty-two men from the state succumbed to influenza at Camp Dix, and Private Candelaria passed away on Sunday 6 October.[38]

Spanish Flu on the Civilian Home Front

In the final two months of World War I, the home front in New Mexico witnessed death stalk and strike down men, women, and children in numbers never before experienced. The state's population was about 350,000, and between 1,500 and 5,000 civilian New Mexicans died from influenza, which means that the population loss ranged from 0.4 percent to as much as 1.4 percent of the total population. Nationwide, 650,000–675,000 died in a total population of 106 million, or slightly more than 0.5 percent. The imprecision in New Mexico's data was an inevitable result of it being the only state that did not collect vital statistics. This lapse was decried at the time, with public unrest focused on "state medical authorities for their disorganization and general unpreparedness in dealing with the [influenza] epidemic." New initiatives spearheaded by women's groups in 1919 resulted in a statewide health board, greater attention to well-baby and infant care, and programs to improve public health.[39]

As the number of victims mounted, only the U.S. Public Health Service's medical officers at Fort Stanton and East Las Vegas provided continuous contact with city, county, and state officials to track the number of sick, tally deaths, and report on the flu's spread and decline. But statistics unknown to New Mexicans then are grim reminders of the true toll in human lives during 1918–19: civilian deaths among New Mexicans from influenza were greater than the state's 195 combat deaths by a multiple of between 7.5 (for 1,500) and 25 (for 5,000).[40]

In relation to the rest of the country, influenza arrived late in New Mexico—at the end of September 1918. *La Bandera Americana* printed a first article in Albuquerque about its spread from the East on 27 September. The next day Deming recorded its initial victim—seventeen-year-old Joel Anderson Smyer, who may have been the state's first civilian flu fatality. By early October outbreaks were occurring statewide without regard to race, gender, or where or how people lived. Though Mountainair's *El Independiente* claimed on 5 October that "the influenza is being combated effectively," the only consistent action taken to stem its spread involved reverting to practices enforced in 1917–18. Wartime mobilization prepared Americans to confront a crisis and accept restrictions on individual rights when imposed by officials. For its part the federal government's most important role in coping with the influenza pandemic came in how it empowered state and local officials to exercise coercive authority. This delegation of power conditioned Americans to accept and obey decrees.[41]

Actions taken by Farmington officials to combat the spread of influenza were representative of how communities responded across the state: "There had been six weeks of quarantine [17 October–28 November]—a ban on meetings, churches, shows, and schools. The fair was cancelled, public places closed, and children were to 'stay at home and not play together.'" Even funerals had to be postponed. Retail businesses cooperated by voluntarily curtailing their hours, restricting the number of shoppers allowed in a store at one time, and requiring everyone entering the store to wear a mask covering their nose and mouth. Companies, including Phelps-Dodge, distributed flyers printed in Spanish and English listing precautions to take. But all these measures did not preclude some citizens from reverting to vigilantism. Across the state vigilantes carrying Smith and Wesson or Colt firearms were sentinels at railroad depots and refused to allow visitors from flu-ridden regions to disembark from trains. Given the alarm over influenza's impact, compliance was high during the limited time that local officials invoked emergency powers to deal with the health crisis—with one exception. On Monday, November 11, the streets filled in towns around New Mexico in defiance of orders prohibiting public gatherings. The largest crowd was in Albuquerque. *La Bandera America* reported, "Ten thousand celebrated the great victory of the Allies on Monday. Huge street processions and flag waving went on all day."[42]

The health dangers posed when people were in close proximity are illustrated in the incidents of influenza at the army hospital in Fort Bayard and at the Pueblo of Isleta. Fort Bayard underwent a fivefold increase in patients during the war, having only three hundred in April 1917 but just over 1,500 on 1 January 1919. It remained primarily a tuberculosis facility, but gassed soldiers arrived throughout 1918. Among nearly 750 staff at the hospital, 129 personnel were felled by the virus in October 1918. These cases accounted for 10 percent of all the influenza patients, and just over a thousand of the TB and gassed patients came down with the flu. Fortunately the majority of these patients recovered, but eighty-three of them did succumb to influenza at Fort Bayard in 1918. No comprehensive records exist for the total number of staff who died from the flu. The Bureau of Indian Affairs sent a physician to Albuquerque to treat influenza victims in nearby pueblos in late October and early November 1918. He reported that eighty-nine in the Pueblo of Isleta died during his ten days of medical service, with ten expiring his first full day at the pueblo. He noted that, even "with death staring them in the face at every corner," he was rarely able to get the sick to leave the crowded rooms into which they congregated. As a result, few survived. Among Navajos, different circumstances yielded similar high death rates. The ill were kept apart and great distances separated hogans, and yet Navajos in northwest New Mexico died in numbers missionaries found dismaying.[43]

The Meaning of Death

One New Mexico scholar recently lifted a veil of silence that has long shrouded the influenza pandemic by reading newspaper descriptions about the victims. In doing so she was left "almost exhausted from sorrow." That same feeling sweeps over anyone who comes across the extensive records loved ones provided the state's Board of Historical Service. The more than 6,800 pages assembled to record deaths of men in uniform humanized the deceased and helped the survivors edit memories to find meaning in a death.[44]

The most obvious of these interpretations was religious, and at that level the construction of death's meaning had been evolving for several centuries when World War I ended. After the Civil War, Americans clung ever more tightly to the centuries-old Christian tradition of *ars moriendi*, a Good Death. Its central tenets were the expectation that preparing oneself to die set a course whereby the deceased passed away peacefully, free of suffering and pain, and ready to enter the hoped-for afterlife. But these traditional ideas had, by the late nineteenth century, "been to a considerable degree separated from their explicitly theological roots." What remained was still a reassuring message, but one that did not account for an obvious and increasingly common reality beginning in the late 1880s—the prevalence of deaths that were wrenching for all involved. These instances included children dying from such diseases as diphtheria and smallpox, and adults committing suicide.[45]

In the several decades after the Civil War, the idealized Good Death version of the transition from life to death increasingly diverged from the reality of people's final days. It held no comfort for all who witnessed or suffered through an agonizing death. Then came World War I, which brought to the fore a darker, even malevolent, sense of death that further punctured the prevailing remnants of a benign passing. The horrors of the battlefield—slaughters amid the brutality of mechanized warfare—compelled survivors to confront the viciousness of death in combat. The random and unrelenting violence of war seemed to confirm the vision of the leading literary naturalist of the era, Theodore Dreiser—that the universe was indifferent to man's fate.

New Mexican servicemen's thoughts about death, the afterlife, or their relation to a supreme being were rarely documented. What is known about how New Mexicans in uniform viewed their future is pragmatic and concrete; they understood the importance of purchasing a term life insurance policy in case they never left France alive or returned disabled. Insurance policies were aggressively pushed at training camps and especially to those in the AEF. The government estimated that 95 percent of all men in uniform carried death and disability insurance for coverage ranging between $1,000 and $10,000. More than $1.2 billion dollars in policies were purchased in the first twelve months of the war. Monthly premiums were based on age, and between $6.30 and $10.08 was automatically deducted from holders' pay for a $10,000 policy. To promote purchases, soldiers were strongly encouraged to use their three-dollar-a-month supplemental allotment, paid for AEF service, to buy a $5,000 policy. The term policy (at the same premium) could remain in effect for five years after the war and then be transferred to a private insurer.[46]

In the maw of war where shrapnel decapitated and shredded bodies, the expectation of a peaceful, painless death was itself a casualty of the ubiquitous disfigurement soldiers saw on the battlefield, gruesome scenes one scholar recently described graphically: "The dead hung on nets of barbed wire, rotted half-buried in shell craters. Some soldiers were obliterated entirely, atomized.... Others were violently dismembered, their limbs, skulls, fingers, even teeth transformed into deadly projectiles." The sight and smell of such carnage prompted one returning New Mexico soldier, who fought in the Meuse-Argonne offensive, to recoil from revisiting the scenes in his recollections. "Please excuse me," he wrote. "I can't tell you anymore of my experiences. May do it at a future date. Hope you don't take this as an insult for them times are too fresh in my memory yet."[47]

On the home front in New Mexico, insight into how people interpreted death is found in the vocabulary, or frame of reference, used to describe it. Nuevomexicanos expressed sentiments similar to those of Evaristo Gurule of Tierra Amarilla in Rio Arriba County, whose twenty-four-year-old son, Pvt. Francisco Gurule in the 123rd Infantry of the 31st Division, died at Hoboken, New Jersey, in the influenza epidemic. The father invoked a celestial allusion to describe his son's passing: "He was called upon to answer the summons of his Creator to enter into the Eternal Mansion, which his spirit did on 21 October 1918." No Euro-American used similar faith-based images. Instead, a secular tone was invoked, such as in describing the fate of 256 naval personnel, including nineteen-year-old petty officer Frederick B. Golding from Silver City. He perished in the mysterious sinking of the USS *Cyclops* off the coast of Brazil on 4 March 1917, perhaps the victim of German saboteurs. An article describing the incident ended in a somber tone of naturalism, hoping "that these men met their death swiftly, and with short-lived struggle 'without sharks and birds of prey to watch their agony.'"[48]

The different frame of reference invoked by a Nuevomexicano and a Euro-American in describing the moment of death likely came from differences in their religious inclinations. A sampling from religious preferences recorded on the servicemen's questionnaires does indeed point to a sharp divide in religious orientations. From among a total of 1,400 service questionnaires reviewed, 310 (22 percent) were randomly selected for tabulation. Item three on the questionnaire sought information on church affiliation. The respondents in the sample were 170 Euro-Americans and 140 Nuevomexicanos. Of these, fifty-seven Euro-Americans (34 percent) and eleven Nuevomexicanos (8 percent) replied "none" or provided no answer. Two variables wrapped the thickest layers of religious insulation around New Mexico soldiers—ethnicity and Catholicism. Among the Nuevomexicanos, 116 (83 percent) self-identified as Catholic (or *Católico*). For Euro-Americans, twenty (12 percent) listed their affiliation as Catholic, and the five highest percentages of Protestant denominational membership were as follows: Methodist, 16 percent (twenty-seven members); Episcopalian, 9.4 percent (sixteen); Protestant/Christian, 8.2 percent (fourteen); Baptist, 6 percent (eleven); and Presbyterian, 5.8 percent (ten). The remaining 9 percent of Euro-Americans listed five other Protestant denominations, and three individuals were of the Jewish faith. Among the 9 percent of Protestant Nuevomexicanos, the church affiliation was just over 2 percent each for Methodists, Baptists, and Christian/Protestants. The obvious omission in the data for Nuevomexicanos involved the Presbyterians, who although present in the state since the 1850s were not represented in data collected. What can be extrapolated from the data are well-known trends of that era: Nuevomexicanos were overwhelmingly Catholic, and Protestantism was in its second decade of adherents drifting away from religion.[49]

What bereaved families really wanted to know were details of how their loved one had met his end. The search for such information was rarely a quick or straightforward process, but the quest was widely understood as an obligation surviving servicemen had to the kin of their deceased comrades. The wife of Pvt. Sixto R. Chavez of Puerto de Luna in Guadalupe County, from the 109th Infantry of the 28th Division, received an official notice of her husband's death six months after he was killed in action on 17 August 1918 during the Vesle River campaign at age twenty-seven; however, she was provided no information about how he died. This information only came when some of his fellow soldiers returned. She learned that "witnesses say he was blown to pieces by a shell. That a shell struck a house which was where he was at the time. . . . Not enough of the body left to bury." The emotional impact of learning such news was unrecorded, but an account of being obliterated was a perverse twist to a Good Death—though instantaneous and therefore painless, it was a horrible end to life.[50]

The six months it took for the 28th Division to report Private Chavez's battlefield death was quite common. For the army the meaning of death was often utilitarian; it accelerated the need for replacement soldiers, and after the armistice the army had to reduce a backlog of notifications of next of kin. The 28th Division had 2,551 battlefield deaths and 11,429 wounded, and given the rate at which replacement troops—such as the soldiers from New Mexico—shuffled in and out as well as the inability to identify bodies hit by artillery, it is little wonder that record keeping was imperfect and follow-up slow. Few officers knew anything about individual enlisted men they commanded, and the volume of correspondence they were charged with preparing was so daunting that commanders, especially in the Regular Army, often used a boilerplate when writing to next of kin. This formatted letter has been succinctly described by a scholar as "usually containing only three stock messages: the man in question was loved by his comrades, he was a good soldier, and he died painlessly." Such letters also wrapped the deceased in the flag of patriotic duty and "reassured the recipient that their loved one had not died in vain and carried the implicit exhortation to the bereaved to make sacrifices of their own." Regular Army officers held firmly to notions of a Good Death in their letters to families of the deceased, uniformly stressing what was patently untrue—that the end came quickly and painlessly.[51]

One of the best postwar novels, William March's *Company K,* drew on experiences from the Regular Army's 2nd Division, particularly the battle at Belleau Wood. One brief section became the best known, and it lampooned platitudes passed off as sincere and honest condolences in notification-of-death letters. That Belleau Wood seared the lives and minds of its survivors is seen in the next-of-kin letters sent Annie Hamby, the mother of nineteen-year-old Cpl. Benjamin J. Hamby of the 2nd Division from Grant County. Though the information provided her had little relation to the formatted letter many grieving families received, its impersonal tone was of scant comfort. The lieutenant who commanded her son's company wrote Annie Hamby a six-sentence message eight months after Corporal Hamby's death. He tersely informed her that her son "was killed in action on June 13, 1918, by shrapnel fire. At the time of his death he was with the company in Belleau Wood on the Chateau Thierry Front. The company was in the lines as Infantry and your son was in a shell hole with a couple of companions (neither of whom are with the company now) when the shrapnel hit him. He died soon after being wounded and was buried that night near the place he was wounded." Although the lieutenant avoided boilerplate platitudes, his clipped communication has the ring of a practiced explanation. But what is most noticeable is the absence of empathy; it is devoid of emotional support and offers no condolences or sympathy. The format further dehumanized the message; it was sent as a memorandum using in its heading "Subject: Death of Corporal Benjamin Hamby." The trauma of the battle likely left the commanding officer emotionless, perhaps overcome by a "sense of disconnectedness that occurs to all who return from war."[52]

Fifty-one weeks after Corporal Hamby's death, a fellow soldier who had been in his company since May 1917 wrote Annie Hamby. He began his eight-sentence missive by stating, "I have intended to write this letter to you for a long time. I hope you will pardon the delay." He described Corporal Hamby as "loved by every man in the company because of his desire to do the right thing." The letter's author mixed genuine emotion—"extending heartfelt sympathy to you in your dark hours of grief"—with flourishes that likely were stock phrases—"died with a smile on his face and a word of cheer to his other comrades." The brevity of each letter needs to be understood as examples of how Belleau Wood imprinted its horror onto survivors.[53]

In contrast to the Regular Army's practices in next-of-kin letters, National Guard and National Army officials seldom resorted to stock phrases. In these notifications the most authentic and forthright information came from fellow soldiers. The parents of Pvt. Royal C. Boehrig from Grant County received an extensive account of his death, at age twenty-six, from Sgt. Ira J. Swingle of the National Army's 356th Infantry, 89th Division. He reported that Private Boehrig was hit by shrapnel in the left ankle as H Company prepared to cross the Meuse

River on 10 November. He was immediately evacuated to an aid station and soon was sent to Hospital No. 50, but things went from bad to worse: "He had two operations then foot removed then later his leg taken off, which was during January. He died February 12th, 1919 . . . of septicemia." The sergeant said that Boehrig was "always held in the highest esteem as a soldier and for his willingness and promptness to do his part."[54]

Next-of-kin notifications from the Regular Army are seldom found in the state's casualties files, and as a result many families "remained forever in ignorance about the last moments of their dead husband, father, or son." Not surprisingly, the absence of such information prompted many complaints to the Board of Historical Service, such as from the father of Pfc. Edmund C. Baca from Mora County, who was in the Regular Army's 5th Division and died at age twenty-five after the St. Mihiel offensive. Fourteen months after his son's death, Hurculano Baca said, "I have never been able to find out any details of his death."[55]

On occasion the War Department was pressured to inform a family member of the death of a loved one, which resulted in a formal—almost ritualized—process. One such instance involved Pvt. (Mechanic) Clarence G. Kepple of Artesia, who was assigned to the National Army's 356th Infantry of the 89th Division and at age twenty-six was killed in action on 23 September on the St. Mihiel front. It is likely that a congressional request prompted the War Department to ask the division's commanding officer, Maj. Gen. Frank L. Winn, to reply to Alice Kepple. The general did so on 30 March 1919, six months after her son died. In his three-paragraph letter he "express[ed] [his] sympathy" for her loss. He offered no details of his death but rather placed it in the context of duty and worthy sacrifice: "You must find a certain pride in his soldier's death and in the knowledge that he fought his good fight in the just cause of our country." He concluded with a one-sentence observation about Private Kepple's character and contributions that rings true to his military record: "His services were valued by his commander and he did well his part in the Great War." Although Kepple's usual duties were as a mechanic, he served as a runner that fateful morning and shuttled messages between company headquarters and the platoon officers leading the attack.[56]

Details of Private Kepple's death were explained to his mother in a page-and-a-half letter from the company commander, Capt. Matthew Winters, dated 26 April 1919. He apologized for the delay in contacting her but explained, "We did not know the [parents'] address." He matter-of-factly reported, "Your son was detailed as a runner. . . . So far as I have been able to ascertain, there was no witness to his death, but it is evident he was killed instantly by shrapnel."

Information on his funeral and burial were also provided, including that his grave was "on the summit of a high hill," a detail likely added as assurance that he was close to Heaven. Almost a third of the letter echoed General Winn's theme that Kepple's death had to be understood as a patriotic sacrifice, which Captain Winters defined as "that Cause which has made the principles of Liberty and Justice paramount throughout the civilized world."[57]

A report prepared by a Paris-based Red Cross official confirmed all information the Army provided Alice Kepple. This final letter went to a Red Cross official at the national headquarters, who forwarded it to her in mid-June 1919. The Red Cross, through its Home Communication Bureau, had been designated early in the war to verify information about AEF servicemen killed or hospitalized, and they were to inform the designated next of kin. Among New Mexico casualties, it was rare that battlefield deaths were known to the Red Cross, but a fairly good system existed for tracking wounded soldiers who died in hospitals, especially at the several dozen largest of among the more than 150 AEF hospitals. Representative of such correspondence were letters sent to Luciano Chavez, father of Pvt. Joaquin Chavez of Alamagordo, assigned to the 110th Infantry of the 28th Division and dead at twenty years old. Red Cross agent Agatha Wexler interviewed a nurse and reported that his son "came here [AEF Hospital No. 3] from the front on the first day of August [Vesle River campaign] with multiple and extensive shrapnel wounds. He passed away on Aug 6th. But I am thankful to say without suffering."[58]

Another Red Cross agent, Horacio Cecil, offered a sanitized version of Joaquin's death several months later: "The cause of his death was a gunshot wound in the leg." He also invoked elements of the Good Death trope—omitting mention of the use of morphine as a pain killer—noting that Chavez "passed away peacefully and without pain on Aug 6, 1918. From the very beginning, everything possible was done for him by the physicians, and nurses and attendants, and I know you will be comforted to hear that he could not have received better and more tender care if he had of been at the best Hospital in America." The letter continued with a detailed description of the burial, which took place "with full military honors at our little military cemetery in the neighboring town.... Our Chaplin conducted the service, and the Mayor of Ministrol made an address. As is customary, there were three volleys over the flag draped casket. Besides the flowers from the hospital, many were brought by the French women and children of the neighborhood." Red Cross agent Cecil ended his narrative with words calculated to reassure Luciano Chavez that his son's death was and would continue to be memorialized: "I am sure you will appreciate it to hear that the French women and children of Ministrol, of their own accord have promised to take care of the graves at our cemetery, and as long as I am stationed at this hospital, I assure you that I shall see that everything is looked after." Agent Cecil's account skewed the notion of the Good Death toward comforting a grieving parent: the funeral tributes, both military and civilian, validated their son's sacrifice; the spontaneous displays of support from the French acknowledged gratitude and showed solidarity; and the pledge to honor and care for the grave site reassured a faraway family that dignity and respect were accorded him.[59]

The need to memorialize a deceased soldier ran deep in the psyche of the survivors. In almost all of the instances cited here, assurances were provided the family that a unit of the Army Quartermaster's Corps Graves Registration Service marked and recorded the site. This paper trail would be crucial to what became known as the repatriation of the deceased between 1920 and 1922. But occasionally soldiers would themselves create a memorial to honor one of their own. The 21st Engineers had more than a hundred New Mexicans, and those in Company E collected money and had a monument erected near where an enemy shell hit a train at the front and killed its engineer, Jesse T. Ritchie of Gallup, on 6 November 1918. In three weeks he would have had his twenty-third birthday. A close friend reported, "The boys of the company bought a marble monument to mark his resting place at Sorcy, where some old French lady has adopted it as a memorial of her own son who was killed and lies somewhere in the mud of Flanders."[60]

Memorializing New Mexicans killed in uniform commanded special attention at the Board of Historical Service. Lansing B. Bloom, an ordained Presbyterian minister, brought to this endeavor the same diligence he applied in plumbing the unexpected death of his twenty-five-year-old brother Raymond. The suffering inflicted from that tragedy pointed him toward ministering to the families of New Mexicans whose fathers, husbands, sons, brothers, cousins, or uncles died in the war. The fifty-three-page file he assembled to document his brother's life—as recalled by family, classmates, friends, and coworkers—became the first and remained the most extensive individual file among the more than four hundred he created. These files were collected during five years and remain an incomparable archive chronicling the ultimate sacrifice rendered by New Mexico's soldiers, sailors, and marines. Raymond Bloom's death transformed Lansing into a minister-at-large. He proved relentless in seeking information from which to draw inspiration to write biographical sketches of men who died in service.

Most of them were about 175 words—the same length as Raymond's—with some shorter and a few longer. Glimpsed in them is a minister's agape love as well as insight into how death was understood in that era.[61]

Lansing Bloom's boss, Dr. Edgar L. Hewitt, only occasionally took an active part in creating the state's war archive. But one of his more frequently found pieces of correspondence was a form letter sent to Spanish-speaking survivors. He employed an empathetic and contemplative tone that acknowledged their loss while also stating a lesson he learned: "I am beginning to understand the fact that our citizens have been so forthcoming in their service to their country because they have left homes in which justice and duty prevail rather than material interests." He also thanked them for "the encouragement your letter gives me." At times the correspondence he referenced is not in the file, so this last stock phrase can seem hollow. But when he replied to Ermelinda Aragon, widowed wife of 3rd Division Pvt. Alonzo Aragon of Dawson, who died of shrapnel wounds in the Meuse-Argonne offensive on 30 October at age twenty-five, it is easy to see that his words are an authentic response to her heartfelt pride in her husband's patriotism and sacrifice:

> My dear husband Alonzo Aragon died on 30 October in France as a result of wounds received while defending the Stars and Stripes of the flag and in defense of the national honor of the United States of America. In spite of my irreparable loss and not withstanding that my little six-month-old daughter and I are left with no more than God's protection, nevertheless I feel proud to be one of the women of America who had a husband whose love for his family and his country exceeded all limits and who willingly offered his life as a sacrifice on the altar of Patriotism during the final battle.[62]

Similar sentiments were expressed by a father, Jesus Garcia, of a village in San Miguel County. At twenty-four years old his son, Pvt. Andres Garcia, assigned to the 110th Infantry of the 28th Division, died on 1 October in the Meuse-Argonne offensive. He was the first man among those drafted from his village to be killed in action, and his father told Bloom, "I feel much pleasure knowing that my son has given his life to free us from the ferocious fury of the German beast."[63]

These statements should not be read through the lens of twenty-first-century cynicism. The pride Sra. Aragon and Sr. Garcia express is a reminder that sometimes people mean exactly what they say, that there is no posturing in their prose. Their words, of course, were precisely what the army and the government wanted all Americans to espouse. Yet their worldview—that defense of the flag and the nation were worth dying for—sprang from conviction supported by their religious faith. In some quarters Sra. Aragon and Sr. Garcia's statements would have been criticized as self-delusion induced by wartime propaganda. Such thoughts went unspoken in New Mexico, and the most visible dissenters in the state were some laborers in mining camps. Antiwar members of the IWW had some adherents among miners. But in the northeastern mining town of Dawson, where Ermelinda Aragon lived and her husband had worked in the coal mine for several years prior to being drafted, antiwar agitation was not the problem it was believed to be in Gallup.[64]

The majority of the state's correspondence with and about deceased servicemen dates from 1919 to 1921, well before a sense of disillusionment with the war settled across America. No condemnation or even criticism was voiced; instead, the emotion closest to the surface was grief. As would be expected, it was ever present, especially among elderly parents whose now deceased son had lived with and helped support them. One such soldier was Pvt. Arturo Montoya of Roy, then in eastern Mora County, a member of the 356th Infantry in the 89th Division. He was assigned to G Company sometime after arriving in France in early July. His final letter home was in late September, then at year's end a letter arrived from the government informing the eighty-seven-year-old father and seventy-five-year-old mother that their twenty-four-year-old son was missing in action. In March and June, Edgar L. Hewitt wrote Jose Maria Montoya seeking updates on Private Montoya's status, and his letter of 26 June noted that "if you wish, you can reply to us in Spanish." The father did so in July not long after receiving formal notice of his son's death. Although Private Montoya had purchased a life insurance policy with a $10,000 death benefit (2017 value: $140,925) to be paid monthly for twenty years at $58.00 (2017 value: $817.37), his father had tried unsuccessfully to learn when they might expect the government's check to ease their poverty and asked Hewitt to assist him.[65]

Private Montoya parents' grief conforms to one arc of war: death, grieving, trying to make sense of what had befallen a family, and worrying about the future. Jose Maria Montoya's letter ends with glimpses of his emotional state. "My son was the one who cared for my wife and me[, and] Arturo Montoya would never leave my side. He cared for us until he was called into the military and now I feel so alone. . . . My wife and I are abandoned."[66]

By July 1919 the Board of Historical Service was moving forward on a plan largely carried out by Lansing B. Bloom. At the end of August he announced,

"We have recently placed on the walls of the Memorial Hall uniform copies of all such pictures which have been furnished us." For more than a year he had been collecting photographs of deceased servicemen to be placed in a memorial room at the Museum of New Mexico. Each letter sent a survivor mentioned the project, which he envisioned as a "perpetual shrine to the [service]men of New Mexico." The memorial room existed for only about ten years.[67]

CHAPTER 8

Veterans' Quest Stories

Seventy-three New Mexicans in the 28th Division marched off transport ships docked at Philadelphia in early May 1919. Soon the entire division passed in review before military and civilian dignitaries flanking the Liberty Bell, whose "base was swaddled in wreaths." These soldiers were the largest number of New Mexicans accorded public celebrations upon their arrival. All other returning troops from the state disembarked in New York or New Jersey, and only divisions from those states received any fanfare. New Mexicans, along with most returning soldiers, were met by representatives of state clubs and invited to visit while on liberty passes freely given during the several weeks spent in nearby camps. To ensure New Mexico's returning servicemen enjoyed the welcome mat put out by New York City, Governor Octaviano A. Larrazolo authorized spending $5,000 ($80,729 in 2017), drawn against the wartime allocation fund, to pay for representatives in New York City to host the state's soldiers while they awaited train rides home.[1]

The first large number of New Mexicans in the AEF had returned to New York in late March—more than a hundred national guardsmen from the 40th Division. Over the next six months more than 5,500 of the state's soldiers would be greeted dockside by staff of the Rocky Mountain Club. This West 44th Street club offered a safe haven in the city. Here they were welcomed, given snacks and soft drinks, received a printed message from the governor, read state newspapers, collected mail, and were provided tickets to theatrical performances. To further ensure their safety, hundreds of deputized men on provost guard duty, including Pfc. Lawrence E. Valentine from a village in Guadalupe County, patrolled the streets. Valentine let the liberty troops take in "the bright lights of Broadway" but kept them from straying into nearby Hell's Kitchen. He reported seeing "some pretty active duty on Broadway" during four and a half months until his discharge at the end of May 1919. A women's auxiliary, organized among those with ties to the state and living in or near New York City, visited "New Mexico boys in the hospitals" as well as in camps.[2]

Finally trains arrived to take soldiers to an army discharge center in or near their state of residence, which for almost all New Mexicans meant traveling to Ft. Bliss in El Paso. Once there, outprocessing took a few days, during which they received a sixty dollar federal bonus, were allowed to keep their uniform (and battlefield souvenirs), were handed a train ticket, and were sent unceremoniously—and often alone—to their hometowns. Most local communities did honor their ex-servicemen during 4th of July celebrations in 1919, with Gallup's parade for McKinley County veterans described as the "biggest in [the] whole Southwest." Only Roswell's Battery A of the 146th Field Artillery returned in mass. Fifty-three of its members arrived in Roswell on 3 July, and a week later the city held a two-mile-long parade to honor them. Afterward a huge barbeque served each of eight thousand people a pound of donated beef and mutton. Also in the afternoon, a memorial plaque was dedicated at the courthouse honoring the county's deceased soldiers and sailors, and that night a dance lasted until 2:00 A.M.[3]

Dissonance

The public events welcoming veterans contrasted markedly with the political angst expressed six months earlier. Across the country the challenge of melding ex-servicemen into civilian life occasioned much anxiety among state and federal officials after the armistice. Thirty-six governors and governors-elect gathered for three days at Annapolis, Maryland, in mid-December 1918 at a National Governors Association meeting, where "practically the entire time of the conference" was devoted to "conditions arising out of the war." Uppermost in their minds was the impact returning soldiers would have on states and their communities and the uncharted steps by which peacetime practices would replace wartime mobilization of civil society and the economy. The governors' agenda included discussion of veterans' employment, veterans' welfare and health, war memorials, adult English-language literacy, public health, and child welfare.

Efforts to institutionalize these measures set the veterans' postwar legislative agenda and "would establish a social contract between the nation and those who fought its battles."[4]

Incoming Republican governor Larrazolo unveiled his blueprint for how New Mexico should adjust to postwar needs in his message to the Fourth Legislature at the opening of its sixty-day session in mid-January 1919. His proposals echoed issues highlighted a month earlier at the governors conference. Among his twenty-one recommendations for legislative action, one-third dealt with two broad issues: the state's obligations to its soon-to-return veterans and correcting social—and especially health—problems exposed during the war. Larrazolo's recommendations were brief and suggestive, and he left all details to the lawmakers. He no doubt believed that the state's veterans—and the public at large—could quickly resume their lives upon enactment of his proposals. Nothing of the sort happened.[5]

Governor Larrazolo's approach to veterans' issues in New Mexico was often a variant of what ex-servicemen had seen too much of in the military—delegate, designate, and disappear. Whenever possible the governor deferred to the federal government, taking the position that legislators needed to "be prepared, by appropriate legislation enacted at [this] time, to cooperate with the federal government in the execution" of initiatives the president and Congress advanced. News of the most ambitious of these federal programs reached hundreds of New Mexican soldiers in the 356th Infantry, aboard the troop transport USS *Agamemnon,* through a short article in the ship's newspaper on Thursday, 22 May 1919. In a column opposite summaries of the ship's boxing tournament, the paper reported that President Wilson endorsed secretary of the interior Franklin K. Lane's plan for providing land to returning soldiers.[6]

Government distribution of land to veterans had a long history in America dating to the 1760s, and it had been especially important to Union Civil War veterans seeking homesteads in the West. Secretary Lane had first advanced his idea in late summer 1918, and in the following year it met with widespread enthusiasm. By late spring 1919 governors in forty states had endorsed the proposal, including Larrazolo. Five days prior to the notice in the *Agamemnon Daily News*, Secretary Lane met with bipartisan leaders in Congress to discuss steps to turn his plan into law. Agreed at that meeting was the need for $500 million, with one quarter of it to come from the states, to be spent "to put soldiers and sailors to work at current wages on a great reclamation scheme, and afterward sell them farms and implements to be paid for in installments." The federal legislation became the eponymous Mondell bill introduced by House majority leader Frank W. Mondell, a Wyoming Republican.[7]

The Fourth New Mexico Legislature hitched itself to the national bandwagon Secretary Lane was steering in the capital and passed a law creating the Soldier Settlement Board (SSB) on 16 March 1919. The four-member board was to work with the federal government to secure reclamation projects to bring water and veteran-settlers to formerly arid lands. The chairperson of the SSB immediately began discussions with federal officials about reclamation in San Juan County, which revived long-standing interest in irrigation using the Animas River. But complications soon arose, and as the state's veterans returned home in ever greater numbers during the summer of 1919 the SSB became mired in political and legal wrangling. The state's veterans soon realized that, although they were done fighting for their country in France, they were going to have to fight at home to secure benefits. This first conflict in New Mexico, though, did not have much direct participation by veterans. Instead, it was primarily a clash among the state's politicians. The rise and demise of the SSB is a case study of political narrow-mindedness derailing attempts to aid the state's veterans. The arc of the SSB's brief existence—created mid-March 1919 by the legislature and terminated 1 March 1920 after adverse court rulings—included obstacles and setbacks that veterans would encounter in various forms throughout the 1920s in their quest to reintegrate into civilian life.[8]

After creation of the U.S. Reclamation Service in 1903 the government and private developers took an active interest in irrigation projects to open up hundreds of thousands of acres for agricultural use in northwest New Mexico. One key supporter from the outset remained a vocal proponent in 1919—attorney and engineer Jay Turley, whose practice was in Santa Fe. His advocacy of irrigation and development during fifteen years had been as tireless as it was ambitious, seeking "the reclamation of an area larger than the State of Delaware," but all he had to show for it was "some thirty-four lawsuits" primarily contesting water rights. Turley was also a veteran, having served in the AEF for fifteen months as a major in the Special Staff and Liaison Service, where he used his fluency in French, Spanish, Portuguese, and Italian to conduct business with the Allies to secure supplies for the AEF. Prior to heading to France in November 1917, he "offered the big San Juan Irrigation Projects, the Water-rights, etc., of which are in my name, to the Secretary of the Interior for development for the Soldiers returning; the U.S. Government has made thorough investigations and, I am informed, is considering taking over our interests and projects."[9]

Turley's scheme was a pipe dream. No one in Washington took an interest in his legally entangled and high-priced project. Governor Larrazolo likewise urged the federal government to fund reclamation projects to aid veterans, but he did so mainly to achieve one of his long-sought goals—and that of many western lawmakers: returning public lands to the states. It, too, was a pipe dream. By wrapping his land grab in the guise of veterans' assistance, Larrazolo believed western states could gain control over 225 million acres held by the federal government. If free to use these lands as they saw fit, each state could sell them to pay their one-quarter share of the cost of reclamation projects.[10]

Governor Larrazolo "took the lead in the move to have the public lands ceded to the Public Land States" by inviting the twenty-five governors of the western public land states to a special two-day conference on cession convened immediately prior to a meeting of the National Governors Association in Salt Lake City held 18–22 August 1919. Eighteen governors from public land states attended and approved a petition endorsing the land transfer and forwarded it to Congress, where it was dead on arrival. Two decades of federal policy could not be undone so quickly by entreat.[11]

August marked the zenith—and the beginning of the demise—of the SSB. In rapid succession the board's existence was challenged by two legal actions within six weeks, between 11 August and 17 September. First the state's attorney general ruled that the SSB had no authority to borrow money to contribute toward a quarter of the reclamation expenses. Shortly thereafter two members of the board, who "positively opposed" reclamation, expressed their concerns to U.S. attorney Summers Burkhart in mid-September. He promptly secured a temporary injunction alleging "that the bill creating the board was unconstitutional," an action that became permanent in a federal court ruling in Santa Fe on 13 January 1920.[12]

In the same week that the federal court ruled against the SSB, Governor Larrazolo was in Washington, D.C., leading a delegation of four western governors lobbying to have "all of the public domain ceded to commonwealths in which they are located" and seeking an appropriation of $250 million for reclamation of arid lands. Most of the western governors, though, no longer supported Larrazolo's campaign and instead sought only federal funding for irrigation. Among servicemen, though, support for "federal help to put soldiers on farms" remained strong. A poll of 13,000 enlisted men conducted by the veterans' magazine *Home Sector* reported that 87 percent approved the idea in February 1920. But the political forces pushing land cessation encountered a strong countercurrent in the newly formed American Legion. The SSB chairman had appealed for its support in the fall, but the group declined because "the reclamation scheme seemed too limited in scope" to justify the investment required. In the last week of the thirty-day session of the state's legislature in mid-February 1920, the New Mexico house overwhelming endorsed a resolution backing the Mondell bill, but in the session's final hours Larrazolo leaned heavily on senators to kill the resolution, arguing that it undercut his cession plan. A week later the SSB closed its doors forever, not only signaling the end for the governor's land scheme but sounding an alarm for the Mondell bill's fate. In mid-April it became apparent that Congress, and particularly Republican members of the House from districts east of the Mississippi River, opposed it because only watersheds in the West benefited.[13]

Ex-servicemen who were homesteaders eagerly looked forward to returning to the land in 1919, but their high hopes would be repeatedly crushed throughout the 1920s. Veterans who held homesteads in New Mexico were cruelly abused by circumstances beyond their control. Veterans had bought into a trifecta of bad luck: recurring drought, falling prices, and restricted access to capital—all capped off by the onset of the Great Depression. Especially hard hit were farmers and homesteaders in the northeast quadrant of the state, whose attorney for the judicial district reported in 1924, "I estimate that fully one-third of our people are gone, many never to return." The land had not nurtured New Mexico's veterans, particularly in the eastern part of the state, and many moved to neighboring states.[14]

Dissonance, or a clash between what was said and what occurred, began in the waning days of the Fourth Legislature in early March 1919 in deliberations over several veterans' issues, including the SSB. For some Nuevomexicano veterans, though, dissonance likewise existed when praise for their military service failed to shield them from discrimination, especially in employment. The contradiction between words and actions emerged shortly after the war ended. Nuevomexicano poet Felipe Maximiliano Chacón in a celebratory poem, "Oda a Los Heroes," heralded the Nuevomexicanos' return from Europe. The opening lines proclaimed, "With pride overflowing in the soul / In the midst of the grandeur of victory / I want to express, your courage triumphant, / My admiration for your everlasting glory." But glory proved fickle. A group of Nuevomexicanos from Deming organized as the Liga Protectora de Obreros Hispano-Americanos (Hispanic-American Workers Protective League) in late spring 1921. They vigorously protested to the governor that local road contractors would not hire them even though all were American citizens and many were ex-servicemen. The state said its hands were tied since it was a federal project. Nine years later, as the Great Depression settled in, a veteran in Socorro County, Rafael B. Rivera, in his poem "Para Todos Protección—Menos Para El Hispano" ("Security for Everyone—Except for the Hispano), published in 1930, contrasted Anglo-American and Nuevomexicano job prospects:

> Now in this moment
> The hard times arrived
> The Anglo has work
> But the Mexican does not
> What happened?
> Where is the security?
> Remember the war
> When the fight came
> All were Americans. . . .
> But now the Anglo is working
> And the Mexican is in the street.

The prevalence of discrimination and racism fueled Rivera's dissonance:

> In the war it happened differently
> That was the world war
> They wanted all races
> To put up a fight
> Oh, the poor Mexican
> Now he is not recognized
> We are not Americans.[15]

Memorials

Debate on New Mexico House Bill 4 began shortly after 9:00 P.M. on Wednesday, 5 March 1919, with two impassioned addresses seeking authorization for the Museum of New Mexico to buy and remodel the adjacent armory building to become a memorial "to commemorate the services of New Mexico men and women in the Great War." Republican representative Liberato Baca of Santa Fe County opened the debate and for half an hour had the rapt attention of those still occupying the house. "Even the democrats who it was known were going to oppose the bill gave him their closest attention." Baca brought to the chamber three visual aids: a map of the state's counties on which were placed gold stars for each serviceman killed in the war; two large framed collections of photographs of many of the state's deceased soldiers; and an artist's rendering of the remodeled armory. All three items had been prepared by the Historical Service office. Baca stated his case bluntly:

> If any citizen of New Mexico can read the Roll of Honor [of the deceased], and look upon the faces of those splendid boys, and not feel his heart swell with pride that we have been represented by such manhood as these, or if after looking upon them he begrudges the few cents in taxes which every citizen would have to pay in order to do them honor, let him take himself and his money out of the State, and hide in some wilderness or desert where gratitude and honor are unknown.[16]

The first opponent to speak was Republican William Blanchard of Lincoln County. "The house filled up the minute he took the floor and one could have heard a pin drop as he spoke for the opponents. . . . Mr. Blanchard said the question was not as to whether a memorial should be built. We are all agreed on that. The issue is whether this is the proper and adequate form of memorial." The object of Blanchard's criticism was the drawing of the proposed memorial. Artist Kenneth M. Chapman had produced an architectural drawing of a war memorial building with the assistance of his employer, museum director Hewett. The Museum of New Mexico was housed in the recently renovated Palace of the Governors, and both men envisioned "wrapping the Palace portal around the east end of the building to reach a remodeled National Guard armory." Such a change would add another building to the re-creation of the capital city done in Santa Fe, or Pueblo, style. This regional architectural movement, which had begun in 1909, was spearheaded by Hewett and inspired by mission churches at nearby pueblos as well as historic Spanish construction in public buildings such as the Palace of the Governors. But it was controversial. Blanchard tapped into the criticism directed at the city's architectural renovation. He reminded the legislators that he sat in the house when the Palace's refurbishing was debated, and "I opposed that proposal as I oppose this one." He framed his argument in blatantly racist terms. The Palace had become "a monument to the Pueblo Indians," and connecting it to a renovated armory to house a war memorial was merely "another tribute to the ascendency of the Pueblo Indians."[17]

Four Democrats also spoke in opposition, each making reference to the need for "a suitable memorial for the soldiery of this state," but also one that was a "properly conceived memorial, which this was not." The Democrats also likely took into account that Baca used this speech as "the opening of his campaign for congress," and they had no interest in aiding a Republican seeking higher office. These five vocal opponents of the war memorial were Euro-Americans, and their opposition can be seen as expressing resentment over surrendering the gains of manifest destiny—the conquest of the West and its native peoples.[18]

The house passed the memorial bill largely along a party line vote of twenty-three to thirteen. Attempts to defuse opposition occurred in the senate and centered on uncoupling the war memorial from the reconstruction of the armory in the Santa Fe style. Respected and senior Republican politicians led these efforts. Former territorial governor L. Bradford Prince offered land near Fort Marcy as a site for "a conspicuous and important" new building that would "represent both the glory of the soldier and the patriotism of the people." In the senate former territorial attorney-general George W. Prichard cut the Gordian knot. Though privately complaining about "this notion of Indian architecture for everything that comes along," publically he said nothing about the design and instead sought to shift attention to the question of funding, arguing that "it is the people's affair, state-wide in its purposes, in which the people themselves can, and no doubt would prefer to voluntarily donate the sum required, [rather] than to have another tax law passed." He secured passage of a special state charter that authorized raising money through "popular subscription." At the beginning of September, Prichard announced that "state-wide [fund-raising] organization and publicity" would soon start, but it never did. Obstacles were the massive compound he proposed, which included an auditorium able to seat three to four thousand, together with the estimated price tag—a quarter of a million dollars ($3.5 million in 2017). Neither of these resonated with the public.[19]

In the immediate aftermath of the war, the federal government had a mixed record regarding memorials. Congress set aside land on the Mall for the George Washington Victory Memorial Hall "to commemorate the patriots of 1776 and the men of 1917," a project enlisting high-ranking military officers and requiring ambitious fund-raising in each state. This national effort—a grandiose version of the state's Memorial Hall Association—included a proposed massive multistory building costing an estimated $8 million dollars ($112.7 million in 2017) to be paid for through donations. Interest in public subscription never took off, in no small measure because the 1921 national convention of the American Legion firmly opposed it and instead called for building hospitals and rehabilitation facilities to treat veterans. But a de facto national war memorial did emerge when the congressionally authorized Tomb of the Unknown Soldier was dedicated on 11 November 1921. At that ceremony, New Mexico was formally represented by two veterans—one Nuevomexicano and one Euro-American. The grief-stricken in the state and across the nation universally embraced the new monument at Arlington National Cemetery. This solitary soldier's symbolic anonymity validated forever the sacrifices of all deceased servicemen from the war and in many people's minds of that era served as a national war memorial.[20]

Local grassroots efforts to honor deceased soldiers did not become entangled in politics because that would profane the grief of a neighbor. Instead, as seen at Roswell, a plaque at the county courthouse imbedded remembrance of sacrifice into a universally respected symbol of community. Deming placed on the courthouse lawn its monument honoring the town's one soldier killed in combat—Claude Close Howard. Bernalillo County recorded thirty-one names on a bronze plaque dedicated in October 1919 at the courthouse, with another half-dozen names added in the next several years. The American Legion in Deming memorialized Claude Howard by naming the local post in his honor, and statewide scores of World War I casualties became namesakes of American Legion posts, including Charles de Bremond in Roswell, Hugh Carlisle in Albuquerque, and Casiano Trujillo in Tucumcari. Both sacred and secular groups created memorials. In Albuquerque a few churches prepared small memorials, including St. John's Cathedral and Immaculate Conception Church, whose memorial honored local deceased Catholic servicemen. Several towns added Pershing to the list of street names, and newly incorporated Hot Springs dedicated three streets to wartime leaders: Pershing, Foch, and (treasury secretary) McAdoo. Las Cruces named a street to honor Joseph Quesenberry. An athletic stadium in Roswell commemorating the service of Colonel de Bremond became the state's last World War I memorial of the interwar decades when dedicated in 1927.[21]

The War Mothers, active since the summer of 1917 in New Mexico, formed the core of the American Legion's Women's Auxiliary beginning in early 1920 when the national organization embraced the mothers, wives, widows, aunts, sisters, and daughters of servicemen. These women figured prominently in creating local memorials, beginning with Arbor Day activities in Albuquerque to honor fallen heroes such as Private Luis Otero, who had enlisted in the spring of 1917, served with the Regular Army's 3rd Division, and died when "gassed by the Germans one dreary morning" along the Marne River in mid-July 1918. The Women's Auxiliary spread rapidly, with Roswell having a particularly large and active chapter throughout the 1920s. All auxiliaries turned out for the annual

Memorial Day poppy sales, which was their major fund-raising event for decades and was a symbolic public memorial to the war's victims. Statewide membership totaled 772 women in 1930 and, as the Great Depression began to settle onto the state, twenty-two towns' auxiliaries raised $1,808.98 from poppy sales ($26,394 in 2017). The majority of the money was allocated to the Auxiliary's Child Welfare Committee in each community to aid local children of living and deceased ex-servicemen, charity offered in the spirit of a living memorial to the survivors.[22]

Conflicting Policies and Priorities

Parochialism tinged with racism prevailed in New Mexico's Fourth Legislature, but more than just narrow-mindedness was evident. Fiscal policy became a deep divide in deliberations about the state's obligation to help veterans and their families. Governor Larrazolo and a majority in the legislature urgently made a "plea of economy," which observers described as "stand[ing] out more plainly than any other in the work of the legislature." A recurring formula was to shift fiscal responsibility, in whole or in part, to other parties when addressing postwar issues. For example, Larrazolo wanted corporations to do more to support the state and its citizens, a campaign that grew more intense in the Fifth Legislature and ultimately cost Larrazolo his party's renomination in 1920. One of the governor's early skirmishes with business interests came when he pushed a bill to address the inability of many draftees to understand English. His legislation would have required that corporations set up and staff schools on their premises to teach English as well as reading and writing. Businesses, and particularly mining firms, took a pick axe to this proposed legislation and killed it.[23]

The 1919 legislature witnessed intense lobbying by women mobilized during the war years. The WASCD sought to create social welfare services, especially aimed at offering health care for mothers and children. Governor Larrazolo likewise pushed for this legislation and signed into law the bill creating the state's first public health department on 25 April. But meager state funding hampered its formation until the federal government stepped in and paid the salary of the first director, allowing him to set up and administer the department until 1921. The state continued to underfund the department, but again the federal government assisted, expanding its support by underwriting the salary of health department employees throughout the 1920s. At the end of the decade the federal government paid the salary of numerous health department employees in most counties. For example, Santa Fe County in 1929–30 had twelve health department employees fully funded by the federal government, including a medical doctor and two nurses, and through matching federal dollars an additional ten positions were supported, including one medical doctor. As one distinguished scholar noted, "The federal government kept the health department afloat" in the state in the 1920s. Another major infusion of federal money for infant welfare and maternal health came in 1921 with the passage of the Federal Maternity and Infancy Act, popularly known as the Sheppard-Towner Act. Only with federal funding did the state sustain public health care in the 1920s, a social welfare project seen as vital to the nation's military and long sought by WASCD activists. This advocacy pushed the state into the sphere of public health and anticipated returning veterans mobilizing to force federal action on their health care demands, a movement unleashed in 1920 and 1921.[24]

Government officials at the state and national levels would invoke fiscal tightfistedness as their first response when addressing veterans' issues throughout the 1920s. But a determined opposition existed in veterans' organizations, the largest and most politically savvy of which was the American Legion. Ironically, that group was founded in Paris on the very day New Mexico's Fourth Legislature wrapped up its session in mid-March 1919. Although the collective will of the government and veterans emerged at great remove from one another, they would quickly collide as each sought to impose its priority on the other: fiscal restraint versus benefits for veterans.

Lt. Col. Theodore Roosevelt Jr. and three fellow officers set in motion events in January 1919 that led to creation of the American Legion when approximately five hundred men gathered for a two-day meeting in Paris in mid-March. That convention did not raise high the banner of a cause, though bedrock principles would be announced over the next twenty months. Instead, in the spring of 1919 it opted for ambiguity and set forth general ideals: "perpetuate principles of justice, freedom, and democracy . . . ; inculcate the duty and obligation of the citizen to the State; preserve the history and incidents of our participation in the war; cement the ties of comradeship formed in service." *Stars and Stripes* enthusiastically endorsed the American Legion and presciently proclaimed it "a worthy successor to the G.A.R. [Grand Army of the Republic]." This Union Army fraternal organization had evolved into the nation's most powerful political lobby in the decades after the Civil War, especially in securing disability pensions. Similarly, World War I veterans would quickly realize that lobbying was needed to ensure that Congress recognized and provided aid to the countless men whose lives were fractured in the war.[25]

To raise up the American Legion in New Mexico, Roosevelt turned to Capt. Bronson Cutting, whom he had befriended at Groton School and Harvard. It was not immediately apparent that the new veterans' organization would take root, because returning New Mexicans were slow to join. A report on the state's recruitment recited the obstacles faced in mid-July 1919: "Owing to great area, sparse population, and inadequate railway facilities, the work of starting the Legion has been fraught with many difficulties." Slow growth followed, and by the end of August posts existed in only six counties. At the end of the year fewer than 10 percent of veterans submitting servicemen's questionnaires claimed membership.[26]

About two hundred men gathered in Albuquerque for the state's first Legion convention in mid-October 1919. Governor Larrazolo addressed them on the final day and spent about equal amounts of time on each of three topics sure to appeal to the assembled men: praise for "having written a most glorious and proud page" through their recent service; assurances that the newly created SSB would attend to their "future comfort and happiness"; and condemnation of agitators and "mobbers" who "would destroy this Republic and establish the Soviet over its ruins." Tucked in between the second and third comments was his brief justification for refusing to back a state bonus bill: "Our state is not overly rich with money. We are poor and we must conserve our resources."[27]

State budgets can always be read as evidence of who has the most political clout in competition over how money is spent. In the postwar years in New Mexico, veterans had a moral claim to public support, but it took a while to convert it into the common coin of the political realm—voting strength. An example of how they were shunted aside is the ease with which the state parried an appeal by veterans to pay a one-time bonus of thirty dollars. To do so the state would have incurred an expense of at least $420,000 ($5.9 million in 2017), which Larrazolo deemed too costly; however, he was disingenuous in invoking empty coffers. He did not mention—nor was it public knowledge—that at the war's end the balance remaining from the state's wartime appropriation could cover such a one-time expenditure. The most generous characterization of Larrazolo's fiscal policy is that it was situationally responsive; that is, in the first nine months of his administration he approved discretionary disbursements from the wartime appropriation that drew down the balance by more than $135,000 ($1.9 million in 2017). The governor approved seven of the eight expenditures of war appropriation money in the closing days of the Fourth Legislature, which raises the possibility that special interests secured their priorities. Given that the governor always sought to support the state's largest employers—livestock and agricultural interests—it is not surprising that more than half the amount released paid for extermination of what livestock raisers called "predatory wild animals and rodent pests"—mainly mountain lions, coyotes, and prairie dogs. Similarly the state's farmers received assistance through a loan program funded through the wartime appropriation. The money borrowed was used to purchase seed, but because the amounts were aggregated rather than separated by year in the ledger sheets only a guesstimate—$20,000 ($281,851 in 2017)—can be made for the appropriation in 1919. About 43 percent of the total amount loaned to farmers during the war years was repaid, but Nuevomexicanos were heavily represented among the defaulting borrowers. The governor wrote off these loans as uncollectable. What is clear in these transactions is that, had it been a priority for the governor, he could have allocated the $45,000 ($634,164 in 2017) initially sought for a war memorial.[28]

Several of the governor's smallest discretionary disbursements aided veterans in meaningful but largely symbolic ways, all of which are long-forgotten today. The Historical Service office, undeterred by the legislature's clumsy handling of the proposed war memorial, pursued its own initiative for a war memorial room in the Palace of the Governors. Such a room opened in November 1919, and for six more years Lansing Bloom continued to gather photographs and biographical data using $6,000 ($84,555 in 2017) carried over from the wartime appropriation. Display of military artifacts had displaced the photographs and dominated the room by 1929.[29]

Among the Living and Dead

One modest appropriation the state made in 1920 directly aided the loved ones of deceased veterans. The consequences of death reached far beyond the battlefield, and among the survivors the search for a new beginning was often a wrenching wait to bring home loved ones for reburial in their community. In the process, the Rocky Mountain Club of New York helped about 180 New Mexico families, acting as an intermediary in what was called repatriation of the dead between 1920 and 1922.[30]

New Mexico men who died overseas or at sea totaled 305 out of nearly 75,000 casualties in the AEF. Of this total, 268 lost their lives in France, four succumbed to their wounds while in English hospitals, three died in Russia, and two passed away while in the Army of Occupation in Germany. An additional fourteen died at sea and for another fourteen there are too few details to identify where they died or were buried. Most of the fourteen who died aboard a ship succumbed to complications from the influenza pandemic and were buried at sea, including five who had enlisted in the navy.[31]

The AEF followed practices to identify and bury deceased soldiers that had evolved since the Civil War. For nearly forty years after the Confederate surrender at Appomattox, the federal government haltingly conducted grave registration for Union soldiers, which meant locating what were usually mass graves, identifying the bodies, and arranging reinterment in a national cemetery. The AEF conducted all the same steps but faced different circumstances in deaths overseas, and they unilaterally decided to create national cemeteries abroad as permanent repositories. But the American public—and especially the mothers and wives of the deceased—quickly disabused Pershing of his assumption that the army retained sole authority over burial decisions. Mothers had pleaded with the War Department to return soldiers' bodies to the United States throughout 1918, and such requests became more voluminous, insistent, and organized under the auspices of the Bring Home the Soldier Dead League in 1919. This mass movement coalesced newspapers, members of Congress, lobbyists, and grieving families into a formidable pressure group, forcing the AEF to heed their call for homeland burials.[32]

The War Department began writing the designated next of kin for each AEF man buried abroad in late 1919 and asked whether he should be returned. Of a total of 74,770 notifications mailed, 59 percent wanted their deceased loved ones repatriated and 30,921 designated burial in AEF cemeteries. The repatriation process took two years and ended on 2 April 1922 with a special commemorative service in New York City for "the last shipment of [1,500] bodies from overseas." In New Mexico the percentage seeking repatriation was higher than the national average: 66 percent of next of kin opted for reburial in the United States, and ninety-three of the 277 New Mexicans among AEF deceased (34 percent) remained in six American cemeteries in France and one in England (see map 2).[33]

The first stateside step toward reinterment of New Mexicans began when the Rocky Mountain Club received flag-draped coffins at docks in New York City and New Jersey. Each plain oak casket contained a sealed metal tube holding the remains. When placed on a train a wreath was added, and an escort accompanied the casket on a four-day train trip to El Paso, after which it was transferred to the town closest to the next of kin. Correspondence between the club and the state's Republican governor, Merritt C. Mechem, recording activities for six months between 13 May 1921 and 3 November 1921 is representative of their work: forty-nine soldiers' remains were shipped to thirty-six different communities. Eleven communities received multiple caskets, with the most (four) sent to Las Cruces. In the choice of site to reinter these soldiers, next of kin for forty-five elected a local private cemetery and only four chose the state's national cemetery in Santa Fe. The ability to customize tombstone inscriptions coupled with proximity to family tipped decisions toward local reburials. Among these forty-nine deceased, twenty-six (53 percent) were Nuevomexicanos and twenty-three (47 percent) were Euro-Americans. Fourteen (29 percent) had been in the 28th Division, six (12 percent) were in the 89th Division, and the remaining twenty-nine men (59 percent) came from twenty other units. The single largest repatriation in this six-month period came when seven coffins reached the state on 13 August 1921.

The mother of Luis Otero had her son returned. He had died at age twenty-four, and his was the first coffin Albuquerque received. An impressive cortage of religious, civic, military, and public officials assembled to accompany the funeral procession, with all flags in the city flown at half-mast. The city commission urged all employers to permit former servicemen to participate in the military honors accorded Otero, and more than two hundred ex-soldiers and some former sailors wore their uniform. On Monday, 19 October, the *Albuquerque Morning Journal* ran this banner above its masthead: "All Albuquerque Should Help Honor the Memory of Luis Otero Tuesday Morning," and an estimated fifteen hundred or more did so. The day after the funeral a *Journal* editorial titled "The Voice of Luis Otero" implored everyone to heed "the words which the life of Luis Otero speaks to you. . . . [Seek] opportunity to serve."[34]

Only Otero's return elicited this outpouring of public support, and the reasons reveal various meanings of commemoration and community. The city's turnout was an expression of both collective mourning and community solidarity. The public's response became an occasion for the city and its citizens to lay to rest grief and sorrow in the wake of deaths from war and sickness and begin to move toward a healing of memories. Likewise in this particular burial were gathered a city's universal reactions of empathy and respect, sentiments badly tarnished by politicians in their tug-of-war over memorials in 1919 but now refurbished by the public. The display of public support also pulled patriotism from the fringes of vigilantism and recentered it on an individual sacrificing his life. Such a repositioning of patriotism was sought by the *Albuquerque Morning Journal* in exhorting all citizens to participate and "honor the memory" of Luis Otero. This community-wide embrace of a dead soldier accelerated the transformation from religious to secular in prevailing conceptions of a Good Death. In accepting home a flag-draped coffin, the community's display of support and respect bestowed on Otero's mother and siblings affirmed the son's generous and selfless sacrifice—achieving a Good Death in the minds and hearts of the city's citizens.

The grassroots resistance to permanent overseas burial had a counterpart in the late 1920s when public opinion again mobilized to support women whose loved ones remained buried abroad. A campaign to convince Congress to pay for round-trip passage and two weeks in France had moved in fits and starts since first proposed in 1919. The intended beneficiaries were Gold Star mothers and widows if they had not remarried. President Wilson had endorsed a WCCND proposal to create the designation Gold Star mother in late May 1918, and ten years later this group's appeals to Congress were a hallowed reminder that the inexorable scythe of warfare left a deep, searing wound in these women. As a salve for the pining and grief of Gold Star mothers, Congress appropriated $5 million ($71.3 million in 2017) in early March 1929, and in early May 1930 the first ship carrying Gold Star mothers sailed from New York. Departures occurred annually through 1933 from May to September.[35]

A total of 11,440 mothers and widows were eligible, and about 6,693 (59 percent) accepted the offer. Of those making the Gold Star pilgrimage (as it came to be known), 55 percent did so in 1930, with 3,653 women transported in a total of twenty crossings that year. The majority of pilgrims were between sixty-one and sixty-five years old, and many had infirmities rendering them, in the opinion of one annoyed participant, "totterers [who] should have a keeper." But few personal aides were available in 1930 and 1931, so other Gold Star mothers assisted them.[36]

Among Gold Star mothers in New Mexico, nineteen women qualified for a pilgrimage—twelve Euro-Americans and seven Nuevomexicanas—but only four Euro-Americans actually participated. The first New Mexican Gold Star mother to go to France, Mrs. J. J. Payne, left Albuquerque in late June 1930 and traveled by train to New York City, where she was met by an officer from the army's Quartermaster Corps, the unit in charge of the pilgrimage. After resting three days in one of three midtown hotels, she and 101 other mothers boarded the SS *America* on 2 July, the tenth sailing of the summer, and arrived at Cherbourg nine days later.[37]

The next day they took a train to Paris, and after several days' rest and memorial events, buses transported sixty-two pilgrims to the Meuse-Argonne cemetery, twenty-three to the St. Mihiel cemetery, and seventeen to the Vesle River (Oise-Aisne) cemetery. After a night's rest at a small town near the cemetery of her loved one, the next morning Mrs. Payne placed a wreath beside a prepositioned commemorative bouquet of poppies framed by small American and French flags. For most mothers, the next hour or so was a tearful reunion as described by one observer: "On each of these graves . . . an individual sorrow was poured forth in sobs which came from the heart to the lips, after twelve years." Many a visit ended in quiet contemplation and with a gentle pressing into pages of a remembrance book both poppy petals and greenery from the wreath. A uniform headstone stood sentinel—a white marble cross on which were incised name, rank, unit, state, and date died. Headstones were slightly more than three feet high and spaced a body length apart on all sides. Once back in Paris, a week of tourist activity was available to pilgrims, then a return to Cherbourg and boarding the *America,* which discharged its passengers in New York on 2 August. A key fact is not revealed in the sketchy records of Mrs. Payne's trip. She did not share the same last name as her deceased loved one, so we do not know which cemetery she visited or of his service and death. But Mrs. Payne finally knew all.[38]

The other three New Mexico Gold Star mothers were among the 689 pilgrims who sailed in 1933. Only five crossings were made that summer; two New Mexican Gold Star mothers embarked 1 June on the SS *Harding,* and the third boarded the SS *America* on 10 August. The only woman identified among these three is Cora Rogers from Artesia. She was the sole surviving relative of Lt. Harry Rogers, who was killed in action during the "Lost Battalion" siege. A military escort attended to each mother when individual attention was needed stateside, and in France the women were divided into small groups with up to twenty-three military escorts provided. Because they were guests of the U.S. government, every effort was made to ensure a safe, comfortable, and worry-free trip, and the government spent on average $840 per pilgrim ($12,263 in 2017).

For all four New Mexico women the emotional quest to be reunited with their loved ones was surely similar to what an observer described in 1930: "They got up at last, and each one of them, after having fondled the name of their son on this, for them, unique marble . . . and before entering the autocar, took in a sorrowful glance, the whole cemetery . . . and [collected] the remembrance of which the heart of these Mothers will take with them to the other end of the world."[39]

The Politics of a New Social Contract

The war's impact on New Mexican veterans, as well as their parents, wives, and families, accelerated transformations in America's social and political life that had been gathering momentum since the late nineteenth century. In the decade after the war's end a fundamental transition occurred. Individualism began being replaced by a more complex set of social, political, and economic relations in which mobilization and interdependency came to the fore. For ex-servicemen in New Mexico this meant making themselves heard by politicians at the local, state, and national levels, including through the advocacy of the American Legion.

At its inception the Legion was one of a number of veterans associations that sprang up after the war, but within three years it became the most listened-to voice among these groups. The attention the Legion commanded came in part through wrapping itself in the American flag and supporting strident anti-Bolshevik and anti-immigrant policies that dominated fear-based politics in the immediate postwar period. But the enduring power of the Legion resided in its ability to mobilize nearly one million members in elections—a number that grew significantly with suffrage to include spouses, widows, mothers, and other females in an extended family. New Mexico membership in the Legion was, at most, 3,700 World War I veterans, but in pursuit of a new social contract these men—and all veterans—were a political presence at all levels in the interwar decades.

The November 1920 election brought New Mexico veterans into politics as crusaders against an entrenched status quo. A headline in the *Santa Fe New Mexican* conveyed the spirit behind their initial political activity in October 1920: "Glittering Promises Made Soldiers When They Marched Away, by Court House Gang, Are All Forgotten Now." The Santa Fe County veterans' complaints were twofold: a lack of respect shown them, no doubt a reference to the failed war memorial proposal, and a desire to bring "clean government to the people." The latter echoed the state's Democratic Party campaign theme that called out Republicans for raising taxes, engaging in cronyism, yielding to corporate interests, and misspending country road funds. The veterans created a fusion party of Democrats, independents, and progressive Republicans—followers of the recently deceased Theodore Roosevelt as well as supporters of Bronson Cutting. In Santa Fe County their nominee for superintendent of schools was army veteran Charles Gooch, recently returned from Siberia. He pledged better schools as a means to create more responsible and informed citizens but failed in his bid. Miguel Otero Jr., an air corps officer, ran as a Republican for a house seat from Santa Fe, but he too lost.[40]

Although this first foray in local politics proved disappointing, veterans had announced their presence for the future. Their next push came in seeking political appointments to state agencies, and in this effort they had powerful allies among recently enfranchised women, who mounted "determined opposition" to force inclusion by "demanding that either one of their sex, or else a world war veteran, be appointed" by victorious Republicans to positions in state agencies. Such agitation did yield results when the Democrats won the election of 1922 and James F. Hinkle became governor. Hinkle placed veterans in the sixteen state executive departments based on a formula of "one ex-servicemen [appointed to an] official position for every 125 [Democratic] votes cast by them." The state highway department and the state penitentiary had twenty-four of the forty-six allotted staff positions for veterans, 52 percent of all their allotted government jobs. Based on the ratio reported, 5,750 veterans voted Democratic, which was just over 8 percent of the reported "70,000 votes cast for the Democratic party." Thereafter each party's political patronage was carefully tallied for veterans throughout the 1920s and 1930s.[41]

In the election of 1924, S. Omar Barker became the first veteran to win a seat in the state legislature. He served in the house as a representative from San Miguel County, the first Democrat elected to the house in that county in at least a dozen years. Barker had worked for the U.S. Forest Service in 1917, went overseas with the 20th Engineers, and emerged as a prolific regional writer after his discharge. He assessed his efforts as doing "less harm than some members and less good than some, but found politics too destructive of one's sense of humor" and did not seek reelection.[42]

Other veterans made inroads in politics in 1924. For example, Doña Ana County Republicans nominated two "veterans of the world war from across the ocean" to run for office in local elections. When the state Republican Party met in convention it responded favorably to "resolutions by the ex-servicemen, who were members of the convention," and selected three veterans for statewide office. The most significant political action of the veterans at the state convention, though, came in their support for the election of Holm O. Bursum, seeking a full term as U.S. senator in his own right after filling out the term of Albert B. Fall, who had resigned after being appointed secretary of the interior in 1921. In "pledging the support of the 10,000 ex-servicemen in the state for Holm O. Bursum for United States senator" in 1924, these Republicans backed a leading congressional voice on veterans' issues.[43]

Upon entering the Senate in 1921, Bursum had become an unusual presence in the Republican Party. Hated and opposed by his predecessor Fall, Bursum needed to establish his credibility with fellow senators, which could not happen if his only credential was Governor Merritt C. Mechem's certificate of appointment. Four years remained in Fall's term, and Bursum opted to take a risky route to Washington. He engineered a special election to fill the post and handily defeated his Democratic opponent, an electoral victory that allowed him to meet fellow senators as equals. They soon reciprocated and appointed him chair of the Committee on Pensions.[44]

Bursum's election showed the depth of his desire to be taken seriously on the national stage, which was no easy feat in the Sixty-Seventh or Sixty-Eighth Congress. He sought to bridge an intraparty split that pitted progressive Republicans against adherents of the big-business conservatism represented by President Warren G. Harding, who was overwhelming popular with New Mexico's major mining and cattle- and sheep-raising interests. In erecting a proverbial "political big tent," Bursum sought to serve veterans by promoting social welfare legislation while simultaneously working for protectionist tariff legislation and an unabashedly pro-business agenda. He was actually comfortable espousing both positions because he connected with each on a personal level. On the one hand, he had numerous acquaintances among veterans of nineteenth-century wars, but also during his twenty-five years as a political insider as well as rancher and stock raiser he steadfastly showed fealty to the view that all legislation aiding businesses helped everyone.[45]

As chair of the Senate Committee on Pensions, Bursum was at the center of a major welfare expansion, one opposed by secretary of the interior Fall, who oversaw the government's Pension Bureau within his department, as well as by President Harding and, after his death in August 1923, his successor Calvin Coolidge. Bursum's three adversaries believed the government had fulfilled its obligations to the disabled and wounded veterans in initiatives such as disability compensation, rehabilitation, and vocational education. Data released in mid-April 1921 reported that "2,073 veterans in this state [New Mexico] had been approved to receive instruction . . . in some new job, craft, or profession as a result of injuries or illnesses contracted during the Great War." The Albuquerque office for veteran rehabilitation and vocational training handled most of these cases, and a report on these men's recovery and training between 1921 and 1925 ran to thirty-seven pages. They could receive assistance for up to eighteen months, during which time they received a monthly salary of at least $100 ($1,362 in 2017) or if they had dependents $130–$170 ($1,771–$2,315 in 2017).The training options available ranged widely across four general categories: professional, commercial, agricultural, and trade and industry.[46]

The latter two programs enrolled the most veterans, and the following two ex-servicemen were representative of beneficiaries. Pvt. Lloyd S. Gipson from

Lincoln County returned from Siberia with a severe injury to his right leg. He had completed the eighth grade in school and worked seven years as a farm and ranch hand before being drafted, and in the fall of 1920 he was enrolled as a vocational student at Colorado Agricultural College. Manuel C. Gonzales of Atrisco in Bernalillo County, a laborer at a freight depot prior to the war, spent thirteen months hospitalized recovering from tuberculosis. Upon discharge in late 1919 he entered a vocational training program seeking to study either auto mechanics or poultry raising.[47]

The first major step Congress took to aid veterans was to consolidate postwar programs within the newly established Veterans Bureau in August 1921. The legislation also placed existing federally operated hospitals, including Public Health Service facilities already serving veterans such as Fort Bayard and Fort Stanton in New Mexico, under the Veterans Bureau. Providing medical care to wounded veterans had overwhelmed both private and public facilities, and Fort Bayard was likewise often overwhelmed both before and after becoming a Veterans Bureau hospital. Among veterans' correspondence about Fort Bayard, expressions of "thanks and gratitude" such as offered by the relative of a veteran recuperating there from battlefield wounds were more than offset by complaints, such as a Roswell AEF veteran lodged in claiming that "we are not getting the [medical] treatment from our Government." When Fort Bayard became a Veterans Bureau facility in 1922, it returned to providing care for TB patients only. By the late 1920s the divide in opinion about Fort Bayard swung decidedly toward a unanimous clamor for investigations and removal of belligerent and abuse staff who, in the view of the American Legion veterans at the hospital and statewide, were "trying to make jails of Veterans Bureau Hospitals." The fractious relations between more than 450 veterans and leadership at Fort Bayard prompted the state's Legion to seek improvements repeatedly into the early 1930s. An ally in these efforts was U.S. senator Bronson Cutting, who knew that Fort Bayard's Legion post was often the largest in the state.[48]

In the Veterans Bureau's turbulent first two years, dissatisfaction over health care was common and almost always justified. The agency's troubles included its first director being convicted of fraud and kickbacks and imprisoned. Matters improved dramatically under Frank T. Hines, who served as director from 1923 to 1945. He began a multipronged campaign to reorganize how the government dealt with its veterans. Included was a plan Congress passed and President Hoover signed into law in July 1930 creating a new Veterans Administration (VA) under Hines that combined three hitherto independent agencies—Veterans' Bureau,

Bureau of Pensions, and National Homes for Disabled Volunteer Soldiers. He also vigorously pursued hospital construction and expanded treatment for physical disabilities and mental disorders, with a veterans hospital being approved for Albuquerque in December 1929. The 259-bed facility opened in August 1932. A national leader of the Disabled American Veterans was instrumental in securing its approval through donation of 500 acres east of the Albuquerque airport. This allowed the association to "salvage from the wreck of a great dream" a hospital for veterans in New Mexico, a project the Disabled American Veterans pursued unsuccessfully in 1921–22.[49]

The Albuquerque VA hospital was initially planned for treatment of physical illnesses only, but local pressure for care of mental illnesses compelled the addition of a thirty-two-bed unit for such care. Throughout the 1920s, though, New Mexico had limited capacity for in-hospital rehabilitation and vocational training, so the state's veterans needing such services typically went to California or Colorado to recuperate as well as take advantage of occupational training opportunities. Some of the state's veterans returned from the war mentally incapacitated, and this number had risen to 135 by the mid-1930s. Their initial institutionalization usually occurred at the state facility in Las Vegas, but soon all were transferred out of state to private facilities and then, after the mid-1920s, sent to veterans' hospitals in California, Arkansas, and Wyoming. A niece's recollection of her uncle, institutionalized for over forty years in a VA facility in Wyoming, is representative of their condition: "He never remembered anything or anyone. He once in a while used to remember a French girl from the War; otherwise his mind was blank." A report on a Nuevomexicano veteran institutionalized for more than a decade in an Arkansas VA hospital noted, he "reacts to hallucinations continually; that is, he talks to imaginary voices that he hears coming out of the air."[50]

Creating medical facilities for veterans in the 1920s set the federal government on a course that soon made it the nation's largest hospital system and health care provider. Senator Bursum had voted for the Veterans Bureau in 1921 and thus had a hand in laying the foundation for the welfare state. Three years later he had an even greater role in shaping and passing the most important extension of benefits to all veterans in that era—the World War Adjusted Compensation Act of 1924, which provided veterans' compensation for each day they served stateside or in the AEF, but it was in the form of bond certificates redeemable in 1945. The road to that legislative success had been rocky and occasioned confrontations with Secretary Fall and presidents Harding and Coolidge, none of whom wanted to spend public money on veterans they considered able-bodied. After Harding's death, Calvin Coolidge remained adamantly opposed to providing additional benefits to veterans. He bluntly dismissed such attempts as "unsound financially, unfair to taxpayers, and destructive of patriotism." Coolidge stated his veto case in straightforward language: "We owe no bonus to able-bodied veterans. . . . No way exists by which we can either equalize the burden or give adequate financial reward to those who served the nation in both civilian and military capacities in time of war. The respect and honor of their country will rightfully be theirs forever. But patriotism can neither by bought nor sold. It is not material, it is spiritual." Coolidge, as did all conservatives, regarded the fiscal impact of the bill as ruinous to the economy's recovery. This was the position of his treasury secretary, Andrew Mellon, but it was a view rejected by most Americans. Massive budget surpluses existed—$313 million in fiscal year 1922 and over a billion dollars the next fiscal year—and this reserve enabled Congress to override Coolidge's veto.[51]

Senator Bursum's view of veterans' service and the government's obligation to them was succinctly, and sympathetically, stated in two letters in 1921 and 1922. The first responded to an influential Pennsylvania Republican and veteran, whom he told in April 1921 that he expected to be assigned to a committee "that will place me in position to better look out for ex-servicemen." Responding to a veteran from Corona, in Lincoln County, in February 1922, Bursum said: "As far as I am individually concerned, I believe in being as liberal [in providing benefits] as we possibly can toward the young men of our country, who so gloriously maintained the American traditions and standards during the recent World's War."[52]

Senator Bursum kept his pledge to "look out for ex-servicemen," which meant that like Sisyphus he endlessly pushed his bills on behalf of veterans in an uphill struggle against formidable foes in his own party. Between 1921 and 1924 he sponsored three separate major bills World War I veterans lobbied to enact. One passed but received a presidential veto that Congress failed to override: to repay World War I veterans for money deducted from their military paychecks for such service-related expenses as allotments and insurance and to compensate veterans in an amount equal to the additional allowances paid civilian employees of the U.S. government during the war. Two other pieces of major veterans legislation cleared the Senate but not the House. One allowed retirement benefits for a class of temporary U.S. Army officers disabled during World War I; the other granted World War I veterans homesteads upon proof of ninety days' residence. Bursum's one major legislative success for veterans came with passage of the World War Adjusted Compensation Act. [53]

When Congress recessed in the summer of 1924, Bursum campaigned vigorously for reelection, and he made visiting veterans a priority, including American Indians statewide. He spent a day at Laguna Pueblo with a representative of the Pension Bureau in late August "to take depositions as to Indians entitled to pensions—amount of back pay for Bonus bill [will] be about $30,000 [$427,721 in 2017]." He hoped his work on behalf of American Indian veterans would be rewarded with their vote after Congress passed and President Coolidge signed the Indian Citizenship Act of 1924 in June, done largely to acknowledge the service of more than 12,000 American Indians in World War I. Bursum supported the bill and was bitter that New Mexico exercised its control over voter qualifications to deny them that privilege until 1948. Bursum's appeal to ex-servicemen figured prominently in his campaign, and some veterans reciprocated with letters of support directed to veterans statewide, urging them to vote on 4 November "to help the man who has always helped you in the past and one on whom you can depend in the future." Despite all that Senator Holm O. Bursum had done for veterans, he lost his reelection bid in November to Democrat Sam G. Bratton by fewer than three thousand votes.[54]

The pro-veteran legacy of Senator Bursum was continued by Senator Bronson M. Cutting, the state's sole Republican U.S. senator beginning in 1927. Cutting had held the rank of captain and was attached to the American Embassy in London as a military liaison, and although he did visit the front in northeast France he had only nominal contact with troops while overseas. But after the war he developed a keen interest in veterans and their problems. He had purchased the *Santa Fe New Mexican* prior to the war, which gave him a voice in state politics that few could match, and during the 1920s he expanded his political base through support of veterans. On his 1919 service questionnaire, he identified his current occupation as "Vice-chairman, American Legion, New Mexico branch," and his duties for the next year included organizing the Legion in New Mexico, Arizona, Oklahoma, and Texas and serving on the Legion's national board. Under his guidance membership in New Mexico reached 2,557 in fifty-one posts in August 1920, and he became commander of the American Legion post in Santa Fe in 1922. But he was also transitioning from increasing membership to organizing veteran support for political purposes. He decided to actively assist the 1922 reelection campaign of Democratic senator Andrieus A. Jones, who was a supporter of veterans' legislation. This campaign "emerges as the turning point in Cutting's career," and veterans' votes carried him into office six years later when he won the seat vacated when Jones died in 1927, winning in the 1928 election a position he briefly filled when Republican governor Richard Dillon appointed him.[55]

Cutting's personal envoy to Legion posts, particularly those in Nuevomexicano communities, was Herman G. Baca, who had thrown himself into Legion organizing upon his discharge from the navy. He both founded the post in Belen and turned it into the largest for membership in the state within four months and soon was elected first state commander. Baca's successes caught Cutting's attention, and he quickly became "Cutting's eyes and ears in New Mexico." For sixteen years he was Cutting's "closest political associate and informally served as his secretary in New Mexico. Baca kept Cutting informed about developments in the American Legion, Veterans Bureau, and other organizations throughout the state." His fluency in Spanish helped solidify support among Nuevomexicano veterans and in their broader community.[56]

Bursum and Cutting clashed during the former's reelection campaign in 1924. A large chasm separated their philosophies over the role of government and whom it served. It was not enough to work on behalf of veterans—as both men had done. Cutting saw government as an agent to improve the lives of all citizens. Bursum, an old guard Republican, believed in a hierarchy of assistance in which aiding big business was preeminent, and the Senate afforded him ample opportunity to do so. To the delight of the New Mexico Wool Growers Association, he fought successfully to reauthorize the administration's tariff legislation that put a high duty on imported wool in 1922, which drove up prices for consumers on all products containing wool. In the wake of that action he noted to a business associate in Albuquerque that the "anti-wool tariff men . . . are squealing—trying to make charges that we are wool growers and have no right to vote or otherwise be active in the matter of wool [tariff] schedules." He went on to assert that "nothing in the Constitution would disenfranchise anyone who happened to be interested in a line of industry."[57]

Bursum's dismissal of all notions of conflict of interest tripped him up in his reelection campaign of 1924. Democrats—funded by Cutting—revealed that he had pushed for a deal with officials in Washington and Mexico to broker the sale of New Mexico cattle valued at up to $1.5 million dollars to ranchers in northern Mexico. Bursum was to receive a $100,000 commission ($1.4 million in 2017) for his efforts. Details of this arrangement came to light and, given the recent revelations that Albert Fall accepted money for oil leases in the Teapot Dome scandal, Bursum's cattle deal imploded. Bursum, as did Fall, merely accepted that it was permissible to create favorable business conditions that benefited a few without regard to their propriety or impact on ordinary citizens, practices since labeled crony capitalism.[58]

Bursum's embrace of crony capitalism appalled Cutting. He stated his philosophy of public service in the immediate aftermath of the Bonus Army March in late July 1932. This tragic event flowed directly from the terms of the Adjusted Compensation bill. With its passage, lobbying began to allow veterans to cash in their bonds, and pressure for immediate redemption began building just prior to the stock market crash of 1929. The Great Depression added urgency to the veterans' demands in the early 1930s, leading to the infamous and ill-fated Bonus Army March that saw an estimated 45,000 protesters, including about 17,000 veterans, encamp near the Capitol and lobby Congress early in the summer of 1932. An estimated fifty-nine ex-soldiers living in New Mexico participated in the Bonus March. Their voices and those of all the protesters failed to sway Congress, but public revulsion over their brutal removal by army troops—in which two veterans died and more than a thousand were wounded—lingered and pricked consciences when Cutting told reporters: "I came in contact with many of the bonus army veterans, and every day I met some of the New Mexico members who were camped in Anacostia [Flats]. I knew a few of them personally." Cutting drew a stark contrast between his views and the support Bursum and conservative Republicans gave to the legislative agenda of big business. Cutting said, "If they [Bonus Marchers] had organized themselves into a corporation, they might have been welcomed by the powers that be. They probably would have been met with nice, fat steaks instead of tear [gas] bombs."[59]

The demand for early payment animated veterans politics until Congress overrode President Franklin D. Roosevelt's veto of a bill in late January 1936 that authorized payment beginning in June. About 80 percent of eligible recipients—2.56 million veterans—redeemed their bonds in 1936–37, which injected about $1.6 billion dollars ($28 billion in 2017) into the economy. During his Senate career Cutting's willingness to aid the state's veterans brought him about ten thousand written requests requiring a reply and follow-up, and collectively they fill thirty-eight archival boxes in his official records. He was a consistent and steadfast advocate for veterans, and typical of his support was a pledge to a constituent in early March 1935: "I shall continue to fight to get a square deal for all disabled veterans."[60]

Cutting's fight on veterans' behalf would be cut short when he died in a plane crash near Atlanta, Georgia, on 6 May 1935. That accident was the final and most devastating blow to the veteran-based constituency Cutting had ably marshaled since 1922. Preceding his death, though, was another major reversal that unfolded beginning in late 1932 and continued for nearly two years. During that time the American Legion's national executive committee censured, threatened to revoke New Mexico's charter, and suspended some of the Legion's statewide officers after a finding of serious violations "of the Constitution of The American Legion, which in part [Article 2, Section 2] is as follows: 'The Legion shall be absolutely non-political.'" The report succinctly—but without naming individuals involved—described the "intense partisan political situation in New Mexico" that led to their actions: "Officers of The American Legion of this department, for at least the past few years, have been prominently identified with various political factions. Newspapers generally have commented upon The American Legion being in the thick of the political struggles and contests in New Mexico."[61]

The principal, unnamed focus of the findings was Senator Cutting. His willingness to freely mix Legion business and political activity went back much longer than "the past few years" cited in the official investigation. He had signaled his intention to challenge the nonpartisan stance of the Legion's constitution when he was state chair of the Committee on Rules and Order of Business in September 1921. He wanted the state council to "go to the National Convention with strong resolutions to amend the American Legion constitution to permit the American Legion to get into politics. . . . [He did not] believe we should get into partisan politics—that is, go Democratic or Republican. We have got to stand as an independent body, ready to swing the entire force of the American Legion one way or another for the benefit of the ex-serviceman." The national leadership never clearly delineated their lobbying activities from political pressure at the ballot box, and for a dozen years Cutting defined his own boundaries, which crossed into partisan politics.[62]

For its part, the American Legion acknowledged overt political activity in reporting in 1928, "We have now 53 members of the American Legion in the House of Representatives and 14 in the United States Senate." One of these senators was Bronson Cutting, and two years later the Legion's national executive committee named him to its eleven-member National Distinguished Guest Committee. But the 1932 national election changed everything both in America and between the Legion and Cutting. For ten years leading up to that election, Cutting had built and coordinated what one scholar called a "Biparty Third Force." A key reason for his clout was his mobilization and control of the vote of veterans, especially among Nuevomexicano ex-servicemen. The essence of how he used his voting bloc as leverage is seen in one statistic: four men were elected governor of New Mexico from 1922 through 1932—three Democrats and one Republican—and each secured the office with the active support of Bronson Cutting. His willingness to back men of both parties came to a head in 1932 when he endorsed Democratic candidates Franklin D. Roosevelt for president and his longtime political mentor Arthur Seligman for reelection as governor. Cutting's endorsements in 1932 so angered both old guard Republicans and Democrats that each set out to end his political career.[63]

It is not clear who nudged the national executive committee of the American Legion to launch an attack against Cutting, but two New Mexicans were prominent in the fight. One was the forty-four-year-old head of the state's Republican Party, Edward L. Safford. He was a World War I veteran and had served as a captain in the 40th Division as commander of a military police company. He was a stalwart of the old guard Republicans and regarded Cutting as a renegade who needed to be replaced by a party loyalist. The leading foe from the Democratic Party was forty-four-year-old Dionisio ("Dennis") Chavez, who had avoided military service with an exemption. A two-term member of the House of Representatives, he planned to run against Cutting in the election for U.S. senator in 1934. Chavez hoped to gain Nuevomexicano votes long given to Cutting and, in doing so, sought to exploit an ethnic division the Legion's executive committee decried in its report:

> Advantage has been taken of the situation in New Mexico relative to the Legion population thereof. There are a great number of native Americans of Spanish descent who served honorably and faithfully in the World War. These folks have a high regard for The American Legion and are proud of their American loyalty and descent. Likewise there is a large element of Anglo-Saxon descent who also takes pride in their service to their country. Partisan politicians have attempted, and with some success, to militate these two groups against each other. A sorry picture is the result. American Legion posts have been alienated from each other by reason of the fact that some posts are predominantly native [Nuevomexicano] and others Anglo-Saxon.[64]

Cutting outpolled Chavez by 1,284 votes in November 1934, an outcome the loser formally challenged. Cutting died returning to Washington after consulting with advisors in the state about his defense of the election results, a vote tally upheld and validated by the Senate shortly after the airplane crash. Democratic governor Claude E. Tingley quickly appointed Chavez to the vacant seat, and the two men began fusing Nuevomexicanos, including ex-servicemen, with the Democratic bloc. As remarkable as was Tingley's legacy in creating jobs through public works projects—funded by millions of federal dollars—another enduring accomplishment was shifting political power from Republicans to Democrats. By doing so he redirected veterans' influence in elections, making them just one more interest group in an emerging coalition of labor, teachers, farmers, small business owners, and women.[65]

Political Coda

Governor Tingley delivered separate addresses to the states' Legionnaires and the women of the Legion Auxiliary at their annual convention in Las Vegas in mid-August 1937. His remarks did the predictable—lauded the more than five hundred assembled and provided a summary of his administration's noteworthy achievements. Tingley's speeches came at a high-water mark in his political fortunes. He stood before these audiences having built a reputation for fostering public welfare since taking office in January 1935, including working on behalf of veterans in securing jobs and relief benefits for the unemployed. He expected that doing so would prompt veterans to transfer their votes and loyalty to himself and the Democratic Party. He was equally solicitous toward women and understood their importance and role in postwar politics and social progress.

The governor addressed the Auxiliary women about a matter of special concern to them—"our public welfare service in New Mexico." The issue had been actively pursued by women during wartime mobilization and throughout the 1920s and into the 1930s, particularly to improve the health of infants and children. Tingley admitted "the seriousness of the problem of our infant death rate" and quickly turned to touting the forthcoming opening of his wife's project to help children with polio—the Carrie Tingley Hospital in Hot Springs (Truth or Consequences).[66]

The governor's address to the Auxiliary women resonated with issues that many women voters cared about deeply, but it also was an approach that tracked with the Democratic Party's outreach. It likewise harkened to and perpetuated the dual track followed during wartime mobilization in which women and men had separate domains. As had been true during wartime mobilization, organizing New Mexico women proved vexing throughout the 1930s in large part because, as a Roswell woman explained to Eleanor Roosevelt in mid-September 1932, "it's very difficult to arouse a great amount of enthusiasm until our own state convention."

The underlying problem was the same one encountered during wartime mobilization—too few women with organizational and leadership skills. A woman in Tatum explained the situation to a woman Democratic leader in Washington, D.C., in October 1941: "I find it harder to interest the Democratic women in the larger towns—they have so many clubs and societies of various kinds, that they only take an interest during the campaigns." Last-minute participation of women became the norm, but their turnout grew with each election. Jennie M. Kirby, vice-chair of the state's Democratic State Central Committee, informed an official at the Democratic National Committee in late summer 1934 that their statewide meeting drew "something like 100 women" from "practically every county," and it was "a very enthusiastic meeting." Interest and participation improved dramatically in 1936 when, for example, predominantly Hispanic San Miguel County had "approximately thirteen hundred women members of the Roosevelt-Garner Club" backing nominees for president and vice-president.[67]

The national Democratic Party instituted rules that provided for 50:50 representation of women in the political organization beginning in 1934, which for New Mexico ended a rift opened when Democratic governor Arthur Seligman (1931–d. September 1933) quashed an effort to form Women's Democratic clubs. His death opened the way for Democratic women to do what wartime mobilization had also allowed them—be heard and contribute their talents. Almost immediately the State Central Committee had equal membership by gender and "thirty out of the thirty-one counties in the state [had] a woman for vice-chair." The women's electoral goal in 1934 became an election mantra for over a decade: "to poll the largest women's vote in the state." It can be assumed that many women who voted had first been mobilized on the home front in World War I and were therefore attuned to appeals aligned with maternalist politics and volunteerism.[68]

The Democratic women in New Mexico had a comparatively unchallenged position during the 1930s because Republican women had only a small network of clubs with between three hundred and five hundred members statewide. Their main activity during election seasons was hosting a tea reception at the party's statewide conventions. Not until February 1939 did the state's Republican women affiliate with the National Federation of Republican Women's Clubs, but no evidence was found of a concerted outreach to New Mexico women in the Legion Auxiliary. More than twenty years after wartime mobilization ended and women were released to their prewar routines, each political party had revived a call to arms among women, but this time enlisting them in partisan politics. Democratic outreach to women in New Mexico began earlier than among Republicans, appealed more broadly, and had far greater participation, in part through contact and coordination with Legion auxiliaries.[69]

The political goal among the state's ex-servicemen centered on creating a social contract aiding veterans during the interwar decades. It emerged piecemeal, with setbacks as common as successes, which forced ex-servicemen to keep their issues before politicians and the public. In pressing the federal government to heed their demands for benefits, veterans in the 1920s and 1930s were an important part of that era's "struggle over entitlements and the emergence of the welfare state." The greatest public policy contribution of World War I veterans came during World War II when President Roosevelt signed the Servicemen's Readjustment Act in June 1944. Popularly known as the GI Bill, it became both the most sweeping social welfare legislation of its time and also the most significant postwar legacy of World War I veterans. Its passage marked the end of a twenty-five-year struggle to establish a social contract between veterans and their government. It provided an array of benefits to the veterans of World War II that allowed them upon discharge to resume their lives without having to fight their government for needed help. World War I veterans had waged that campaign—and finally won.[70]

CHAPTER 9

Double

William A. Easley from Alto village in Lincoln County was a private 1st class in the AEF's 146th Field Artillery and "started for home July 22, 1919," after seven months with the Army of Occupation. When he submitted his service questionnaire in late November, he was twenty-two years old, reported a flesh wound as his only injury while in combat, and shortly after returning had found work as a "motor mechanic," a field in which he had taken courses prior to the war. On the surface Easley's reentry into civilian life seemed to be going well, but comments on his questionnaire revealed anxiety. He claimed that because of Prohibition "all rights have been taken from us," and the removal of alcohol made "the United States a living hell to any soldier who spent a long hitch in the American Expeditionary Forces." He resented proscriptive legislation New Mexico voters approved in 1917, and statewide enforcement of Prohibition began a year later—and nationwide in 1920. But what most disturbed him was "the way the war was conducted." He felt that what he called "the great uncalled for war ... should never be explained to our people at home for it was carried out in such way that I and all others I have talked to are ashamed of our service with the United States Army and National Guard organizations."[1]

Easley did not elaborate on his criticism of the AEF, so we are left to wonder about the referent. Was it the high and needless loss of life, especially the toll taken by enemy machine guns, or perhaps the behavior of soldiers far from home succumbing to wine and women to escape the gory reality of the frontlines, or something else? But on one level it is a distraction to speculate on what he may have had on his mind; instead, what is most important is the fact that something weighed heavily on his conscience when he got home. It is in focusing on what is known—that a seed of discontent had been planted during his AEF combat experiences—that brings us to an answer to two related questions most frequently posed to historians: What is the takeaway here? How do we identify the most salient or important theme?

Resilience and Brokenness as Double

Of the many possible ways to address questions like those Easley inspires, I take my cue from Robert Coles, psychiatrist and public intellectual. He wrote, "In the last chapter of *Middlemarch,* George Eliot asks a question many college teachers have put to themselves: 'Who can quit young lives after being long in company with them, and not desire to know what befell them in their after-years?'" Eliot's question becomes mine in regard to the interwar years. "After being long in company with" men and women of New Mexico during World War I and having sketched the state's wartime ambiance in an attempt to fulfill Edgar L. Hewett's pledge that one day "the historian [will] interpret such times and events as these and assign them to their proper place," and having provided eyewitness testimony from New Mexican draftees, national guardsmen, and Regular Army infantrymen about combat, I realize that, as important as those accounts are, what is most essential lies elsewhere. It is the postwar lives of veterans and their families that most reveal war's impact. Finding out "what befell them in their after-years" has been an often illusive quest, but one that reveals the complexity of the human spirit—at times irreparably broken, often resilient, and frequently both at once.[2]

Found in some public documents about William Easley's postwar life are elements of tragic reversals along with strands of strength and vitality. What is known is that by 1925 Easley lived in Denver, worked as a machinist, had married, and had a son, William, the following year. He brought his wife Cynthia and son to Lincoln County a few years later, where his daughter Leatrice was born in 1928. He opened and operated a restaurant in the Lincoln National Forest and his family lived there. Sometime in the early 1930s he relocated the family to Pima County, Arizona, where his son died in 1934. William worked as an attendant at a "Government Hospital"—a VA facility in Tucson—and earned $1,062 a year in 1940 ($18,494 in 2017). He died at age forty-six in 1943 and was buried in Tucson.[3]

A contrasting experience—with greater degrees of adversity and lesser amounts of forbearance—are found in the life of navy Petty Officer 1st class Eli S. Rodriguez from Santa Fe. He was twenty-six years old when he completed his service questionnaire in December 1919. On it he made sweeping, optimistic predictions about resuming civilian life, which he said had been made better during the war because of "great moral changes within our Political and Social Circles. Prohibition, Education, Suffrage, Labor, Industry, and Religion are all going thru a great evolution and are advancing with great strides." Rodriguez's assessment of political and social change occurring as a great evolution advancing with great strides was an oversimplification. The actual course of events in the nation—and in his personal life—was more complicated than he forecast. Rather than a linear, unimpeded path toward the future, switchbacks and obstacles abounded.[4]

Eli Solomon Rodriguez served in naval aviation in England and helped assemble airplanes and ferried them to bases in France. He had completed three years of college in Ohio when he enlisted in the navy in September 1917. After the war, though, he struggled to regain a life direction. He lived with his parents and siblings early in 1920 but was unemployed. He is not found in the 1930 census, but he does show up in the 1940 census, which provides information on his life in 1935 as well. By the mid-1930s he resided in Los Angeles. Still in California in 1939, he worked twenty weeks and earned a total of $300 ($5,262 in 2017). By mid-April 1940 he was living at a large VA residence outside Milwaukee and was divorced. With the outbreak of World War II men up to age sixty-five were required to register for the draft, and when he did so Rodriguez stated that he was unemployed and lived in a Detroit hotel. He died at age fifty-seven in 1950 and was interred in the national cemetery in Denver.[5]

The vignettes of Easley and Rodriguez during their post–World War I lives encapsulate a reality for a number of ex-servicemen from New Mexico. Once they shed their uniform upon discharge, they could not so readily put aside their wartime experiences. The designations "citizen-soldier" and "veteran" revealed an essential double that enveloped them in the interwar years, especially for those who had been at or near the front. Their time abroad was forever a part of who they were, especially because most of their experiences were unlike anything in their civilian lives. The wartime citizen-soldier became two men in one throughout the 1920s and 1930s—veteran and civilian. Civilians who spent the war on the home front were often aware of this double but cast it in hopeful terms. One New Mexico journalist noted that "as one . . . talks with the men who have been mustered out, or recalls days even amidst the discomforts and terrible scenes at the front, there is apt to be born the wish that the country might retain something of the community life that was fostered under the aegis of war." But veterans inhabited two intertwined communities at once: they returned to civilian life but brought into it their new status as veterans and the attendant physical and psychological struggles. The link between the two often included health conditions they could neither escape nor erase even as they struggled to understand their meaning. And some among the state's veterans were outside any community. For them, World War I was a disturbing trauma—one that profoundly impacted their psychological and physical well-being and was experienced as intensely personal and isolating.[6]

Veterans forever carried two separate sets of experiences, each with its distinct characteristics. The portion formed from the residue of war became larger and larger for many veterans during the interwar years, and these effects can be likened to lengthening shadows; that is, wartime trauma persisted in veterans' lives, especially in physical and mental health consequences, and became encumbrances. No one typical New Mexico veteran can be conjured as a prototype to encompass all the many lived realities between 1919 and 1941. Rather, the stories of many individuals open up anew the interwar years and provide a fuller understanding of their double lives—veterans as civilians.

Attention to double in the lives of veterans as civilians is not a projection of the present onto the past. It was at the heart of how Sigmund Freud grappled with the psychological impact of World War I, especially beginning in 1919. As literary scholar Michael Clark observed, "Freud says that the everyday soldier was prone to neuroses due to the very nature of combat." The war's mechanized brutality and wanton slaughter precipitated traumatized consciousness, which led Freud to shift from seeking the origin of neurosis in an individual's psychic development in early childhood to identifying effects imposed through traumatic societal events such as war. Clark summarized this change in Freud's approach: "The conflict is between the soldier's old peaceful ego and his new warlike one, and it becomes acute as soon as the peace-ego realizes what danger it runs of losing his life owing to the rashness of its newly formed parasitic double. It would be equally true to say that the old ego is protecting itself from a mortal danger by taking flight into a traumatic neurosis." Today little of merit remains in Freud's claims that neurosis originates when "mortal danger" is recognized by the "peaceful ego." Still, though Freud's suggested etiology is now dismissed, the notion of double retains utility in explaining war's impact on the body and mind. It is important to consider how brokenness carried as war's pain and wounds—including mental illness—was present in the lives of veterans, overwhelming some but more often existing alongside its double—an unbowed resilience.[7]

Trauma in Ex-servicemen's Lives

Pfc. George W. Pannell from Quay County and Pfc. Rolla A. Parker of Carrizozo in Lincoln County were, respectively, in the 4th Division and 89th Division, and each went into the military in 1917 and entered their division's military police. Pannell wrote a single sentence about his military service: "I had some real experiences but I don't care to relate them." He returned to farming in Quay County but does not appear in federal census records from 1920, 1930, or 1940. Parker mentioned that he was shell-shocked, had the flu, and went to a hospital in Bordeaux a few days before the armistice, but otherwise he was unable to talk about his time in the AEF: "I wish I could explain just to the dot all I would like to as what I went through in France but can't." As MPs in frontline units, they likely shared two experiences: dealing with combat deserters and being shelled and gassed.[8]

These two New Mexicans offered capsule versions of their experiences on their questionnaire in 1919. Clearly each man left France wrestling with wartime memories, but we are not told anything about the human drama and events they witnessed. But their time in the AEF left them with a storehouse of anguish that could not be discarded upon returning to New Mexico. Military police carried recollections of their AEF activities for decades, and in fact the last World War I service report received—submitted in January 1961—was from an MP in the 40th Division, Alva Warren McDougal. He was nineteen when he enlisted in the New Mexico National Guard, leaving his home in Deming "determined to see France and possibly Germany." In looking back more than forty years, he summarized his military duty as being "a few experiences bad, and some good." But the only AEF incident he recounted was a confrontation with his company commander over his refusal to obey a patently ill-conceived order, which brought a severe rebuke from the captain, who "let me off with a talking too, and told me what he thought of me, and what he hoped for me, which was not very pleasant." This encounter deeply affected him, and half of his questionnaire's narrative was a belated retort. He took enormous satisfaction in his achievements. Two and a half years after returning to New Mexico, McDougal left the state to visit his wife's home in Maine. They ended up staying, and he worked more than forty years as an electrician, the last twenty years of his career in the Portsmouth naval shipyard. His five children's accomplishments were likewise a source of great pride. All completed college, several received graduate degrees, and one graduated from the U.S. Naval Academy. His service report became a healing of memories. McDougal lived another twenty-five years, dying in 1986.[9]

Upon leaving the service in 1919, Parker returned to Carrizozo in Lincoln Country, where he celebrated his twenty-fourth birthday at the end of October. Runners on the front rarely survived for three weeks, but Parker had made it through seven weeks and two days before being tagged for hospitalization for shell shock. "Shell shock was, and indeed remains, the signature injury of World War I." Today it is known as post-traumatic stress disorder, and the sketchy information we have about Parker's life during the interwar years has red flags for that disorder: divorce, multiple moves, and protracted hospitalization. He married in about 1925, but five years later he lived alone at a boarding home in San Jose, California, and worked as an attendant at a garage. By 1935 he was a long-term in-patient at the VA hospital in San Mateo, midway between Palo Alto and San Francisco. He was still a patient there in 1940, and among the 1,120 residents were Parker and four other ex-servicemen from New Mexico—two Nuevomexicanos and two Euro-Americans.[10]

The postwar lives of McDougal and Parker highlight the different impacts the war had on individuals. Their varying experiences, and especially health consequences, distribute along a continuum ranging from squall to tsunami. McDougal was closer to the former in carrying nagging bitterness for decades. Parker was at the opposite end. Each man, though, fits into a sphere recently described by a distinguished scholar of intellectual history, Dominick LaCapra, who observed in 2014 that "it is astonishing how little historians recognize the significance of individual and collective trauma even when they write of events and processes in which it is prevalent, such as genocides [and] wars." One source of the hesitancy to address trauma, he suggests, is the need to "infer traumatic experiences," which is constrained because "a prevalent tendency [exists] in professional historiography to resist speculation, even when it is properly framed." Discussing historical trauma requires ensuring it is "properly framed," and doing so for World War I is forever linked to what combat troops endured—mud, blood, shelling, poison gas, and all too often mercurial leaders. The accounts left by Privates Parker and McDougal—and others introduced in this book—are evidence of the obvious: frontline experiences had lasting, adverse consequences in men's postwar lives. At the most basic level, it made killers of these men, a reality they typically carried secretly into civilian life.[11]

Two questions are foremost in considering trauma among New Mexicans in World War I: What was their trauma, and how did it manifest in veterans' lives? An astute definition of trauma has recently been offered by university president and distinguished professor of intellectual history Michael S. Roth: "Trauma is how a memory becomes a charismatic wound, an injury that attracts everything to it. In trauma, the recollected past causes suffering, and the traumatic event has a magnetic appeal that pulls a wide constellation of experience (often, an individual's whole life) into its orbit." The metaphor of a charismatic wound attracting to it a wide constellation of experience encompasses trauma as psychological assaults, when a veteran would be ambushed by flashbacks, or memory run amok, such as in PTSD. One entry point to a discussion of trauma's impact on ex-servicemen's mental and physical health is the statement of Pfc. Rolla A. Parker, an MP in the 89th Division. He reported that during the St. Mihiel and Meuse-Argonne offensives "our Division was under shell-fire ninety-five days without rest." He served with the military police until 16 September but was then transferred to the 354th Infantry and assigned as a runner, duties he fulfilled on the front until relieved on 6 November and sent to a hospital in Bordeaux. There he was treated for both flu and shell shock.[12]

The VA facility Parker inhabited beginning in the 1930s originated as U.S. Public Health Service Hospital Number 24 but had served veterans since the 1920s. Already in 1930 one Euro-American from New Mexico was a resident in-patient, and three others—together with Parker—had been residents since at least 1935; all five were still in-patients in 1940. Insufficient information exists on the military experience of the two Euro-Americans to speculate about their need for hospitalization, but fragmentary records exist for the two Nuevomexicanos. One, Abelino Rivera, had been a national guardsmen with the 40th Division. His entire account of his AEF experience reads, "Served in France for eleven months." He was a sergeant cook, so it is possible he was at or near the front, and in 1930 he was forty-seven years old, married, and farming in Mora County. The other ex-serviceman, Fernandes Gallegos, was forty-two years old in 1930, was married, and worked as a mechanic for the railroad in Albuquerque. In the AEF he served in an unspecified unit as a machinist and moved around to Services of Supply camps. Parker self-reported shell shock, and in addition as a runner he must have been exposed to poison gas on the Meuse-Argonne front. No doubt some combination of those two combat-related conditions contributed to the multiyear hospitalization of the two Nuevomexicanos.[13]

Given the prevalence of shelling and gas at and near the front, perhaps the best measure of the war's impact is found in VA data on what were called neuropsychiatric cases. Official reports on all VA patients found that neuropsychiatric admissions increased steadily year after year, and ten years after the armistice they accounted for half of all in-patients. They had been 18.4 percent (4,133) of the 22,461 veterans in hospitals in 1921, the first year for which data are available. Seven years later, in-patient neuropsychiatric cases were exactly half of all VA admissions (13,092 of 26,139 patients), and just four years later neuropsychiatric admissions were 59.6 percent of all hospitalizations (20,157 of 33,795 in-patients) in June 1932. The number of neuropsychiatric patients had grown steadily with each passing year, and this trend continued until the beginning of World War II. At its opening in 1932, the Albuquerque VA hospital had just thirty-two beds out of 259 for neuropsychiatric cases, and the treatment provided was surely short-term or acute care. Referrals from this facility to long-term care facilities were common.[14]

Both the national and state American Legion continuously monitored neuropsychiatric hospitalizations, but the closest attention came at the national level and was conducted on two fronts. One was through the bureaucracy to secure benefits on behalf of mentally ill patients, with their first fight being to secure neuropsychiatric treatment for veterans when the diagnosis was not tied to service-connected incidents. The second campaign was a continuous push at Congress for money to build more hospitals to handle the backlog of needed beds. In 1929 the American Legion reported that 2,243 neuropsychiatric veterans, aside from the 7,217 in nongovernmental institutions, were awaiting hospitalization. The immediate need for nearly 9,500 new beds for neuropsychiatric cases was the first wave of an ominous trend—a nearly twenty-year projection for ever greater numbers of in-patients. In 1929 a Legion official reported, "Over 52,000 World War veterans are receiving compensation for service connected with neuropsychiatric disabilities. We are told by experts that the peak of the neuropsychiatric load will not be reached until 1947." Within New Mexico attention to neuropsychiatric cases was a subset within a broad array of veteran claims, "a broad field of work which [in 1938] includes compensation, pensions, insurance, hospitalization, civil service, social services and social security." All these activities were classified as "rehabilitation, [which] will always be the most important and exacting program of the American Legion in this [state's] Department."[15]

Why had neuropsychiatric treatment become so large a medical issue among World War I veterans? Sights, sounds, and smells seared the memories of citizen-soldiers, marring their lives and recurring as nightmares. During the war most New Mexicans—along with most other Americans—had heard about shell shock and the enemy's use of poison gas. But when the troops returned home in 1919, suddenly what had been merely words, and therefore abstract and remote, became an immediate presence on farms and ranches and in villages, small towns, and cities throughout the state. Gas-related deaths among recently returned veterans proved especially wrenching for communities such as Tucumcari, which buried Casiano Trujillo—one of the state's first volunteers—in late September, or Roswell, where the funeral procession for Charles M. de Bremond brought the town to a halt on 9 December. But by 1920 attention began to shift to the repatriation of bodies, which had begun in earnest in New Mexico. It took an unusual event, such as the sudden death of a promising young man like twenty-nine-year-old Charles Gooch of Santa Fe in mid-October 1922, a member of the state's American Legion executive committee, to refocus attention on how the war continued to assault some ex-servicemen's health and dramatically shortened their lifespan. In reporting Gooch's death from a cerebral hemorrhage, the *Santa Fe New Mexico* observed that "it is thought likely the trouble was due to a blow on the head received in the Siberia campaign." Health consequences of the war often shortened the veteran's life, as with Charles Gooch's head trauma, but more often they went undiagnosed for a decade or more, especially for heart and lung diseases and diabetes, all the while hastening an early death.[16]

Widespread awareness of the war's cumulative toll in causing irreversible damage to organs and hastening death did not receive medical attention until the 1990s when exposure to mustard gas finally received sustained investigation. What emerged was that alongside psychological impacts were physiological changes tied to breaking apart the essential mechanics of cell reproduction, which lead to a new trauma—disease. Causal links between mustard gas and skin cancer, leukemia, and suppression of the immune system were established in 1993. These medical conditions were residual, traumatic effects of war. The illnesses attributed to exposure to mustard were the result of the body being attacked by poisonous chemicals, which amounted to taking a sledgehammer to one's DNA. A malicious disruption of "memory" occurred when the cell's normal "recall" of the processes for replicating its healthy state was broken apart. This internal trauma at the cellular level no doubt had some role in the extended in-patient treatment and then death in the early 1940s of various veterans, including Abelino Rivera, who died at age fifty in 1944.[17]

The most devastating and irreversible traumas led to declarations of mental incapacity. Such instances began occurring during the war and continued thereafter. The number of such cases among the state's veterans had risen to 135 in the mid-1930s. The men's initial institutionalization usually occurred at the state facility in Las Vegas, but all were transferred out of state to private hospitals and then, after the mid-1920s, sent to U.S. Public Health Service hospitals in California, Arkansas, and Wyoming—all of which became Veterans Administration facilities in 1930. Twenty-four-year-old Joseph Wesley Akers of Otero County had his skull crushed while among the fifty or so New Mexicans assigned to the Spruce Production Division in the Pacific Northwest, a logging operation to harvest spruce trees for timber to build airplanes. His squadron was responsible for building a railroad spur line in some of the most rugged country in western Washington's Olympic Peninsula, a ripped landscape of "great canyons and ravines, amid steep, rock-hard slopes with impenetrable underbrush. . . . much of the spruce country received an annual rainfall that averaged 135 inches." Hazards were everywhere, and accidents inevitable. The one that befell Akers was a blow to the head by a piece of metal called a fishplate, which was bolted to the ends of two rails to hold together a section of track. He survived the blow but was mentally incapacitated. He entered the "New Mexico asylum for the insane" in Las Vegas on 12 September 1919. He was there for the 1920 census but had been sent to a government hospital in Little Rock as of the 1930 census and remained there until he died in 1962. The origin of the mental incapacity of Antonio Mascarenas of San Miguel County is not known, but after he returned from the AEF he lived at home for about seven years until he required hospitalization. For the remaining thirty-six years of his life his only memory was not of family or farm but of a girl he knew briefly in France.[18]

The long-term institutionalization of many thousands of veterans was an inevitable result of the prevailing medical model during the interwar decades. But it was not the only option, although it would take decades for mental health specialists to embrace other practices largely overlooked in the interwar years. Three such alternative models existed, and each was grounded in tapping into a sense of community as a source of collective healing. American Indians in New Mexico traveled to Oklahoma to participate in healing ceremonies after returning from the war. Their sacred rituals typically lasted four days, during which time one's body and spirit were cleansed of the detritus of war through such instrumentalities as the sweat lodge and fasting. Rituals and strong, supportive kinship bonds helped many American Indians, but they were not always enough to quiet all the effects of trauma. A New Mexico Navajo, Tom Ration, recalled in an interview in 1968 some friends from the reservation going off to "first war, 1918, first world war." Ration had been hospitalized with pneumonia when the draft registration occurred in June 1917, but a good friend—Sam Chissum—signed up and was inducted. He "came back gassed from this poison gas," and over the years "he lived with us off and on, Sam Chissum, he was hard of hearing from all the shooting I guess, big guns going off." When the interviewer asked, "Did you talk to Sam about any of his war experiences or any of those Indians that served," the response was typical of veterans: "They didn't talk about it much. . . . He always want to forget it." Chissum died in the early 1960s, having had tuberculosis "from this poison gas he got."[19]

Combat veterans rarely open up to nonveterans about their wartime memories for a couple of reasons. For one, it is too difficult to put into words and create a narrative of the two most traumatic events of a battlefield—seeing the harm you inflict on others and watching a buddy die. In addition, the listener is curious but rarely empathetic and often appalled when the chaos, fear, and grisly reality of the maw of war are revealed. In such circumstances many veterans befriended others who went through the same traumas, which gave rise to a second model of community as a source of healing. This version existed in the comradeship veterans found in affiliating with clubs or veterans' organizations. In Albuquerque, as a family member recalled many decades later, Italian American veterans often participated in the Columbus Club as a way to socialize and surround themselves with familiar cultural and Catholic religious norms. In a similar way, American Legion posts provided an opportunity to be at ease and reconstruct one's sense of self in the kinship of those who were going through similar travails after returning home, including struggling with depression, flashbacks, nightmares, hypervigilance, anger issues, and suicidal thoughts.[20]

A brief item in the potpourri of humor titled "Whitecaps" that appeared in a transport ship's daily newspaper was a harbinger of both postwar psychological reactions and the need to connect with other veterans to share experiences. The "Whitecaps" entry cautioned against diving into street manholes when a car backfired. Although the account made light of a startle reflex, the issue was real and widespread. British artillery and infantry officer Robert Graves reported that once he was home "the noise of a car backfiring would send me flat on my face, or running for cover." The startle reflex was especially common among shell-shocked soldiers. The hypervigilance, mood swings, nightmares, depression, flashbacks, and startle reflex of shell shock were freely acknowledged as part of what many soldiers brought home from World War I. So prevalent was it that it became the subject of an article in an August 1919 issue of *American Legion Weekly,* a first-person account by a writer identified only as "Shell Shock." In it he traced the origin of his "restless, jumping feeling back to the front" and the many bombardments of high-explosive shells, which stalked him stateside and left him with an "irritable temper," nervousness, and "fits of melancholy that come from nowhere at all." Only when he realized other veterans had the same reactions did he begin to be at ease in their company.[21]

A third healing community emerged with the founding of Alcoholics Anonymous in 1935. Many American veterans used alcohol to quiet the voices of dead comrades heard in their dreams, a wrenching confrontation compounded by survivor's guilt, and a drama played out in solitary pain but bravely revealed in war hero and distinguished British poet Siegfried Sassoon's "Sick Leave" (1918). One of the most common traits of World War I veterans was masking their lives in the AEF by pulling a curtain of humor across battlefields while toasting the past, which is what infantryman Joshua Lee, who trained at Camp Cody, did in his ballad "The Battle of Cognac" (1919). So popular did this light-hearted paean to "wine and women" become that he recited it as a freshman congressman for President Roosevelt and newly elected congressmen invited to the White House in the mid-1930s. An undetermined number of self-medicating ex-servicemen, spurred by a desire to find a path to sobriety, began attending Alcoholics Anonymous. Personal contacts and word of mouth were the usual routes of introduction in AA's formative years between 1935 and 1940. As a result, verifiable evidence of AA meetings in New Mexico eluded detection for the pre–World War II years.[22]

Divided Mind

Relocation became a common pattern among the state's postwar veterans. Throughout their time in the military they had packed up and moved numerous times. After a peripatetic year or two while in uniform, at least a quarter of New Mexico's ex-servicemen left their communities shortly after being discharged, and many of these men seem to have drifted away to other states. Veterans across the country were on the move in late 1919, a trend the federal government labeled "general restlessness from the war." A federal agency found that "more than half the men changed their residence [within six months] after mustering out of the service." In New Mexico veterans confronted a species of double in their decisions about where home would be. It stemmed from a divided mind—having to choose between opportunity and obligation, a new path or an old pattern.[23]

The postwar experiences of a pair of veterans—brothers Candido C. Rodarte (b. 1894) and Alfredo S. Rodarte (b. 1895), from the village of Rodarte in Taos County—highlight the search for a new home. Candido was a navy petty officer who had sailed to numerous ports in the Far East. He returned to Taos County and briefly managed a sawmill but was soon unemployed. Sometime in the 1920s he moved to Los Angeles and began working for the U.S. Post Office, the government agency that hired the second-largest number of veterans in the interwar years (after the Veterans Bureau/VA). His brother Alfredo, a corporal attached to the 89th Division's artillery, had gone directly to Los Angeles after the war and was also hired by the post office. The brothers lived a few miles apart; Alfred bought a home about a mile west of the historic Mexican American communities in Chávez Ravine, and Candido purchased his home several miles northwest of his brother's house. They each married and began a family. Candido's wife was from New Mexico, Alfredo's from New York. The choices the Rodarte brothers made to resolve their divided mind typified three recurring transitions in the interwar years: the move from rural to urban, away from New Mexico (and often to California), and from enlisted man to government employee. Both men were buried in the Los Angeles area: Alfredo in 1975 and Candido in 1988.[24]

The appeal of California as a land of opportunity proved strong for a number of New Mexico veterans. Nuevomexicano Pvt. Felipe P. Barela, from Sierra County, at twenty-three years old served in an ambulance unit with the 331st Field Hospital when it deployed to Italy in July 1918. During the last week of March 1919 he sailed from Genoa to Marseille and departed for the United States in early April. He left carrying a lifelong affection for Italy, and sometime between 1935 and 1940 he departed Albuquerque with his wife and three of their children and relocated to Los Angeles. He took a job as a hospital orderly, moved into an Italian neighborhood, and died there in 1969. Frank Beaman promptly relocated to Southern California after the war. He had been a salesman in Albuquerque before being drafted, and he turned thirty-two in mid-October 1918, just a few weeks after arriving in Vladivostok. When his troop transport docked in San Francisco a year later, he was discharge from the army three days before his thirty-third birthday. He headed south to Los Angeles, found work as a salesman and driver for a laundry company, and married late in 1920. Twenty years later he remained employed as a salesman for a dry cleaning company and had divorced. Nine days after his fifty-fourth birthday he died, and he was buried in the Los Angeles National Cemetery in October 1940.[25]

The brief sketches of four veterans who settled in California in the interwar decades bring to the fore some patterns in their experiences—particularly the search for employment opportunities. The need to find steady work and provide for a family is also an implicit critique of New Mexico's economy between the wars, one revealing its in-grained weaknesses—the lack of employment opportunity as well as the shrinking viability of subsistence farming and ranching. One approximation of the influence these two economic constraints exerted is found in data compiled only for Lincoln County, whose draft officials researched 148 men whose service questionnaires Santa Fe officials informed them were returned undeliverable between early October and late December 1919. The county board's research and data provided information on ethnicity, age, marital status, and prewar occupation of men no longer residing in the county and who often had moved outside New Mexico. A sample of sixty-four men proportionate to the three-to-one ratio of Euro-Americans (forty-eight) to Nuevomexicanos (sixteen) in the unclaimed letters revealed greater occupational diversity for the former: one-third of the Euro-Americans had a trade skill such as auto mechanic, railroad brakeman, carpenter, painter, butcher, or druggist, whereas only one Nuevomexicano did (teamster). Work as a "laborer" was cited by twelve Nuevomexicanos, and three listed "farmer." Among the two-thirds of Euro-Americans not having trade skills, just five were identified as "laborer," eleven cited "rancher," fifteen were "farmers," and one was unemployed prior to military service. Four Euro-Americans in the sample were married versus just one among the Nuevomexicanos, which meant that almost all of the men in each group had only themselves to answer to for their life choices. In the sample the majority of Euro-Americans were between twenty-one and twenty-five years old when entering the military, whereas the majority of Nuevomexicanos were between twenty-six and thirty-one. Each group no doubt knew enough of what the future held for them at home that they wanted to try something different. What seems evident is that farmers and ranchers in both groups realized the difficulty of resuming work in Lincoln County and decided to try elsewhere. Similarly, the skilled workers who moved realized that a change might improve their job prospects.[26]

In the shift toward larger land holdings and commercial agriculture beginning in the 1930s, not only were the number of new smallholdings dramatically reduced with the termination of homesteading after passage of the Taylor Grazing Act in 1934, but also adversely affected were existing family-owned subsistence farms and ranches, especially in traditional Nuevomexicano settlements in the state's north-central and east-central regions. These properties' low to nonexistent integration into a cash economy necessitated an annual migration of wage earners in which "about one member of every village family was leaving home each year to find work" by 1929. But "when opportunities for outside income disappeared with the onset of the depression, great numbers of Hispanic laborers returned to their home villages," although a few subsistence farmers who worked seasonally tending sheep continued to work out of state. One such was World War I veteran Jacobo Romero of El Valle in Taos County, who was the fourteenth of thirty-five men from the county taken in the August 1918 draft. After discharge he resumed his routine of sheepherding in Utah and Wyoming and continued to do so during the interwar years. This work and its wages (supplemented by bootlegging during Prohibition and cooking at a Civilian Conservation Camp in the late 1930s) allowed him to accumulate sufficient cash to slowly purchase from brothers and sisters much of the farmland and the house that had been subdivided among siblings upon their father's death. He continued to live and farm this land until his death in 1985. Some subsistence farmers replicated Romero's activity, and though several federal programs existed to help such farmers in the 1930s, including the Resettlement Administration and its successor the Farm Security Administration, the acreage the government acquired allowed only a very few Nuevomexicanos access to grazing.[27]

The Great Depression accelerated depopulation of villages as opportunity seekers migrated, often to nearby cities in search of jobs. For example, Santa Fe's population increased 180 percent between 1920 and 1940, from 7,236 to 20,325, while the populations of Albuquerque and Las Cruces rose, respectively, 134 percent and 111 percent. The statewide population increase was 48 percent in the interwar decades, rising from 360,350 in 1920 to 531,818 twenty years later; however, three predominantly Nuevomexicano counties near Santa Fe—Rio Arriba, Taos, and San Miguel—had smaller increases of 30 percent, 45 percent, and 22 percent, respectively, signs of outmigration in varying degrees.[28]

In a small sample of ex-servicemen with an equal number of Euro-Americans and Nuevomexicanos living in the capital city in 1930, only 27 percent had entered the service as residents of either the city or county, meaning that almost three of every four ex-servicemen living and working in Santa Fe had relocated there in the 1920s. They held jobs either restricted to urban settings or more plentiful there than in smaller communities. Three main occupational categories accounted for 80 percent of the employment of these relocating veterans: 36 percent in craft work (e.g., carpenter, plumber, shoe maker), 30 percent in commerce (e.g., clerk in various enterprises, barber, merchant), and 14 percent in government (e.g., prison guard, city inspector, National Guard NCO).[29]

Opportunity for employment also acted as a magnet in eastern New Mexico between 1920 and 1940, drawing ex-servicemen away from farming and into other lines of work, principally for the railroad or at a mine, and by 1940 into Works Progress Administration (WPA) employment for those unable to find steady jobs. Illustrative of these trends are veterans who entered the service from

Trementina, a small agricultural community midway between Las Vegas and Tucumcari. Twenty-three men from the village served in World War I: one was killed in action defending Château-Thierry as a soldier in the 3rd Division; one died in France during the influenza pandemic in mid-October 1918; one—Juan B. Aragon—received a medical discharge, although he outlived all the others, dying at age ninety-seven; and eight had insufficient data to allow tracking them in the interwar years. Of the remaining twelve veterans, all Nuevomexicanos, five resumed their lives in Trementina in 1920 but one would die in 1929. Of the four veterans remaining in Trementina in 1930, two were farming and two were occasional laborers. Of the eleven surviving ex-servicemen in 1930, only two continued to farm in Trementina throughout the 1930s. In that decade one ex-serviceman became a miner in Dawson, and four others went to work for the railroad. By 1940 only one of these men continued with the railroad in Tucumcari and the other three worked in town as WPA laborers for the federal government.[30]

Interwar America and Double

The end of World War I left New Mexico—and the nation—at a crossroads. Just as a literal double marked the lives of veterans as civilians, so too did a figurative double envelop citizens on the home front during the war and vex the political order throughout the interwar years. Early in 1920 a woman active in wartime mobilization succinctly described the political and social double vying in America:

> Throughout the [First World] War there ran two currents of thought, almost side by side and often intermingling. One was a desire that the war machinery should be available after the war for reconstructing the social fabric and making America all that true Americanism might desire it, that the cooperative spirit developed under the war needs might be salvaged. . . . the other was a distinct fear that organizations built up for war needs might be perpetuated during peace times until they became a heavy incubus on the social structure, that the personal liberty yielded for the sake of national strength should not be returned.[31]

Progressivism channeled the first current of thought, and New Mexico's and most other veterans found it congruent with many of their demands for benefits. Veterans repeatedly thrust upon the postwar political generation a fundamental question that continues to be addressed in the twenty-first century: What is the federal government's proper role in people's lives? The answer provided veterans in the interwar years oscillated between rejecting and embracing their expectations. But the trend was toward a transition to a welfare state through growing acceptance of the principle that in certain instances, most notably for veterans, the government had an obligation to provide assistance including free health care and disability pensions. These benefits along with initiatives of President Franklin D. Roosevelt's New Deal such as Social Security (passed in 1935) were steps toward providing for the well-being of citizens in times of distress, principally the Great War and the Great Depression.

Of the many initiatives the federal government undertook during the administration of President Roosevelt and his New Deal, perhaps the two most immediately beneficial to veterans in New Mexico and elsewhere were Works Progress Administration jobs and work provided through Civilian Conservation Corps (CCC) camps. These programs helped keep families in food and shelter when employment and money were especially scarce in the 1930s. Jacobo Romero from El Valle in Taos County was a typical beneficiary. Income from his farm was insufficient to support himself, his wife, and their sons and daughters, but his work as a cook in one of the CCC camps in northern New Mexico provided money that kept them on their land. The largest number of the state's veterans found employment with the WPA, including men from Trementina who migrated to Tucumcari. In both programs the veterans were middle-age and usually had families to support; the government programs allowed men otherwise down-and-out in their prospects to earn some money and, more important, to retain a sense of self-worth during years aptly described "as the worst hard time."[32]

The CCC aided both rural and urban areas, and a VA assessment noted that the agency in 1936 "assisted a large number of veterans throughout the state in obtaining work in the veterans' contingent of the CCC. . . . Preference [was] given to veterans in appointments to positions in the Facility in Albuquerque." Veterans began enrolling in CCC camps throughout the state after an executive order President Roosevelt signed in May 1933, a response to a second veterans' Bonus Army March on Washington, D.C. As part of a massive program to put the unemployed to work, he authorized recruiting out-of-work veterans as well as unemployed young men (many of whom would one day serve in World War II). This initiative recast the notion of service the government had imposed upon soldiers during World War I. Service in the army, and especially in the AEF, had meant powerlessness before often capricious authority and commands, but President Roosevelt inverted the relationship. He put the army in charge of opening camps for a quarter of a million unemployed men in less than three months. After just seven weeks, sixteen camps operated in New Mexico. During its nine years, the CCC employed more than 50,000 men at 237 camps built in the state. Some of the camps, including at Albuquerque and near Carlsbad, were primarily for veterans, who in general were at least a dozen years older than the typical CCC enrollees. In many camps older, skilled veterans worked as Local Experienced Men teaching the younger men marketable trades. Although the camps used quasimilitary regimentation, their underlying structure reversed the locus of power, placing the government in the service of unemployed veterans.[33]

1941

Blanche Lucero, vice-chair of the New Mexico State Democratic Central Committee, received an appreciative note acknowledging receipt of her hand-written, three-page report in early November 1941. She had dutifully responded to a request from the Roosevelt administration for states to provide information to be used in compiling a National Defense Survey. Beginning in January 1941, President Roosevelt took the first of several public steps to safeguard against unpreparedness in an increasingly hostile world. Congress quickly appropriated $1.8 billion from which New Mexico had received $13,397,000 ($222.2 million in 2017) by 1 August 1941. The state's Democratic governor, John Mills, together with the adjutant general coordinated and oversaw home-front initiatives undertaken as National Defense projects. The largest block of money went to facilities projects in the state for the War and Navy departments, totaling $4,221,000 ($70 million in 2017). Within that amount, airport expansion and roadwork were given priority. For the latter, "18 percent of employment on road projects was involved in defense road work." National Defense money also went toward vocational training programs in high schools: "With 3,670 students enrolled for the courses, about 60% of the mechanics who have taken this training have been successful in finding employment in aviation plants and machine shops [out-of-state]. Training includes such courses as airplane engine mechanics, all types of welding, aircraft maintenance, related metal work, etc." In addition, New Deal programs aligned in numerous ways in support of National Defense programs: "WPA projects in the state having a direct bearing on National Defense reflect a total cost of $3,878,659 [$64.3 million in 2017], and consist of constructing airports, defense housing projects, barracks, access roads, and armories. An airbase was established at Albuquerque and an arsenal built at Fort Wingate."[34]

The National Youth Administration provided employment so that "1,427 New Mexico youth will be enabled to continue their education during the 1941–42 school year." These youth and many other youngsters also received school lunches through a program that distributed food valued at $95,000 ($1.6 million in 2017). Twenty-eight of the "CCC camps operating in the state with 2,655 enrollees" ensured that their "training program fits into the defense picture, and boys can readily fill vacancies left by those men who go into defense industries." The various National Defense initiatives stimulated employment, and state and federal offices made a total of 20,051 job placements in 1940. The state's workers on federal defense projects received $3,070,000 ($50.9 million in 2017) in salaries during thirty-two months beginning 1 January 1939, which did much to end Depression-era hardships.[35]

Political, economic, and social change championed by men and women who had gone through World War I created a foundation, or societal infrastructure, upon which New Deal programs and National Defense projects expanded prior to America's entry into World War II. The groundwork laid in the activism of these men and women who came to adulthood during World War I and the 1920s greatly aided ramping up for World War II. In that process international events, culminating in public acknowledgment of German rearmament in 1935, validated the grassroots efforts the World War I generation pursued during the interwar decades: healthier youth as a result of better infant and child care; improved nutrition through school lunch programs; a more educated populace especially through vocational training; and more adults experienced in organizing and leading groups. Regrettably the American Legion's call for a larger standing army, better training of officers, and peacetime conscription gained little traction in Congress or with the American public, including the several million veterans not affiliated with the Legion. As a result the efforts tallied in the National Defense Survey of 1941 remained well short of what would be needed in the aftermath of Japan's attack on Pearl Harbor on 7 December 1941 and America's entry into World War II.[36]

Using New Mexico as a case study, the years 1916–41 had many periods of double, or concurrent and generally contrasting trends. Between 1916 and 1919, civilian home-front activities experienced oscillations and countercurrents, including patriotism and vigilantism, cooperation and coercion, service and control, modernity and orthodoxy, as well as gender, ethnic, and racial divisions. For men in uniform double always centered on the personal and their simultaneous status during war as citizen-soldier and, after returning home, as war veteran-cum-civilian. But the political, economic, and social arenas likewise encompassed double, and it shaped the lives of all men and women through peace and war, reform and reaction, maternalism and mobilization, change and continuity, and opportunities and obstacles.

But between 1919 and 1941, perhaps the most pervasive double was anxiety and activism. The men and women who had been the mainstay of the home front faced immediate economic challenges in rising prices and declining income, a squeeze that farmers and ranchers experienced as a decade-long foretaste of the coming Great Depression. Many of the state's returning citizen-soldiers were caught in this dilemma as well. They had eked out a living before going to war and now had to figure out how to resume their livelihood in conditions stacked against subsistence farming and ranching. The economic condition of the state was succinctly described in 1927: "In material possessions our people in New Mexico are not affluent. The average wealth per capita is low. The great majority live by simple pursuits—small farming, stock raising, and various forms of wage earning." In addition, most of the combat veterans carried home burdens unique to their experience in the AEF—physical disabilities, mental disorders, or both. They mobilized and broke political barriers to create a new social compact that provided veterans with comprehensive and free health care, pensions, and compensation to somewhat offset higher salaries paid civilians during the war. Their successes came as a result of gaining the ear of politicians who heard in their demands a new, powerful constituency.[37]

When viewed broadly, the political contest for veterans' votes in New Mexico engaged some talented and controversial figures, none more so than Bronson Cutting and Dennis Chavez. The intersection of their political careers between 1931 and 1935 is a fascinating instance of double in the sense of contrasting personal and political values. Following the lead of progressive Republican Cutting, a veteran and political pied piper, many ex-servicemen began to drift toward the Democratic Party in 1922. Thereafter, when Republican Cutting sided with the other party as the best choice for New Mexicans, veterans voted according. They also elected him as a Republican U.S. senator in 1928, reelected him in 1934, but also followed his lead in supporting Democrat Franklin D. Roosevelt's campaign for the White House in the fall of 1932.

Veterans were not a monolithic voting bloc, of course. As a result competition for the veterans' vote intensified, which led to Democrat Dennis Chavez seizing opportunities to provide veterans attentive constituent services. As the state's U.S. representative (1931–35) he cultivated contacts to assist them in securing benefits. He served on House committees for Veteran Legislation and Veteran Insurance during his first term and was particularly attentive to Nuevomexicanos in appealing decisions of the VA. He considered them the majority among the state's veterans—which they were not—and hoped to attract new voters from among them. Beginning in 1932 his field representative in northern New Mexico sought out Democratic Nuevomexicano veterans because "our Democratic boys are all disallowed [as VA claimants] and Republicans are receiving [all disability] compensation." Concurrent with the American Legion's 1933 probe into Cutting's political use of the organization, Chavez moved quickly to exploit what he saw as an opportunity to consolidate Legionnaires' support for him through patronage. His brother, David, was mayor of Santa Fe and recommended that he appoint to the politically prominent position of postmaster in Albuquerque "an ex-serviceman and a former state Commander [who] has many Legion friends," someone who in turn had his own small network of jobs to dispense. Patronage became a favorite means Chavez used to attract and hold the loyalty of veterans and others. His practices became so flagrantly coercive among WPA hires in the run-up to the 1938 election that the abuses precipitated a congressional inquiry and contributed significantly to passage of the Hatch Act of 1939, which prohibited political activity among executive department appointees and employees.[38]

To piece together what New Mexicans encountered between 1916 and 1941 requires allowing them to reveal themselves—to listen to voices long silent. As one scholar described it, such an approach "is not to follow a frictionless course but to enter a field of force and will to power, to attend to both the sound and sense therein and their rival and reciprocal energies." Such an approach is also a pursuit of double in seeking "to attend to both the sound and sense" and simultaneously to consider "their rival and reciprocal energies." In hearing World War I era voices we need to return to Pfc. William A. Easley's comment in this chapter's opening—that the war "should never be explained to our people at home for it was carried out in such way that I and all others I have talked to are ashamed of our service." One way to understand what Easley may have had in mind is to contrast two reports Benjamin Read solicited from AEF soldiers, who returned home to Santa Fe in early summer 1919, with the lofty rhetoric he invoked in his address to departing Nuevomexicano soldiers in late August 1918 when he spoke passionately about soldiers going forth into battle "defending civilization" and being "champions of liberty and guardians of justice."[39]

The two returning soldiers—Pvt. Jack D. Trainor of the 356 Infantry, 89th Division, and Cpl. Andres S. Ribera, 109th Infantry, 28th Division—related in detail scenes from their battles and their "dread" after seeing buddies' bodies torn apart by shrapnel and lying motionless in the mud. Nowhere was there a hint of any noble purpose propelling them forward. They wanted only to survive what Trainor called "a hell on earth." He summarized his experiences in the AEF as "seeming like a bad dream," the opposite of Read's heroic and even romantic expectation that as "valiant sons of New Mexico, [you will] touch, and if possible, eclipse the glories of Sparta." Read's address was rousing and patriotic, but it was absent any sense of the maw of war. The words of the respected Nuevomexicano intellectual and the war weariness of the two returning veterans epitomized the collision of hope and disillusion that would, within several years, characterize reactions to World War I.[40]

What emerged was not an either-or choice between optimism and pessimism. Instead the two existed simultaneously, albeit in varying degrees. For those of the home front, including Read, learning "about life and doings as a soldier" personalized the horrors inflicted by shrapnel and poison gas, and these stories could not be ignored or dismissed. Instead they created a cognitive dissonance that became the double to their naive jingoism. Read had sent the men to camp with the reminder that "from the far ends of the earth generations alive today and ones to come until the end of time, see us; and they watch us with eager anticipation fighting against the enemies of fair government and against diabolical tyranny." Trainor had helped rid France of its enemy, but he was disappointed when, upon departing Brest for New York on 16 May 1919, "there was not one Frenchman there to see us off. Of course, they were there when we arrived." The contrast between Read's words and those from the two reports is perhaps the most deeply embedded double of the postwar decades, which existed in some degree within each veteran and many American civilians—patriotic words and lofty ideals clashing with disillusion and war-weariness.[41]

Legacies from World War I in New Mexico and across the nation gained renewed importance after the attack on Pearl Harbor. Those who had tended the home front and especially the veterans who lived through World War I and the decades of the 1920s and 1930s possessed a repertoire of skills that proved invaluable when called upon to make sacrifices and meet obligations during World War II. Home-front mobilization in the first world war became a dress rehearsal for similar activities when food conservation, war bond sales, and hyperpatriotism were revived during World War II. Moreover, those who came of age during World War I raised and sent off to the military many of the men and women hailed as the Greatest Generation.[42]

Notes

Abbreviations

AGC-HS	Adjutant General Collection—Historical Service, New Mexico State Records Center and Archives, Santa Fe, NM
ALD	American Legion Department of New Mexico, New Mexico State Records Center and Archives, Santa Fe, NM
AMJ	*Albuquerque Morning Journal*
BIFR	Bureau of Investigation Field Report
CSWR	Center for Southwest Research and Special Collections, University Libraries, University of New Mexico, Albuquerque, NM
Ellis Scrapbook	Scrapbook of Col. Richard T. Ellis, National Archives and Records Administration II, College Park, MD
Larrazolo Papers	Governor Octaviano A. Larrazolo Papers, New Mexico State Records Center and Archives, Santa Fe, NM
LBA	*La Bandera Americana* (Albuquerque)
Lindsey Papers	Governor Washington E. Lindsey Papers, New Mexico State Records Center and Archives, Santa Fe, NM
NARA I	National Archives and Records Administration I, Washington, DC
NARA II	National Archives and Records Administration II, College Park, MD
NARA-Atlanta	National Archives and Records Administration, Atlanta, GA
NARA-Denver	National Archives and Records Administration, Denver, CO
NMSRCA	New Mexico State Records Center and Archives, Santa Fe, NM
NYT	*New York Times*
Prichard Papers	George W. Prichard Family Papers, Center for Southwest Research and Special Collections, University Libraries, University of New Mexico, Albuquerque, NM

Read Collection   Benjamin M. Read Collection, New Mexico State Records Center and Archives, Santa Fe, NM
RGHC   Rio Grande Historical Collections, Archives and Special Collections Department, Branson Library, New Mexico State University, Las Cruces, NM
SCD   [New Mexico] State Council of Defense
SFNM   *Santa Fe New Mexican*
WCCND   Women's Committee of the Council of National Defense
WWIVS   World War I Veterans Survey, U.S. Army History and Education Center, Carlisle, PA

Chapter 1

1. Secretary of State, *New Mexico Blue Book*, 7 (quote), 63–114.
2. Pond, "At the Front." See Bibliography for the three editions.
3. The archive holding the Jewish servicemen's questionnaires—collected as a sample from the more than 100,000 Jewish men in uniform—is accessible through Ancestry.com, World War I, American Jewish Committee Office of War Records. Krouse, *North American Indians*, 12–16.

    The recently available digital access to a number of large collections of public documents—including city directories, census records, draft registration cards, [Federal]Bureau of Investigation investigations, grave registrations and headstone applications for veterans, and world war military records—provides unprecedented research capabilities, especially through key word searches using state and/or surnames. I accessed these six collections of public records through the commercially available digital archives found on Ancestry.com.
4. Hewett, "Preface," in Bloom, *New Mexico in the Great War*, vii.
5. Bloom to New Mexico State Council of Defense, 2 September 1918, New Mexico State Records Center and Archives, Santa Fe, NM [hereafter NMSRCA], Adjutant General Collection—Historical Service [hereafter AGC-HS], S10894 F4; Twitchell to Lindsey, 30 September 1918, AGC-HS, S10894 F2; Ribera to Read, 18 June 1919; and Trainor to Read [June 1919], NMSRCA, Benjamin M. Read Collection [hereafter Read Collection], S8425 F54.
6. Obituaries, AGC-HS, S10902 F5; Raymond C. Bloom, January 1920, AGC-HS, S10902 F53.
7. Cappon, "Collection," 735–36, 741 (quote). Cappon tallied twenty states as collecting war records, but today at "Online World War I Indexes and Records—USA," www.militaryindexes.com, twenty-six states are listed as holding statewide military records for 1917–19. Gutiérrez, *Doughboys*, 176–200, discusses state war records. Leland to Twitchell, 20 December 1917, AGC-HS, S10894 F4; *Report of the American Historical Association for the Year 1917*, 113–36; National Board for Historical Service to New Mexico State Council of Defense, 15 August 1917, AGC-HS, S10894 F3.
8. Holtby, *Forty-Seventh Star*, 39–66; Danburg, "State Council," 38 (quote).

9. Bernstein, "First Issue"; Bloom to Springer, 26 January 1919; and Twitchell to Lindsey, 5 November 1918, AGC-HS, S10894 F2; Bloom to Hewett, 8 January 1919, AGC-HS, S10894 F11; Chauvenet, *Hewett and Friends*.
10. Patterson, *New Deal*, is a model I looked to in re-visioning state-federal relations.
11. Kennedy, *Over Here*, 94–143; Rothbard, "War Collectivism."
12. Hewett, "Cost," 145.
13. "Officials at Conference," *New Mexico Legionnaire*, 3, NMSRCA, American Legion Department of New Mexico [hereafter ALD], S6494, F1931; Udall, "Roadmap," 476.
14. Joe G. Wilson Jr., 30 November 1919, AGC-HS, S10900 F33; Rubin, *Last of the Doughboys*.
15. Harris and Sadler, *Great Call-Up*.
16. Boghardt, *Zimmermann Telegram*.
17. Bloom, "To the Colors," 115.
18. Hewett, "Preface," in Bloom, *New Mexico in the Great War*, vi.
19. "Died in Service," 21 June 1920, AGC-HS, S10902 F1.
20. Hewett, "Preface," in Bloom, *New Mexico in the Great War*, vii.
21. Day to "Dear Bro," 14 June 1918, AGC-HS, S10903 F3; Harry M. Day, 5 June 1917, U.S. World War I Draft Registration Cards, 1917–1918, National Archives and Records Administration, Atlanta, GA [hereafter NARA-Atlanta] (available online); Harry M. Day, 2 February 1921, AGC-HS, S10903 F3.
22. "Col. De Bremond Meets Parents," *Roswell Daily Record*, 14 January 1919, 1; Kelly, *History*, 166.
23. "The Big Parade," Wikipedia online encyclopedia, https://en.wikipedia.org/wiki/The_Big_Parade.
24. Crane, *Red Badge of Courage*, 7–39, 23, 26, 35 (quotes).
25. "Recuerdos," 29 December 1918, AGC-HS, S10905 F86; Bloom, "To the Colors," 121.
26. Berg, *Wilson*, 438.
27. Takaki, *Strangers*, 7–8.
28. Harvey to Haddox, 7 April 1919, AGC-HS, S10897 F13; Coles, *Call of Stories*, 31–91.
29. Clark, *Sleepwalkers*, 562; Graves, *Good-bye*, 202; Mullaney, *Unforgiving Minute*, 360.
30. Reynolds, *Long Shadow*, 87 (quote)–101.
31. On revisionist views of disillusionment literature, see Gutiérrez, *Doughboys on the Great War*, 41–45; Trout, *Memorial Fictions*, 118–31, 147–71; Schaffer, *America in the Great War*, 194–97; and Morris, *Ambulance Drivers*. "Index of Deceased Veterans," 24 November 1939, AGC-HS, S10902 F9.
32. Linderman, *Embattled Courage*, 1.
33. Taylor, *Origins*, 22–43.

Chapter 2

1. "Los Ferrocarrileros," *La Bandera Americana* (Albuquerque) [hereafter *LBA*], 3 May 1918, 2 (quote); "Henry J. Lang," *Albuquerque Morning Journal* [hereafter *AMJ*], 29 April 1918, 5 (quote); Horgan, *Mountain Standard Time*, 201; "Mob Law," *AMJ*, 7 April 1918, 4; Eaton to Springer, 11 April 1918, AGC-HS, S10910 F31.

2. "The Third Party," *AMJ*, 31 July 1912, 12.
3. "Los Ferrocarrileros," *LBA*, 3 May 1918, 2.
4. "Beware of Mob," *Santa Fe New Mexican* [hereafter *SFNM*], 27 April 1918, 3. The identical article appeared in many newspapers, e.g., "Governor Warns," *Deming Headlight*, 3 May 1918, 4.
5. "Lynching," *Christian Science Monitor*, 5 April 1918, 1.
6. "The Collinsville Lynching," *New York Times* [hereafter *NYT*], 6 April 1918, 14; "Lynching Law," *Chicago Daily Tribune*, 12 April 1918, 6; "Disloyalist," *Chicago Daily Tribune*, 20 April 1918, 1; Luebke, *Bands of Loyalty*, 1–14; Schwartz, "Lynching."
7. "Cabinet Discusses," *NYT*, 6 April 1918, 15.
8. *Santa Fe New Mexican* quoted in Simmons, *Albuquerque*, 354–55; Melzer and Mingus, "Art to Crush the Kaiser"; Melzer, "Stage Soldiers," 39–40.
9. "The Huns," *AMJ*, 24–26, 28–29 April 1918, 1; "New Exhibits," *AMJ*, 11 October 1917, 7, is an early example of atrocity-scene art created in New Mexico, one originating when the New Mexico State Council of Defense raffled a painting titled *Kultur in Belgium* as part of a fund-raising campaign. Ponsonby, *Falsehood*; Horne and Kramer, *German Atrocities*.
10. "Mob Law," *AMJ*, 7 April 1918, 4; Eaton to Springer, 11 April 1918, AGC-HS, S10910, F31; Ganzhorn, 15 April 1918, RG 65, FBI, Old German Files, Bureau of Investigation Field Report [hereafter BIFR], CF17582. Readers wishing to examine the documents cited are best served by commercially available Ancestry.com under the Fold3 collection. At the Ancestry site click on Fold3, World War I, Old German Files, then execute a search using the case file number. Additionally, the extant materials for FBI investigations records to 1922 are declassified and held in RG 65 at NARA II in College Park, MD. They are available on 595 rolls of microfilm.
11. Wilson, "Third Annual Address," 7 December 1915, quoted at Peters and Woolley, "The American Presidency Project," www.presidency.ucsb.edu/ws/?pid=29556; Wren, 1 August 1917, BIFR, CF39619.
12. Kennedy, *Over Here*, 60–62; Hofstadter, *Paranoid Style*, 3–4, 31–32.
13. Capozzola, *Uncle Sam*, 173–205; Jensen, *Price of Vigilance*; Jensen, *Army Surveillance*, 111–210.
14. Jensen, *Price of Vigilance*; Gregory to Lindsey, 16 November 1917; and Briggs to Moxley, 23 August 1917, NMSRCA, Governor Washington E. Lindsey Papers [hereafter Lindsey Papers], S14118 F203; Jaehn, *Germans in the Southwest*, 29–30; Higham, *Strangers*, 196. American Protective League correspondence at National Archives and Records Administration II, College Park, MD [hereafter NARA II], RG65.5, FBI, exists for only five states: AR, CA, KS, NY, and NC.
15. Melzer, "Exiled"; "Se Deporte," *La Voz del Pueblo*, 14 July 1917, 1; Melzer, "World War I," 69–70, 90nn11–12; Fornoff to Lindsey, 12 August 1917, Lindsey Papers, S14118 F180.
16. Pollard to Lindsey, 1 August 1917, Lindsey Papers, S14118 F180.
17. Harris and Sadler, *Plan de San Diego*, 102–66; Wren, 11 May 1917, BIFR, CF17582; Gonzales and Massmann, "Loyalty Questioned."
18. Briggs to Moxley, 23 August 1917, Lindsey Papers, S14118 F203 (quote); Diaz, 26 September 1917, BIFR, CF22746; Harris and Sadler, *Plan de San Diego*.

19. On the administrative history of the Bureau of Investigation, see RG 65, FBI, OGF, CF14800. The agents were Maximo H. Diaz, A. R. Gere, Pearce C. Rodey, E. B. Sisk, Joe Solanas, E. E. Winter, and John K. Wren. The actual dates each agent served in New Mexico could not be determined, although approximate dates were found for Agent Rodey (June 1917 to March 1918, at which time he entered the army and went to France). On the draft status of Diaz, see memorandum Bielaski to [U.S.] Attorney General, 27 December 1917, RG 65, FBI, OGF, CF136724. In addition, three other field agent filed reports in 1918: Fred Fornoff, John W. Ganzhorn, and Hyman Harris, although the latter was in New Mexico only when an investigation required a person who spoke and read German. Daniel, *World War I Era*.
20. Brubaker to Boyles, 24 June 1918, BIFR, CF38642; Wilson, "Ranger."
21. "Alleged Slacker," *AMJ*, 21 June 1917, 1; see the following BIFRs: Diaz, 16 September 1917, CF42948; Rodey, BIFR, 30 September 1917, CF63773; Rodey, 1 January 1918, CF115714; Rodey, 28 February 1918, CF150645; Nuenhoffer to Bielaski, 18 November 1918, CF14800; Delgado [informant], field report, 10 August 1918, CF265770; and Diaz to Breniman, 18 March 1918, CF 14800.
22. "Another Plea," *AMJ*, 29 April 1918, 3; Bielaski to Burkhart, 14 January 1918; and Burkhart to Bielaski, 31 January 1918, BIFR, CF90047.
23. Ganzhorn, 15 April 1918, BIFR, C17582.
24. Marvin and Ingle, *Blood Sacrifice*.
25. Solanas, 3 September 1917; and Burkhart to Solanas (telegram), 29 August 1917, BIFR, CF47986; Burkhart to Diaz, 24 July 1918, AGC-HS, S10910 F31.
26. Rodey, 12 June 1917, BIFR, CF23766; Burkhart to Solanas, 23 June 1918, BIFR, CF250116.
27. Recter to Barnes, 3 November 1917, BIFR, CF150777.
28. Burkhart to Winter, 27 June 1918, BIFR, CF273685; Gere to Breniman, 4 March 1919, BIFR, CF14800.
29. Gere to Breniman, 4 March 1919, BIFR, CF14800.
30. Samson [Denver office], 19 June 1917, BIFR, CF22746.
31. Sixty-Sixth Congress, 1st Session, *Hearings Before the Joint Commission*, 7; Johnson, "Wilson, Burleson, and Censorship," 48.
32. Post office numbers for 1917 are an extrapolation based on data from U.S. Post Office Department, *Reports of Site Locations*. That number (259) was added to the 634 known to exist in 1912 at statehood. Harris, 4 May 1917, BIFR, CF14310.
33. Diaz, 24 May 1917, BIFR, CF17677. Diaz to various sheriffs and postmasters, 29 August 1917, BIFR, CF52665; Solanas, 7 December 1917, BIFR, CF133108.
34. Rodey, 6 June 1917, BIFR, CF22746. Dillon's argument was a crude version of a critique Randolph Bourne elaborated during the war—"War is the health of the state"—a point of view that has retained its currency among some opponents of war from the 1960s to the present; as quoted in Clayton, *Forgotten Prophet*, 266.
35. Diaz, 12 October 1917; Diaz, 16 October 1917; and Burkhart to Barnes, 18 October 1917, BIFR, CF22746; *Schenck v. United States*, 249 U.S. 47 (1919).
36. Rodey to Diaz, 9 December 1917; White [El Paso, TX], 10 July 1919; and White, 13 March 1920, BIFR, CF22746; "S. Burkhart," *Albuquerque Journal*, 15 May 1932, 1.

37. "Don't Be So Sure of Your Job" [1921], NMSRCA, Governor Merritt C. Mechem Papers, S14136 F218.
38. Bujac to New Mexico Adjutant General, 5 June 1917, BIFR, CF22811.
39. Hudspeth to all postmasters, 15 January 1918, Box 13 Fld 3, U.S. Marshal (NM), MSS 322 BC, Center for Southwest Research and Special Collections, University Libraries, University of New Mexico, Albuquerque, NM [hereafter CSWR]; also at MSS 322 BC, CSWR: "List of German Alien," 6 May 1918; and "List of German Enemy Aliens—Female," 28 November 1918, Box 13 Fld 6; Long to Seligman, 18 September 1918, 30 October 1918; and Smith to Hudspeth, 19 December 1918, Box 13 Fld 5; Solanas, 30 October 1918, BIFR, CF311351; Diaz, 12 October 1918, BIFR, CF309973; Daniel, *World War I Era*, iv–xviii, 1–178.
40. "House Committee Investigating," *SFNM*, 29 November 1919, 1; Report, War Department's Military Intelligence Division to Burke, 9 May 1920, BIFR, CF77098; Bolles to Hoover, 17 January 1921, BIFR, CF202600.
41. Murray, *Red Scare*; Schmidt, *Red Scare*.
42. Lucero, *Acts, Memorials and Resolutions*, 6 (quote); Suzanne Stamatov, "Washington E Lindsey," Office of the State Historian, New Mexico History.org, http://newmexicohistory.org/people/washington-e-lindsey.
43. "A memorandum of the past and future functions," 22 March 1918, National Archives and Records Administration II, College Park, MD [hereafter NARA II], RG 62, Council of National Defense, Field Division, Box 966; Springer, *Report of the Council of Defense*. Legislation creating the Council of National Defense was not repealed until 6 September 1966. When created, it constituted the first federally directed civilian defense effort in U.S. history.

    The following New Mexicans served on the New Mexico State Council of Defense; an asterisk denotes the executive committee's members: Secundino Romero, chair, of Las Vegas; W. A. Hawkins, Three Rivers; *C. R. Brice, Roswell; J. M. Sully, Santa Rita; Eufracio Gallegos, Gallegos; *Charles Springer, chair, Cimarron; *Benigno. C. Hernandez, Canjilon; Eduardo M. Otero, Los Lunas. The two members who resigned were R. E. Putney and Rafael Garcia, the latter sheriff of Bernalillo County. The organization's official history is New Mexico, Council of Defense, *Final Report of the Council of Defense*.
44. Within weeks of the mandatory registration two new counties were officially formed—Lea and De Baca.
45. Chapter 4 continues the discussion of the New Mexico National Guard in 1916–18. Memorandum Ruppe to Commanding Officer, 17 December 1916, NARA II, RG 407, AGO, NG, Box 311; "Guide to the Records of the Adjutant General," in "New Mexico Council of Defense," Series 18, AGC-HS, 40; "Draft Records for New Mexico District Board, 1917–1918," Boxes 1–2, MSS 82 BC, CSWR; "Selective Service Board" [1919], NMSRCA, Governor O. A. Larrazolo Papers [hereafter Larrazolo Papers], S14129 F162. At the outset of World War II, and while in his early eighties, Hernández again served on the Selective Service Board of New Mexico.

46. Fornoff to Lindsey, 12 August 1917, Lindsey Papers, S14118 F180; Risdon to Lindsey, 7 August 1917; Tumulty to Lindsey, 20 September 1917; and Wilson to Tumulty, 19 September 1917, Lindsey Papers, S14118 F181.
47. Risdon to Lindsey, 7 August 1917, Lindsey Papers, S14118 F181.
48. Springer to Redington, 30 September 1918; and Mills to Danburg, 2 September 1918, AGC-HS, S10910 F31.
49. Melzer, "Stage Soldiers," 23–42.
50. Link, *Papers of Woodrow Wilson*, 73 (quotes); Lucero, *Acts, Memorials and Resolutions*, 5.
51. "Believe State," *AMJ*, 21 May 1917, 2.
52. Telford to Lindsey, 12 May 1917; Springer to Jackson, 14 June 1917; Danburg to Jones, 11 April 1918; Danburg to Nordhaus, 6 May 1918; Danburg to Carroll, 4 February 1919; and Danburg to Darrah, 19 March 1919—all AGC-HS, S10908 F5.
53. McKean to State Council of Defense, 8 December 1917, AGC-HS, S10908 F5.
54. "Report of the Examination" [1920], Larrazolo Papers, 7–9, S14129 F163. Citing figures different from those reported by the state auditor, Bloom, *New Mexico in the Great War*, 32, reported a 61 percent collection rate, but he gave no source for his data.
55. *Proceedings of the Fourth Annual Meeting*, 36–37; Woodward to Hinkle, 5 February 1924, Governor James F. Hinkle Papers, NMSRCA, S14145 F218.
56. "A Patriotic Campaign," *AMJ*, 27 April 1917, 6; "County Agents Now," *AMJ*, 4 October 1917, 6; County [Annual] Reports, January–December 1917, NARA II, RG 83, Records of the Bureau of Agricultural Economics, Box 165.
57. "Wheat Futures," *AMJ*, 15 August 1917, 1; Danburg, "State Council of Defense," 32.
58. Larrazolo to State Council of Defense, 13 March 1919, Larrazolo Papers, S14129 F163.
59. La Follette and La Follette, *Robert M. La Follette,* 761–931; Thelen, *Robert M. La Follette*, 141 (quote); "The Case," *AMJ*, 7 October 1917, 1.
60. For transcript, see Library of Congress, Manuscripts Division, Washington, DC, La Follette Family Papers, B: Box 240.
61. Wray, "America's Unguarded Gateway," 312, 314–15.
62. "Proud and Loyal State," 487 (quote); "Harvey and Wray," *AMJ*, 28 August 1918, 1; "Junta de Indignación," *LBA*, 16 August 1918, 1; Gonzales, "'La Junta de Indignación.'"
63. "Anti-Hearst," *AMJ*, 22 June 1918, 3; Sarasohn, "Election of 1916," 286, 289, 296–97; "Hearst Case," *AMJ*, 10 August 1918, 5; Walter, "Press and Public Life," 83–84, 84 (quotes). Holtby, *Forty-Seventh Star*, 90–91.

Chapter 3

1. "Fate of War," *SFNM*, 16 April 1917, 1; "President Sounds," *AMJ*, 16 April 1917, 1; Link, *Papers of Woodrow Wilson*, 73, 74–75 (quotes); "National Advice," *NYT*, 6 May 1917, 4.
2. Link, *Papers of Woodrow* Wilson, 74–75 (quote); "Patriotic Production League" and "Roswell Farmers," *SFNM*, 16 April 1917, 7.

3. Ferguson to Myers, 12 June 1917; and Ferguson to precinct leaders and newspapers, 29 May 1917, George W. Prichard Family Papers [hereafter Prichard Papers], MSS 187 BC, Box 12 Fld 7, CSWR; "Roswell," *AMJ*, 20 May 1917, 6.
4. "Appeal Made," *AMJ*, 15 April 1917, 6 (quote); Miller, *Isabella Greenway*, 84–109; Bailey to Lindsey, 18 July 1917, Prichard Papers, MSS 187 BC, Box 13, Fld 4, (quote).
5. Skocpol, Ganz, and Munson, "Nation of Organizers," 542 (quote); Clemens, "Organizational Repertoires," 760–63, 781–83.
6. Miller, *Isabella Greenway*, 3–83; Miller and McGinnis, *Volume of Friendship*, 129 (quote); Patterson, *American New Woman*.
7. Koven and Michel, *Mothers of a New World*.
8. Blair, *Woman's Committee*, 137 (quote); "News of Club," *AMJ*, 6 May 1917, 2; "Food Bill," *AMJ*, 17 May 1917, 3 (quotes).
9. Miller and McGinnis, eds., *Volume of Friendship*, 133 (quote); Miller, *Isabella Greenway*, 87.
10. Blair, *Woman's Committee*, 26.
11. Clarke, *American Women*; Skocpol et al., "Nation of Organizers," 537–41; Wood, *History of the General Federation*; Catt and Shuler, *Woman Suffrage*.
12. Henderson, "Women's Part," 55.
13. Biographical information on Amanda Lindsey and Maude Prichard culled from Prichard Papers, MSS 187 BC, Boxes 12–13.
14. Blair, *Woman's Committee*, 36 (quote); Nordhaus to Peixotto, 26 July 1918, MSS 187 BC, Box 12 Fld 1; Nordhaus to Prichard, 31 July 1918, MSS 187 BC, Box 12 Fld 1; and Paterson to State Chairman, 17 December 1918, MSS 187 BC, Box 13, Fld 4, Prichard Papers.
15. Wood to Lindsey, 23 May 1917, Prichard Papers, MSS 187 BC, Box 14, Fld 7 (quote); "Coordination" (memorandum), 10 September 1918, Box 779, RG 62, Council of National Defense, State Council Section, NARA II; Report from McKinley County to Lindsey and Prichard [Spring 1918], Prichard Papers, MSS 187 BC, Box 12, Fld 1; "National Council" [subcommittee list prepared by WCCND] [Summer 1917], Prichard Papers, MSS 187 BC, Box 13, Fld 1.
16. Porter to Lindsey, 20 November 1917, Prichard Papers, MSS 187 BC, Box 13, Fld 3. The WCCND initially prescribed these thirteen subcommittees be formed: Organization, Registration, Food Production and Victory Garden, Food Administration and Conservation, Women in Industry, Child Welfare, Health and Recreation Service, Education and Americanization, Moral and Spiritual Forces, Liberty Loan, Home and Foreign Relief, Home Economics, and Public Markets. Three additions were made in the spring of 1918: Women's Land Army, Publicity, and Liberty Choruses.
17. Bureau of the Census, *Fourteenth Census*, Vol. 2, 103–14, 1275, 1352; Jensen, "Canning," 365, rounds up to 60 percent the population of Hispanic women.
18. Bureau of the Census, *Fourteenth Census*, Vol. 2, 114; Clarke, *American Women*, 319–20; "Visita del Secretario," *LBA*, 26 April 1918, 1; Britton, *American Indians*, 133 (quote).
19. "Great Patriotic," *AMJ*, 10 April 1917, 2, 4; Mitchell, *Coyote Nation*, 15; Wesley, *History of the National Association*, 501–6.

20. Bureau of the Census, *Fourteenth Census,* Vol. 3, 15, 119, 525–30; Henderson, "Women's Part," 58 (quote).
21. *General Federation of Women's Clubs,* 137–38; "Society News," *AMJ,* 30 September 1917, 2; "News of Club," *AMJ,* 6 May 1917, 2; Council of National Defense circular, 15 May 1917, Prichard Papers, MSS 187 BC, Box 13, Fld 1; SCD, "Definite Report" [September 1918], MSS 187 BC, Box 12, Fld 1; WCCND, Press Release, 18 September 1918, MSS 187 BC, Box 13, Fld 4; and circular "To 11,000,000 Patriotic Women" [late August 1918], MSS 187 BC, Box 12, Fld 1—all in Prichard Papers; "Belen," *AMJ,* 23 June 1918, 3; Jensen, "Canning," 365–66.
The first and oldest woman's organization in New Mexico is the Woman's Christian Temperance Union; see O'Leary-Siemer, "Roots."
22. Gibson and Lennon, *Historical Census Statistics,* tab. 6; Schackel, *Social Housekeepers,* 121; Nostrand, *El Cerrito,* 107; Leonard and Loomis, *Culture;* Roberts to Prichard, 12 August 1918, Prichard Papers, MSS 187 BC, Box 12, Fld 1.
23. Roberts to Prichard, 12 August 1918, MSS 187 BC, Box 12, Fld 1 (quote); and Pearman to Madame Chairman, 15 March 1918, MSS 187 BC, Box 13, Fld 3 (quote), Prichard Papers.
24. Sánchez, Spude, and Gómez, *New Mexico,* 200.
25. Jensen, "Canning," 365–66; International Child Welfare League of New York City, "Report" [New York, 1918], Prichard Papers, MSS 187 BC, Box 4, Fld 4; and circular, Council of National Defense to SCD, 2 February 1918, Prichard Papers, MSS 187 BC, Box 13, Fld 3 (quote); Nostrand, *El Cerrito,* 94–95; "Society of State," *AMJ,* 3 June 1917, 2; "Las Cruces," *AMJ,* 15 July 1917, 4 (quote); "Clovis," *AMJ,* 18 November 1917, 6.
26. Hernandez to Lindsey, 19 July 1918, Prichard Papers, MSS 187 BC, Box 13, Fld 3; "Socorro," *AMJ,* 29 July 1918, 5 (quotes); Jensen, "Canning," 372–74.
27. "Atención Sacerdotes,"*LBA,* 9 August 1918, 2 (quote); "Cocinas de Demonstración," *La Estrella,* 5 May 1918, 1 (quote); "Abran Vds Una Cocina," *La Estrella,* 25 May 1918, 4.
28. "Mercado de Trigo," *LBA,* 19 April 1918, 2; "La sociedad Hoover," *LBA,* 16 August 1918, 2; "Cada Bushel," *LBA,* 21 June 1918, 2; "Se Necesita," *El Centinela,* 31 May 1918, 2; "El Major Alimento," *LBA,* 7 June 1918, 2, which also noted "and with good tortillas and a little chile on the side, for us, nothing is better."
29. "¡Sostenga Vd!" *La Estrella,* 25 May 1918, 1; "Salieron Hoy," *El Independiente* [Mountainair], 25 May 1918, 1; Smith, "New Mexico's Wartime Food Problems," Part 1, 349–51.
30. Miller, *Isabella Greenway,* 87; "Christmas Membership," *Tucumcari News,* 17 January 1918, 2; "War Conditions," *AMJ,* 3 June 1917, 2; "La Cruz Roja," *LBA,* 24 May 1918, 2; Rivera letter to editor, *El Nuevo Mexicano (Seminario) de Santa Fe,* 29 December 1918, 3 (quote); Tomas Rivera, 5 November 1919, AGC-HS, S10899 F11; "Red Cross Ladies," *Tucumcari News,* 17 January 1918, 2; About Us, American Red Cross, www.redcross.org.
31. Nash, *Life of Herbert Hoover,* 3–113.
32. "The President Urges," *AMJ,* 16 May 1917, 4.

33. On internal tensions inherent in the war's "ideology of voluntarism," see Hall, "Wilson," 42–44, and Guth, "Herbert Hoover." Gamble, "Savior Nation," 9–10 (quote); Cuff, "Herbert Hoover"; "The President Urges," *AMJ*, 16 May 1917, 4; "President Sounds," *AMJ*, 16 April 1917, 1 (quote); Schaffer, *America in the Great War*, 31–64.
34. "The President Urges," *AMJ*, 16 May 1917, 4; "Food Bill," *AMJ*, 17 May 1917, 3; "The President Appoints," *AMJ*, 20 May 1917, 1; "Wilson Orders," *NYT*, 17 June 1917, 1 (quotes).
35. "Women Will," *AMJ*, 18 June 1917, 1; "Both Houses of Congress," *AMJ*, 18 June 1917, 1; "Wilson Orders," *NYT*, 17 June 1917, 1.
36. "Will Register," *AMJ*, 11 July 1917, 6.
37. Lindsey to Nutter [September 1917], Prichard Papers, MSS 187 BC, Box 12 Fld 1; "Mrs, Grunsfeld," *AMJ*, 7 September 1917, 3; Hernandez to Lindsey, 19 July 1918, Prichard Papers, MSS 187 BC, Box 13, Fld 3; Miller, *Isabella Greenway*, 87 (quote); Nash, *Life of Herbert Hoover*, 97–98.
38. "A Proclamation," *AMJ*, 10 October 1917, 2; Smith, "New Mexico's Wartime Food Problems," Part 1, 375; Address, "Patriotism" [mid-October 1917], Prichard Papers, MSS 187 BC, Box 12, Fld 1; Kingsbury, *For Home and Country*, 179–94; Blair, *Woman's Committee* 56–63, 108 (quote); Henderson, "Women's Part," 58; Hoover Institution Library and Archives, United States, Food Administration Records, Collection No XX066, 6-H States Administration Records, (New Mexico) Box 23, Fld 8, (Massachusetts) Box 22, Fld 10–12, (New York) Boxes 23–27, (Ohio) Box 28 Fld 3.
39. Smith, "New Mexico's Wartime Food Problems," Part 2, 1–54, 39–40 (quote).
40. Ibid., 361–62, 378–80; "New Exhibits," *AMJ*, 11 October 1917, 7 (quote); Mullendore, *History of the United States Food Administration*.
41. Clarke, *American Women*, 44–60; Smith, "New Mexico's Wartime Food Problems," Part 1, 375 (quote); Wilson, "Address," 13 May 1918, Prichard Papers, MSS 187 BC, Box 13, Fld 2.
42. Smith, "New Mexico's Wartime Food Problems," Part 2, 7–8, 12; Smith, "New Mexico's Wartime Food Problems," Part 1, 380–81; Circular "Libraries," 2 April 1918, Prichard Papers, MSS 187 BC, Box 12, Fld 1; Jensen, "Canning," 375–76.
43. Smith, "New Mexico's Wartime Food Problems," Part 2, 12; Heinz to Department of Food Supply, 7 January 1918, Prichard Papers, MSS 187 BC, Box 13, Fld 7; Speech, Hoover to the National Conference of the WCCND, 15 May 1918, Prichard Papers, MSS 187 BC, Box 12 Fld 4 (quote); Veit, *Modern Food*.
44. Jensen, "Canning," 367–77; "Plan for Paving," *AMJ*, 9 April 1918, 8; Smith, "New Mexico's Wartime Food Problems,: Part 2, 378; Smith, "New Mexico's Wartime Food Problems," Part 1, 358–59.
45. Jensen, "Canning," 374.
46. "Local Items," *AMJ*, 6 December 1917, 6; "Miss Tura Hawk," *AMJ*, 21 September 1918, 2; "Farmers Gather," *AMJ*, 13 January 1918, 5; "Will Lecture," *AMJ*, 29 January 1918, 8; Lindsey to Hawk, 6 March 1918, Prichard Papers, MSS 187 BC, Box 12, Fld 1; Jensen, "Canning."

47. "Many Notables," *AMJ*, 9 June 1918, 4 (quotes); Prichard to Madam Chairman [May 1918], Prichard Papers, MSS 187 BC, Box 12, Fld 1 (quote); "Muchas Madres," *La Estrella*, 6 July 1918, 1 (quotes); "Wonderful Program,"*AMJ*, 26 June 1918, 3 (quotes).
48. "Experts to Tell," *AMJ*, 22 January 1918, 3; report, Demonstrator Bertha Becker, 30 July–4 August 1917, Prichard Papers, MSS 187 BC, Box 13, Fld 5 (quotes); Moir to Lindsey, 20 February 1918, Prichard Papers, MSS 187 BC, Box 13, Fld 3 (quote).
49. Creel, *How We Advertised*, 213 (quote); Axelrod, *Selling the Great War*.
50. Creel, *How We Advertised*, 192 (quotes); "Assist Spanish Press," *AMJ*, 12 June 1918, 3 (quote); "Reunión de Periodistas," *LBA*, 21 June 1918, 1 (quote).
51. "Los Patriotas Entregan," *El Independiente*; 27 April 1918, 4 (quotes); "No Comeremos," *El Independiente*, 25 May 1918, 3 (quote); "Mercado de trigo," *LBA*, 19 April 1918, 2.
52. Huey to Lindsey, 6 April 1918, Prichard Papers, MSS 187 BC, Box 13, Fld 8; "Breve Patriótico Discurso," *LBD*, 19 April 1918, 1 (quote); Report "Fourteen Minute Women's Speakers' Bureau," n.d., RG 62, CND, Committee on Women's Defense Work, News Department, Box 596, NARA II.
53. County-by-county leadership forms [c. September 1917], Prichard Papers, MSS 187 BC, Box 12, Fld 1; county-by-county reports [c. spring 1918], Prichard Papers, MSS 187 BC, Box 13, Flds 3,7, 8.
54. Huey to Lindsey, 6 April 1918, Prichard Papers, MSS 187 BC, Box 13, Fld 8.
55. Asplund, "Civilian Activities," 44.
56. "Breve Patriótico," *LBA*, 19 April 1917, 1 (quote); report, "Fourteen Minute Women's Speakers' Bureau," n.d., RG 62, Council of National Defense, Committee on Women's Defense Work, News Department, Box 596, NARA II; "El Condo," *La Estrella*, 27 April 1918, 1. For the third bond drive the simple interest rate rose to 4.5 percent per year redeemable in 1923. Although *La Estrella* promised to provide another list of purchasers, it never appeared.
57. WCCND circular to State Councils, 3 April 1918, Prichard Papers, MSS 187 BC, Box 12, Fld 1 (quote); Peters to Lindsey, 18 April 1918, Prichard Papers, MSS 187 BC, Box 13, Fld 2; Ferguson to Dear Sir, 28 June 1918; and Springer to Ferguson, 13 July 1918, NMSRCA, Adjutant General Collection, State Council of Defense materials, S10910 Fld 4 (quote).
58. Trumbull to Ferguson, 3 August 1918; U.S Department of Agriculture Farm Help Specialist to Ferguson, 8 July 1918; and Whitehall to Ferguson [Summer 1918], Prichard Papers, MSS 187, Box 12. Fld 1.
59. "Statement of the Work of the Cost of Living Division of the Bureau of Investigation for the Fiscal Year 1919–1920," n.d., Box 1; "Department of Justice, Division of Women's Activities," n.d., Box 1; Special Assistant to U.S. Attorney General to Burkhardt, 27 January 1920, Box 3; Special Assistant to U.S. Attorney General to Johnson, 8 December 1919, Box 7; and U.S. Attorney General to Larrazolo, 7 February 1920—all in NARA II, RG 60, High Cost of Living Division, Letters Sent.
60. Circular, "Department of Justice, Division of Women's Activities," Box 1; circular, "Division of Women's Activities, Special Campaign," n.d., Box 1; and circular, "Division of Women's Activities, Platform," n.d., Box 1 (quotes)—all in ibid.

61. Patterson, *New Deal*, 17 (quotes); Noggle, *Into the Twenties*; U.S. Attorney General to Larrazolo, 13 October 1920, NARA II, RG 60, High Cost of Living Division, Letters Sent, Box 7; Clayton, *Forgotten Prophet*, 225–37.
62. Jensen, "'Disenfranchisement,'" 17–19; Sixty-Fifth Congress, Senate, 1st Session, Committee on Woman Suffrage, "Woman Suffrage"; Center for Legislative History at NARA I, RG 233, *Guide to the Records*, Judiciary Committee and Related Committees, Committee on Woman Suffrage.
63. Whaley, *Nina Otero-Warren*, 77–94; circular, "Senator [Miles] Poindexter [R-WA] Urges," 30 August 1917, Prichard Papers, MSS 187 BC, Box 12. Fld 1.
64. Clarke, *American Women*, 62.

Chapter 4

1. "Tucumcari Boy," *Tucumcari News*, 4 July 1918, 1; and "Jose F. Trujillo," *Tucumcari News*, 8 August 1918; Jose F. Trujillo, 11 December 1919, AGC-HS, S10905 F100; "Enlisted Men, Regular Army," n.d., AGC-HS, S10882 F3.
2. "Six Weeks," 281; "Enlisted Men, Regular Army," n.d., AGC-HS, S10882 F3; Gutiérrez, *Doughboy*, 14 (quote).
3. "Lucero," *AMJ*, 21 May 1917, 8 (quote); "Twenty-One," *AMJ*, 26 April 1917, 4; "Navy Enlistments," n.d., AGC-HS, S10882 F9; "Marine Corps," n.d., AGC-HS, S10882 F1; Palmer Ketner, n.d., AGC-HS, S10902 F5, Bloom, "To the Colors," 114.
4. Crowell and Wilson, *Road to France*, 387–407.
5. Joseph Quesenberry, 23 April 1920, AGC-HS, S10905 F22.
6. Bloom, "To the Colors," 116; Pershing, *My Experiences*, vol. 1, 81–86, 104–5, 210.
7. "New Mexico Boy," *Tucumcari News*, 17 January 1918, 1; Pershing, *My Experiences*, vol. 1, 134–35, 156–57; vol. 2, 204–6; Walter, "Life in Camp," 123–34; Collins, *Fighting Engineers*.
8. Adolph Abeyta, 11 November 1919, AGC-HS, S10895 F1b.
9. Simmons and Davies, *Twentieth Engineers*; "Fifty Men," *AMJ*, 6 July 1917, 2; Chapman to Bloom, 28 November 1917; Pooler to Bloom, 2 July 1918; Kerr to Bloom, 20 August 1918; and "Men of District 3" [1917] (quote), AGC-HS, S10882 F12.
10. "List of Men from New Mexico" [January 1918], AGC-HS, S10882 F3; Woodward, *American Army*, 176, 178.
11. "Guardsmen Start," *AMJ*, 20 June 1917, 3; "Eddy Leads," *AMJ*, 5 July 1917, 2; Simmons, *Albuquerque*, 354; Simmons, "New Mexicans Mustered," *SFNM*, 23 January 2010, 4; "Sunburned Veterans," *San Diego Union*, 20 October 1917, 6; Welsh, "Beyond the Call."
12. "Printer-Soldier," *AMJ*, 6 July 1917, 2; "Deaths and Funerals," *AMJ*, 1 September 1917, 2; Hodgin, *War Service*, 4.
13. Wright, *History of the Sixty-Sixth*, 85–106; Carl Fantacci, 11 October 1919, AGC-HS, S10896 F22.
14. "Camp Kearny," *San Diego Union*, 13 October 1917, 1; "Camp Population," *San Diego Union*, 2 November 1917, 6; "Sunburned Veterans," *San Diego Union*, 20 October 1917, 6 (quote); Bokovoy, *San Diego World's Fair*.

15. Clark, *American Expeditionary Force*, 279; *History of the Fortieth*, 36–38, 73–81; Robert B. Haynes, 6 July 1918, AGC-HS, S10897 F16.
16. "Jovenes," *LBA*, 20 December 1918, 1; [father] Griego y Armijo to Hewett, 26 December 1918, AGC-HS, S10903 F86.
17. Mahoney to Fall, and Mahoney to Scott, 11 April 1917, A. B. Fall Family Papers, MS 8, Box 7, Fld 20, Rio Grande Historical Collections, Archives and Special Collections Department, Branson Library, New Mexico State University, Las Cruces, NM [hereafter RGHC]; "Deming Gets It," *Deming Graphic*, 11 June 1917, 1; Provost Marshal General to Reid, 17 August 1918, Lindsey Papers, S14118 F191; "Deming," *AMJ*, 4 October 1917, 2.
18. Lindsey to WCCND [September 1917], NARA II, RG 112, Deming F, Box 288; Hudspeth to U.S. Attorney General, 28 September 1917; and Popenoe to Sanitary Corps, 30 January 1918, Box 39, Correspondence, MSS 322 BC, CSWR.
19. Berg to Seligman, 29 July 1918; and U.S Marshal to Gere, 16 September 1918, Box 13 F5, MSS 322 BC, CSWR (quote); "Special Train," *Deming Headlight*, 29 March 1918, 1.
20. Bloom, "To the Colors," 111.
21. "Notice," *Farmington Times-Hustler*, 31 May 1917, 2. The 1917 draft form had fifteen questions, and the form in June 1918 changed some of the questions and added others for a total of twenty-eight questions.
22. "Have Registered," *AMJ*, 6 June 1917, 2; "Proclamation," *Roswell Daily Record*, 4 June 1917, 1 (quote); "Registration," *AMJ*, 5 June 1917, 1; "State to Make," *AMJ*, 2 June 1917, 2.
23. "333," *Tucumcari News*, 7 June 1917, 1 (quote); telegram Crowder to Lindsey, 1 August 1917, Lindsey Papers, S14118 F185.
24. "Institutional History" within "Inventory," MSS 82 BC, CSWR; Bloom, "To the Colors," 111 (quote).
25. "Eddy County," *AMJ*, 4 July 1918, 5; "Report of Accounts," 28 February 1918, Lindsey Papers, S14118, F188.
26. Lindsey Papers, S14118 F185–F194; memorandum Reid to Local Boards, 11 January 1918, S14118 F187; Brooks W. Harmon, 17 November 1919, AGC-HS, S10897 F14.
27. "Draft Lottery," *Washington Post*, 21 July 1917, 1; "Men Drawn," *Tucumcari News*, 2 August 1917, 1; "45 Men Accepted," *Tucumcari News*, 23 August 1917, 1; Casper Allen, U.S. World War I Draft Registration Cards, NARA-Atlanta.
28. Pedro Pablo Borquez, U.S. World War I Draft Registration Cards, NARA-Atlanta; Pedro Borquez, 27 October 1919, AGC-HS, S10895 F24; "Report of Accounts," 28 February 1918, Lindsey Papers, S14118 F188; Casper Allen, June 1917, U.S. World War I Draft Registration Cards, NARA-Atlanta; Bloom, "To the Colors," 111 (quote).
29. Kennedy, *Over Here*, 162; Mead, *Doughboys*, 352; "Draft List," *AMJ*, 2 August 1917, 2.
30. Asplund, "Civilian Activities," 41.
31. "71 Percent," *Washington Post*, 21 July 1917, 2; Ramírez, *To the Line of Fire*, 22 (quote).
32. Survey of 364 soldiers, AGC-HS, S10895—74 total distributed as Euroamericans 32, Nuevomexicanos 42; S10896—44 total distributed as Euroamericans 28, Nuevomexicanos 16; S10897—66 total distributed as Euroamericans 37, Nuevomexicanos 29;

S10898—48 total distributed as Euroamericans 13, Nuevomexicanos 35; S10899—54 total distributed as Euroamericans 30, Nuevomexicanos 24; S10900—78 total distributed as Euroamericans 53, Nuevomexicanos 25. Survey of 190 soldiers: Euroamericans, S10897, 35 surnames Haas to Hawk; S10898, 60 surnames McA to McR; Nuevomexicanos, S10896, 35 surnames Gabaldon to Garcia; S10898, 60 surnames all Montoya. Ethnicity is attributed based on surname and given name.

33. "New Mexico Draft Board Records," n.d., Box 3, MSS 82 BC, CSWR; La Farge, *Santa Fe*, 66.
34. Kennedy, *Over Here*, 154–56, 163 (quote); "New Mexico Draft Board Records," n.d., Boxes 1–2, MSS 82 BC, CSWR.
35. "Eddy County," *AMJ*, 4 July 1918, 5; "Exemptions," *AMJ*, 18 August 1917, 5 (quote); telegram Crowder to Reid, 6 August 1917, Lindsey Papers, S14118 F185.
36. "Draft Board's," *AMJ*, 3 September 1917, 8; Dennis Chavez, 21 May 1917, U.S. World War I Draft Registration Cards, NARA-Atlanta.
37. Memorandum Provost Marshal General to New Mexico Adjutant General, 27 October 1917, Lindsey Papers, S14118 F185.
38. "New Mexico Draft Board Records," n.d., Boxes 1–2, MSS 82 BC, CSWR.
39. Wolford to Baca, 4 December 1917, AGC-HS, S10891 F1; "New Mexico Draft Board Records," n.d., MSS 82 BC, Boxes 1–2, CSWR; Mead, *Doughboys*, 363 (quote).
40. "County Reports," December 1917, AGC-HS, S10899 F1, 3, 5, 8, 9.
41. "Grant County's," *AMJ*, 4 October 1917, 4.
42. U.S. Army Heritage and Education Center, Carlisle, PA, World War I Veterans Survey [hereafter WWIVS], 89th Division, 356th Infantry, Rudolph A. Forderhase, Book 1; Barkley, *Scarlet Fields*, 1–18; "Sunburned Veterans," *San Diego Union*, 20 October 1917, 6 (quote).
43. Matthews and Wecter, *Our Soldiers Speak*, 357 (quote); Mohr, *Holy Sh** t227–34.
44. Telegram Wood to Baca, 25 October 1917, Lindsey Papers, S14118 F185; English, *History of the 89th*, 19–30; "Rookies," *Trench and Camp* [Camp Upton, NY] 1, no. 1 (8 October 1917): 3.
45. [Staff], "Wooden Horses," 337 (quote); Rainey, "Ambivalent Warfare," 34 (quote); Moore, "Wooden Guns," 316–18; Rainey, "Questionable Training of the AEF," 92–93.
46. Bloom, "To the Colors," 119; "Albuquerqueans," *AMJ*, 29 July 1917, 2 (quote); Miguel A. Otero Jr., 8 October 1919, AGC-HS, S10898 F 34; Sanchez, "Julius (Julio) Sanchez."
47. [Cora] Rogers to "Dear Sir," 11 February 1919, AGC-HS, S10905 F40; Rogers to "Dear Aunt," 6 September 1917, 27 October 1917, AGC-HS, S10905 F40.
48. Rogers to "Dear Aunt," 6 September 1917, 3 November 1917, 12 January 1918, and 14 April 1918, AGC-HS, S10905 F40.
49. White, *Taos Society*, 107n9, 111n10 (quotes); *El Palacio* 5 (31 August 1918), 148, 154 lists range finder paintings sent to Camp Funston and Camp Cody.
50. U.S. Army, Office of the Surgeon General, *Medical Department*, vol. 4, 70.
51. "List of Men Drafted and Sent to Camp Funston," December 1917, AGC-HS, S10889 F4, S10890 F3, F7; "Fighting against Tuberculosis," *NYT*, 6 January 1918, 42; Harries and Harries, *Last Days*, 134; Byerly, "Army Sanctuary."

52. "Fighting against Tuberculosis," *NYT*, 6 January 1918, 42.
53. "Governor Lindsey," *AMJ*, 16 December 1917, 1 (quotes); "Tubercular Committee," *AMJ*, 1 March 1919, 8.
54. Sixty-Fifth Congress, Senate 2nd Session, *Investigation of the War Department*; "Gorgas Severely Denounces," *AMJ*, 19 December 1917, 1 (quote); "Clean Up Week," *Deming Headlight*, 29 March 1918, 1.
55. Bushnell to Lindsey, 23 May 1918, NARA II, RG 112, Office of the Surgeon General, Box 289, States F/New Mexico.
56. Holtby, *Forty-Seventh Star*, 39–66; Melzer, *Captain Maximiliano Luna*, 96–119.
57. Elder to Lindsey, 18 June 1918, Lindsey Papers, S14118 F210 (quote); "Disabled Men," *AMJ*, 12 July 1918, 8; "State Victims," *AMJ*, 12 July 1918, 2; "Praises," *AMJ*, 4 July 1918, 1 (quote).
58. Memo Reid to Provost Marshal General, 31 July 1918, Lindsey Papers, S14118 F190.
59. Kennedy, *Over Here*, 157–58; Ford, *Americans All*.
60. Francis George Townsend, 21 May 1920, AGC-HS, S10900 F15.
61. Dario Lucero, U.S. World War I Draft Registration Cards, NARA-Atlanta; Dario Lucero, 15 October 1919, AGC-HS, S10898 F2.
62. U.S. Army, Office of the Surgeon General, *Medical Department*, vol. 13, section 4, 205–16, 205 (quote), 207 (quote); Odell, "New Spirit," 140 "General Order #2," 2 July 1918, NARA I, RG 393, Miscellaneous Memorandum and Correspondence, Box 30, Camp Meade, MD (quote).
63. "Making Americans," *NYT*, 22 September 1918, 40 (quote); Ford, *Americans All*.
64. Brown, "Porto Rico for War," *Washington Post*, 7 November 1917, 2; Wilson, *Maneuver and Firepower*, 63–64, 76n39.
65. Luther P. Garcia, 12 December 1919, AGC-HS, S10896 F33 (quote); personal communication, Anthony Chavez, Albuquerque, April 2014.
66. "Despida," *LBA*, 30 August 1918, 1 (quote); "Carta," *LBA*, 4 October 1918, 4 (quote); Geronimo S. Barboa and Toribio Trujillo, U.S. World War I Draft Registration Cards, NARA-Atlanta.
67. Allen, *1918 Camp Pike*; Cleto Enriquez, 20 October 1919, AGC-HS, S10896 F19 (quote).
68. Juan B. Gallegos, 6 November 1919, AGC-HS, S10896 F31.
69. Joseph H. Gonzalez, 9 September 1919, AGC-HS, S10897 F3.
70. Read, "Discursito," Read Collection, S8425 F53.

Chapter 5

1. Marshall, *Memoirs*, 8, 13.
2. "Record Crowd," *NYT*, 6 July 1917, 3.
3. "Celebration," *AMJ*, 7 July 1917, 1; "Great Welcome," *AMJ*, 16 August 1917, 1–2; "U.S. Troops," *Roswell Daily Record*, 16 August 1917, 1; Mosier, *Verdun*, 12–17; Yockelson, *Borrowed Soldiers*. The other eight divisions placed temporarily in the British Expeditionary Force were these: one Regular Army, 4th; three National Guard, 28th, 33rd, 35th; four National Army, 77th, 78th, 80th, and 82nd.

4. Fraser to Bloom, 19 August 1919, AGC-HS, S10896 F26. This correspondence precedes the formal questionnaires and is one of the few such statements gathered in the summer of 1919. Bloom knew the family.
5. Coffman, *War to End*, 132-34.
6. Le Naour, "Le Sexe et la Guerre," 103 (quote), 105.
7. Ibid., 105, 116; Many versions of "Mademoiselle from Armentières" are available online. I used the Robert W. Gordon "Inferno" Collection, Archive of Folk Culture, American Folklife Center, Library of Congress. Gordon, a longtime researcher and archivist at the LOC, collected marching songs from among World War I veterans in the early 1920s. For samples from this collection, search "Armentieres" at Jack Horntip Collection, www.horntip.com/mp3/all_mp3s_on_website.htm.
8. Leonardo Lucero, 28 November 1919, AGC-HS, S10898 F3; Le Naour, "Le Sexe et la Guerre," 114-16; Yockelson, *Forty-Seven Days*, 77-78, 325.
9. Joseph Quesenberry, 23 April 1920; and telegram Pershing to Bullard, 11 March 1918, AGC-HS, S10905 F22; Thomas, *History of the A.E.F.*, 66.
10. Thomas, *History of the A.E.F.*, 68-71; Greenhalgh, *French Army*, 271-311; "Foreign Deaths, Regular Army," n.d., AGC-HS, S10902 F1; Joseph Quesenberry, 23 April 1920, AGC-HS, S10905 F22.
11. Grotelueschen, *AEF Way*, 59-141; Woodward, *American Army*, 224-32, 232 (quote); Eisenhower, *Yanks*, 121-34; Thomas, *History of the A.E.F.*, 70-78; U.S. Army, Cochrane, "1st Division at Cantigny," 69-74; Col. Robert R. McCormick Research Center, Honor Roll, "A History of the First Division," 1 March 1941, 13-15, First Division Museum at Cantigny Park, Colonel Robert R. McCormick Research Center, Wheaton, IL.
12. William H. Goodwin, n.d.; and Delfino Gonzales, n.d., AGC-HS, S10902 F5.
13. Homsher, *American Battlefields*.
14. Frank McCrarey, 20 November 1919, AGC-HS, S10898 F4; Miller, "Bayonets, Blood, and Beyond."
15. Eisenhower, *Yanks*, 141-48.
16. Clark, *Devil Dogs Chronicle*, 135-211, 145 (quote); John Watson Barr, n.d. (quote); and Palmer Ketner, n.d., AGC-HS, S10902 F5.
17. Clark, *Devil Dogs Chronicle*, 185 (quote); Schaffer, *America in the Great War*, 199-212.
18. Grotelueschen, *AEF Way*, 200-279; Homer E. Weathers, n.d.; and Frank C. McDermott, AGC-HS, S10902, F5. Three marines present at Belleau Wood—William March (1894-1954), 5th Regiment; John W. Thomason Jr. (1893-1944), 5th Regiment; and Thomas Boyd (1898-1935), 6th Regiment—wrote critically acclaimed, timeless fictional accounts of their war experiences: Boyd, *Through the Wheat*; Thomason, *Fix Bayonets!*; and March, *Company K*.
19. Wright, *History of the Sixty-Sixth*, 109-10.
20. Ibid., 110-11, 374 (quote); Frank R. Jeffrey, "Brief History," n.d., 1-4, de Bremond Family Papers, MS 105, Box 7 Fld 2, RGHC; "From Old Roswell," *Roswell Daily Record*, 8 January 1919, 1, 4; Votaw, "Robert Rutherford McCormick," 130-35.
21. George Hall, 17 July [1920?], AGC-HS, S10903 F100; Verdie J. McReynolds, 11 May 1920; and father to Hewett, 26 August 1918, AGC-HS, S10904 F63; Aparicio Rael,

19 December 1919, AGC-HS, S10905 F23 (quote); Association of the 110th Infantry, *History of the 110 Infantry*, 49–58.
22. Thomas, *History of the A.E.F.*, 127.
23. Greenhalgh, *French Army*, 312–15.
24. Johnson and Hollman, *Soissons*; Neiberg, *Second Battle of the Marne*.
25. Eisenhower, *Yanks*, 162–78.
26. Kenneth Burns, 23 February 1920 (quote); and Mull to Wheeler, 25 July 1918, AGC-HS, S10902 F70; Raines, *Getting the Message Through*, 165–201, 176 (quote).
27. Society of the First Division, *History of the First Division*, 99–142, 121 (quote), 123 (quote), 127 (quote); Earl Elliott, n.d., AGC-HS, S10902 F5; Edmonds, *Military Operations*, 259 (quote). For an oblique and completely sanitized version of the Scottish burial detail, see Society of the First Division, *History of the First Division*, 141.
28. Jose Felipe Archuleta, 3 January 1920, AGC-HS, S10902 F28; Society of the First Division, *History of the First Division*, 128 (quote)–33, 140–41.
29. Greenhalgh, *French Army*, 321–36; Neiberg, *Second Battle of the Marne*, 155–59; Woodward, *American Army*, 82; Grotelueschen, *AEF Way*, 4–5 (quote), 172 (quote). See also Allen, *Toward the Flame*, 139.
30. Benjamin W. Kemp, 16 November 1919, AGC-HS, S10897 F31.
31. Grotelueschen, *AEF Way*, 4–5; Association of the 110th Infantry, *History of the 110th Infantry*, 62; Lt. Col. Bare, quoted in "The Battle of Croix Rouge Farm—After the Battle," Croix Rouge Farm Memorial Foundation, www.croixrougefarm.org (search "Bare"). The battle site is now a museum maintained by this American foundation.
32. Association of the 110th Infantry, *History of the 110th*, 58–70, 59.
33. Benjamin W. Kemp, 16 November 1919, AGC-HS, S10897 F31.
34. Liberato Jaramillo, n.d., AGC-HS, S10902 F1; Jose Leon Madrid, 21 March 1921, AGC-HS, S10904 F69.
35. Ribera to Read, 18 June 1919, Read Collection, S8425 F54. Ribera's service report, written four months later, makes no mention of these details; see Andres Ribera, 13 October 1919, AGC-HS, S10899 F16.
36. Benjamin W. Kemp, 16 November 1919, AGC-HS, S10897 F31; Allen, *Toward the Flame*, 200–82; Lewis, "Challenge of the Vesle," 5–7, 25; Foulenpont to "Muy senores," AGC-HS, S10903 F6.
37. Compilation: "Died in Service," 21 June 1920, AGC-HS, S10902 F1; Dan K. Yaple, n.d., AGC-HS, S10902 F5.
38. Delfin Sabedra, 20 November 1919, AGC-HS, S10899 F24.
39. Ibid.; Bureau of the Census, *Fifteenth Census*, "Sabedra, Delfin," New Mexico, Valencia County, 1930, Enumeration District 31-9, Sheet 5A; Seventy-Third Congress, House, 1st Session, *Proceedings of the 14th National Convention*, "Address of Josephus Daniels," 11 (quote).
40. Mosier, *Verdun*, 241–308.
41. Pond, "At the Front," 138 (quote); *With 'F' Company*, 8 (quote); Hatler, *Company 'B' 356 Infantry*, 8 (quote).
42. Adolph Abeyta, 11 November 1919, AGC-HS, S10895 F1b.

288   *Notes*

43. Pablo S. Romero, 20 December 1919, AGC-HS, S10905 F45; Clark, *American Expeditionary Force*, 65.
44. U.S. Army, Cochrane, *89th Division Comes into the Line*, 4–6; Pond, "At the Front," 140.
45. Freemantle, *Chemists' War*, 187–97, and specific poisons 314–315, 319; U.S. Army, Cochrane, *89th Division Comes into the Line*, 7 (quote).
46. McGrath, *War Diary of 354th Infantry*, 21–169; Jones, *History and Roster*, 46–142; U.S. Army, Cochrane, *89th Division Comes into the Line*, 13–16; Rivera to Bloom, 24 May 1919, AGC-HS, S10899 F11; John B. Vellar, 24 October 1919, AGC-HS, S10900 F25; Memo [Maj. Davis] to [Brig. Gen. Winn] the Commanding General, "Gas Attacks of 7 August 1918," Box 14639, NARA II, RG 120, American Expeditionary Forces, Records of Divisions, 89th Division; Gonzales to Bloom, 7 June 1919, AGC-HS, S10897 F2.
47. U.S. Army, Cochrane, *89th Division Comes into the Line*, 10 (quote); U.S. Army, Cochrane, *89th Division in the Bois de Bantheville*, 88 (quote).
48. U.S. Army, Cochrane, *89th Division Comes in the Line*, 33; Damiano C. de Baca, 15 October 1919, AGC-HS, S10896 F11; WWIVS, 89th Division 356th Infanty, Rudolph Forderhase, Book 1, 13–14; Jesse R. Cross, 15 November 1919; and Cross [father] to Board of Historical Service, 2 January 1919, AGC-HS, S10902 F115.
49. Wright, *History of the Sixty-Sixth*, 128–30; "Ammunition Status, August [1918]," Box 13103, NARA II, RG 120, American Expeditionary Forces, Records of Divisions, 41st Division.
50. Wright, *History of the Sixty-Sixth*, 128–130 (quotes); "Ammunition Status, 146th F.A." [September 12–16 1919]; and "Situation des Munitions, Le Captaine Landron" [September 1918], Box 13103, NARA II, RG 120, American Expeditionary Forces, Records of Divisions, 41st Division.
51. English, *History of the 89th*, 60; War College, Historical Section, *Eighty-Ninth Division*, 19 (quote).
52. Manuel Rodrguez, 27 October 1919, AGC-HS, S10899 F19.
53. Jack Douglas Trainor, 10 October 1919, AGC-HS, S10900 F17; Trainor to Read [June 1919], Read Collection, S8425 F54; Crumrine, *History of Company 'L,'* 6.
54. Trainor to Read [June 1919], Read Collection, S8425 F54.
55. Marshall, *Memoirs*, 147; War College, Historical Section, *Eighty-Ninth Division*, 20; WWIVS, 89th Division, 356th Infantry, Forderhase, Book 4, 6; Wright, *Meuse-Argonne Diary*, 21–23.
56. WWIVS, 89th Division, 356th Infantry, Forderhase, Book 4, 5–6; Keller [sister] to Historical Association, AGC-HS, S10897 F31; Bloom to Aschbacher, 23 April 1919, AGC-HS, S10895 F12.
57. Wright, *Meuse-Argonne Diary*, 20–26; American Battle Monuments Commission, *89th Division*, 14–16; Marshall, *Memoirs*, 137–58.

Chapter 6

1. Ferrell, *America's Deadliest Battle*, 45.
2. Yockelson, *Forty-Seven Days*, 159–68; Ferrell, *America's Deadliest Battle*, 151–52, 152 (quote).

3. U.S. Army, *Final Report of Gen. John J. Pershing*, 46.
4. The following extended account from Sibley is drawn from WWIVS, Sibley, 28th Division, 109th Infantry, in addition to sources noted.
5. Zaloga, *French Tanks*, 20–41, 41 (quote).
6. Faulkner, "Disappearing Doughboys," 7–25; Harries and Harries, *Last Days of Innocence*, 391–92.
7. "Died in Service," 21 June 1920, AGC-HS, S10902 F1, 28th Division KIA: Pvt. Simon Garcia (29 September, 110th Infantry, Rio Arriba County); Pvt. Albino G. Montoya (30 September, 109th Infantry, Las Cruces); Pvt. Andres Garcia (1 October, 110th Infantry, San Miguel County); Pfc. Jose C. Montoya (1 October, 110th Infantry, Santa Fe); Pvt. Alfonso T. Maestas (2 October, 110th Infantry, Mora County); Pvt. Carl D. Yancey (5 October, 110th Infantry, Socorro County); Pvt. Evangolisto Gonzales (6 October, 110th Infantry, Silver City); Pvt. Jesus Martinez (6 October, 109th Infantry, Taos County); Pvt. Charles Klenck (8 October, 109th Infantry, Lincoln County); and Pvt. Donaciano Martinez (8 October, 109th Infantry, Rio Arriba County).
8. Mastriano, *Alvin York*, 1–9, 93–160. Recent historical archaeology and GPS data have enabled identification of the location of York's exploits; see Nolan, "Battlefield Landscapes," 41–138; and Beattie, "Continuing the Search for York," 20–28.
9. Rogers to "Dear Aunt" [Cora Rogers], 14 May, 13 July, 27 July, 17 August, 20 September, 28 September 1918, and Whittlesey to [Cora] Rogers, 24 May 1919, AGC-HS, S10905 F40.
10. Adler, *History of the Seventy-Seventh*, 150 (quote); Ferrell, *Five Days*, 12–43, 80–81. No definitive figures exist for the total number of AEF or enemy soldiers involved in the Charlevaux Mill skirmishes.
11. Johnson and Pratt, *Lost Battalion*, 33–34 (quote); Grotelueschen, *AEF Way*, 323–24 (quote); memo Alexander to U.S. Army Adjutant General, 13 December 1919, Box 13103, NARA II, RG 120, "Operations of the 41st (1st Depot) Division," AEF, Records of Divisions, 41st Division.
12. "Lost in Forest," *AMJ*, 9 October 1918, 1.
13. Johnson and Pratt, *Lost Battalion*, 55–56 (quotes); Ferrell, *Five Days*, 81.
14. Slotkin, *Lost Battalions*, 364–94; Clifford, *World War I Memoirs of Robert P. Patterson*, 63.
15. Whittlesey to [Cora] Rogers, 24 May 1919; and Distinguished Service Cross citation, n.d., AGC-HS, S10905 F40; Grotelueschen, *AEF Way*, 321 map 20; Harry Rogers, n.d., AGC-HS, S10902 F5; "Lost in Forest," *AMJ*, 9 October 1918, 1.
16. Ferrell, *America's Deadliest Battle*, 148 (quote)–56; Huelfer, *"Casualty Issue,"* 64–68; Bloom, "To the Colors," 116. Total number of New Mexicans in combat is an extrapolation: the 195 combat casualties are assumed to be the 8 percent casualty rate for the AEF, which equates to having 2,438 of the state's men on the battlefield, which I round up to 2,500. Total casualty rate means killed in action, died of combat wounds, and wounded. As compared to the 8 percent total casualty rate for the AEF, the other major combatant nations had these total casualty rates: Austria-Hungary, France, and Russia, each 76 percent; Germany, 64 percent; Italy, 39 percent, British Empire, 37

percent. Stated another way, the death toll during seven weeks in the Meuse-Argonne offensive was nearly half that of Vietnam in ten years (1963–73).
17. Marshall, *Memoirs of My Service*, 138.
18. Wright, *Meuse-Argonne Diary*, 55–56, 60.
19. Ibid., 59; Elbert E. Brown, 9 November 1919, AGC-HS, S10895 F27; Isaac Quintana, 25 October 1919, AGC-HS, S10899 F18; Biterbo Gallegos, [mother] to Hewett, 17 December 1918, AGC-HS, S10903 F40; Abe Cawyer, 23 October 1919, AGC-HS, S10905 F37; Pedro Fresquez, 13 October 1919, AGC-HS, S10896 F28.
20. WWIVS, 89th Division, 356th Infantry, Forderhase, Book 4, 1–3; U.S. Army, Cochrane, *89th Division in the Bois de Bantheville*, 5–10, 8 (quote); Trainor to Read [Summer 1919], Read Collection, S8425 F54 (quote).
21. WWIVS, Foderhase, 89th Division, 356th Infantry, Book 4, 2 (quote); Wright, *Meuse-Argonne Diary*, 62–63, 108.
22. Hernon, *The Great Rescue*, 248 (quote); Greenhalgh, *Foch in Command*, 407–94.
23. "Speech of Major General Summerall . . . October 17, 1918," Box 1, NARA II, RG 120, World War I Organizational Records, 89th Division; Wright, *Meuse-Argonne Diary*, 78–80, 80 (quote); Ferrell, *Reminiscences of Conrad S. Babcock*, 126–27, 127 (quote), 142 (quote).
24. U.S. Army, Cochrane, *89th Division in the Bois de Bantheville*, 51–52; Ferrell, *Reminiscences of Conrad S. Babcock*, 128, 130.
25. Conrado Lucero, 19 June 1919, "He recibido una carta," AGC-HS, S10898 F2; Atanacio Springer Garcia, n.d., "Died in Service," AGC-HS, S10902 F1, F5.
26. WWIVS, Forderhase, 89th Division, 356th Infantry, Book 4, 5–15, Book 5, 1–10.
27. This section drawn from Wright, *History of the Sixty-Sixth*, 131–35; Report from HQ 146th FA, "An Account of the 146th Field Artillery" [1919]; and 146th FA, "Ammunition Status, 11 October–11 November, Expended," Box 13106, NARA II, RG 120, AEF, Records of Divisions, 41st Division.
28. Armijo, "Lest We Forget," *El Palacio*, 103.
29. Trainor to Read [summer 1919], Read Collection, S8425 F54. An abbreviated version of his narrative is with his service questionnaire: Jack Douglas Trainor, 19 October 1919, AGC-HS, S10900 F17. Andres S. Ribera, 18 June 1919, Read Collection, S8425 F54.
30. WWIVS, Forderhase, 89th Division, 356th Infantry, Book 5, 2.
31. Wright, *Meuse-Argonne Diary*, 166; Adolfo Ortiz, 15 October 1919, AGC-HS, S10898 F35.
32. Damiano C. de Baca, 15 October 1919, AGC-HS, S10896 F11; Reginald E. Baird, n.d., AGC-HS, S10902 F5; Hugh Calvin Wharton, 17 February 1921, AGC-HS, S10905 F134; Jose Eligio Madrid, April [1919], AGC-HS, S10904 F67; Arturo Montoya, AGC-HS, S10904, F108; Leon B. Vaughan, n.d., AGC-HS, S10902 F5; Royal C. Boehrig, 4 August 1920, AGC-HS, S10902, F54.
33. Augustine Martinez, 7 November 1919, AGC-HS, S10898 F13.
34. Ibid.; WWIVS, Forderhase, 89th Division, 356th Infantry, Book 5, 5–7.
35. Persico, *Eleventh Month*, 7; 146th FA, "Ammunition Status, 11 October–11 November, Expended," Box 13106, NARA II, RG 120, AEF, Records of Divisions, 41st Division.

36. "Died in Service," 21 June 1921, AGC-HS, S10902 F1.
37. Wright, *Meuse-Argonne Diary*, 162. Quotations are from a reply to "World War I: Wasted Lives on Armistice Day," HistoryNet, 12 June 2006, www.historynet.com/world-war-i-wasted-lives-on-armistice-day.htm, by Josehp Garcia's son, Donald G. Garcia.
38. "Carta de un Soldado," *LBA*, 3 January 1919, 1.
39. Trainor to Read [summer 1919], Read Collection, S8425 F 54; Wright, *Meuse-Argonne Diary*, 156–66.
40. Association of the 110th Infantry, *History of the 110th Infantry*, 113–14 (quote); Adolfo Abeyta, 11 November 1919, AGC-HS, S10895 F1b (quote).
41. WWIVS, 89th Division, Forderhase, 356th Infantry, Book 5, 9; Herring, *Trifling with War*, 274–75.
42. "Gen. March Tells of Cruelty," *NYT*, 24 July 1919, 1, 3; "William A. Poe," 21 March 1920, AGC-HS, S10899 F9.
43. Keene, *Doughboys*, 151–54.
44. "A.M. Bergere" [1919], Read Collection, S8425 F54.
45. Graves, *America's Siberian Adventure*, 5.
46. Richard, *When the United States Invaded;* Trani, "Woodrow Wilson and the Decision," 453–59; Graves, *America's Siberian Adventure*, 5–10. Strictly speaking, the military's use of the word "Siberia" in reference to Vladivostok is erroneous. Vladivostok is in a Pacific shore region to the east of the Siberian region border.
47. Woodward, *American Army*, 256–75, 257 (quote); Trani, "Woodrow Wilson and the Decision," 459 (quote); Graves, *America's Siberian Adventure*, chaps. 1–4; Richard, *When the United States Invaded*, chaps. 1–3; Bullock, *Russian Civil War;* Mohr, *Czech-Slovak Legion*.
48. Graves, *American's Siberian Adventure*, 137–39.
49. Charles Gooch, 17 February 1920, AGC-HS, S10897 F5.
50. McMaster, "International Military Police."
51. Frank Beaman, 20 December 1919; and Beaman, "Siberian Stuff," 4–8, AGC-HS, S10895 F19; U.S. Army, Office of the Surgeon General of the Army, *Medical Department*, vol. 8, 966–69.
52. Brooks Lee, n.d., AGC-HS, S10902 F5; Brooks Lee, 5 June 1917; and Nestor Lopez, 6 June 1917, U.S. World War I Draft Registration Cards, 1917–1918, NARA-Atlanta (quote); Woodward, *American Army*, 274; Beaman, "Siberian Stuff," 6 (quote).
53. Charles Gooch, "Saving Russia," *SFNM*, 7 April 1919, 6.
54. Carl A. Russell Papers, Polar Bear Expedition Digital Collections, Bentley Historical Library, University of Michigan, https://quod.lib.umich.edu/p/polaread; Terrell D. Thompson, 5 June 1917, U.S. World War I Draft Registration Cards, 1917–1918, NARA-Atlanta; Bureau of the Census, *Twelfth Census*, "Willminner, Emil H." [later changed the spelling to Willmunger], New Mexico, 2 June 1900, Enumeration District 20, Sheet 2; Ralph Voylles, 5 June 1917, U.S. World War I Draft Registration Cards, 1917–1918, NARA-Atlanta.
55. Bureau of the Census, *Twelfth Census*, "Archibeque, Antonio," New Mexico, 11 June 1900, Enumeration District 104, Sheet 5.

56. Woodward, *American Army*, 262–67; "Died in Service," 21 June 1921, AGC-HS, S10902 F1; Moore et al., *History of the American Expedition*, 51 (quote); Trani, "Woodrow Wilson and the Decision," 444, 459–61.
57. WWIVS, Forderhase, 89th Division, 356th Infantry, Book 5, 21–22; Augustin Martinez, 9 November 1919, AGC-HS, S10898 F13; Harry Rogers," n.d., AGC-HS, S10905 F40.
58. U.S. Army full-text citations for award of the Distinguished Service Cross, Home of Heroes, *www.homeofheroes.com/valor/02_awards/02_dsc.html*; "Decorations and Citations of New Mexico's Men," n.d., AGC-HS, S10912 [no folder number]; Bureau of the Census, *Fifteenth Census*, "Garcia, Amado," Acoma Pueblo, New Mexico, 7 April 1930, Enumeration District 31-35, Sheet 3B; Bureau of the Census, *Sixteenth Census*, "Martinez, Lauriano," Chacon, New Mexico, 2 May 1940, Enumeration District 17-17, Sheet 3B.
59. Home of Heroes, *www.homeofheroes.com/valor/02_awards/02_dsc.html*.
60. Leonard C. Hoskins, n.d., AGC-HS, S10902 F2; Bryan Mudgett, n.d., AGC-HS, S10902 F5; Benjamin I. Berry, n.d., AGC-HS, S10902 F2 (quote).
61. 31 October 1919, AGC-HS, S10896 F7; Bureau of the Census, *Fifteenth Census*, "Crockett, Oren Overton," San Diego town, California, 9 April 1930, Enumeration District 37-138, Sheet 9B; Floyd H. Wells, 26 October 1919, AGC-HS, S10900 F30; Bureau of the Census, *Fifteenth Census of the United States*, "Wells, Floyd H.," Deaver, Wyoming, 7 April 1930, Enumeration District 2-34, Sheet 2A.

Chapter 7

1. Pecho A. Mondragon, 20 November 1919, AGC-HS, S10898 F23. A vivid account of a U-boat torpedo sinking a ship is Larson, *Dead Wake*, 147–49.
2. Crowell and Wilson, *Road to France*, 321 (quote); Pershing, *My Experiences*, vol. 1, 78 (quote).
3. Arthur C. Edwards, 18 October 1919, AGC-HS, S10896 F18; Bureau of the Census, *Fifteenth Census*, "Edwards, Arthur C.," Oakland, CA, 7 April 1930, Enumeration District 1-143, Sheet 7A.
4. William A. Ott, 1 November 1919, AGC-HS, S10898 F34; Bureau of the Census, *Fifteenth Census*, "Ott, William A.," Boston City, 7 April 1930, Enumeration District 13-59, Sheet 11.
5. Alfred T. Hubbard, 24 November 1919, AGC-HS, S10897 F19; Bureau of the Census, *Fifteenth Census*, "Hubbard, Alfred T.," Aztec town, 10 April 1930, Enumeration District 23-2, Sheet 6B. On background to patrolling the U.S. coastline May to September 1918, see Koerver, *German Submarine Warfare*, 614–50.
6. Clarence W. Thorne, 16 December 1919, AGC-HS, S10900 F11; Bureau of the Census, *Fifteenth Census*, "Thorne, Clarence W.," Los Griegos, Bernalillo County, 22 April 1930, Enumeration District 1-27, Sheet 14B. For a discussion of Dutch ships and their wartime status, see Kruizinga, "NOT Neutrality."
7. Joseph D. Paiz Jr., 22 October 1919, AGC-HS, S10899 F4; Bureau of the Census, *Fifteenth Census*, "Paiz, Joseph D., Jr.," Albuquerque, 4 April 1930, Enumeration District 1-13, Sheet 3B.

8. Reyes A. Sanchez, 25 February 1920, AGC-HS, S10899 F28; Bureau of the Census, *Fifteenth Census,* "Sanchez, Reyes A.," Albuquerque, 18 April 1930, Enumeration District 1–21, Sheet 16B.
9. Charles L. Johnson, 1 December 1920, AGC-HS, S10897 F29; Bureau of the Census, *Fifteenth Census,* "Johnson, Charles L.," Wolf, OK, 2 April 1930, Enumeration District 67–40, Sheet 1B.
10. Alfred T. Hubbard, 24 November 1919, AGC-HS, S10897 F19.
11. Brown, "USS New Mexico," 1–2.
12. Meliton Felix Otero, 24 November 1919, AGC-HS, S10898 F34; Bureau of the Census, *Fifteenth Census,* "Otero, Meliton Felix," Albuquerque, New Mexico, 17 April 1930, Enumeration District 1–6, Sheet 16B; Edward Ross Selover, 15 December 1919, AGC-HS, S10899 F34.
13. Lino Gonzales, 12 November 1919, AGC-HS, S10897 F4; Bureau of the Census, *Fouteenth Census,* "Gonzales, Lino," Lemitar, New Mexico, 13 January 1920, Enumeration District 150, Sheet 16B; Commonwealth of Pennsylvania, World War II Veterans Compensation Bureau, Box 296, Gonzales, Lino, available under Veteran *Compensation* Application Files, *WWII,* 1950–1966, Ancestry.com. After *World War II,* the *Commonwealth of Pennsylvania* paid honorably discharged *veterans* and those still in service a bonus *compensation*. This collection includes more than 1.1 million *f*iles.
14. Davis, *Sweeping the North Sea Barrage,* 10–21.
15. Morton Seligman, 10 January 1920, AGC-HS, S10899 F34; "Morton Seligman Helps," *SFNM,* 12 December 1922, 7; "Dillon and Cutting Make Request," *SFNM,* 14 July 1928, 5.
16. Justus C. Adams, 2 January 1920, AGC-HS, S10895 F3.
17. Davis, *Sweeping the North Sea Barrage,* 83–137; Bureau of the Census, *Sixteenth Census,* "Adams, Jake," Milam, TX, 30 April 1940, Enumeration District 166 Sheet 15B.
18. "New Exhibits Added," *AMJ,* 11 October 1917, 7; "Will Give Cowboy Ball," *AMJ,* 19 July 1917, 2.
19. "Wonderful Program," *AMJ,* 26 May 1918, 3; Walter, "Art, Drama, and Literature," 106.
20. The papers left by B. J. O. Nordfeldt are sketchy in comparison to Henderson's material from the war years. Walter, "Art, Drama, and Literature," 106 (quote); Henderson to [wife Alice Corbin] Henderson, 19 October 1918 (quote) and 24 October 1918 (quote); and Henderson to Emergency Fleet Corporation, 15 December 1918, Archives of American Art, Smithsonian Institution, Washington, DC, Box 1, William Penhallow Henderson Papers, Camouflage Service Records, Smithsonian Institution, Washington, DC.

Using the massive space of a ship's hull as his canvas may have had two effects on Henderson's later art: removing any qualms about the scale of mural work while also attuning him to appreciate "the expansiveness of the Pueblo Kiva mural tradition." Typescript, William H. Spurlock, 1973, "Federal Support for the Visual Arts," 66, Box 6 in the Henderson Papers.

21. Lewis and Hagan, *Peculiar Alchemy*, ably covers Hewett's thirty-nine years as founding director of the School of American Archaeology/Research. Hewett's personality, captured in the sobriquet El Toro, is conveyed in Bernstein, "First Issue of *El Palacio*," 36–43.
22. Brunhouse, *Sylvanus G. Morley*; Shapiro, "Sylvanus Griswold Morley," 59–65.
23. Harris and Sadler, *Archaeologist Was a Spy*.
24. Herman G. Baca, 22 November 1919, AGC-HS, S10895 F13.
25. Weaver and van Bergan, "Death from 1918 Pandemic," 538–46; Byerly, *Fever of War*, 55–61; Barry, *Great Influenza*, 91–115; Opdycke, *Flu Epidemic*; Martinez, "Their Harrowing Experience."
26. Oxford et al., "Hypothesis," 940–45, 941 (quote); Erkoreka, "Origins of the Spanish," 190–94; González Bombardiere, "La Pandemia Olvidada," 2 (quote); "Sigue la Epidemia," *El Sol* (Madrid), 26 May 1918, 4; "La Fiebre," *El Sol*, 28 May 1918, 1 (quote).
27. González Bombardiere, "La Pandemia Olvidada," 2–3. On H1N1, see Martinez, "Their Harrowing Experience," especially her discussion and citations to research done by Centers for Disease Control, 6–8, 101fn6, and chap. 1.
28. Jordan, *Epidemic Influenza*, 65 (quoted); Erkoreka, "Origins of the Spanish," 193.
29. Raymond Curtis Bloom, January 1920, AGC-HS, S10902 F53; Sopar, "Pandemic," 1901 (quote).
30. Local Draft Board Socorro County Form 1029, 4 June 1919, AGC-HS, S10887 F2; [R] Bloom to "Dear Mother," 6 March 1918; and Maxey to Bloom, 25 February 1920, AGC-HS, S10902 F53 (quotes); Raymond Curtis Bloom, U.S. World War I Draft Registration Cards, NARA-Atlanta; "Santa Fe Pays Homage," *AMJ*, 27 March 1918, 5.
31. Sopar, "Pandemic," 1900–1901; "Influenza of 1918 (Spanish flu) and the US Navy," Naval History and Heritage Command, www.history.navy.mil/research/library/online-reading-room/title-list-alphabetically/i/influenza/influenza-of-1918-spanish-flu-and-the-us-navy.html; "Died in Service," 21 June 1920, AGC-HS, S10902 F1.
32. "Died in Service," 21 June 1920, AGC-HS, S10902 F1; "Soldier Rest, Thy Warfare's O'er," Kipling Wade, n.d., AGC-HS, S10905 F119 (quote).
33. Telegrams, 31 October 1918, Lindsey Papers, S14118, F178.
34. "Died in Service," 21 June 1920, AGC-HS, S10902 F1; Hodgin, *War Service*, 4, 7. Killed in action was Howard E. Morrow; dying of disease were Floyd Leslie Bradley, Hugh A. Carlisle, and William Lampton.
35. Hugh A. Carlisle, 17 December 1919; and [wife] to Hewett, 22 December 1918, AGC-HS, S10902 F83. Fictionalized accounts of communicable disease aboard transport ships are Cather, *One of Ours*, 292–319; and Dos Passos, *Three Soldiers*, 40–42.
36. Lewis B. Robinson, 26 October 1919, AGC-HS, S10899 F17; Harold Hugh Edwards, n.d., AGC-HS, S10896 F18; Hernon, *Great Rescue*, 240–46, 252–55.
37. Candido Montoya [December 1919]; and Montoya to "Mi muy apreciable Papa," 16 September 1918, AGC-HS, S10904 F109; Melzer, "Dark and Terrible Moment, 227.
38. "Onofre N. Candelaria," 19 July 1920; and [wife] to Hewett, [El] Presidente, 31 January 1919, AGC-HS, S10902 F77.

Notes 295

39. Schackel, *Social Housekeepers*, 13–19; J. W. Kerr, "Public Health Administration in New Mexico, n.d., Lindsey Papers, S14118 F178; Spidle, *Doctors of Medicine*; Prichard to Eylar, 26 August 1918, Prichard Papers, MSS 187 BC, Box 12, Fld 1; Melzer, "Dark and Terrible Moment," 222–35, 229 (quote). Martinez, "Their Harrowing Experience," 22–95, is incomparable as a carefully researched yet poignant multicultural history of urban and rural New Mexico during the flu epidemic.
40. Kerr to City and County Health Officers, 4 November 1918; Kerr to Health Officers [26 October 1918]; Memorandum Kerr to Secretary State Board of Health [31 October 1918]; and Memorandum Kerr to Secretary State Board of Health [31 October 1918]—all Lindsey Papers, S14118 F178. "Died in Service," 21 June 1920, AGC-HS, S10902 F1.
41. "Influenza Española," *LBA,* 27 September 1918, 1; Carolyn O'Mara Smyer, "Joel Anderson Smyer," n.d., Centers for Disease Control and Prevention, www.cdc.gov/publications/panflu/stories/state.html, search "Smyer, Carolyn O'Mara"; "La Influenza Esta Siendo Combatida," *El Independiente,* 5 October 1918, 3.
42. Waybourn, *Homesteaders to Boomtown,* 70–71, 71 (quote); "La influenza Española," *LBA,* 11 October 1918, 1; "La Influenza Española," *LBA,* 18 October 1918, 4; Lauren Gray, "Influenza Epidemic in New Mexico 1918," Office of the New Mexico State Historian, http://newmexicohistory.org/people/influenza-epidemic-in-new-mexico-1918; "The Great Pandemic of 1918: State by State," address by Mike Leavitt, Secretary of the U.S. Department of Health and Human Services, 28 March 2006, FluTrackers. com, https://flutrackers.com/forum/forum/welcome-to-the-scientific-library/-1918-pandemic-data-stories-history/14750-the-great-pandemic-of-1918-state-by-state [scroll to New Mexico]; "Noticias Importantes," *LBA* 15 November 1918, 1.
43. Memorandum [Major] Welles to Surgeon General, 18 May 1920, RG 112, Office of the Surgeon General, General Hospital Fort Bayard; and "Consolidated Daily Report," 1918 and 1919, Box 1238, NARA II; Memorandum Richardson [M.D.] to Lonergan, 20 December 1918, RG 75, Bureau of Indian Affairs, NARA-Denver, online NARA exhibit "The Deadly Virus," www.archives.gov/exhibits/influenza-epidemic/records-list. html (quote); Reagan, "Flu among the Navajos," 131–38.
44. Personal communication, Kim Martinez, 7 July 2015; "Wounded Men Correspondence" [1918–1924], AGC-HS, S10905 F2, F3; "Biographical Sketches of Men Who Died in Service," n.d., AGC-HS, S10905, F5. Typical of newspaper announcements of flu deaths are these from *La Bandera Americana*: "Muy Lamentable Muerte," 11 October 1918, 4; "Carlos Lorenzo Hubbell," 18 October 1918, 1; and "Con Profundo Dolor," 18 October 1918, 1.
45. Faust, *This Republic of Suffering,* 6–30, 7 (quote); Lesy, *Wisconsin Death Trip.*
46. "AEF Men Carry $1,250,000,000," *Stars and Stripes* 1, no. 11 (19 April 1918), 1, 2; Alan Bruce [president of the New Mexico Underwriters Association], "War Risk Insurance," 1st Annual Convention of the American Legion of New Mexico [16–18 October 1919], typescript minutes, 13–14, ALD, S6495 F1.
47. WWIVS, Sibley, 28th Division; Kinder, "Iconography of Injury," 340 (quote); William Adair, 17 October 1919, AGC-HS, S10895 F3 (quote).

48. [Evaristo] Gurule to Caro Senor [Bloom], AGC-HS, S10903 F93; E. K. Roden, "The Mystery of the U.S.S. Cyclops," clipping in Frederick B. Golding, AGC-HS, S10903 F67, 52.
49. Religious affiliation data, whether stated or omitted, were collected for Euro-Americans and Nuevomexicanos from two selections: 40 percent of the sample for each group was drawn from questionnaires randomly selected in AGC-HS, S10895–10900; a second selection, and 60 percent of the sample, was designed to gather an equal number of Euro-American and Nuevomexicano respondents: Euro-Americans, S10897 F12–15, 24, and S10898 F4–6; Nuevomexicanos, S10896 F28–32, and S10898 F24–26.

    I thank my brother, Dr. Ralph B. Holtby, for helping with this tabulation and especially for sharing his experiences as an army field combat medic in Vietnam (1968–69) relative to soldiers' faith and their attitudes toward religion and survival as he observed it in his platoon and company.
50. Sixto R. Chavez service questionnaire [completed for the widow], 3 April 1919, AGC-HS, S10902 F95.
51. Clark, *American Expeditionary Force*, 129; Hanson, *Unknown Soldiers*, 227 (quotes).
52. March, *Company K*, 101–2. McE Chase to Hamby, 22 February 1919, AGC-HS, S10903 F102 (quote); Wood, *What Was Asked of Us*, xvi (quote).
53. Fulkerson to [Annie] Hamby, 5 July 1919.
54. Royal C. Boehrig service questionnaire [completed by Louis Boehrig], 4 August 1920, AGC-HS, S10902 F54.
55. Hanson, *Unknown Soldiers*, 228 (quote); Edmund C. Baca service questionnaire [completed by Herculano Baca], 10 November 1919, AGC-HS, S10902 F32.
56. Winn to Kepple, 30 March 1919, AGC-HS, S10904 F18.
57. Winters to Kepple, 26 April 1919, AGC-HS, S10904 F18.
58. Wexler to Chavez, 8 August 1918, AGC-HS, S10902 F91.
59. Cecil to Chavez [October 1918], AGC-HS, S10902 F91.
60. Jesse T. Richards, n.d., AGC-HS, S10902 F5; Clarence E. Habiger, 5 November 1919, AGC-HS, S10897 F12 (quote).
61. Casualty files are in NMSRCA, AGC-HS, S10902–905.
62. Hewitt to [Beatrice] Ortega, 12 December 1918, AGC-HS, S10904 F136 (quote); Alonzo Aragon, U.S., World War I Draft Registration Cards, 1917–1918, NARA-Atlanta; Hewitt to [Ermelinda V.] Aragon, 28 December 1918; and [Ermelinda V.] Aragon to Hewitt, 12 December 1918, AGC-HS, S10902 F25 (quote).
63. [Jesus] Garcia to Senores, 6 January 1919, AGC-HS, S10903 F50.
64. Bennett and Howlett, *Antiwar Dissent and Peace Activism*.
65. Arturo Montoya, 11 November 1919; Hewitt to Montoya, 26 June 1919 (quote); and Montoya to "Esta es en respuesta," July 1919, AGC-HS, S10904 F108.
66. Montoya to "Esta es en respuesta," July 1919, AGC-HS, S10904 F108.
67. Bloom to Montoya, 30 August 1919, AGC-HS, S10884 F1.

Chapter 8

1. Association of the 110th Infantry, *History of the 110th Infantry*, 124 (quote), 126; Larrazolo to Springer, 28 February 1919, NMSRCA, Governor Octaviano A. Larrazolo Papers [hereafter Larrazolo Papers], S14129 F163; "Rocky Mountain Club," *AMJ*, 24 March 1919, 7.
2. "New Mexico National Guard," *SFNM*, 24 March 1919, 6; Lawrence E. Valentine, 20 December 1919, AGC-HS, S10900 F24; "Soldiers Arrive" [early April 1919], unidentified newspaper clipping in file of Tomas Rivera, 8 November 1919, AGC-HS, S10899 F11.
3. Pencak, *Encyclopedia of the Veteran*, 468–69; "Gallup Celebration," *SFNM*, 9 July 1919, 7 (quote); "Battery Boys Welcomed," *Roswell Daily Record*, 3 July 1919, 1; "Greatest Parade Ever," and "Yesterday Was One Great Day," *Roswell Daily Record*, 11 July 1919, 1.
4. "40 Governors," *Washington Post*, 16 December 1918, 5 (quote); Dickson and Allen, *Bonus Army*, 3 (quote).
5. "Much Progressive Legislation," *AMJ*, 16 January 1919, 1, 6.
6. "Washington," *Agamemnon Daily News*, 22 May 1919, 4. This ship, on its sixteenth voyage as a troop transport, was the seventh-largest in the navy's transport fleet and could carry a total of 5,867 men; see "The Twelve Big Transports," *Agamemnon Daily News*, 19 May 1919, 3.
7. "Farms for Veterans," *NYT*, 17 May 1919, 12 (quote); "Land for Soldiers," *NYT*, 29 May 1919, 19; Wecter, *When Johnny Comes Marching*, 375–84.
8. Report, Young to Larrazolo, "Soldier Settlement Board," 14 February 1920, 3–4, Larrazolo Papers, S14129 F161; "What the New Mexico Legislature," *AMJ*, 19 March 1919, 6; "Rush Expected," *AMJ*, 21 August 1907, 2.
9. Turley to McElroy, 26 July 1919, AGC-HS, S10900 F20 (quotes); "San Juan County Water," *AMJ*, 22 November 1909, 3.
10. Turley to McElroy, 26 July 1919, AGC-HS, S10900 F20; Report, Young to Larrazolo, "Soldier Settlement Board," 14 February 1920, 3–10, Larrazolo Papers, S14129 F161.
11. Report, Young to Larrazolo, "Soldier Settlement Board," 14 February 1920, 5 (quote), Larrazolo Papers, S14129 F161.
12. Ibid., 7; "Young Urges American Legion," *SFNM*, 28 January 1920, 6 (quote).
13. "Western Governors," *AMJ*, 11 January 1920, 1 (quote); "Gov. Larrazolo Urges," *AMJ*, 10 January 1920, 1; Wecter, *When Johnny Comes Marching*, 371–72; "New Mexico Legislature," *AMJ*, 22 February 1920, 1; "Mr. Mondell's Warning," *NYT*, 9 February 1920, 8 (quote); "Republicans Split," *NYT*, 20 April 1920, 17.
14. Woodward to Hinkle, 5 February 1924, NMSRCA, Governor James F. Hinkle Collection, S14145 F218.
15. Chacón, *Obras*, 17–24, 17; Montoya to Mechem, 22 May 1921, NMSRCA, Governor Merritt C. Mechem Papers, S14136 F211; Rivera, *El Defensor del Pueblo*, 1 August 1930, 3. I am indebted to Professor A. Gabriel Melendez for bringing Chacón's poem to my attention.
16. Armijo, "Lest We Forget," 99 (quote); "Baca War Memorial," and "Eloquent Tribute," *SFNM*, 6 March 1919, 2, 4 (quotes).

17. "Baca War Memorial," *SFNM*, 6 March 1919, 2 (quote); Wilson, *Myth of Santa Fe*, 135 (quote) and fig. 86; "New Mexico War Memorial," 50. I am indebted to Professor Jon Hunner for bringing this article to my attention. Munson, *Kenneth Chapman's Santa Fe*, chaps. 4, 6.
18. "Baca War Memorial Bill," *SFNM*, 6 March 1919; Wilson, *Myth of Santa Fe*, 146–48.
19. "Prince Offers Fort Marcy," *SFNM*, 12 March 1919, 4 (quote); "Communicated" [1919], Prichard Papers, MSS 187 BC, Box 5 Fld 2 (quote); "Col. Prichard," *SFNM*, 1 September 1919, 4 (quote).
20. Trout, *On the Battlefield of Memory*, 19 (quote)–21; "To Erect National Memorial," *SFNM*, 26 January 1920, 4; Atwood to Mechem, 16 February 1922; Mechem to Atwood, 18 February 1922; and Mechem to Weeks, 28 October 1921, NMSRCA, Governor Merritt C. Mechem Papers, S14136 F216; Trout, *Memorial Fictions*, 23–25.

The George Washington National Victory Memorial Building site was relinquished in 1937, and the National Gallery of Art was built instead. The 1st and 2nd Divisions did create memorials in the nation's capital in 1924 and 1936, respectively, but not until 2006 did a national World War I memorial emerge—in Kansas City, with the reimagining and rededication of the Liberty Memorial, originally opened in 1926.
21. "Erect Monument," *Deming Headlight*, 21 August 1921, 1; "Dedicación del Memorial," *LBA*, 24 October 1919, 1. Today this memorial is in its third location—at the New Mexico Veterans Memorial in Albuquerque, about fifty yards north of the entrance. Memo [Bloom to Montoya] copy to Renehan, 14 October 1919; Montoya to Bloom, 21 July 1920; and Bloom to Vallient, 17 November 1922, AGC-HS, S10884 F1. The Catholic memorial is preserved in the basement at St. Mary's School; personal communication, Mary DeSaulniers, November 2015. "Battery A Members," *AMJ*, 18 October 1926, 8.
22. "American Legion Meeting," *AMJ*, 15 January 1920, 5; 'Women Eligible," *AMJ*, 25 February 1920, 2; "The Voice of Luis Otero," *AMJ*, 20 October 1920, 2 (quote); "American Legion and Disabled Soldiers," *AMJ*, 13 March 1921, 2; ALD, State [Women's] Auxiliary, S5911 Ledger Book 1, Book 2, 233, 261–65. The top five sales came from Albuquerque ($329.38), Roswell ($282.16), Gallup ($214.53), Santa Fe ($175.00), and Artesia ($149.26).
23. Kettleborough, "Legislative Notes and Reviews," 275–76 (quote); Gonzales, "Race, Party, and Class," 102–6.
24. WCCND, memorandum "To Save the Lives" [Fall 1918], Prichard Papers, MSS 187 BC, Box 12, Fld 2, which provided in conjunction with the "Year of the Child" a four-and-a-half-page agenda for state action to be pursued through April 1919. Schackel, *Social Housekeepers*, 14–22 19 (quote); "Santa Fe County," NMSRCA, Governor Richard C. Dillon Papers, S14156 F20.
25. "Caucus to Plan," *Stars and Stripes* 2, no. 6 (14 March 1919), 1, 3; "American Legion to Unite," *Stars and Stripes* 2, no. 7 (21 March 1919) 1, 3 (quotes); McConnell, *Glorious Contentment*; Pencak, *For God and Country*; Rumer, *American Legion*, 8–109.
26. "New Mexico," *American Legion Weekly*, 11 July 1919, 11. Question three on the questionnaire provided New Mexico ex-servicemen two lines for responses. The first asked about "Church affiliation" and the second queried on "Lodges, trade unions, etc."

27. Typescript of minutes, "Governor Larrazolo Addresses," 1st Annual Convention of the American Legion of New Mexico" [16–18 October 1919, Albuquerque], ALD, S6495 F1, 40, 42, 45, 43.
28. Bloom to Gabaldon, 28 October 1922, AGC-HS, S10896 F28; "Report of the Examination [by the State Traveling Auditor]," 1 October 1920, Larrazolo Papers, S14129, F163. The 1919 expenses are discussed in eight pieces of correspondence in this folder between Larrazolo and Springer, dated 28 February 1919, 12 March (two), 13 March (two), 15 March, 17 March, and 8 July.
29. Bloom to Winston, 14 June 1919, AGC-HS, S10887 F1; Hewett, "Historical Service," 172–74; Bloom to Cooper, 21 February 1924, AGC-HS, S10905 F148; [George] Quesenberry to Bloom 31 July 1924, AGC-HS, S10899 F10; Bloom, "Trophies of the Great War," 205–7; Doak, "Opportunities Offered," 8.
30. See fifteen letters, Rocky Mountain Club to Governor [Merritt C. Mechem], 13 May 1921 to 3 November 1921, NMSRCA, Governor Merritt C. Mechem Papers, S14136 F216. The Rocky Mountain Club served seven other midwestern and western states.
31. "Died in Service," 21 June 1920, AGC-HS, S10902 F1. AEF burials are found in American Battle Monuments Commission at www.abmc.gov using "New Mexico" as keyword search.
32. Faust, *This Republic of Suffering,* 213–46; Budreau, *Bodies of War,* 37–50.
33. Budreau, *Bodies of War,* 63–81; Seventy-First Congress, Senate, 1st Session, S26, Bratton, "Deceased Soldiers from New Mexico Buried in Permanent American Cemeteries in Europe": Aisne-Marne American Cemetery (five New Mexicans); Brookwood American Cemetery in England (three); Meuse-Argonne American Cemetery (thirty-three); Oise-Aisne American Cemetery (thirty); Somme American Cemetery (two); St. Mihiel American Cemetery (seven); Suresnes American Cemetery, Paris (thirteen). By way of comparison, Arizona had 127 AEF casualties, with Euro-Americans accounting for 94 percent.
34. "Body of Local Hero Arrives Here Tonight," *AMJ,* 17 October 1920, 4; "Luis Otero, Killed in France," and "All Albuquerque Should Help," *AMJ,* 18 October 1920, 1 (quote); "Whole City to Join Today in Honoring Hero," *AMJ,* 19 October 1920, 1; "Taps Sounded for Soldier Hero," and "The Voice of Luis Otero," *AMJ,* 20 October 1920, 1, 2 (quote).
35. Budreau, *Bodies of War,* 95–99, 198–208; Graham, *Gold Star Mother Pilgrimages;* Potter, "World War I Gold Star Mothers"; Noll, "Crosses," 14–17, 52; Wilson, "War Mother Goes 'Over There'"; "6,000 Women to Visit" clipping [*New York Herald,* 15 March 1930] in Scrapbook of Col. Richard T. Ellis, NARA II, RG 92, Office of the Quartermaster General, Gold Star Pilgrims, Container 2 [hereafter Ellis Scrapbook].
    The following discussion of the Gold Star mothers pilgrimages is based on information in the Ellis Scrapbook as well as Gold Star Mothers, RG 92, Office of the Quartermaster General, Gold Star Pilgrims, Container 1, Flds 1, 2, and 4, along with other sources cited above.
36. Robinson to Ellis, 3 September 1931, Ellis Scrapbook.
37. "10th Gold Star Unit," clipping [*New York Herald* (Paris ed.), 9 July 1930], Ellis Scrapbook.

38. Typescript, "At the Cemetery of Belleau Wood," 5 June 1930, Ellis Scrapbook (quote). Neither the *Albuquerque Journal* nor the *Santa Fe New Mexican* had an article on Mrs. Payne's pilgrimage in the summer of 1930.
39. Ibid.
40. "Glittering Promises," *SFNM,* 20 October 1920, 6; "Good Government Trio," *SFNM,* 22 October 1920, 1; "How to Vote," *SFNM,* 20 October 1920, 4.
41. "Women Busy as Office Seekers," *AMJ,* 4 December 1920, 3 (quote); "Recapitulation of Vote" [1923], Governor James F. Hinkle Papers, NMSRCA, S14145 F202 (quote). See Governor Richard C. Dillon Papers, NMSRCA, Box 1, F20, for a Republican governor's tally of political patronage.
42. "Barker, S. Omar," in Raines, *Writers and Writing,* 19–20.
43. "El Boleto Republicano," *La Estrella,* 18 October 1924, 2 (quote); "Prager Miller Nominated," *Roswell Daily Record,* 25 September 1924, 1 (quote).
44. Hamm, *Bursums of New Mexico,* 129–31.
45. Fernland, "Senator Holm O. Bursum," 436–37, argues that Bursum made an opportunistic political calculation to appear to embrace progressive Republican policies as a way to separate himself from Fall's influence and shadow. Bursum's genuine commitment to aiding veterans complicates this reading of his motives.
46. Wardwell to Director Veterans Bureau, 6 October 1925, NARA-Denver, RG 15, Department of Veterans Affairs, Federal Board for Vocational Education, 1917–1933, Records of the Albuquerque Regional Office, Box 1.
47. Lloyd S. Gipson, 25 October 1920, AGC-HS, S10896 F37; Manuel C. Gonzales, 26 November 1919, AGC-HS, S10897 F4; Cooley to Bursum, 11 June 1923, Holm O. Bursum Papers, MS 305, Box 56 Fld 25, RGHC.
48. Gonzales to "Muy Señor mio," 7 June 1919, AGC-HS, S10897 F2; William A. Easley, 22 November 1919, AGC-HS, S10896 F18 (quote); "Ninth Annual Convention of the American Legion, Department of New Mexico [1927]," ALD, S6495 F7, 28–29 (quote).
49. Wecter, *When Johnny Comes Marching,* 385–405; "Memorial to War Mothers," *AMJ,* 10 October 1921, 3; J. H. Toulouse, "A History of the Work," *Albuquerque Journal,* 14 August 1932, 9 (quote).
50. [Hines], *Annual Report of the Administrator . . . 1935,* 92; "Joseph Wesley Akers," 16 October 1919, AGC-HS, S10895 F3; Bureau of the Census, *Fourteenth Census,* "Akers, Joseph W.," 14–15 January 1920, Las Vegas, NM, Enumeration District 180, Sheet 14A; Bureau of the Census, *Fifteenth Census,* "Akers, Joseph W.," 10 April 1930, Little Rock, AR, Enumeration District 60-77, Sheet 7A; "Akers, Joseph Wesley," U.S. Headstone Applications for Military Veterans, 1925–1963, Ancestry.com; Sandoval to Keleher and McLeod, 1 August 1969, "Guardianship of Antonio Mascarenas, Final Report and Account," Probate Court of Mora County, Deceased No. 587, 1969, District Court, County of San Miguel (quote); I am indebted to Michael Keleher for sharing this information. Hospital Manager to Gibson, 16 October 1935, Dennis Chavez Papers, MSS 394 BC, Box 211, F196, CSWR (quote).
51. "A Brief Summary of the Record of Senator Bursum's" [1924], Holm O. Bursum Papers, MS 305, Box 54, Fld 16, RGHC; "Text of the President's Message," *NYT,* 16 May 1924, 1–2; Keene, *Doughboys,* 174.

52. Bursum to Heinz, 8 April 1921, Holm O. Bursum Papers, MS 305, Box 55, Fld 15(A), RGHC; Bursum to Keegan, 1 February 1922, Holm O. Bursum Papers, MS 305, Box 55, Fld 8, RGHC.
53. "A Brief Summary of the Record of Senator Bursum's" [1924], Holm O. Bursum Papers, MS 305, Box 54, Fld 16, RGHC; Michael Cooney, "Records in Three Cases" [1924], Holm O. Bursum Papers, MS 305, Box 54, Fld 20, RGHC.
54. Nina Otero-Warren, diary entry 24 August 1924, NMSRCA, A. M. Bergere Family Papers, Box 5, F38; "Appreciates Bursum," *AMJ,* 28 September 1924, 6 (quotes).
55. Lowitt, "Bronson Cutting and the Early Years," 152–58; Cutting to Wood, 24 November 1920, Bronson M. Cutting Papers, Library of Congress, Manuscripts Division, Washington, DC, MSS 17566, Box 5. This document outlines well before his 1922 action why the split in the Republican Party in New Mexico necessitated his support of Democrats.
56. Lowitt, *Bronson M. Cutting,* 81–86, 103–9, 185–86 (quote).
57. Bursum to Reid, 31 July 1922, Holm O. Bursum Papers, MS 305, Box 55, Fld 2, RGHC.
58. Fernland, "Senator Holm O. Bursum." The complex financing for this cattle "deal" can be studied in eighty-five pages, double-sided, in Records of War Finance Corporation, Agricultural Loan Agency, NARA-Denver, RG 154, Ledgers of Transferred Accounts, V. 263.
59. Dickson and Allen, *Bonus Army;* "Aim to Hold Bonus Army," *Albuquerque Journal,* 22 June 1932, 8; "Santa Feans Join," *SFNM,* 22 June 1932, 1. Ex-serviceman V. W. Baker led the New Mexico protesters, but he seems not to have entered the military from New Mexico. "Chavez Agrees," *Albuquerque Journal,* 31 July 1932, 10 (quote). Ortiz, *Beyond the Bonus March.*
60. Telser, "The Veterans' Bonus," Bronson M. Cutting Papers, Library of Congress, Manuscripts Division, Washington, DC, MSS 17566, Containers 43–81. Of the total of 116 containers, these thirty-eight are one-third of the collection; the quotation is from Cutting to Williams, 1 March 1935, Box 71.
61. [American Legion] National Executive Committee, *Digest of Minutes, National Executive Committee Meeting,* "Committee on New Mexico Situation," 20–21 November 1933, Indianapolis, IN, 25–27; and "New Mexico Commission Report," 3–4 May 1934, 41–43, ALD, S30292 F1 and F2.
62. Cutting, "Minutes of the Third Annual [New Mexico] American Legion Convention," Silver City, 22–24 September 1921, 3, ALD, S6495 F1.
63. Seventieth Congress, 2nd Session, *Proceedings of the Tenth National Convention of the American Legion,* 145 (quote) [also ALD, S5908 F1]; [American Legion] National Executive Committee, Digest of Minutes, National Executive Committee Meeting, 13–14 November 1930, Indianapolis, IN, 24, ALD, S30292 F1; Holmes, *Politics in New Mexico,* 139–214, 160 (quote); Keleher, *Memoirs,* 165–77; Lowitt, *Bronson M. Cutting,* 107–9.
64. Edward L. Safford, 7 October 1919, AGC-HS, S10899 F24; [American Legion] National Executive Committee, Digest of Minutes, National Executive Committee Meeting, "Committee on New Mexico Situation," 20–21 November 1933, Indianapolis, IN, 26 (quote), ALD, S30292 F1.

65. Holmes, *Politics in New Mexico*, 160–74, 199–205.
66. "Governor Outlines State's," *Las Vegas Daily Optic*, 14 August 1937, 1, 4.
67. Robinson to Roosevelt, 15 September 1932, Box 44; Foreman to Tillett, 5 October 1941, Box 93; Kirby/Vigil to Dewson, 2 October 1936, Box 46; and Kirby to Wolfe, 31 August 1934, Box 46—all Democratic National Committee, Women's Division, 1933–44, Correspondence, Franklin D. Roosevelt Presidential Library, Hyde Park, NY.
68. Wolfe to Kirby, 24 November 1934; Quoted Kirby to June [Wolfe], 4 January 1935; Kirby to Wolfe, 4 June 1935; and Quoted Kirby to Wolfe, 12 October 1934—all Box 46, Democratic National Committee, Women's Division, 1933–44, Correspondence, Franklin D. Roosevelt Presidential Library, Hyde Park, NY.
69. "Week's Social Calendar," and "Republican Women Gathering at Tea," *Albuquerque Journal*, 16 August 1936, 7, 17.
70. Keene, *Doughboys*, 174–75 (quote), 205–14; Frydl, *G.I. Bill*.

Chapter 9

1. William A. Easley, 22 November 1919, AGC-HS, S10896 F18.
2. Coles, *Call of Stories*, 67; Hewett, "Preface," in Bloom, *New Mexico*, vii.
3. William A. Easley, U.S. City Directories, 1822–1995, Denver 1925, Ancestry.com; Bureau of the Census, *Fifteenth Census*, "Easley, William A.," Lincoln County, unincorporated area, 18 April 1930, Enumeration District 14–11, Sheet 1A; Bureau of the Census, *Sixteenth Census*, "Easley, William A.," Pima, AZ, 15 April 1940, Enumeration District, 10–67, Sheet 8B; Easley, William A., Find a Grave Index, Ancestry.com.
4. Eli S. Rodriguez, 8 December 1919, AGC-HS, S10899 F18.
5. Ibid.; Bureau of the Census, *Fourteenth Census*, "Rodriguez, Eli S.," Santa Fe City, 7 January 1920, Enumeration District 131, Sheet 8; Bureau of the Census, *Sixteenth Census*, "Rodriguez, Eli S.," 11 April 1940, Waukesha, WI, Enumeration District 67–51, Sheet 6B; U.S. World War II draft registration cards are known as the "Old Man's Registration" or the "Old Man's Draft," for those men whose year of birth was from 28 April 1877 to 16 February 1897, and are held at NARA-St. Louis. Rodriguez, Eli Solomon, *Find A Grave Index*, Ancestry.com.
6. Walter, "Life in Camp."
7. Clark, *Dos Passos's Early Fiction*, 78–79 (quotes); Fixico, *Indian Resilience and Rebuilding*.
8. George W. Pannell, 24 October 1919; and Rolla Aaron Parker, 21 December 1919, AGC-HS, S10899 F4.
9. Alva Warren McDougal, 10 January 1961, AGC-HS, S10898 F5.
10. Jones et al., "Shell Shock," 1641 (quote); "History of PTSD in Veterans," U.S. Department of Veterans Affairs, www.ptsd.va.gov/public/ptsd-overview/basics/history-of-ptsd-vets.asp; Junger, *Tribes*.

    Bureau of the Census, *Fifteenth Census*, "Parker, Rolla A.," San Jose, CA, April 1930, Enumeration District 43–51, Sheet 3A; Bureau of the Census, *Sixteenth Census*,

"Parker, Rolla A.," San Mateo, CA, Veterans Administration Facility, 10 April 1940, Enumeration District 41-68, Sheet 11B. The other New Mexico veterans at this facility recorded in the Sixteenth Census are these four: Fernandez[s] Gallegos, Sheet 10B; Abel[ino] Rivera, Sheet 8B; Samuel Sachs, Sheet 6A; and Clyde E. Smith, Sheet 4B.

11. LaCapra, *Writing History, Writing Trauma*, x, xxxiii.
12. Roth, *Memory, Trauma, and History*, xviii; Rolla A. Parker, 21 December 1919, AGC-HS, S10899 F4.
13. Abel[ino] Rivera, 21 November 1919, AGC-HS, S10899 F11; Fernandez[s] Gallegos, 2 December 1919, AGC-HS, S10896 F30.
14. Treasury Department, *Annual Report of the Director*, 26; Seventieth Congress, 2nd Session, *Proceedings of the Tenth Annual National Convention*, 128; [Hines], *Annual Report of the Administrator . . . 1933*, 43.
15. "National Commander's Report," in Seventy-First Congress, 1st Session, *Proceedings of the Eleventh Annual National Convention*, 13 (quote); "Rehabilitation," in *19th Annual Convention*, Raton, 4–6 August 1938, ALD, S6495 F11, 18 (quote).
16. "Casiano Trujillo Dies," *Tucumcari Sun*, 26 September 1919, clipping in AGC-HS, S10886 F3; "Lt. Col. Charles M. de Bremond Died," *Roswell Daily Record*, 8 December 1919, 1; "Funeral," *Roswell Daily Record*, 10 December 1919, 1; "Brave Veteran of Siberia Dies," *SFNM*, 16 October 1922, 2.
17. Fox et al., "Evaluating the Community Health," 96–98; Marmar et al., "Course of Posttraumatic Stress."
18. [Hines], *Annual Report of the Administrator . . . 1935*, 92; Joseph Wesley Akers, 16 October 1919, AGC-HS, S10895 F3 (quote); Williams, "Spruce Production," 7 (quote); Bureau of the Census, *Fifteenth Census*, "Akers, Joseph Wesley," Las Vegas, NM, 14–15 January 1920, Enumeration District 180, Sheet 14A; Bureau of the Census, *Sixteenth Census*, "Akers, Joseph Wesley," Little Rock, AR., 10 April 1930, Enumeration District 60-77, Sheet 7A; Akers, Joseph Wesley, U.S. Headstone Applications for Military Veterans, 1925-1963, Ancestry.com.
19. Britten, *American Indians in World War I*, 85; interview Tom Ration by Terry Carroll, 11 October 1968, American Indian Oral History Collection, MSS 314 BC, Transcript Tape 358, [true] Side 1, 12–14, CSWR.
20. Personal communication, Mary Nicola Menicucci, Albuquerque, January 2015.
21. "Whitecaps," *Agamemnon Daily News*, 22 May 1919, 3; Graves, *Good-bye*, 268; "H.[igh] E.[xplosive] and Breaking Glass," *American Legion Weekly* 1, no. 8 (22 August 1919), 14, 17; Jones et al., "Shell Shock."
22. Lee, *Battle of Cognac*. Lee (1892–1967) trained at Camp Cody in 1917 and then went overseas early in 1918. He was a Democrat elected to the U.S. House of Representative for one term (1935–37) and then one term as a U.S. senator from Oklahoma (1937–43). Searches of the *Albuquerque Journal* and the *SFNM* for the period 1935–40 yielded no results for Alcoholics Anonymous.
23. "One-Third of a Million," *SFNM*, 26 September 1919, 2.
24. Candido Carlos Rodarte, 14 November 1919, AGC-HS, S10899 F18; Bureau of the Census, *Fifteenth Census*, "Rodarte, Candido Carlos," Los Angeles, CA, April 1930,

Enumeration District 12–63, Sheet 3B; Bureau of the Census, *Sixteenth Census,* "Rodarte, Candido Carlos," Los Angeles, CA, 24 April 1940, Enumeration District 60–1059, Sheet 11A.

Alfredo S. Rodarte, 22 March 1920, AGC-HS, S10899 F18; "Civil Service," in Seventy-Second Congress, 1st Session, *Proceedings of the 13th National Convention,* 181–83; Bureau of the Census, *Fifteenth Census,* "Rodarte, Alfred S.," Los Angeles, CA, 5 April 1930, Enumeration District 19–718, Sheet 7B. Alfredo Anglicized his name to Alfred in the 1930 and 1940 census.

25. Wiskup and Christmas, "Hispanic New Mexicans and World War I," session paper, Historical Society of New Mexico annual conference, 8 May 2015, Albuquerque, NM. I am deeply appreciative of Ms. Wiskup's assistance with this biographical sketch of her cousin, Pvt. Felipe P. Barela, and Ms. Christmas's invaluable help in deciphering penmanship and misspellings in a particularly challenging Spanish-language serviceman's questionnaire. Clark, *American Expeditionary Forces,* 294–95; Bureau of the Census, *Sixteenth Census,* "Barela, Philip," Los Angeles, 23 April 1940, Enumeration District 60–1077 Sheet 22B; in this census, Felipe and his wife Maria Anglicized their names as Philip and Mary, and twelve of their neighbors on the same side of Casanova Street were born in Italy. Frank Beaman, 20 December 1919, AGC-HS, S10895 F19; Bureau of the Census, *Fifteenth Census,* "Beaman, Frank," 11 April 1930, Los Angeles, Assembly District 58, Enumeration District 19–165, Sheet 10B; Bureau of the Census, *Sixteenth Census,* "Beaman, Frank," Huntington Park, Los Angeles County, Enumeration District 19–516, Sheet 61A; Beaman, Frank, *U.S., Headstone Applications for Military Veterans, 1925–1963,* Ancestry.com.

26. "Lincoln Country War Records Returned Unclaimed," 22 December 1919, AGC-HS, S10885 F8.

27. deBuys, *Enchantment and Exploitation,* 206 (quote); Forrest, *Preservation,* 16 (quote), 138–50; Jacobo Romero, "Persons Registered 1918 Class (21 Years)," Taos County, n.d., AGC-HS, S10890, F11; deBuys and Harris, *River of Traps,* 14, 56, 103–4, 120; Wager-Smith, "Resettlement Administration," especially 8B.

28. Williams, *New Mexico in Maps,* 153, 237–52.

29. The survey drew on two sources: "Santa Fe County Men in Service" [1919], AGC-HS, S10886 F9, and Bureau of the Census, *Fifteenth Census,* Santa Fe Precinct 18, 4 April 1930, Enumeration District 25–14, beginning at Sheet 6A with Jose Romero and ending with Willie Knight; Santa Fe Precinct 3, 9 April 1930, Enumeration District 25–3, beginning at Sheet 11A with William J. Mayor and ending with Valentin Garcia; and Santa Fe Precinct 18, 9 April 1930, Enumeration District 25–4, Sheet 12A beginning with Nasario Garcia and ending with Jose Lujan.

30. George H. Hall, 7 July 1920, AGC-HS, S10903 F100; Solomon A. Brogdon, "Men in Service from San Miguel County," n.d., AGC-HS, S10886 F8; Juan B. Aragon, *Find A Grave Index,* Ancestry.com. The twelve Trementina veterans who were located emerged in records from some combination of these sources: U.S. Census data from 1920, 1930, 1940; U.S., World War I Draft Registration Cards, 1917–1918, n.d.,

NARA-Atlanta; NMSRCA war service forms; and Find A Grave Index, Ancestry.com. The following veterans were identified: Crisantos Aragon (5 December 1919, AGC-HS, S10895 F7); Emiterio Aragon (3 December 1919, AGC-HS, S10895 F7); Seferino Aragon (30 December 1919, AGC-HS, S10895 F7); Paul E. Blea (31 January 1920, AGC-HS, S10895 F23. Blea served in Siberia and was in at least five shooting skirmishes; Francisco Encinias (no AGC-HS record found); Nicacio Garcia (no record); Martin Gonzales (no record); Albino Romero (12 December 1919, AGC-HS, S10899, F19); Francisco Ambrosio Sandoval (no record); Pedro Antonio Tenorio (no record); Tiburcio Tenorio (no record); and Bacilio Trujillo (no record).
31. Blair, *Woman's Committee*, 133.
32. Veteran and civilian accounts of daily life in Depression era New Mexico are abundant in Franklin D. Roosevelt Library, President's Personal File, Box 20; and Papers of Harry L. Hopkins, Boxes 58, 74–76, 121, National Archives and Records Administration, Hyde Park, NY. An outstanding overview of the New Deal in New Mexico is Sánchez, Spude, and Gómez, *New Mexico*, 225–55. See also Egan, *Worst Hard Time*.
33. Gibson, "Veterans' Administration"; Melzer, *Coming of Age*.
34. Lucereo to Tillett, 5 November 1941, Democratic National Committee, Women's Division, Box 117, Franklin D. Roosevelt Library, National Archives and Records Administration, Hyde Park, NY.
35. Ibid.
36. Personal communication, Frank Montoya, Albuquerque, August 2008; personal communication, Ralph Trujillo, Albuquerque, July 2010; personal communication, Alicia Montoya, Albuquerque, March 2015.
37. Hewett, "Cost and the Gain," 142.
38. Chavez to Griffith, 20 January 1933, Fld [no number, precedes Fld 158]; Trujillo to Chavez, 9 May 1932, Fld 67 (quote); Chavez to Trujillo, 16 May 1932, Fld 67; [David] Chavez to [Dennis] Chavez [1933], Fld 135 (quote); and San Miguel County Nuevomexicano veteran to Chavez, 5 November 1933, Fld 133—all Dennis Chavez Papers, MSS 394, Part 3, Series VIII, Box 211, CSWR; Porter, "Senator Carl Hatch."

Correspondence of veterans to and from Chavez is restricted access material to which I was granted limited use and could research only the files for the years Chavez was in the House of Representatives (1931–35), which meant only Box 211 could be opened. Boxes 212–214, covering the years 1936–40, were closed to me. I also agreed to the condition that no veteran's name would be cited and the only identification would be to county and ethnicity.
39. Stoler, *Along the Archival Grain*, 44–53; William A. Easley, 22 November 1919, AGC-HS, S10896 F18; Read, "Discursito a . . . los Soldados," 27 August 1918, Read Collection, S8425 F53.
40. Jack D. Trainor [June 1919], Read Collection S8425 F54; Read, "Discursito a . . . los Soldados," 27 August 1918, Read Collection, S8425 F53.
41. Andres S. Ribera, 18 June 1919, Read Collection S8425 F54; Read, "Discursito a . . . los Soldados," 27 August 1918, Read Collection, S8425 F53; Jack D. Trainor [June 1919], Read Collection, S8425 F54.

42. Brokaw, *Album of Memories*. Key civilian and military leaders in World War II had served during World War I, and their careers were launched in that era; see Larrabee, *Commander in Chief*; Eisenhower, *Bitter Woods*; Clifford, *World War I Memoirs of Robert P. Patterson*.

Bibliography

Archives

Archives of American Art, Smithsonian Institution, Washington, DC
    William Penhallow Henderson Papers
    B. J. O. Nordfeldt Papers

Center for Southwest Research and Special ollections, University Libraries, University of New Mexico, Albuquerque, NM
    MSS 82 BC, New Mexico [Draft] District Board, 1917–1918
    MSS 187 BC, George W. Prichard Family Papers
    MSS 314 BC, American Indian Oral History Collection
    MSS 322 BC, U.S. Marshal (NM)
    MSS 394 BC, Part 3 Series VIII, Dennis Chavez Papers

First Division Museum at Cantigny Park, Colonel Robert R. McCormick Research Center, Wheaton, IL

Franklin D. Roosevelt Library, National Archives and Records Administration, Hyde Park, NY
    Democratic National Committee, Women's Division
    Papers of Harry L. Hopkins
        Confidential Political File, New Mexico
        FERA-WPA Field Reports, New Mexico
    President's Personal File, New Mexico

Hoover Institution Library and Archives, Palo Alto, CA
    United States, Food Administration Records, New Mexico

Library of Congress, Manuscripts Division, Washington, DC
   Bronson M. Cutting Papers
   La Follette Family Papers
   John J. Pershing Papers
Library of Congress, Veterans History Project of the American Folklife Center
   World War I, 89th Division
      Hubert Joseph Wesselman Collection
National Archives and Records Administration I, Washington, DC
   Record Group 15—Department of Veterans Affairs
   Record Group 233—Judiciary Committee and Related Committees
   Record Group 393—U.S. Army Continental Commands, 1821–1920
National Archives and Records Administration II, College Park, MD
   Record Group 60—Department of Justice
      High Cost of Living Division
   Record Group 62—Council of National Defense
   Record Group 65—[Federal] Bureau of Investigation
      Old German Files, 1909–1921
   Record Group 83—Bureau of Agricultural Economics
   Record Group 92—Office of the Quartermaster General
   Record Group 120—American Expeditionary Forces
      Records of Divisions, 41st
      Records of Divisions, 89th
   Record Group 407—Adjutant General Office, National Guard
National Archives and Records Administration, Atlanta, GA
   U.S. World War I Draft Registration Cards, 1917–1918
National Archives and Records Administration, Denver, CO
   Record Group 15—Department of Veterans Affairs
      Federal Board for Vocational Education
   Record Group 75—Bureau of Indian Affairs
   Record Group 154—War Finance Corporation
      Agricultural Loan Agency
National Archives and Records Administration, St. Louis, MO
   World War II Draft Registration Cards, 1940–1945
National World War I Museum and Memorial, Kansas City, MO
   World War I, 89th Division
   Transport Ships Newspaper Collection
New Mexico State Records Center and Archives, Santa Fe
   Adjutant General Collection—Historical Service, Accession 1973-019
   Adjutant General Collection—[State] Council of Defense, Accession1973-019
   American Legion Department of New Mexico, Accession 1959-007
   A. M. Bergere Family Papers, Accession 1975-024

Benjamin M. Read Collection, Accession 1959–179
Governor Richard C. Dillon Papers, Accession 1959–101
Governor James F. Hinkle Papers, Accession 1959–099
Governor Octaviano A. Larrazolo Papers, Accession1959–097
Governor Washington E. Lindsey Papers, Accession1959–096
Governor Merritt C. Mechem Papers, Accesion 1959–098
Governor Clyde K. Tingley Papers, Accession 1959–104

Rio Grande Historical Collections, Archives and Special Collections Department, Branson Library, New Mexico State University, Las Cruces
    MS 8—A. B. Fall Family Papers
    MS 105—de Bremond Family Papers
    MS 305—Holm O. Bursum Papers

U.S. Army History and Education Center, Carlisle, PA
    World War I Veterans Survey, 28th Division, 109th & 110th Infantry
        William M. Sibley, Journal
    World War I Veterans Survey, 89th Division, 355th & 356th Infantry
        Rudolph Forderhase, "We Made the World Safe!!??" Books 1–5

U.S. Government Publications, 1901–1960

American Battle Monuments Commission. *89th Division: Summary of Operations in the World War.* Washington, DC: GPO, 1944.
———. *American Armies and Battlefields in Europe.* Washington, DC: GPO, 1938.
Blair, Emily Newell. *The Woman's Committee, United States Council of Defense: An Interpretive Report, April 12, 1917 to February 27, 1919.* Washington, DC: GPO, 1920.
Gibson, Campbell J., and Emily Lennon. *Historical Census Statistics of the Foreign-Born Population of the United States, 1850–1990.* Working Paper No. 29. Washington, D.C.: Bureau of the Census, 1999.
Leonard, Olen E., and Charles P. Loomis. *Culture of a Contemporary Rural Community: El Cerrito, New Mexico.* Washington, DC: Department of Agriculture, Bureau of Agricultural Economics, 1941.
U.S. Post Office Department. *Reports of Site Locations, 1837–1950, New Mexico*, Microcopy 1126, Reels 382 and 385. Washington, DC: National Archives, General Services Administration, 1980.

Executive Branch

Bureau of the Census
Twelfth Census of the United States Taken in 1900. Washington, DC: U.S Census Office, 1901.
Thirteenth Census of the United States Taken in 1910. Washington, DC: GPO, 1911.
Fourteenth Census of the United States Taken in 1920. Washington, DC: GPO, 1921.
    Volume 2: *General Report and Analytical Tables.* Washington, DC: GPO, 1921.
    Volume 3: *Population.* Washington, DC: GPO, 1922.

Fifteenth Census of the United States Taken in 1930. Washington, DC: GPO, 1931.
Sixteenth Census of the United States Taken in 1940. Washington, DC: GPO, 1941.
Treasury Department
Annual Report of the Director of the Bureau of War Risk Insurance for the Fiscal Year Ending June 30, 1921. Washington, DC: GPO, 1921.
U.S. Army
Cochrane, Rexmond C. "The 1st Division at Cantigny, May 1918: Gas Warfare in World War I." Army Chemical Center, MD: U.S. Army Chemical Corps Historical Office, 1958.
———. *The 89th Division Comes into the Line, August 1918*. Army Chemical Center, MD: U.S. Army Chemical Corps Historical Office, 1958.
———. *The 89th Division in the Bois de Bantheville, October 1918*. Army Chemical Center, MD: U.S. Army Chemical Corps Historical Office, 1960.
Final Report of Gen. John J. Pershing: Commander-in-Chief American Expeditionary Forces [1 September 1919]. Washington, D.C.: GPO, 1920.
Office of the Surgeon General of the Army. *The Medical Department of the United States Army in the World War*, Vol. 4: *Mobilization Camps and Embarkation*. Washington, DC: GPO, 1927.
———. *The Medical Department of the United States Army in the World War*, Vol. 8: *Field Operations*. Washington, DC: GPO, 1925.
———. *The Medical Department of the United States Army in the World War*, Vol. 10: *Neuropsychiatry*. Washington, DC: GPO, 1929.
———. *The Medical Department of the United States Army in the World War*, Vol. 13: *Physical Reconstruction*, Section 4, *Development Battalion*. Washington, DC: GPO, 1927.
———. *Report to the Secretary of War: Influenza and Pneumonia Pandemic of 1918*. Washington, DC: GPO, 1919.
War College. Historical Section. *The Eighty-Ninth Division, 1917–1919*. Washington, DC: Army War College, 1924.
Veterans Affairs
[Frank T. Hines]. *Annual Report of the Administrator of Veterans' Affairs for the Year 1933*. Washington, DC: GPO, 1934.
———. *Annual Report of the Administrator of Veterans' Affairs for the Year 1935*. Washington, DC: GPO, 1935.

Legislative Branch

Sixty-Fifth Congress, Senate, 1st Session. Committee on Woman Suffrage, "Woman Suffrage: Hearing before the Committee on Woman Suffrage. Washington, DC: GPO, 1917.
Sixty-Fifth Congress, Senate, 2nd Session. *Investigation of the War Department, Hearings before the Committee on Military Affairs, for the Purpose of Inquiring from the Different Branches of the Service of the War Department as to the Progress Made . . . in Connection with the Present War*, 2 vols., 12 December 1917–29 March 1918. Washington, DC: GPO, 1919.

Sixty-Sixth Congress, 1st Session. *Hearings Before the Joint Commission on Postal Salaries,* October 14, 1919, vol. 2 Washington, DC: GPO, 1919.

Seventieth Congress, 2nd Session. *Proceedings of the Tenth Annual National Convention of the American Legion,* San Antonio, TX, 8–11 October 1928. Washington, DC: GPO, 1929.

Seventy-First Congress, Senate, 1st Session, Senate Document No. 26, [U.S. Senator Sam G.] Bratton, "Deceased Soldiers from New Mexico Buried in Permanent American Cemeteries in Europe," 17 September 1929. Washington, DC: GPO, 1929.

Seventy-First Congress, 1st Session. *Proceedings of the Eleventh Annual National Convention of the American Legion,* Louisville, KY, 30 September–3 October 1929. Washington, DC: GPO, 1930.

Seventy-Second Congress, 1st Session. *Proceedings of the 13th National Convention of the American Legion,* Detroit, MI, 21–24 September 1931. Washington, DC: GPO, 1932.

Seventy-Second Congress, 2nd Session. *Proceedings of the 14th National Convention of the American Legion* (Portland, OR, 12–15 September 1932). "Address of Josephus Daniels." Washington, D.C.: GPO, 1932, 9–16.

Newspapers and Magazines

Agamemnon Daily News [Transport Ship France to New York]
Albuquerque Morning Journal and *Albuquerque Journal* (beginning 1925)
American Legion Weekly and *The American Legion Monthly* (beginning 1925)
La Bandera Americana (Albuquerque)
Chicago Daily Tribune
Christian Science Monitor
El Combate (Wagon Mound)
El Defensor del Pueblo (Socorro)
Deming Headlight
La Estrella (Las Cruces)
Farmington Times-Hustler
El Independiente (Mountainair)
Las Vegas Daily Optic
Los Angeles Times
New York Herald
New York Times
Roswell Daily Record
Santa Fe New Mexican
El Sol (Madrid, Spain)
San Diego Union
Stars and Stripes (Paris)
Trench and Camp (Camp Upton, NY, and Camp Cody, NM)
Tucumcari News
Washington Post

Books, Theses, and Dissertations

Adler, J. O., ed., *History of the Seventy-Seventh Division: August 25th 1917–November 11th 1918*. New York: WHC Printers, 1919.

Allen, Desmond Walls. *1918 Camp Pike, Arkansas, Index to Soldiers' Naturalizations*. Conway, AR: Arkansas Research, 1988.

Allen, Hervey. *Toward the Flame: A Memoir of World War I*. Introduction by Steven Trout. Reprint of 1926 ed. Lincoln: University of Nebraska Press, 2003.

Association of the 110th Infantry. *History of the 110 Infantry (10th Pa.) of the 28th Division, U.S.A., 1917–1919*. Greensburg, PA: The Association, 1920.

Axelrod, Alan. *Selling the Great War: The Making of American Propaganda*. New York: Palgrave Macmillan, 2009.

Barkley, John Lewis. *Scarlet Fields: The Combat Memoir of a World War I Medal of Honor Hero*. Introduction by Steven Trout. Lawrence: University Press of Kansas, 2012.

Barry, John M. *The Great Influenza: The Story of the Deadliest Pandemic in History*. New York: Penguin, 2005.

Bennett, Scott H., and Charles F. Howlett, eds. *Antiwar Dissent and Peace Activism in World War I America: A Documentary Reader*. Lincoln: University of Nebraska Press, 2014.

Berg, A. Scott. *Wilson*. New York: G. P. Putnam's Sons, 2013.

Bloom, Lansing B., ed. *New Mexico in the Great War*. Santa Fe, NM: El Palacio Press, 1927.

Boghardt, Thomas. *The Zimmermann Telegram: Intelligence, Diplomacy, and America's Entry into World War I*. Annapolis, MD: Naval Institute Press, 2012.

Bokovoy, Matt. *The San Diego World's Fair and Southwestern Memory, 1880–1940*. Albuquerque: University of New Mexico Press, 2005.

Britton, Thomas A. *American Indians in World War I: At War and at Home*. Albuquerque: University of New Mexico Press, 1997.

Brokaw, Tom. *An Album of Memories: Personal Histories from the Greatest Generation*. New York: Random House, 2001.

Brunhouse, Robert L. *Sylvanus G. Morley and the World of the Ancient Mayas*. Norman: University of Oklahoma Press, 1971.

Budreau, Lisa M. *Bodies of War: World War I and the Politics of Commemoration in America, 1919–1933*. New York: New York University Press, 2010.

Bullock, David. *The Russian Civil War, 1918–1922*. Oxford, UK: Osprey, 2008.

Byerly, Carol R. *Fever of War: The Influenza Epidemic in the U.S. Army during World War I*. New York: New York University Press, 2005.

Capozzola, Christopher. *Uncle Sam Wants You: World War I and the Making of the Modern American Citizens*. New York: Oxford University Press, 2008.

Catt, Carrie Chapman, and Nettie Rogers Shuler. *Woman Suffrage and Politics: The Inner Story of the Suffrage Movement*. New York: Charles Scribner's Sons, 1923.

Chacón, Felipe Maximiliano. *Obras de Felipe Maximiliano Chacón: Prosa y Poesía*. Albuquerque: La Bandera Americana, 1924.

Chauvenet, Beatrice. *Hewett and Friends: A Biography of Santa Fe's Vibrant Era*. Santa Fe: Museum of New Mexico Press, 1983.

Clark, Christopher. *The Sleepwalkers: How Europe Went to War in 1914*. New York: HarperCollins, 2012.
Clark, George B. *The American Expeditionary Force in World War I: A Statistical History, 1917–1919*. Jefferson, NC: McFarland, 2013.
———. *Devil Dogs Chronicle: Voices of the 4th Marine Brigade in World War I*. Lawrence: University Press of Kansas, 2013.
Clark, Michael. *Dos Passos's Early Fiction, 1912–1938*. Selinsgrove, PA: Susquehanna University Press, 1987.
Clarke, Ida Clyde. *American Women and the World War*. New York: D. Appleton, 1918.
Clayton, Bruce. *Forgotten Prophet: The Life of Randolph Bourne*. Baton Rouge: Louisiana State University Press, 1984.
Clifford, J. Garry, ed. *The World War I Memoirs of Robert P. Patterson: A Captain in the Great War*. Knoxville: University of Tennessee Press, 2012.
Coffman, Edward M. *The War to End All Wars: The American Military Experience in World War I*. New York: Oxford University Press, 1968.
Coles, Robert. *The Call of Stories: Teaching and the Moral Imagination*. Boston: Houghton Mifflin, 1989.
Collins, Francis A. *The Fighting Engineers: The Minute Men of Our Industrial Army*. New York: Century, 1918.
Cooper, John Milton, Jr. *Pivotal Decades: The United States, 1900–1920*. New York: W. W. Norton, 1990.
———. *The Warrior and the Priest: Woodrow Wilson and Theodore Roosevelt*. Cambridge, MA: Belknap Press of Harvard University Press, 1983.
Creel, George. *How We Advertised America*. New York: Harper and Brothers, 1920.
Crowell, Benedict, and Robert F. Wilson. *The Road to France*: Vol. 2: *The Transportation of Troops and Military Supplies, 1917–1918*. New Haven: Yale University Press, 1921.
Crumrine, Sergeant Albert. *History of Company 'L' 356th Infantry, 89th Division*. Trier, Germany: J. Lintz, 1919.
Daniel, Karen Stein. *World War I Era Alien Enemy Registrations for New Mexico, 1918*. Albuquerque: New Mexico Genealogical Society, 2016.
Davis, Noel, Lt. USN, *Sweeping the North Sea Barrage*. Department of the Navy Mine Force: North Sea Minesweeping Detachment, 1919.
deBuys, William. *Enchantment and Exploitation: The Life and Hard Times of a New Mexico Mountain Range*. Albuquerque: University of New Mexico Press, 1985.
deBuys, William, and Alex Harris. *River of Traps: A Village Life*. Albuquerque: University of New Mexico Press, 1990.
Dickson, Paul, and Thomas B. Allen. *The Bonus Army: An American Epic*. New York: Walker, 2004.
Doak, Mary Woodward. "Opportunities Offered by the School of American Research and the Museum of New Mexico for Study and Research in the Social Sciences." M.A. Thesis, Texas Technological College, 1929.
Edmonds, James E. *Military Operations, France and Belgium, 1918*, Vol. 3: *May–July: The German Diversion Offensives and the First Allied Counter-Offensive*. London: Macmillan, 1938.

Egan, Timothy. *The Worst Hard Time: The Untold Story of Those Who Survived the Great American Dust Bowl*. Boston: Houghton Mifflin, 2006.

Eisenhower, John S. D. *The Bitter Woods: The Dramatic Story, Told at All Echelons—from Supreme Command to Squad Leader—of the Crisis That Shook the Western Coalition: Hitler's Surprise Ardennes Offensive*. New York: G. P. Putnam's Sons, 1969.

———. *Yanks: The Epic Story of the American Army in World War I*. New York: Simon and Schuster, 2001.

English, George. *History of the 89th Division: From Its Organization in 1917, through its Operations in the World War, the Occupation of Germany and until Demobilization in 1919*. Denver: Smith-Brooks, 1920.

Faust, Drew Gilpin. *This Republic of Suffering: Death and the American Civil War*. New York: Alfred A. Knopf, 2008.

Ferrell, Robert H. *America's Deadliest Battle: Meuse-Argonne, 1918*. Lawrence: University Press of Kansas, 2007.

———. *Five Days in October: The Lost Battalion of World War I*. Columbia: University of Missouri Press, 2005.

———. *Reminiscences of Conrad S. Babcock: The Old U.S. Army and the New, 1898–1918*. Columbia: University of Missouri Press, 2012.

Fixico, Donald. *Indian Resilience and Rebuilding: Indigenous Nations in the Modern American West*. Tucson: University of Arizona Press, 2013.

Ford, Nancy Gentile. *Americans All: Foreign-Born Soldiers in World War I*. College Station: Texas A&M University Press 2001.

Forrest, Suzanne. *The Preservation of the Village: New Mexico's Hispanics and the New Deal*. Albuquerque: University of New Mexico Press, 1989.

Freemantle, Michael. *The Chemists' War, 1914–1918*. Cambridge, UK: Royal Society of Chemistry, 2015.

Frydl, Kathleen J. *The G.I. Bill*. New York: Cambridge University Press, 2009.

General Federation of Women's Clubs, Sixth Biennial, Official Proceedings [Los Angeles, 1902]. Detroit, MI: John Bornment and Sons, 1902.

Graham, John W. *The Gold Star Mother Pilgrimages of the 1930s: Overseas Grave Visitations by Mothers and Widows of Fallen U.S. World War I Soldiers*. Jefferson, NC: McFarland, 2005.

Graves, Robert. *Good-bye to All That*. Revised ed. Garden City, NY: Doubleday Anchor, 1957.

Graves, William S. *America's Siberian Adventure, 1918–1920*. Reprint of 1931 ed. New York: Peter Smith, 1941.

Greenhalgh, Elizabeth. *Foch in Command: The Forging of a First World War General*. Cambridge, UK: Cambridge University Press, 2011.

———. *The French Army and the First World War*. Cambridge, UK: Cambridge University Press, 2014.

Gross, Norman, ed. *Noble Purposes: Nine Champions of the Rule of Law*. Athens: Ohio University Press, 2007.

Grotelueschen, Mark E. *The AEF Way of War: The American Army and Combat in World War I*. New York: Cambridge University Press, 2007.

Gutiérrez, Edward A. *Doughboys on the Great War: How American Soldiers Viewed Their Military Service*. Lawrence: University Press of Kansas, 2014.
Hamm, Ron. *The Bursums of New Mexico: Four Generations of Leadership and Service*. Socorro, NM: Manzanares Street, 2012.
Hanson, Neil. *Unknown Soldiers: The Story of the Missing of the First World War*. New York: Alfred A. Knopf, 2006.
Harries, Meirion, and Susie Harries. *The Last Days of Innocence*. New York: Random House, 1997.
Harris, Charles H., and Louis R. Sadler. *The Archaeologist Was a Spy: Sylvanus G. Morley and the Office of Naval Intelligence*. Albuquerque: University of New Mexico Press, 2003.
———. *The Great Call-Up: The Guard, The Border, and The Mexican Revolution*. Norman: University of Oklahoma Press, 2015.
———. *The Plan de San Diego: Tejano Rebellion, Mexican Intrigue*. Lincoln: University of Nebraska Press, 2013.
Hatler, M. Waldo. *Company 'B' 356 Infantry, American Expeditionary Forces*. Schweich, Germany: n.p., 1919.
Hernon, Peter. *The Great Rescue: American Heroes, an Iconic Ship, and the Race to Save Europe in WWI*. New York: HarperCollins, 2017.
Herring, Ray DeWitt. *Trifling with War*. Boston: Meador, 1934.
Herteg, Johan den, and Samuël Kruizinga, eds. *Caught in the Middle: Neutrals, Neutrality, and the First World War*. Amsterdam: Amsterdam University Press, 2011.
Higham, John. *Strangers in the Land: Patterns of American Nativism, 1860–1925*. 2nd ed. New Brunswick: Rutgers University Press, 2002.
History of the Fortieth (Sunshine) Division: Containing a Brief History and Roster of All the Units under the Command of Major General Frederick S. Strong, 1917–1919. Los Angeles: C. S. Hutson, 1920.
Hodgin, C. E. *War Service of the University of New Mexico*. University of New Mexico Bulletin 33. Albuquerque: University of New Mexico, 1919.
Hofstadter, Richard J. *The Paranoid Style in American Politics and Other Essays*. Cambridge: Harvard University Press, 1964.
Holmes, Jack E. *Politics in New Mexico*. Albuquerque: University of New Mexico Press, 1967.
Holtby, David V. *Forty-Seventh Star: New Mexico's Struggle for Statehood*. Norman: University of Oklahoma Press, 2012.
Homsher, David C. *American Battlefields of World War I: Château-Thierry—Then and Now*, vol. 1. San Mateo, CA: Battlefield Productions, 2006.
Horgan, Paul. *Mountain Standard Time*. New York: Farrar, Straus, and Cudahy, 1962.
Horne, John, and Alan Kramer. *German Atrocities, 1914: A History of Denial*. New Haven: Yale University Press, 2001.
Huber, Michel. *La Population de la France pendant la Guerre, avec un Appendice sur les Revenus avant et après la Guerre*. New Haven: Yale University Press, 1931; Paris: Les Presses Universitaires de France, 1931.

Huelfer, Evan Andrew. *The "Casualty Issue" in American Military Practice: The Impact of World War I*. Westport, CT: Praeger, 2003.

Jaehn, Tomas. *Germans in the Southwest, 1850–1920*. Albuquerque: University of New Mexico Press, 2005.

Jensen, Joan M. *Army Surveillance in America, 1775–1980*. New Haven: Yale University Press, 1991.

———. *The Price of Vigilance*. Chicago: Rand McNally, 1968.

Johnson, Douglas V., II, and Rolfe L. Hollman Jr. *Soissons, 1918*. College Station: Texas A&M University Press, 1999.

Johnson, Thomas M., and Fletcher Pratt. *The Lost Battalion*. Introduction by Edward M. Coffman. Reprint of 1938 ed. Lincoln: University of Nebraska Press, 2000.

Jones, Carlisle L. *History and Roster of the 355th Infantry, 89th Division*. Lincoln, NE: Society of the 355th Infantry, n.d. [1920s].

Jordan, Edwin O. *Epidemic Influenza: A Survey*. Chicago: American Medical Association, 1927.

Junger, Sebastian. *Tribes: On Homecoming and Belonging*. New York: Twelve, 2016.

Keene, Jennifer D. *Doughboys, the Great War, and the Remaking of America*. Baltimore: Johns Hopkins University Press, 2001.

———. *World War I: The American Soldier Experience*. Reprint of 2006 ed. Lincoln: University of Nebraska Press, 2011.

Keleher, William A. *Memoirs: Episodes in New Mexico History, 1892–1969*. Reprint of 1969 ed. Santa Fe, NM: Sunstone Press, 2008.

Kelly, J. R. *A History of New Mexico Military Institute, 1891–1941*. Albuquerque: University of New Mexico Press, 1953.

Kennedy, David M. *Over Here: The First World War and American Society*. New York: Oxford University Press, 2004.

Kingsbury, Celia Malone. *For Home and Country: World War I Propaganda on the Home Front*. Lincoln: University of Nebraska Press, 2010.

Koerver, Hans Joachin. *German Submarine Warfare, 1914–1918, in the Eyes of British Intelligence: Selected Sources from the British National Archives, Kew*. Berlin, Germany: LIS Reinisch, 2010.

Koven, Seth, and Sonya Michel, eds. *Mothers of a New World: Maternalist Politics and the Origins of Welfare States*. New York: Routledge, 1993.

Krouse, Susan Applegate. *North American Indians in the Great War*. Lincoln: University of Nebraska Press, 2007.

LaCapra, Dominic. *Writing History, Writing Trauma*. 2nd ed. Baltimore: Johns Hopkins University Press, 2014.

La Farge, Oliver. *Santa Fe: The Autobiography of a Southwestern Town*. Norman: University of Oklahoma Press, 1959

La Follette, Bella Case, and Fola La Follette. *Robert M. La Follette (June 14, 1855–June 25, 1925)*, vol. 2. New York: Macmillan, 1953.

Larrabee, Eric. *Commander in Chief: Franklin D. Roosevelt, His Lieutenants, and Their War*. Reprint of 1987 ed. Annapolis, MD: U.S. Naval Institute Press, 2004.

Larson, Eric. *Dead Wake: The Last Crossing of the Lusitania.* New York: Crown, 2015.
Lee, Joshua Bryan. *The Battle of Cognac, and Other Soldier Rhymes.* Reprint of 1919 ed. Oklahoma City: Harlow, 1948.
Lesy, Michael. *Wisconsin Death Trip.* Reprint of 1973 ed. Albuquerque: University of New Mexico Press, 2000.
Lewis, Nancy Owen, and Kay Leigh Hagan. *A Peculiar Alchemy: A Centennial History of SAR.* Santa Fe, NM: SAR Press, 2007.
Linderman, Gerald F. *Embattled Courage: The Experience of Combat in the American Civil War.* New York: Free Press, 1987.
Link, Arthur S., ed. *The Papers of Woodrow Wilson,* vol. 42. Princeton: Princeton University Press, 1983.
Linker, Beth. *War's Waste: Rehabilitation in World War I America.* Chicago: University of Chicago Press, 2011.
Lovejoy, Arthur O. *Essays in the History of Ideas.* Baltimore: Johns Hopkins University Press, 1948.
Lowitt, Richard. *Bronson M. Cutting: Progressive Politician.* Albuquerque: University of New Mexico Press, 1992.
Lucero, Antonio, comp. *Acts, Memorials and Resolutions of the Legislature of the State of New Mexico, Passed at Its Extraordinary Session.* Santa Fe, NM: State Record Printer, 1917.
Luebke, Frederick C. *Bands of Loyalty: German-Americans and World War I.* De Kalb: Northern Illinois University Press, 1974.
Marshall, George C. *Memoirs of My Service in the World War, 1917–1918.* Boston: Houghton Mifflin, 1976.
Martinez, Kim A. "Their Harrowing Experience: A Social History of the Spanish Influenza in New Mexico, 1918–19." M.A. Thesis, Adams State University, Alamosa, CO, 2015.
Marvin, Carolyn, and David W. Ingle. *Blood Sacrifice and the Nation: Totem Rituals and the American Flag.* New York: Cambridge University Press, 1999.
Mastriano, Douglas V. *Alvin York: A New Biography of the Hero of the Argonne.* Lexington: University Press of Kentucky, 2014.
Matthews, William, and Dixon Wecter, *Our Soldiers Speak, 1775–1918.* Boston: Little, Brown, 1943.
McConnell, Stuart. *Glorious Contentment: The Grand Army of the Republic.* Chapel Hill: University of North Carolina Press, 1997.
McGrath, John F. *War Diary of 354th Infantry: 89th Division.* Trier, Germany: J. Lintz, 1919.
Mead, Gary. *The Doughboys: America and the First World War.* New York: Overlook Press, 2000.
Melzer, Richard A. *Captain Maximiliano Luna: A New Mexico Rough Rider.* Albuquerque: Rio Grande Press, 2017.
———. *Coming of Age in the Great Depression: The Civilian Conservation Corps Experience in New Mexico, 1933–1942.* Las Cruces, NM: Yucca Tree Press, 2000.
———, ed. *Sunshine and Shadows in New Mexico's Past: The Statehood Period, 1912–Present.* Los Ranchos, NM: Rio Grande Books, 2012.

Meyer, G. J. *The World Remade: America in World War I*. New York: Bantam Book, 2016.
Miller, Kristie. *Isabella Greenway: An Enterprising Woman*. Tucson: University of Arizona Press, 2004.
Miller, Kristie, and Robert H. McGinnis, eds. *A Volume of Friendship: The Letters of Eleanor Roosevelt and Isabella Greenway, 1904–1953*. Tucson: Arizona Historical Society, 2009.
Mitchell, Pablo. *Coyote Nation: Sexuality, Race, and Conquest in Modernizing New Mexico, 1880–1920*. Chicago: University of Chicago Press, 2005.
Mohr, Joan McGuire. *The Czech-Slovak Legion in Siberia, 1917–1922*. Jefferson, NC: McFarland, 2012.
Mohr, Melissa. *Holy Sh*t: A Brief History of Swearing*. New York: Oxford University Press, 2013.
Moore, Joel R., et al. *The History of the American Expedition Fighting the Bolsheviki: Campaigning in North Russia, 1918–19*. Detroit, MI: Polar Bear, 1920.
Mora, Anthony P. *Border Dilemmas: Racial and National Uncertainties in New Mexico, 1848–1912*. Durham, NC: Duke University Press, 2011.
Morris, James McGrath. *The Ambulance Drivers: Hemingway, Dos Passos, and a Friendship Made and Lost in War*. Boston: Da Capo Press, 2017.
Mosier, John. *Verdun: The Lost History of the Most Important Battle of World War I, 1914–1918*. New York: New American Library, 2013.
Mullaney, Craig M. *The Unforgiving Minute: A Soldier's Education*. New York: Penguin, 2009.
Mullendore, William C. *History of the United States Food Administration*. Stanford, CA: Stanford University Press, 1941.
Munson, Marit K., ed. *Kenneth Chapman's Santa Fe: Artists and Archaeologists, 1907–1931—The Memoirs of Kenneth Chapman*. Santa Fe, NM: School of Advanced Research Press, 2008.
Murray, Robert K. *Red Scare: A Study in National Hysteria, 1919–20*. Minneapolis, MN: University of Minnesota Press, 1955.
Nash, George H. *The Life of Herbert Hoover: Master of Emergencies, 1917–1918*. New York: W. W. Norton, 1996.
Neiberg, Michael S. *The Second Battle of the Marne*. Bloomington: Indiana University Press, 2008.
New Mexico, Council of Defense. *Final Report of the Council of Defense of the State of New Mexico, May 10th 1917 to May 31st, 1920*. Santa Fe, NM: Council of Defense, 1920.
Noggle, Burl. *Into the Twenties: The United States from Armistice to Normalcy*. Urbana: University of Illinois Press, 1974.
Nolan, Thomas Justus. "Battlefield Landscapes: Geographic Information Science as a Method of Integrating History and Archaeology for Battlefield Interpretation." Ph.D. dissertation, Texas State University-San Marcos, 2007.
Nostrand, Richard Lee. *El Cerrito, New Mexico: Eight Generations in a Spanish Village*. Norman: University of Oklahoma Press, 2003.
O'Leary, Cecilia Elizabeth. *To Die For: The Paradox of American Patriotism*. Princeton: Princeton University Press, 1999.

O'Leary-Siemer, Clare Denise. "Roots of the New Mexico Women's Movement: Missionaries and the New Mexico Woman's Christian Temperance Union." M.A. thesis, University of New Mexico, 1997.

Opdycke, Sandra. *The Flu Epidemic of 1918: America's Experience in the Global Health Crisis*. New York: Routledge, 2014.

Ortiz, Stephen R. *Beyond the Bonus March and GI Bill: How Veteran Politics Shaped the New Deal Era*. New York: New York University Press, 2010.

———, ed. *Veterans' Policies, Veterans' Politics: New Perspectives on Veterans in the Modern United States*. Gainesville: University Press of Florida, 2012.

Patterson, James T. *The New Deal and the States: Federalism in Transition*. Princeton: Princeton University Press, 1969.

Patterson, Martha A. *The American New Woman Revisited, 1894–1930*. New Brunswick: Rutgers University Press, 2008.

Pearl, James, ed. *Picture This: World War I Posters and Visual Culture*. Lincoln: University of Nebraska Press, 2009.

Pencak, William A., ed. *Encyclopedia of the Veteran in America*, vol. 1. Santa Barbara, CA: ABC-Clio, 2009.

———. *For God and Country: The American Legion, 1919–1941*. Boston: Northeastern University Press, 1989.

Pershing, John J. *My Experiences in the World War*, 2 vols. New York: Frederick A. Stokes, 1931.

Persico, Joseph E. *Eleventh Month, Eleventh Day, Eleventh Hour: Armistice Day 1918 and Its Violent Climax*. New York: Random House, 2004.

Ponsonby, Arthur. *Falsehood in War-Time*. New York: Dutton, 1928.

Proceedings of the Fourth Annual Meeting of the New Mexico Cattle and Horse Growers' Association. Las Vegas, n.p., 1918.

Radosh, Ronald, and Murray N. Rothbard, eds. *A New History of Leviathan*. New York: E. P. Dutton, 1972.

Raines, Lester, ed. *Writers and Writing of New Mexico*. Las Vegas: New Mexico Normal University, 1934.

Raines, Rebecca Robbins. *Getting the Message Through: A Branch History of the U.S. Army Signal Corps*. Washington, D.C.: Center of Military History, 1996.

Ramírez, José A. *To the Line of Fire: Mexican Texans and World War I*. College Station: Texas A&M University Press, 2009.

Report of the American Historical Association for the Year 1917. Washington, DC: American Historical Association, 1918.

Report of the Proceedings of the Statewide Coordination Meeting of Federal Agencies Operating in New Mexico. Santa Fe, NM: National Emergency Council, 1936.

Reynolds, David. *The Long Shadow: The Legacies of the Great War in the Twentieth Century*. New York: W. W. Norton, 2014.

Richard, Carl J. *When the United States Invaded Russia: Woodrow Wilson's Siberian Disaster*. Lanham, MD: Rowman and Littlefield, 2012.

Roth, Michael S. *Memory, Trauma, and History: Essays on Living with the Past*. New York: Columbia University Press, 2011.

Rubin, Richard. *The Last of the Doughboys: The Forgotten Generation and Their Forgotten War*. Boston: Houghton Mifflin Harcourt, 2013.

Rumer, Thomas A. *The American Legion: An Official History, 1919–1989*. New York: M. Evans, 1990.

Sánchez, Joseph P., Robert L. Spude, and Art Gómez. *New Mexico: A History*. Norman: University of Oklahoma Press, 2013.

Schackel, Sandra. *Social Housekeepers: Women Shaping Public Policy in New Mexico, 1920–1940*. Albuquerque: University of New Mexico Press, 1992.

Schaffer, Ronald. *America in the Great War: The Rise of the War Welfare State*. New York: Oxford University Press, 1991.

Schmidt, Regin. *Red Scare: FBI and the Origins of Anticommunism in the United States, 1919–1943*. Copenhagen: Museum Tusculanum Press, University of Copenhagen, 2000.

Secretary of State, Manuel Martinez. *The New Mexico Blue Book or State Official Register, 1919*. Santa Fe, NM: Secretary of State, 1919.

Simmons, Marc. *Albuquerque: A Narrative History*. Albuquerque: University of New Mexico Press, 1982.

Simmons, Peter, and Alfred H. Davies, eds. *Twentieth Engineers, 1917–1918–1919*. Portland, OR: Twentieth Engineers, 1920.

Slotkin, Richard. *Lost Battalions: The Great War and the Crisis of American Neutrality*. New York: Henry Holt, 2005.

Snell, Mark A., ed. *Unknown Soldiers: The American Expeditionary Forces in Memory and Remembrance*. Kent, OH: Kent State University Press, 2008.

Society of the First Division. *History of the First Division during the World War, 1917–1919*. Philadelphia: John C. Winston, 1922.

Spidle, Jake. *Doctors of Medicine in New Mexico*. Albuquerque: University of New Mexico Press, 1986.

Springer, Charles. *Report of the Council of Defense of the State of New Mexico*. Santa Fe: n.p., [October] 1918.

Stoler, Ann Laura. *Along the Archival Grain: Epistemic Anxieties and Colonial Common Sense*. Princeton: Princeton University Press, 2009.

Takaki, Ronald. *Strangers from a Different Shore*. Revised ed. Boston: Little, Brown, 1998.

Taylor, A. J. P. *The Origins of the Second World War*. 2nd ed. Greenwich, CT: Fawcett, 1965.

Thelen, David P. *Robert M. La Follette and the Insurgent Spirit*. Boston: Little, Brown, 1976.

Thisted, Moses N. *Pershing's Pioneer Infantry of World War I*. Helmet, CA: Alphabet Printers, 1982.

Thomas, Shipley. *The History of the A.E.F.* Reprint of 1920 ed. Nashville, TN: Battery Press, 2000.

Trout, Steven. *Memorial Fictions: Willa Cather and the First World War*. Lincoln: University of Nebraska Press, 2002.

———. *On the Battlefield of Memory: The First World War and American Remembrance, 1914–1941*. Tuscaloosa: University of Alabama Press, 2010.

Tuchman, Barbara W. *The Guns of August*. New York: Macmillan, 1962.

———. *Practicing History: Selected Essays*. New York: Random House, 1981.

———. *The Proud Tower: A Portrait of the World before the War, 1890–1914*. New York: Macmillan, 1966.

———. *The Zimmermann Telegram*. New York: Viking Press, 1958.

Veit, Helen Zoe. *Modern Food, Moral Food: Self-Control, Science, and the Rise of Modern American Eating in the Early Twentieth Century*. Chapel Hill: University of North Carolina Press, 2013.

Waybourn, Marilu. *Homesteaders to Boomtown: A Pictorial History of Farmington, New Mexico, and Surrounding Area*. Farmington, NM: Farmington Museum Foundation, 2001.

Wecter, Dixon. *When Johnny Comes Marching Home*. Boston: Houghton Mifflin, 1944.

Weiss, Elaine F. *Fruits of Victory: The Woman's Land Army of America in the Great War*. Washington, D.C.: Potomac Books, 2008.

Wesley, Charles H. *The History of the National Association of Colored Women's Clubs: A Legacy of Service*. Washington, DC: The Association, 1984.

Whaley, Charlotte. *Nina Otero-Warren of Santa Fe*. Albuquerque: University of New Mexico Press, 1994.

White, Robert R., ed. *The Taos Society of Artists*. Albuquerque: University of New Mexico Press, 1983.

Williams, Jerry L., ed. *New Mexico in Maps*. 2nd ed. Albuquerque: University of New Mexico Press, 1986.

Wilson, Chris. *The Myth of Santa Fe: Creating A Modern Regional Tradition*. Albuquerque: University of New Mexico Press, 1997.

Wilson, John B. *Maneuver and Firepower: The Evolution of Divisions and Separate Brigades*. Washington, DC: Center of Military History, U.S. Army, 1999.

With 'F' Company 356th Infantry, 89th Division, National Army: From September 5, 1917 to April 20, 1919. Treves: Pomlinus-Druckerd, 1919.

Wood, Mary I. *The History of the General Federation of Women's Clubs for the First Twenty-Two Years of Its Organization*. New York: General Federation of Women's Clubs, 1912.

Wood, Trish. *What Was Asked of Us: An Oral Hisory of the Iraq War by the Soldiers Who Fought It*. Introduction by Bobby Muller. New York: Little, Brown, 2006.

Woodward, David R. *America and World War I: A Selected Annotated Bibliography of English-Language Sources*. New York: Routledge, 2007.

———. *The American Army in the First World War*. New York: Cambridge University Press, 2014.

Wright, William M. *Meuse-Argonne Diary: A Division Commander in World War I*. Edited and Introduction by Robert H. Ferrell. Columbia: University of Missouri Press, 2004.

Wright, William R. *A History of the Sixty-Sixth Artillery Brigade, American Expeditionary Forces*. Denver: Smith-Brooks, 1919.

Yockelson, Mitchell. *Borrowed Soldiers: Americans under British Command, 1918*. Norman: University of Oklahoma Press, 2008.

———. *Forty-Seven Days: How Pershing's Warriors Came of Age to Defeat the German Army in World War I*. New York: New American Library, 2016.

Zaloga, Steven J. *French Tanks of World War I*. Oxford, UK: Osprey, 2010.

Articles and Book Chapters

Armijo, Isidoro. "Lest We Forget," *El Palacio* 6, no. 7 (22 March 1919): 99–109.

Asplund, Rupert F. "Civilian Activities." In Lansing B. Bloom, ed., *New Mexico in the Great War*, 40–54. Santa Fe, NM: El Palacio Press, 1927.

Beattie, Taylor V. "Continuing the Search for York." *Army History*, no. 66 (Winter 2008): 20–28.

Bernstein, Bruce. "The First Issue of El Palacio and Its Vision for the Museum of New Mexico." *El Palacio* 118, no. 4 (Winter 2013): 36–43.

Bloom, Lansing B. "To the Colors." In Lansing B. Bloom, ed., *New Mexico in the Great War*, 108–22. Santa Fe, NM: El Palacio Press, 1927.

———. "Trophies of the Great War." *New Mexico Historical Review* 2, no. 2 (April 1927): 205–7.

Brown, Dick. "USS New Mexico—Glorious Past, Awesome Future." *La Crónica de Nuevo México*, no. 95 (April 2013): 1–2.

Burran, James A. "Prohibition in New Mexico, 1917." *New Mexico Historical Review* 48, no. 2 (April 1973): 133–49.

Byerly, Carol R. "Army Sanctuary for Tubercular Veterans." In Stephen R. Ortiz, ed., *Veterans' Policies, Veterans' Politics: New Perspectives on Veterans in the Modern United States*, 11–37. Gainesville, FL: University Press of Florida, 2012.

Cappon, Lester J. "The Collection of World War I Materials in the States." *American Historical Review* 48, no. 4 (July 1943): 733–45.

"The Case of Senator La Follette." *Current Opinion* 63, no. 5 (November 1917): 1–3.

Clemens, Elisabeth S. "Organizational Repertoires and Institutional Change: Women's Groups and the Transformation of U.S. Politics, 1890–1920." *American Journal of Sociology* 98, no. 4 (January 1993): 755–78.

Cuff, Robert D. "Herbert Hoover, the Ideology of Voluntarism and War Organization during the Great War." *Journal of American History* 64, no. 2 (September 1977): 358–72.

Danburg, Walter W. "The State Council of Defense" in In Lansing B. Bloom, ed., *New Mexico in the Great War*, 22–39. Santa Fe, NM: El Palacio Press, 1927.

Erkoreka, Anton. "Origins of the Spanish Influenza Pandemic (1918–1920) and Its Relation to the First World War." *Journal of Molecular and Genetic Medicine* 3, no. 2 (December 2009): 190–94.

Faulkner, Richard S. "Disappearing Doughboys: The American Expeditionary Forces' Straggler Crisis in the Meuse Argonne." *Army History*, no. 83 (Spring 2012): 7–25.

Fernland, Kevin J. "Senator Holm O. Bursum and the Mexican Ring, 1921–1924." *New Mexico Historical Review* 66, no. 4 (1 October 1991): 433–53.

Fox, Mary, et al. "Evaluating the Community Health Legacy of World War I Chemical Weapons Testing." *Journal of Community Health* 35, no. 1 (February 2010): 93–103.

Gamble, Richard M. "Savior Nation: Woodrow Wilson and the Gospel of Service." *Humanitas* 14, no. 1 (Spring 2001): 4–22.

Gibson, J. R. R. "Veterans' Administration." In *Report of the Proceedings of the Statewide Coordination Meeting of Federal Agencies Operating in New Mexico*, 16A. Santa Fe: National Emergency Council, 1936.

Gonzales, Phillip B. "'La Junta de Indignación': Hispano Repertoire of Collective Protest in New Mexico, 1884–1933." *Western Historical Quarterly* 31, no. 2 (Summer 2000): 161–86.

———. "Race, Party, and Class" In Norman Gross, ed., *Noble Purposes: Nine Champions of the Rule of Law*, 95–109. Athens: Ohio University Press, 2007.

Gonzales, Phillip B., and Ann Massmann. "Loyalty Questioned: Nuevomexicanos in the Great War." *Pacific Historical Review* 75, no. 4 (November 2006): 626–66.

González Bombardiere, Sergio. "La Pandemia Olvidada de 1918." *Revista de Estudios Médico Humanísticos* 14, no. 14 (2007): 1–7.

Guth, James L. "Herbert Hoover, the U.S. Food Administration, and the Dairy Industry, 1917–1918." *Business History Review* 55, no. 2 (Summer 1981): 170–87.

Hall, Tom G. "Wilson and the Food Crisis: Price Control during World War I." *Agricultural History* 47, no. 1 (January 1973): 25–46.

Henderson, Alice Corbin. "The Women's Part." In Lansing B. Bloom, ed., *New Mexico in the Great War*, 55–69. Santa Fe, NM: El Palacio Press, 1927.

Hendricks, Rick. "The Double Sapphire Anniversary of the *New Mexico Historical Review*. *New Mexico Historical Review* 92, no. 1 (Winter 2017): 9–20.

Hewett, Edgar Lee. "The Cost and the Gain." In Lansing B. Bloom, ed., *New Mexico in the Great War*, 142–47. Santa Fe, NM: El Palacio Press, 1927.

———. "Historical Service." *El Palacio* 8, no. 7/8 (July 1920): 172–74.

Holtby, David V. "Historical Reflections on New Mexico Statehood: New Mexico's Economy, a Case Study of Mining to 1940." *New Mexico Historical Review* 88, no. 1 (Winter 2013): 63–94.

———. "The New Mexico National Guard before and during World War I." New Mexico Historical Review 93, no. 1 (Winter 2018): 1–30.

Jensen, Joan M. "Canning Comes to New Mexico: Women and the Agricultural Extension Service, 1914–1919." *New Mexico Historical Review* 57, no. 4 (October 1982): 361–86.

———. "'Disenfranchisement Is a Disgrace': Women and Politics in New Mexico, 1900–1940." *New Mexico Historical Review* 56, no. 1 (January 1981): 5–35.

Johnson, Donald. "Wilson, Burleson, and Censorship in the First World War." *Journal of Southern History* 28, no. 1 (February 1962): 46–58.

Jones, Edgar, et al. "Shell Shock and Mild Traumatic Brain Injury: A Historical Review." *American Journal of Psychiatry* 164, no. 11 (November 2007): 1641–45.

Kettleborough, Charles. "Legislative Notes and Reviews." *American Political Science Review* 13, no. 2 (May 1919): 264–80.

Kinder, John W. "Iconography of Injury." In James Pearl, ed., *Picture This: World War I Posters and Visual Culture*, 340–68. Lincoln: University of Nebraska Press, 2009.

Kruizinga, Samuël. "NOT Neutrality." In Johan den Herteg and Samuël Kruizinga, eds., *Caught in the Middle: Neutrals, Neutrality, and the First World War*, 85–104. Amsterdam: Amsterdam University Press, 2011.

Le Naour, Jean-Yves. "Le Sexe et la Guerre: Divergences Franco-Américaines pendant la Grande Guerre (1917–1918)." *Guerres Mondiales et Conflits Contemporains*, no. 197 (March 2000): 103–16.

Lewis, Edwin Newell. "The Challenge of the Vesle." *American Legion Weekly* 1, no. 7 (15 August 1919): 5–7, 25.

Lowitt, Richard. "Bronson Cutting and the Early Years of the American Legion in New Mexico." *New Mexico Historical Review* 64, no. 2 (April 1989): 143-58.

Marmar, Charles R., MD, et al. "Course of Posttraumatic Stress Disorder 40 Years after the Vietnam War." *JAMA Psychiatry* 72, no. 9 (1 September 2015): 857-951.

McMaster, Christopher T. "The International Military Police and the Allied Intervention in the Russian Civil War." *Student Pulse* 6, no. 4 (2014), www.inquiriesjournal.com/a?id=891.

Melzer, Richard. "A Dark and Terrible Moment: The Spanish Flu Epidemic of 1918 in New Mexico." *New Mexico Historical Review* 57, no. 2 (July 1982): 213-38.

———. "Exiled in the Desert: The Bisbee Deportees' Reception in New Mexico, 1917." *New Mexico Historical Review* 67, no. 3 (July 1992): 269-84.

———. "Stage Soldiers of the Southwest: New Mexico's Four Minute Men of World War I." *Military History of the Southwest* 20, no. 1 (Spring 1990): 23-42.

———. "World War I and the Gallup Deportation to Belen, 1917." In Richard Melzer and John Taylor, eds., *A River Runs through Us: True Tales of the Rio Abajo*, 232-40. Albuquerque: Rio Grande Books, 2015.

Melzer, Richard, and Phyllis Mingus. "Art to Crush the Kaiser: World War I Poster Art in New Mexico." *El Palacio* 88, no. 1 (Spring 1982): 23-30.

Miller, Michael. "Bayonets, Blood, and Beyond." In Mark A. Snell, ed., *Unknown Soldiers: The American Expeditionary Forces in Memory and Remembrance*, 83-98. Kent, OH: Kent State University Press, 2008.

Moore, Earl C. "Wooden Guns in War Time." *Field Artillery Journal* 7, no. 3 (July-September 1917): 316-18.

"Necrology: Washington E. Lindsey." *New Mexico Historical Review* 1, no. 4 (October 1926): 489-90.

"New Mexico War Memorial." *El Palacio* 6, no. 4 (8 February 1919): 50-52.

Noll, John J. "Crosses." *American Legion Monthly* 8, no. 3 (September 1930): 14-17, 52.

Odell, Joseph H. "The New Spirit of the New Army." *Outlook*, 23 January 1918, 140.

"Officials at Conference on Child Welfare." *New Mexico Legionnaire* 2, no. 7 (April 1931): 3.

"Our Military System as It Appeared to America's Citizen Soldiers." *Infantry Journal* 15, no. 10 (April 1919): 771-87.

Oxford, J. S., et al. "A Hypothesis: The Conjunction of Soldiers, Gas, Pigs, Ducks, Geese, and Horses in Northern France during the Great War Provided the Conditions for the Emergence of the 'Spanish' Influenza Pandemic of 1918-1919." *Vaccine* 23, no. 7 (4 January 2005): 940-45.

Pond, Ashley. "At the Front." In Lansing B. Bloom, ed., *New Mexico in the Great War*, 138-41. Santa Fe, NM: El Palacio Press, 1927. Originally published in *The New Mexico Blue Book or State Official Register, 1919*, 112-14 (Santa Fe, NM: Secretary of State, 1919); and republished in *New Mexico Historical Review* 2, no. 1 (January 1927): 17-21.

Porter, David. "Senator Carl Hatch and the Hatch Act of 1939." *New Mexico Historical Review* 48, no. 2 (April 1973): 151-64.

Potter, Constance. "World War I Gold Star Mothers Pilgrimages, Part I." *Prologue Magazine* (National Archives) 31, no. 2 (Summer 1999), www.archives.gov/publications/prologue/1999/summer.

"A Proud and Loyal State." *North American Review* 208, no. 755 (October 1918): 487–93.
Rainey, James W. "Ambivalent Warfare: The Tactical Doctrine of the AEF in World War I." *Parameters: Journal of the U.S. Army War College* 13, no. 3 (September 1983): 34–46.
——. "The Questionable Training of the AEF in World War I." *Parameters: The Journal of the U.S. War College* 22, no. 4 (Winter 1992–93): 83–109.
Reagan, Albert B. "The 'Flu' among the Navajos." *Transactions of the Kansas Academy of Science* 30 (April 1919–February 1921): 131–38.Rothbard, Murray N. "War Collectivism." In Ronald Radosh and Murray N. Rothbard, eds., *A New History of Leviathan*, 66–110. New York: E. P. Dutton, 1972.
Sanchez, Victoria. "Julius (Julio) Sanchez, an Early Aviator, WWI." *Herencia* 22, no. 4 (October 2014): 34–35.
Sarasohn, David. "The Election of 1916: Realigning the Rockies." *Western Historical Quarterly* 11, no. 3 (July 1980): 285–305.
Schwartz, E. A. "The Lynching of Robert Prager, the United Mine Workers, and the Problems of Patriotism in 1918." *Journal of the Illinois State Historical Society* 95, no. 4 (Winter 2002/3): 414–37.
Shapiro, Jason. "Sylvanus Griswold Morley: A Life in Archaeology and Elsewhere." *El Palacio* 118, no. 3 (Fall 2013): 59–65.
"Six Weeks of Recruiting." *Issues and Events* 6, no. 21 (26 May 1917): 281–82.
Skocpol, Theda, Marshall Ganz, and Ziad Munson. "A Nation of Organizers: The Institutional Origins of Civic Voluntarism in the United States." *American Political Science Review* 94, no. 3 (September 2000): 527–46.
Smith, George Winston. "New Mexico's Wartime Food Problems, 1917–1918: A Case Study in Emergency Administration," Part 1. *New Mexico Historical Review* 18, no. 4 (October 1943): 349–85.
——. "New Mexico's Wartime Food Problems, 1917–1918," Part 2. *New Mexico Historical Review* 19, no. 1 (January 1944): 1–54.
Sopar, George A. "The Pandemic in the Army Camps." *Journal of the American Medical Association* 71, no. 23 (7 December 1918): 1899–1909.
[Staff]. "Wooden Horses for Training Recruits." *Field Artillery Journal* 7, no. 3 (July–September 1917): 337–38.
Stevens, Rosemary A. "The Invention, Stumbling, and Reinvention." In Stephen R. Ortiz, ed., *Veterans' Policies, Veterans' Politics: New Perspectives on Veterans in the Modern United States*, 38–62. Gainesville, FL: University Press of Florida, 2012.
Telser, Lester G. "The Veterans' Bonus of 1936." *Journal of Post-Keynesian Economics* 26, no. 2 (Winter 2002/3): 227–243.
Trani, Eugene P. "Woodrow Wilson and the Decision to Intervene in Russia: A Reconsideration." *Journal of Modern History* 48, no. 3 (September 1976): 440–61.
Udall, Tom. "A Roadmap for the Twenty-First Century: A Review Essay of *New Mexico 2050*." *New Mexico Historical Review* 91, no. 4 (Fall 2016): 475–76.
Votaw, John F. "Robert Rutherford McCormick." In Mark A. Snell, ed., *Unknown Soldiers: The American Expeditionary Forces in Memory and Remembrance*, 120–42. Kent, OH: Kent State University Press, 2008.

Wager-Smith, D. R. W. "Resettlement Administration." In *Report of the Proceedings of the Statewide Coordination Meeting of Federal Agencies Operating in New Mexico*, 8A-8E. Santa Fe, NM: National Emergency Council, 1936.

Walter, Paul A. F. "Art, Drama, and Literature." In Lansing B. Bloom, ed., *New Mexico in the Great War*, 89-108. Santa Fe, NM: El Palacio Press, 1927.

———. "Life in Camp and Cantonment." In Lansing B. Bloom, ed., *New Mexico in the Great War*, 123-37. Santa Fe, NM: El Palacio Press, 1927.

———. "The Press and Public Opinion." In Lansing B. Bloom, ed., *New Mexico in the Great War*, 69-88. Santa Fe, NM: El Palacio Press, 1927.

Weaver, Peter C., and Leo van Bergan. "Death from 1918 Pandemic Influenza during the First World War: A Perspective from Personal and Anecdotal Evidence." *Influenza and Respiratory Viruses* 8, no. 5 (September 2014): 538-46.

Welsh, Michael. "Beyond the Call of Duty: World War I at the University of New Mexico. *New Mexico Historical Review* 64, no. 1 (January 1989): 25-38.

Williams, Gerald W. "The Spruce Production Division." *Forest History Today*, Spring 1999, 2-10.

Wilson, John P. "The Ranger and the Saboteur." In Richard A. Melzer, ed., *Sunshine and Shadows in New Mexico's Past: The Statehood Period, 1912-Present*, 125-28. Los Ranchos, NM: Rio Grande Books, 2012.

Wilson, Louis C. "The War Mother Goes 'Over There.'" *Quartermaster Review*, May-June 1930, 21-25.

Wray, Henry. "America's Unguarded Gateway." *North American Review* 208, no. 753 (August 1918): 312-15.

Fiction

Boyd, Thomas. *Through the Wheat: A Novel of the World War I Marines*. Bison Books reprint of 1923 ed. Introduction by Edwin Howard Simmons. Lincoln: University of Nebraska Press, 2000.

Cather, Willa. *One of Ours*. Reprint of 1922 ed. Amherst, NY: Prometheus Books, 2004.

Crane, Stephen. *The Red Badge of Courage and Other Stories*. Edited and with an Introduction by Pascal Covici Jr. New York: Penguin, 1991.

Dos Passos, John. *Three Soldiers*. Reprint of 1921 ed. New York: Modern Library, 2002.

Fitzgerald, F. Scott. *The Great Gatsby*. Reprint of 1922 ed. New York: Scribner, 2004.

Hemingway, Ernest. *A Farewell to Arms*. Reprint of 1929 ed. New York: Scribner, 1967.

March, William. *Company K*. Reprint of 1933 ed. Introduction by Philip Beidler. Tuscaloosa, AL: University of Alabama Press, 1989.

Shaara, Jeff. *To the Last Man: A Novel of the First World War*. New York: Ballantine, 2004.

Thomason, John W., Jr. *Fix Bayonets!* Reprint 1926 ed. Mount Pleasant, SC: Nautical and Aviation, 2007.

Vizenor, Gerald Robert. *Blue Ravens: A Historical Novel*. Middleton, CT: Wesleyan University Press, 2014.

Index of 172 New Mexico Men in Uniform

Key
- * Killed-in-action or died of wounds: 60 men (30 each Euro-Americans and Nuevomexicanos). These 60 men were 31 percent of the state's total of 195 casualties.
- † Died of disease: 9 men (5 Euro-Americans and 4 Nuevomexicanos). These 9 men were 3 percent of the total of the state's 270 men succumbing to illness.
- [N] U.S. Navy: 17 men. These 17 men were 10 percent of the total of 172 men listed below; 94 were Euro-Americans (55%) and 78 were Nuevomexicanos (45%).

  Abbott, Edmund C. (Santa Fe County), 87
  Abeyta, Adolph (Quay County), 84, 177
  Adams, Justus C. [N] (Doña Ana County), 193
  Akers, Joseph Wesley (Otero County), 157
  Alarid, Frank (Bernalillo County), 176
* Aragon, Alonzo (Colfax County), 213
† Archibeque, Antonio (San Miguel County), 183, 184
* Archuleta, Jose Felipe (Union County), 141

  Baca, Damiano C. de (Sandoval County), 151, 174
* Baca, Edmund C. (Mora County), 210
  Baca, Herman G. [N] (Valencia County), 196, 241
  Baca, Adj. Gen. James (Santa Fe County), 104
* Baird, Reginald E. (Eddy County), 174
  Barboa, Geronimo S. (Bernalillo County), 108

Barela, Felipe P. (Sierra County), 179, 260
Barker, S. Omar (San Miguel County), 235
*Barr, John W. (San Miguel County), 135
Beaman, Frank (Bernalillo County), 182, 260
*Berry, Benjamin I. (Lincoln County), 186
†Bloom, Raymond (Socorro County). *See* Subject Index
*Boehrig, Royal C. (Grant County), 174, 209
Borquez, Pedro Pablo (Quay County), 92
Brown, Elbert R. (Lincoln County), 166
Bujac, Etienne de P. (Eddy County), 87
*Burns, Kenneth K. (Rio Arriba County), 140

†Candelaria, Onofre N. (Bernalillo County), 203
†Carlisle, Hugh C. (Bernalillo County), 201
Cawyer, Abe (Grant County), 167
Chaplin, Ivory H. (Grant County), 185
*Chavez, Joaquin (Otero County), 211
*Chavez, Sixto R. (Guadalupe County), 208
Chissum, Sam (McKinley County), 257-58
*Chretien, August (McKinley County), 131
Crockett, Oren (Chaves County), *121*, 186
Crockett, Paris (Chaves County), *121*
*Cross, Jesse R. (Chaves County), 151

*Day, Harry M. (Curry County), 15
De Bremond, Charles M. (Chaves County). *See* Subject Index
*Delgar, Max (Socorro County), 146

Easley, William A. (Lincoln County), 248, 249, 268
Edwards, Arthur C. [N] (Santa Fe County), 188
Edwards, Howard H. (Doña Ana County), 202
*Elliott, Earl (Union County), 140-41
Emerson, Ernest O. (Chaves County), 143
Enriquez, Cleto (Union County), 108

Fantacci, Carl (Chaves County), 86
Fraser, Hugh C. (McKinley County), 128
Fresquez, Pedro (Otero County), 167

*Gallegos, Biterbo (Grant County), 167
Gallegos, Fernandes (Bernalillo County), 254
Gallegos, Juan B. (Guadalupe County), 109

Gallegos, Manuel (Grant County), 167
Garcia, Amado (Acoma Pueblo), 185
*Garcia, Andres (San Miguel County), 213, 289n7
*Garcia, Atanacio (Bernalillo County), 170
Garcia, Joseph (Bernalillo County), 175–76
Garcia, Luther P. (Union County), 107
*Garcia, Simon (Rio Arriba County), 289n7
Gipson, Lloyd S. (Lincoln County), 236–37
*Golding, Frederick B. [N], 207
*Gonzales, Delfino (Quay County), 81, 126, 132
*Gonzales, Evangolisto (Grant County), 289n7
Gonzales, Lino [N] (Socorro County), 192
Gonzales, Manuel C. (Bernalillo County), 237
Gonzalez, Joseph H. (Santa Fe County), 109
Gooch, Charles H., *122*, 181–82, 183, 234, 256
*Goodwin, William H. (Guadalupe County), 132
*Griego, Eliseo (Bernalillo County), 87
†Gurule, Francisco (Rio Arriba County), 207

*Hall, George (Quay County), 138
*Hamby, Benjamin J. (Grant County), 209
Harvey, Levi C. (Torrance County), 18
†Heath, Faris (Eddy County), 86
Hilton, Conrad (Socorro County), 99, *123*
*Hoskins, Leonard G. (San Miguel County), 185
*Howard, Claude Close (Luna County), 225
Hubbard, Alfred T. [N] (San Juan County), 189, 191

*Jaramillo, Liberato (Valencia County), 144
Johnson, Charles L. [N] (Guadalupe County), 190

Keller, John (Lincoln County), 155
Keller, Robert (Lincoln County), 155
Kemp, Benjamin W. (Socorro County). *See* Subject Index
*Kepple, Clarence G. (Eddy County), 210–11
*Ketner, Palmer (McKinley County), 82, 135
*Klenck, Charles (Lincoln County), 289n7

*Lee, Brooks (Grant County), 182
Lembke, Charles H. (Bernalillo County), 99
*Lopez, Nestor (Socorro County), 182
Lucero, Conrado (San Miguel County), 169–70

Lucero, Dario (Santa Fe County), 105, 106, 107
Lucero, Leonard (Rio Arriba County), 129–30
Luthy, Charles F. (Bernalillo County), 99

*Madrid, Jose Eligio (Rio Arriba County), 174
*Madrid, Jose Leon (San Miguel County), 144
*Maestas, Alfonso S. (Mora County), 289n7
Martin, Jack (Sierra County), 143
Martinez, Augustine (San Juan County), 170, 172, 184
*Martinez, Donaciano (Rio Arriba County), 289n7
*Martinez, Jesus (Taos County), 289n7
Martinez, Lauriano (Colfax County), 185
Mascarenas, Antonio (San Miguel County), 257
McCrarey, Frank (Union County), 134
*McDermott, Frank C. (Roosevelt County), 135
McDougal, Alva Warren (Luna County), 252
McFie, John Jr. (McKinley County), 99
*McReynolds, Verdie J. (Curry County), 138
Miller, J. Wickliffe (Bernalillo County), 99
Mondragon, Pecho O. [N] (Colfax County), 187
*Montoya, Albino G. (Doña Ana County), 289n7
*Montoya, Anastasio (Santa Fe County), 182
*Montoya, Arturo (Mora County), 174, 214
†Montoya, Candido (Lincoln County), 202
*Montoya, Jose C. (Santa Fe County), 289n7
*Morrow, Howard E. (UNM student, residence unknown), 86
*Mudgett, Bryan (Eddy County), 185

Ortiz, Adolfo (Santa Fe County), 174
*Otero, Luis (Bernalillo County), 225, 231–32
Otero, Meliton F. [N] (Bernalillo County), 192
Otero, Miguel A. (Santa Fe County), 99, 234
Ott, William A. [N] (Quay County), 188

Paiz, Joseph D., Jr. [N] (Quay County), 190
Pannel, George W. (Quay County), 252
Parker, Rolla A. (Lincoln County), 252
Poe, William A. (Luna County), 178

*Quesenberry, Joseph (Doña Ana County). *See* Subject Index
Quintana, Isaac (Rio Arriba County), 166, 167

*Rael, Aparicio (Guadalupe County), 138

Reid, R. C. (Santa Fe County), 92, 104, 107
Ribera, Andres S. (Santa Fe County), 144–45, 268
*Ritchie, Jesse T. (McKinley County), 212
Rivera, Abelino (Mora County), 254
Rivera, Rafael B. (Socorro County), 222
Rivera, Tomas (Rio Arriba County), 116–17
Robinson, Lewis B. (Grant County), 201
Rodarte, Alfredo S. (Taos County), 259, 260
Rodarte, Candido C. [N] (Taos County, 259, 260
Rodriguez, Eli S. [N] (Santa Fe County), 249–50
Rodriguez, Manuel (Rio Arriba County), 153
*Rogers, Harry (Eddy County). *See* Subject Index
Romero, Jacobo (Taos County), 262, 264
*Romero, Pedro S. (Quay County), 149
Ross, Leo L. (Mora County), 185

Sabedra, Delfin (Valencia County), 146–47
Safford, Edward L. (Santa Fe County), 244
*Salazar, Manuel (Rio Arriba County), 155
Sanchez, Julius (Socorro County), 99
Sanchez, Reyes A. [N] (Socorro County), 190
Seligman, Morton [N] (Santa Fe County), 193
Selover, Edward R. [N] (San Miguel County), 192
Sibley, William N. (Luna County). *See* Subject Index
†Simpson, Charles E. (Taos County), 84
Smith, Robert S. (unknown residence), 155

*Tafoya, Silas (Rio Arriba County), 17
Thorne, Clarence C. [N] (Bernalillo County), 189
Thompson, Terrell D. (San Miguel County), 183
Townsend, Francis C. (San Juan County), 105
Trainor, Jack D. (Santa Fe County), 153, 172, 268
*Trujillo, Casiano (Quay County), 81, 126, 256
*Trujillo, Jose F. (Quay County), 81, 126
Trujillo, Toribio (Bernalillo County), 108
Turley, Jay (Santa Fe County), 219

*Vaughan, Leon B. (Union County), 174
Valentine, Lawrence E. (Guadalupe County), 217
Voylles, Ralph (Roosevelt County), 183

†Waddell, Wilfred (Luna County), 86
Wade, Kipling (San Juan County), 200

Warton, Hugh Calvin (Otero County), 174
*Weathers, Homer E. (Curry County), 135
Willmunger, Emil H. (McKinley County), 183
Wilson, Joe B. (Curry County), 7
Woods, Henry Melvin (San Juan County), 185

*Yancey, Carl D. (Socorro County), 289n7

Subject Index

References to illustrations appear in italic type.

164th Development Battalion: Camp Funston, 104–5; Camp Kearny, 144; Camp Pike, 108–9

1st Division: 16th Infantry Regiment, 126, 132; 18th Infantry Regiment, 130; 26th Infantry Regiment, 140, 141; battlefield positions, 131, *133*, 138, 140–42, 149, 152, *157*; convoy, 82, 83, 126, 128, 192; occupation of Rhineland, 178; parades, 126–28; volunteers, 81, 82. *See also* Pershing, John J.

2nd Division, *133*, 134–36, 138, 140, 152, *157*, 177, 178, 208, 209

3rd Division, *121*, *133*, 134, 137, 140, *157*, 178, 186, 225, 263

4th Division, 87, *133*, 140, 146, *157*, 178, 252

5th Division, *133*, *157*, 210

8th Division (in Russia), *121*, 180, 181, 190

26th Division, 131, 138, 140, 149, 185

27th Division, 128

28th Division, 99, *118–19*, *133*; 109th Infantry Regiment, 143, 144, 146, 158, 161, 208, 268; 110th Infantry Regiment, 161, 176, 178; 112th Infantry Regiment, 146; Marne region offensives, *133*, 137, 140, 143–47; Meuse-Argonne offensive, *157*, 156–61, 176; reburial, 231; return home, 216

30th Division, 128

32nd Division, 146, *157*, 178, 186

34th Division, 88, 105, *114–15*, 202, 203

40th Division: 157th Infantry Regiment, 87; 158th Infantry Regiment, 87, 178; to France, 105, *118–19*; military police, 87, 178–79, 244, 252

41st Division: 66th Field Artillery, 86, *133*, 136, 137, *157*; Battery A, 1st NM Field Artillery, 86. *See also* 146th Field Artillery Battery A

42nd Division, *133*, 138, 140, 143, 152, 175, 178. *See also* La Croix Rouge Farm, Battle, Fr.

77th Division, *119*, *157*, 162–65. *See also* Lost Battalion

82nd Division, 99, *133*, *157*, 161. *See also* York, Alvin C.

83rd Division, 178
85th Division (North Russia), 180, 183–84
89th Division: 353rd Infantry Regiment, 97, 169, 173; 354th Infantry Regiment, 97, 149, 169, 173; 355th Infantry Regiment, 97, 149–50, 152, 173; 356th Infantry Regiment, 97, 148, 151, 152, 153, 154, 155, 166, 167, 169–70, 173, 174, 175, 184, 185, 209, 218, 268; commanding general, 166, 168; to France, 105, 187, 260; Meuse-Argonne offensive, *157*, 165–71, 172–76, 252; occupation of Rhineland, 178, 184, 248; poison gas attacks, 149–51, 166–67, 169, 170; reburial, 231; St. Mihiel offensive, *133*, 147–55, 210
90th Division, *133*, 155, *157*, 178, 185
92nd Division, *157*, 162
94th Division, 107
10th Engineers, 84
20th Engineers, 84, 235
21st Engineers, 84, 148–49, 177, 212
146th Field Artillery Battery A, *117*, *133*; in combat, 137, 138, 144, 147, 151–52, 171–72, 175; homecoming, 217, 248; shells expended, 137, 150, 172, 175; in training, 36, 137
331st Field Hospital (Italy), 179
813th Pioneer Labor Battalion, 203
167th Transportation Corps (Russia), 183

Abeyta, Adolph, 84, 177
Acoma Pueblo, 185
AEF (American Expeditionary Forces), 3, 18; Château Thierry, 134, 137; infrastructure needs, 83; mission extended, 179; organized leisure activities, *123*, 179; Puerto Ricans, 107; return home, 177–78, 248; Spanish-speaking Nuevomexicanos, 107; tactics, 142, 146, 154, 158, 166. *See also* convoy; Marne region offensives; Meuse-Argonne offensive; St. Mihiel offensive
AEFNR (North Russia), 180, 183–84
AEFS (Siberia), 180–83
African Americans: in AEF, 11, 202; National Association of Colored Women's Clubs, 59; veterans, 12; women, 58
Agricultural Extension Service, 45–46; agricultural agents, 46, 71; home demonstration agents, 46, 70, 71, 72
agriculture: exemption, 96; increased productivity, 39, 42, 43, 44, 45, 46, 52. *See also* farmers; gardens; wheat
Aire River, Fr., 156, *157*, 171
Aisne-Marne Offensive, 139–42, 143
Albuquerque, N.Mex.: bureau of investigations, 30, 32, 34; ethnicity and, 23, 24, 37, 38, 59, 63, 268; influenza, 204, 205, 225; mobilization, 23, 25, 37, 40, 52, 53, 59, 60, 64, 69, 71, 72, 74, 81, 90, 95, 108; in uniform, 85, 86, 87, 99, 145, 170, 176, 182, 189, 192, 203; veterans, *117*, 190, 192, 228, 236, 238, 254, 255, 260, 262, 264, 265; vigilantism, 23, 24, 29; women, 225, 231, 232. *See Albuquerque Morning Journal*; *La Bandera Americana*
Albuquerque Morning Journal, 26, 48, 49, 51, 95, 163, 165, 231. *See also* newspapers, New Mexico English-language
Alexander, Robert, 162, 163
Allies: defined, 13, 180; military activity, 25, 131, 138, 139, 140; supporting, 53, 179, 194, 204, 219
American Expeditionary Forces. *See* AEF; AEFNR; AEFS
American Indians: and combat, 185; entering the military, 11; Indian Citizenship Act, 240; influenza pandemic, 204, 205; veterans, 240, 257; women mobilized, 58

Subject Index

American Legion: creation, 227, 240; in New Mexico, 9, 16, 122, 196, 225, 228, 240, 241, 243–44; veterans issues, 39, 221, 224, 234, 245, 255, 258, 266. *See also* Bursum, Holm O.; Chavez, Dionisio "Dennis"; Cutting, Bronson M.

American Legion Women's Auxiliary, 10, 225, 226, 245, 246

American Protective League: *See* surveillance

American sector. *See* Lorraine, or Toul, sector

Amiens, Fr., 127, 131

Argonne Forest, Fr., 85, 128

Arizona, 29, 36, 79, 82, 87, 92, 97, 103

Armistice, 77, 175–77, 182, 204

army. *See* Regular Army; National Army; National Guard

artillery: 75 mm, 86, 153; 155 mm GPF (Grand Puissance Filloux), 117, 137, 151, 171, 172; barrages, 132, 135–36, 137, 138, 139, 140, 141, 142, 143, 144, 145, 146, 150, 152, 153, 154, 156, 165, 166, 167, 172, 173, 175, 177; Camp de Souge, 137; shrapnel from high-explosive shell, 132. *See* 146th Field Artillery Battery A

Asian Americans, 11–12

automatic rifle: Browning, 182; Chauchat, 15

AWOL/desertion, 27, 160, 289n6

Aztec, N.Mex., 53, 96, 105, 115

Baker, Newton D., 40, 90

La Bandera Americana, 25, 49, 62, 63, 108, 203, 204. *See also* newspapers, New Mexico Spanish-language

barbed wire entanglements, 120, 152, 154, 156, 165

baseball, 89, 179

Battery A, 1st New Mexico Artillery, 15, 21. *See* 146th Field Artillery Battery A

Belleau Wood: battle, 134–36; islettes, 139; marines, 134–35

benefits/social contract. *See* veterans

Bernalillo County, N.Mex., 2, 21,71, 72, 85, 87, 94, 188; eyewitnesses from, 17, 87, 99, 108, 170, 175–76, 182, 189, 192, 201, 203, 225, 231–32, 237, 254, 260

Berzy-le-Sec, Fr., 133, 141

Bisbee deportation, 29

Bloom, Lansing B., 4, 7, 17, 212, 214

Bloom, Raymond, 5, 198–99, 212

Board of Historical Service, 4, 5, 6, 14, 205, 210, 212, 214–15, 229. *See also* questionnaire from servicemen

Bois de Bantheville, Fr., 157, 169–71, 173, 177

Bois de Mort Mare (Dead Pond Forest), Fr., 133, 152, 153, 154

bond sales. *See* Liberty bonds

Bonus Army march, 21, 242

Bordeaux, Fr., 83, 121, 127, 136, 137, 159, 252

Bourne, Randolph, 78, 275n34

Brest, Fr., 83, 118, 127, 128, 191, 192, 269

Bureau of Investigation (BI): agents, 30–31, 32, 39, 89; High Cost of Living Division, 77–78; investigations, 12, 27, 29, 30, 31–33, 35; prosecutions, 33–34; Socialist Party of New Mexico, 34–37, 47

Burkhart, Summers: and civil liberties, 31–32, 36–37; as U.S. attorney, 24, 26, 30, 31, 32, 34, 36, 38, 77, 220

Burleson, Albert S. *See* surveillance

Bursum, Holm O.: Congress, 9, 235, 236, 241; veterans issues, 235, 236, 238, 239, 240

Bushnell, George E., 102, 103, 104

California, 89, 92, 192, 200; training camp, 40, 86, 87, 97, 99, 122, 181, 185; veterans, 121, 186, 188, 238, 250, 253, 257, 260

camps: Cody, N.Mex., 30, 64, 88, 100, 103, 104, 106, 114–15, 200, 202, 259; de Souge, Fr., 137; Dix, N.J., 200, 201,

camps *(continued)*
  203; Fremont, Calif., *121*, 181;
  Funston, Kans., 85, 88, 89, 91, 96–101,
  104, 105, 107, *115*, *120*, *121*, 143, 144, 197,
  198, 199, 200; Furlong, N.Mex., 12, 27,
  29; Gordon, Ga., 99; Greene, N.C.,
  86; Hancock, Ga., 99; Hill, Va., 86;
  Kearny, Calif., 69, 86, 87, 97, 102, 103,
  106, *121*, 143, 144, 149, 200; Kitchener,
  N.Mex., 85; Lewis, Wash., 86, 97;
  Logan, Tex., 82, 200; MacArthur,
  Tex., 15, 82, 200; Mills, N.Y., 86, 200,
  201; Pike, Ark., 108, 200; Perry, Ohio,
  83; Travis, Tex., 104, 200; Wheeler,
  Ga., 201
canning, 62, 78
Cantigny, Fr., 131–32, 136, 141
Carlsbad, N.Mex., 23, 25
casualties: AEF, 131, 132, 136, 142, 143,
  144, 146, 149–50, 159, 163, 165, 169,
  175; AEFNR, 183; AEFS, *122*, 182–83;
  Pershing's projections, 82; public
  reaction, 168. *See also* cemeteries;
  "friendly fire"
Catt, Carrie Chapman, 55, 56. *See also*
  Women's Committee of the Council
  of National Defense (WCCND)
cemeteries: AEF, *127*, 201, 230, 232–33;
  Arlington National, 225; local in
  France, 211; national stateside, 199,
  231, 250, 260
censorship, 15, 16
census: of 1910, 91; of 1920, 58, 60, 252,
  257; of 1930, 147, 188, 189, 192, 250, 252,
  257, 262; of 1940, 192, 194, 250, 252
Central Powers, 13
Château Thierry, Fr.: Battery A, 136, 137,
  138; casualties, 138, 209, 263; combat,
  117, *127*, 130, 132, *133*, 134, 139, 142, 143,
  145, *157*
Châtel-Chéhéry, Fr., *157*, 158, 160, 161
Chaumont, Fr., *127*, 128

Chaves County, N.Mex., 2, 15, 33, 85, 94;
  eyewitnesses from, 86, *121*, 143, 151,
  186. *See also* De Bremond, Charles M.
Chavez, Dionisio "Dennis," 95, 244,
  267–68
Cherbourg, Fr., 83, *127*
child health and welfare: maternalistic
  politics, 54, 57, 60, 80, 227, 245–46;
  reforms, 9, 10, 78, 203, 217, 226, 266
Chinese labor: Camp Funston, 197;
  Camp Furlong, 12
churches, 61, 68
citizen-soldier: double with veteran role:
  124, 250, 255, 266; and mobilization,
  10; postwar, 267
Civilian Conservation Corps (CCC), 262,
  264–65, 266
Clemenceau, Georges, 129
Clovis, N.Mex., 7, 37, 60
Colfax County, N.Mex., 2, 25, 39, 91, *114*,
  194; eyewitnesses from, 185, 187, 213
Columbus, N.Mex.: Council of Defense,
  29, 41; raid, 11
Coolidge, Calvin, 238, 239, 240
Committee on Public Information:
  Division of Women's War Work, 73;
  Foreign Languages Press branch, 72
convoy, 83, *118*, 128, 177–78, 181, 187–88,
  201–2. *See also* ships
Council of National Defense (CND), 29,
  39, 40, 46, 55, 57, 62, 65, 72
counties: map, 2. *See also* names of
  individual counties
Curry County, N.Mex., 2, 31, 94;
  eyewitnesses from, 7, 15, 135, 138
Cutting, Bronson M.: American Legion,
  240; death, 242–43, 244; New Mexico
  politics, 9, 228, 240, 241, 242, 243, 244,
  267; veterans, 10, 228, 234, 237, 243,
  245, 267

Daniels, Josephus, 147
dazzle camouflage, *118*, 194

death: battlefield, 14, 15, 17, *118*, *119*, *120*, 131, 132, 138, 141, 144, 146, 149, 151, 164–65, 173; buried at sea, 201, 202, 207, 230; disease and, 14, 86, 197–98, 199, 200; first enlisted and officer in combat, 131; Gold Star mothers, 232–33; meaning of, 17, 146, 151, 165–66, 173, 176, 177, 183, 185, 186, 200, 202, 205–15, 231–32; repatriation of deceased soldiers, 229–32; suicide, 173

de Bremond, Charles M.: 146th Field Artillery, 15, 136; Battery A, 1st Artillery, 11, 86; and citizen-soldier-veteran double, 15–16, 20–21; postwar, 15, 21, 225, 256

Deming, N.Mex.: Bureau of Investigation, 30; Council of Defense, 41; civil-military relations, 88–89, 102; influenza, 203; National Guard, 88; vigilantism, 25, 29

Democrats/Democratic Party: Congress, 78, 79, 236, 240, 241; governor, 39, 235, 244, 265; national, 246, 265; president, 65, 267; state politics, 49, 222, 223, 224, 234, 235, 243, 245, 268

demonstration kitchens, 61, 63, 69

Department of Justice, 27, 28, 30, 35; enemy alien registration, 38; U.S. marshal, 37–38, 89

development battalions, 105–9; instituted, 105, 202; medical referrals, 106; nonmedical referrals, 106; training techniques, 105–6, 107, 108–9

disease: DNA corrupted by poison gas, 256; dysentery/diarrhea, 101, 158, 161, 167; inoculation at camp, 97; measles, 100, 101, 151; meningitis, 101; mumps, 101; pneumonia, 102, 103, 198; venereal disease, 102, 129. *See also* influenza pandemic; tuberculosis

Distinguished Service Cross, *121*, 164, 175, 184–86

Doña Ana County, N.Mex., 2, 46, 60, 71, 75, 76, 83, 94; eyewitnesses from, 193, 202, 289n7. *See also* Quesenberry, Joseph

double role as citizen-soldier and veteran, 15–16, 20–21, *124*, 248–51, 259, 263–64, 266–69

draftees: citizenship conferred, 108; in combat, 109, *120*, *122*, 145; ethnicity, 94, 95, 96; exemptions, 91, 94, 95, 96; honoring deceased, 231; local boards, 91, 92, 93–94, 95; medical screening, 92, 101; from New Mexico, 89, 90, 91, 92, 96, 97, *114*, *120*, *122*; Nuevomexicano nationalism and, 108–9, 223; pay, 95; Puerto Ricans, 107; registration, 40–41, 89; Spanish-speaking, 105–9. *See also* 89th Division; National Army

Eddy County, N.Mex., 2, 45, 87, 90, 94, 99–100, *119*, 162; eyewitnesses from, 85, 86, 174, 185, 210–11. *See also* Rogers, Harry

El Cerrito, N.Mex., 60–61

enemy aliens: development battalions, 106; registration, 35, 37; residing in state, 38

English language, 226. *See* development battalions

enlisted men: AEF, 84, 128, 136, 150, 186, 208; border duty, 40; casualties, 134; navy, 191, 193; training camp, 85; veterans, 220. *See* 1st Division; 28th Division; 89th Division; 146th Field Artillery Battery A; draftees

Espionage Act (1917): origins, 26–27, 35; *Schenck v. United States*, 35; violations, 69

Euro-American men: ethnic presence, 24, 91, 101, 225, 261; military contributions, 11, 93; mobilization, 12, 28, 44; politics, 79, 224; tabulations, 283–84n32, 289n7

Euro-American women: mobilization, 62, 74, 75, 76, 232; reformers, 9, 12; socioeconomic status, 53, 56, 57, 58, 59

Fall, Albert B.: challenge to Senator La Follette, 47–48; heads Interior Department, 235, 236, 241
Fall, Emma Morgan (wife), 61
farmers: debt, 43–45, 221, 229; Federal Farm Loan Act (1916), 45; productivity, 43, 44, 45, 46, 52, 64, 76
Farmington, N.Mex., 89, 185, 200, 204
federal-state relations: federal presence, 9, 19; state-level perspective, 8. *See also* Bureau of Investigation (BI); surveillance
Ferguson, Isabella: background, 53, 54, 79; friendship with Eleanor Roosevelt, 53; and Robert Ferguson (husband), 53, 79; Land Army, 76–77; service army, 52, 64
Fismes, Fr., 127, 133, 143, 145, 146, 185
Fismettes, Fr., 133, 146
Foch, Ferdinand: planning offensive, 138, 146; street honoring, 225; war of attrition, 142, 168
food conservation, 6, 12, 58, 62, 63, 67–74, 75, 77
Forderhase, Rudolph A., 167, 170–71, 177
foresters: in AEF, 83, 84; in New Mexico, 84
Fort Bayard Hospital, N.Mex., 102, 204–5, 237
Fort Bliss, Tex., 81, 82, 217
Four Minute Men, 42–43, 74
Fourteen Minute Women's Speaker's Bureau, 74
"friendly fire," 145, 151, 154

Gallup, N.Mex.: Council of Defense, 41–42; men from, in AEF, 82, 99, 131, 135, 183, 212, 217; miners deported, 29; vigilantism, 25; women's activities, 60

gardens, 43, 51, 52, 53, 78
General Federation of Women's Clubs (GFWC), 54, 56, 58, 59, 60, 67, 74, 77
George V, king of England, 83, 127
German Americans: attacks upon, 23, 24, 25, 28, 35; pro-German activities, 32, 33, 89
Germany, 110; activities in Mexico and Central America, 195; aircraft, 143, 158, 159–60; assessing U.S. Army, 11; reliance on railroads, 142, 168; reported atrocities, 26; spring 1918 offensive, 25, 129; troops retreating, 138, 139, 142, 144, 145, 146, 152, 154, 173
Gold Star Mothers, 232–33
Good Death, 205, 208, 212, 232
Gorgas, William C., 102
Grant County, N.Mex., 2, 52, 91, 94, 97, 140, 201; eyewitnesses from, 167, 174, 182, 185, 201, 209, 289n7
Graves, Robert, 18, 258
Graves Registration Service, 212
Great Depression, 10, 21, 221, 222, 226, 242, 262, 264, 266, 267
Great War. *See* World War I
Grimpettes Wood, Fr., 144–45
Guadalupe County, N.Mex., 2, 6, 33, 96; eyewitnesses from, 109, 132, 138, 190, 208, 217

Harding, Warren G., 238, 239
Hawk, Tura A., 71–72. *See also* Agricultural Extension Service
healing communities: Alcoholics Anonymous, 259; American Indian ceremonials, 257–58; American Legion posts, 258–59
health. *See* child health and welfare
Hearst, William Randolph, 49–50
Henderson, William Penhallow, 194–95
Hernández, Benigno C., 41, 92–93
Hewett, Edgar Lee, 4, 6, 7, 9, 14, 195, 213, 223

Hoboken, N.J., 82, 83
homecoming: New Mexico, 217; New York City, 216–17
home front: influenza, 203–5; mobilization, 8, 35, 47, 51, 53, 54, 61, 62, 65, 79, 246, 267, 269; wartime U.S., 3, 10, 26, 27, 64, 206 250, 263, 269
Hoover, Herbert, as head of Food Administration, 65, 88, 67, 72, 237
Hoover Pledge card, 67, 68
hospitals: AEF, 85, 130, 145, 155, 210, 211, 252; Albuquerque VA, 255; neuropsychiatric illnesses, 254–55; Veterans Administration and, 254, 257
Hundred Days Offensive, 142–77

illegal sales of alcohol, 88
influenza pandemic: Camp Funston, 197–98, 200; deaths, 196–97, 198, 199, 200; impact on civilians, 203–5; impact on the military, 199, 200–201, 202, 230; origins and spread, 196–98, 200, 201; in Spain, 197; U.S. Public Health Service, 203. See also U.S. Navy
insurance: crop, 43; servicemen, 146, 206, 214, 239
Italy, 179, 190
IWW (Industrial Workers of the World), 25, 28–29, 41, 214

Jones, Andrieus A., 78–79, 240, 241

Kemp, Benjamin W., 142–43, 144–45
kitchens: AEF, 137, 146, 159, 160; home front, 59, 61, 63, 70, 72; training camp, 87, 98
Knights of Columbus, 89, *123*, 179

La Croix Rouge Farm, Battle, Fr., 143
Lafayette, Marquis de, 127
La Follette, Robert M., 47–48

Laguna Pueblo, N.Mex., 59, 240
land for veterans, 218, 219–20, 221
Lane, Franklin K., 218
La Rochelle, Fr., 83, *127*
Larrazolo, Octaviano A., 6, 77, 217, 218, 220–21, 226, 228
Las Cruces, N.Mex., 46, 60, 71, 231
Las Vegas, N.Mex., 30, 36, 60, 61
legislature, N.Mex.: benefits for veterans, 218, 219, 227; defending state's reputation, 5–6; financing the war, 39, 40, 43, 46, 47, 77, 91, *114*, 216; fiscal constraints, 226, 227, 228; fourth (1919), 219, 221, 222–24, 226, 227, 228; memorial activity, 212–13, 215, 222–24; war book, 3–4
Le Havre, Fr., 83, *127*, 136, 143
letters and correspondence: Board of Historical Service, 4, 213, 214, 215; Bureau of Investigation, 28, 34, 36; civilian correspondent, 16, 43, 44, 48, 49, 195; death conveyed, 5, 208, 209, 210, 211; home front mobilization, 51, 53, 55, 88; official government business, 63, 77, 91, 103, 104, 214; soldier writing, 15, 17, 18, 65, 109, 174, 202, 214
Lever Act (1917), 65, 66, 67, 69, 77, 78
Liberty Bonds, 6, 12, 23, 25, 35, 59, 64, 74–76, *113*
Lincoln County, N.Mex., 2, 94, 223, 239, 261; eyewitnesses from, 155, 166, 202, 236–37, 248, 249, 252, 268, 289n7
Lindsey, Amanda (wife), 54, 56, 57, 58, 75, 88
Lindsey, Washington E.: and Charles Springer, 6, 24, 41, 56; as wartime governor, 28, 39, 41, 44, 69, 85, 102, 103, 104, 201
London, Eng., 83, 127
Lorraine, or Toul, sector, 84, 128, 130, 147–48, 149, 150
Los Angeles, Calif., *123*, 250, 260

Lost Battalion, *119*, *157*, 161–65; and Charles Whittlesey, 162, 163–64, 165. *See also* 77th Division; Rogers, Harry
Lost Generation, 20
Luna County, N.Mex., 2, 41, 73, 76, 90, 158; eyewitnesses from, 86, 178, 225, 252. *See also* Sibley, William N.
lynching, 24, 25, 26

MacArthur, Douglas, 138
machine gun: AEF unit, 86, 87, 134,170; casualties, 142, 143, 155, 248; combat, 145, 147, 154, 185, 186; enemy use, 134, 139, 140, 141, 158, 160, 161, 164, 170, 173, 174, 176; nests, *119*, 142, 159, 162, 169, 175, 185; training, 100
"Mademoiselle from Armentières," 129
marines: enlistments, 82. *See also* Belleau Wood
Marne region offensives, *133*, 134–47
Marne River, *133*, 134, 136, 139, 142, 145, 225
Marshall, George C., 126, 130, 166
Masonic Lodge, 89
maternalistic politics, 54, 60, 80, 246
McKinley County, N.Mex., 2, 31, 41, 42, 217; eyewitnesses from, 82, 99, 128, 131, 135, 183, 212, 257–58
Memorial Day, 139, 226
memorials, 17, *127*, 212, 215, 217, 222–26, 229
memory, 7, 10, *125*, 127, 231–32, 252, 254; "lest we forget," 18–22
Meuse-Argonne offensive: *157*; combat in, 87, *116–17*, 118–19, *120*, 156–77, 185, 186, 210, 213; and home front, 172; influenza pandemic, 197, 198
Meuse River, *127*, *157*, 171, 173–75, 197, 198
Mézières, Fr., 142, *157*
migration. *See* relocation
Military Police, 87, 178–79, 244. 252
mobilization: civilian, 27, 35, 40, 42, 43, 52, 63, 65, 204, 234, 245, 246; military, 104, 106, *115*, 172, 198, 267; national, 9, 19–20, 36, 269; state, 5, 12, 46, 62, 63, 217, 243; women and, 12, 54, 68, 77, 79, *111*, *112*, 263
Mondell Bill (1919), 219, 220, 221
Montsec, Fr., *133*, 148, 149, 152, 154
Mora County, N.Mex., 2, 33, 46, *125*; eyewitnesses from, 174, 185, 210, 214, 254, 289n7
Morley, Sylvanus G., 195
motion pictures: *The Big Parade* (King Vidor, dir.), 16; *Sergeant York* (Howard Hawks, dir.), 161; *The Lost Battalion* (Burton L. King, dir.), 161–62
Museum of New Mexico, 4, 6, 100–101, 195, 222–23

National Army: and draft, 89–96; exemptions, 91, 94–96; training, 96–101, 114–15. *See also* 89th Division
national defense, in 1941, 265. *See also* preparedness
National Governors Association (NGA): in 1918, 217; in 1919, 220; Governor Larrazolo, 220–21
National Guard: 1st New Mexico artillery, 15, 86, *117*; AEF, 15, 85, *118*, 128, 131, 136, 138, 143–47, 165, 178, 209, 252; border duty, 10, 11, 40, 88, 181, 182, 183; home front mobilization, 37, 40, 69, 86, 88, 97; medical issues, 102, 200, 254; return home, 216, 223, 248, 249, 262; training 37, 40, 69, 85, 97, 114. *See also* 28th Division; 146th Field Artillery Battery A
nationalism: in New Mexico, 5–6; Nuevomexicano, 108–9, 223
New Deal, 264, 265, 266
New Mexico Blue Book, 3, 6
New Mexico Historical Review, 3–4
New Mexico in the Great War (Bloom, ed.), 4, 6, 9, 11, 14, 16–17

Subject Index 341

New Mexico Military Institute, 16, 21, 105
New Mexico State Council of Defense. *See* State Council of Defense (SCD)
newspapers, foreign, *El Sol*, 197
newspapers, military: *Agamemnon Daily News*, 218; *Stars and Stripes*, 227
newspapers, New Mexico English-language: *Farmington Times-Hustler*, 89; *New Mexico War News*, 49, 50, 73; *Roswell Daily Record* 15.See also *Albuquerque Morning Journal*; *Santa Fe New Mexican*
newspapers, New Mexico Spanish-language: *El Centinela*, 62; *El Defensor del Pueblo*, 63; *La Estrella*, 63, 64; *El Independiente*,73–74, 204; *La Revista de Taos*, 62; *La Voz del Pueblo*, 62. See also *La Bandera Americana*
newspapers, outside New Mexico: *Chicago Daily Tribune*, 24; *New York Times*, 11, 24, 67; *San Diego Union*, 97; *Washington Post*, 93
New Women movement, 54, 78, *112*
New York City, 82, 216–17, 230
Nineteenth Amendment. *See* suffrage
Nordfeldt, Bror Julius Olsson, 194
North American Review, 48–49, 108
North Russia, 180, 183–84
Nuevomexicanas: defined, 58; Gold Star mothers, 232; home front, 12, 58, 60–61, 62, 63, 72, 74, 75, 76; political activities, 61, 246, 265
Nuevomexicanos, 185; defined, 6, 104; employment, 221–22, 261, 262; ethnicity, 24, 91, 101, 225, 261; home front, 12, 28, 44, 63, 91; meaning of death, 207, 208, 225; nationalism, 108–9, 223; poetry, 221, 222; political activities, 61, 244, 267–68; reburial, 231; tabulations, 283–84n32, 289n7; in uniform, 11, 65, 81, 85, 87, 93, 101, 103, 104, 109, *114–15*, *116–17*, 148, 268; veterans issues, 10, 221–22, 243–44, 267–68

officers: AEF, 82, 83, 84, 131, 138, 162, 168, 169, 208, 210; AEFS, 180; border duty, 40; casualties, 132, 134, 141, 145, 150, 154, 161, 165, 175; navy, 191, 193, 195, 196; New Mexico, 40, 99, 100, 104, *119*, *123*, 163, 164, 185; postwar, 210, 227, 239, 266; training camps, 40, 85, 86, 87, 107
Oise-Aisne offensive, 142–47
open warfare, 99, 142, 154, 163
Otero County, N.Mex., 2, 61, 76, 257; eyewitnesses from, 99, 157, 167, 174, 192, 211, 225, 231–32, 234
Otero-Warren, Adelina (Nina), 62, 79
"over the top" (phrase), 130, 139, 145, 154, 155

Paris: AEF, *123*, 128, 130, 141, 176; capital, 107, 126, *127*, 130, 131, *133*, 147, *157*, 179, 192, 198, 201, 211, 227, 232, 233; German objective, 25, 134, 136, 137, 138
patriotism: 23–50; contested terrain, 24–25, 47–50, 239; hyperpatriotism, 23, 269; "paranoid style," 27; Patriotic Week, 69; wartime, 6, 32, 42, 52, 92
Pershing, John J.: AEF 1st Division arrives, 126–27; awarding medals, 164, 184; burial decisions, 230; extends AEF mission, 179; interactions with French, 129, 133–34, 138; Meuse-Argonne offensive,158, 164, 168, 178; Micheline Resco, 130; Punitive Expedition, 11, 131, 132; streets honoring, 225; training troops, 98, 128, 132, 142, 163
Pétain, Henri-Philippe, 132, 134
poison gas: arsine (diphenylchlorarsine), 150, 166, 167; battlefield use, 145, 147, 149–50, 152, 160, 166, 167, 172; health consequences, *116–17*, 145, 147, 150, 167, 255, 258; mustard gas (dichloroethyl sulfide), 150, 160, 166, 167, 169, 256; shells, 132, 150, 152; yperite, 151, 172
Pond, Ashley, 3, 148, 150

Pont-à-Mousson, Fr., 149
poppies, 139, 152, 226, 233
Post Office, U.S., 30, 34, 35, 37, 38, 259–60
post-traumatic stress disorder, 20, 135, 253, 254 258–59
preparedness: for World War I, 17–18, 98, 187; for World War II, 265–66
Prichard, George W., 56, 224
Prichard, Maude (wife), 56, 57, 75, 79
prisoners of war, *119*, 128
Prison Farm No. 2, 178
Prohibition, 54–55, 56, 248, 250, 262
prostitution: AEF, 129; training camps, 88
provost marshal general, U.S., 91, 92, 94
Punitive Expedition: *See* Columbus, N.Mex.

Quartermaster Corps, *123*, 127, 128, 232
Quay County, N.Mex., 2, 32, 34, 45, 90, 91; eyewitnesses from, 81, 84, 92, 126, 132, 138, 149, 177, 188, 190, 252, 256
Quesenberry, Joseph, 83, 130–31, 225
questionnaire from servicemen: eyewitness accounts, 7, 14, 18, *123*, 146–47, 149, 153, 169–70, 174–75, 178, 181, 187, 248, 250, 252; navy, 189, 191, 193, 196; numbers, 4, 14; omissions, 16, 130, 167; origin, 5; uses, 207, 228, 240, 261

racism, 5–6, 11, 58–59, 102–4, 222, 223
raiding sorties, 130–31
railroads, 8, 66, 97; government nationalizing, 8, 66, 88; employees in AEF, 83, 84, 177; in Russia, 180–83; transport of U.S. soldiers, 16, 96, 97, 100, 108, *115*, 136–37, 143, 216, 217; workers, 23, 24, 37, 183–84
rain and mud, 15, 84, 126, 139, 144, 147, 148, 149, 153, 158, 159, 160, 169, 171, 180
ranchers, and Stock-Raising Homestead Act (1916), 45

range finder paintings, 100, 195
Read, Benjamin M., 5, 109, 268–69
The Red Badge of Courage (Crane), 16
Red Cross: home front, 3, 43, 53, 64, 65, 89, *111*; in France, 148, 211; in Russia, 181
Red Scare: interpretations of, 38, 39; New Mexico, 37, 38
Regular Army: AEF, 82, *119*, *121*, 126–27, 132, 134, 138, 146, 163–64, 177, 178, 249; AEFS, *122*, 180; Camp Furlong, N.Mex., 12, 27, 29; casualties, 135, 140–42, 165, 186, 208–9, 216, 225; Fort Bliss, Tex., 81, 82; medical screening, 101–2; Punitive Expedition, 10, 11, 82, 131–32; stateside, 5, 6, 10, 11, 12, 15, 19, 27, 29, 34, 37, 82, 83, 84. *See also* 1st–5th Divisions; 8th Division; Pershing, John J.
Reims, Fr., *127*, *133*, 138, 139, 146, *157*
relocation: in New Mexico, *117*, 186, 190, 191, 262, 263; out-of-state, *121*, *123*, 221, 253, 259, 260, 261, 265
repatriation of dead soldiers. *See* deaths
Republicans/Republican Party: Congress, 9, 41, 79, 92, 221, 240, 267; governor, 6, 40, 56, 218, 230, 241, 244; national, 20, 47, 49, 218, 236, 239, 241, 246; president, 238–39; state politics, 6, 39, 57, 69, 79, *114*, 222, 223, 224, 234, 235, 243, 244, 245, 247, 267. *See also* Bursum, Holm O.; Cutting, Bronson M.; Larrazolo, Octaviano A.; Lindsey, Washington E.
rifle and bayonet, 99, 142. *See also* open warfare
Rio Arriba County, N.Mex., 2, 16, 17, 28, 29, 41, 62, 91, 92, 94, 96, 101, 262; eyewitnesses from, 105, 106, 107, *116–17*, 129–30, 140, 153, 155, 166, 167, 174, 207, 262, 289n7
Rocky Mountain Club (New York City), 216, 229, 230

Rogers, Harry: 77th Division, *119*, *157*, 162; background, 99–100; Distinguished Service Cross, 164; Gold Star mother, 233; Lost Battalion, 162–65; Regular Army, 100, 164, 184; training camp, 100
Roosevelt, Eleanor, 53, 54
Roosevelt, Franklin D.: as assistant secretary of the navy, 55; as president, 242, 244, 247, 259, 264, 265
Roosevelt County, N.Mex., 2, 37, 39; eyewitnesses from, 135, 183
Roswell, N.Mex., 11, 30, 37, 60, 90, *121*, 225
Russia: AEFNR, north Russia, 180, 183–84; AEFS, Siberia or far eastern, *122*, 180–83; foreign intervention, 14, 179, 180; revolution in, 13, 37, 180; Russian Civil War, 180; Suchan coal field, 181, 182, 183; Trans-Siberian Railway, 180, 181, 182 . *See also* 8th Division; 167th Transportation Corps

San Diego, Calif., 87, *121*, 186
Sandoval County, N.Mex., 2, 33, 72; eyewitnesses from, 151, 174
San Juan County, N.Mex., 2, 5, 94, 96, 174; eyewitnesses from, 105, 170, 172, 185, 189, 191, 200
San Miguel County, N.Mex., 2, 36, 46, 60–61, 91, 101, 262; eyewitnesses from, 135, 144, 169–70, 183, 184, 185, 192, 213, 235, 257, 289n7
Santa Fe, N.Mex., 25, 38, 60, 67, 90, 94
Santa Fe County, N.Mex., 2, 46, 58, 79, 85, 96, 193, 219, 223; eyewitnesses from, 87, 92, 94, 99, 104 105, 106, 107, *122*, 144–45, 153, 172, 174, 182, 188, 234, 244, 249–50, 268, 289n7
Santa Fe New Mexican, 38, 51, 234, 240, 256. *See also* newspapers, New Mexico English-language
Santa Fe style, 223, 224
Santayana, Jorge (George), 18–19

schools: army, 83, 85, 109, 135, 140, 185, 198; private, 3, 53, 135, 192, 226; public, 10, 60, 61, 62, 68, 71, 96, 99–100, 153, 188, 189, 190, 196, 200, 237, 265–66; School of American Archaeology/Research, 195; teachers, 17, 61, 62, *116–17*, 181, 196, 234
Sedition Act (1918), 27
Service Army, 51–54, 55, 57, 58, 61, 64–66, 77, 80, *111*, 113
Services of Supply (SOS), 128, 130, 165, 178, 254
Shaw, Anna Howard, 54, 55, 56
shell shock. *See* trauma; post-traumatic stress disorder
ships: RMS *Carpatha*, 187; SS *America*, 232, 233; SS *Harding*, 233; USAT *Sheridan*, 181; USS *Agamemnon*, 218; USS *Alert*, 190–91; USS *Brooklyn*, 190; USS *Cyclops*, 207; USS *Dakotan*, 189; USS *George Washington*, 191; USS *Grebe*, 193–94; USS *Leviathan* (*Vaterland*), *118*, 188, 202; USS *Major Wheeler*, 196; USS *McCawley*, 189; USS *Mount Vernon*, 188; USS *Nevada*, 189; USS *New Mexico*, 191–92; USS *Santa Teresa*, 192; USS *Ternate*, 189. *See also* U.S. Navy
Siberia (or far eastern Russia), *122*, 180–83, 237, 291n46
Sibley, William N., 158–61
Sierra County, N.Mex., 2; eyewitnesses from, 143, 179, 260
Signal Corps, 140
Silver City, N.Mex., 60, 97, 102
slackers, 27, 32, 33
sleepwalkers, 18–19
Socialist Party of New Mexico. *See* Bureau of Investigation (BI)
Socorro County, N.Mex., 2, 26, 32, 42, 62, 91, 94, 95, 101; eyewitnesses from, 5, 99, *123*, 142–43, 145, 146, 182, 190, 192, 198–99, 222, 289n7

Soissons, Fr., *127*, *133*, 139, 140, 141, 142, *157*
Soldier Settlement Board. *See* land for veterans
Sommedieue, Fr., *133*, 151
Spanish-speaking soldiers. *See* development battalions
Springer, Charles: background, 6, 56, *114*; as wartime administrator, 6–7, 23–24, 39, 42, 44, 57, 59, 69, 76
spring offensive (1918), 25, 104, 107, 129, 131
Spruce Production Division, 257
State Council of Defense (SCD), 5, 6, 12, 24, 30, 39–41, 72, 92, *114*. *See also* Springer, Charles
Stenay, Fr., 155, *157*, 168, 172, 175
St. Mihiel offensive, 17, 130, 131, *133*, 147–55, 210
St. Nazaire, Fr., 83, *121*, 126, *127*, 128–29, 130
stretcher bearers, 144, 171
submarines. *See* U-boats
suffrage, 54, 55, 61, 71, 78–79, 234–35, 250
sugar, 19, 63, 65, 70, *121*
Summerall, Charles P., 168–69
surgeon general, army, 102, 104, 106
surveillance, 27–30; American Defense Society, 31–32; American Protective League, 28–30

tanks, 158–59
Taos County, N.Mex., 2, 6, 31, 44, 46, 75; eyewitnesses from, 84, 259–60, 262, 264, 289n7
teachers, 17, 61, 62, *116–17*, 181, 196, 234. *See also* schools
temperance, 54, 60, 77, 80
Texas: draftees from, 93; Tejanos in uniform, 93
Tingley, Claude E., 245–46
Torrance County, N.Mex., 2, 52, 72; eyewitness from, 18
Toul, Fr., 128, 130, 147

training: AEF, 130; British and French assistance, 128; in camps, 81–109; daily routine, 97–98; inoculations, 97; troops reassigned stateside, 97. *See also* camps
trauma: Belleau Wood, 135, 209; defined, 253–54; mental incapacity, 256–57; Meuse-Argonne, 156, 160, 206; symptoms, 258; veterans, 250–51, 252–59
Treaty of Versailles, 22, 182, 191
Trementina, N.Mex., 263
trenches: American use, 3, 15, 51, 87, 130, 131, 144, 146–47, 148; German use, 15, 132, 135, 163; and warfare, 18, 19, 85–86, 149, 150, 152–54, 156, 159, 162, 166–67, 186. *See also* poison gas
tuberculosis, 9, 101–2, 103, 104
Tucumcari, N.Mex.: Bureau of Investigation, 30; and draft, 90–91; navy, 188; postwar, 225, 256, 263–64; Red Cross, 64; Regular Army, 81, 126, 132, 149, 177. *See also* Quay County, N.Mex.

U-boats: attacks by, 195; evading, 82, 187
Union County, N.Mex., 2, 34, 42, 43, 60, 96; eyewitnesses from, 107, 108, 134, 140–41, 174
University of New Mexico, 85, 86, 201
U.S. Food Administration (USFA), 12, 62, 65, 69, 72, 77; Ralph Ely, administrator, 68, 69
U.S. Forest Service. *See* 10th Engineers; 20th Engineers; foresters
U.S. Navy: enlistments, 6, 37, 82, *121*, 188–93, 197; headquarters at Brest, 128; honoring deceased, 231; influenza pandemic, 200, 230; marine camouflage, *118*, 194–95; Navy League, 194; North Sea minesweeping, 193–94; Office of Naval Intelligence, 195;

post-armistice role, 191–92; role in war, 187, 189, 192; training stations, 188, 189, 190; U.S. submarines, 191. *See also* ships

Valencia County, N.Mex., 2, 6, 31; eyewitnesses from, 144, 146–47, 196, 241
Verdun, Fr., *133*, 147, 155, *157*, 166, 167, 168
Vesle River, *118–19*, *133*; combat, 144, 145–47, 211
veterans: benefits/social contract, 217–18, 227, 233–34, 236, 238–39, 247, 264; burial stateside, 229–32; reintegration, 8, 15–16, 20–21, 217, 219, 234–35, 236, 247, 248–51, 255; political activities, 10, 221, 224, 227, 234, 235, 247, 267. *See also* double role as citizen-soldier and veteran
Veterans Bureau: Frank T. Hines, administrator, 237; hospitals, 237–38; World War Adjusted Compensation Act, 238, 239
vigilantism, 23–27, *110*
Villa, Francisco (Pancho), 11
Vladivostok, Rus., *122*, 180, 181, 182, 190, 291n46
volunteers: army, 82, 126; civilian: 51–79; navy and marines, 82; voluntarism, 66, 246
Vosges, Fr.: forest, 84; front, 185; mountains, 85, 128, 132

War Industries Board, 8
War Service card, 69–70
wartime appropriations, 39, 40, 43, 46, 47, 77, 91, *114*, 216, 228, 229
wartime socialism, 8, 66, 88
war weariness, 20, 214, 248–49, 268–69
Washington, D.C.: army, 83, 86, 90, 92, 102; Bonus Army March, 242, 264; Bureau of Investigation, 31; navy, 55, 192; as U.S. capital, 12, 24, 25, 58, 220; women, 55, 67, 246
weapons. *See* artillery; automatic rifle; poison gas
welfare state, 9, 226–27, 238–39, 247, 264
western front: combat on, 13, 25, 74, 87, 96, *117*, 131–32, 136–37, 139, 140, 146, 166–67, 172; maps, *127*, *133*, *157*; New Mexicans and, 3, 20, 108, 131–33, 138, 140, 145, 147–50, 166
wheat, 46, 63, 64, 70, 73–74
Wilson, Woodrow: Columbus raid, 11; and deaths, 17; domestic turmoil, 24, 27, 29, 66; draft boards, 91; farmers, appeal to, 43, 51, 66; Gold Star mothers, 232; Lever Act, 65, 67; Paris peace talks, 191; Red Cross, *111*; service army, 51, 52, 53, 65, *111*; veterans, 218
"wine and women," 18, 148, 248, 259
Wood, Leonard, 98
women reformers, 9, 53–54, 78–79, *112*. *See also* maternalistic politics
Women's Auxiliary of the State Council of Defense (WASCD): Land Army, 76–77; Nuevomexicanas, 61, 62; origin, 12, 56–57, 11; participation, 58, 59, 60, 68, 69, 71–75; postwar, 77, 78, 79, 226, 227; structure, 57, 58, 67, 68, 70, 74
Women's Committee of the Council of National Defense (WCCND): activism, 76–77, 79, 88, 232; formation, 55, 56, 57; state organization, 56, 57, 59, 69, 74, 76
Women's Land Army, 76–77. *See also* Ferguson, Isabella
Works Progress Administration (WPA), 264
World War I: AEF/AEFNR/AEFS, 126–86; home front, 23–80; influenza pandemic, 196–205; mourning, memorializing, burying, 205–15, 229–33; navy, 187–96; overview for

World War I *(continued)*
    New Mexico, 3–22; postwar impact, 216–69; recruitment and training camps, 81–109
World War II, 7, 21, 51, 77, *125*, 130, 134, 161, 192, 247, 250, 264, 266, 269

YMCA, 15, 89
York, Alvin C., *157*, 161
YWCA, 89

Zimmermann telegram, 11, *110*

www.ingramcontent.com/pod-product-compliance
Lightning Source LLC
Chambersburg PA
CBHW031426160426
43195CB00010BB/634